BETTER ACTIVE THAN RADIOACTIVE!

OXFORD HISTORICAL MONOGRAPHS

The *Oxford Historical Monographs* series publishes some of the best Oxford University doctoral theses on historical topics, especially those likely to engage the interest of a broad academic readership.

Better Active than Radioactive!

Anti-Nuclear Protest in 1970s France and West Germany

ANDREW S. TOMPKINS

OXFORD
UNIVERSITY PRESS

OXFORD
UNIVERSITY PRESS

Great Clarendon Street, Oxford, OX2 6DP,
United Kingdom

Oxford University Press is a department of the University of Oxford.
It furthers the University's objective of excellence in research, scholarship,
and education by publishing worldwide. Oxford is a registered trade mark of
Oxford University Press in the UK and in certain other countries

© Andrew S. Tompkins 2016

The moral rights of the author have been asserted

First Edition published in 2016

Impression: 1

Published in the United States of America by Oxford University Press
198 Madison Avenue, New York, NY 10016, United States of America

British Library Cataloguing in Publication Data
Data available

Library of Congress Control Number: 2015958681

ISBN 978–0–19–877905–6

Printed in Great Britain by
Clays Ltd, St Ives plc

Acknowledgements

My first thanks are to the many people who consented to be interviewed for this project. Whether their words have made it into the final version of this book or not, I am grateful for the time (and, often enough, food and shelter) that they so generously offered me. I have only been able to describe a fraction of their experiences here, but talking to them taught me more about people, about life, and about myself than I will ever be able to put into words.

Parts of this book deal with difficulties, tensions, and disagreements among these (former) activists. I have tried not to take sides in their debates, but to analyse as best I could what took place behind them and to show how people with diametrically opposed viewpoints worked together in spite of their differences. Everyone that I interviewed spoke with sincerity and conviction. I hope I have done justice to them and to their experiences.

I am profoundly grateful to several archivists who went out of their way to help me find material for my project. In addition to directing me towards invaluable primary source material and stimulating secondary literature, Wolfgang Hertle at the Hamburger Institut für Sozialforschung, Franck Veyron at the Bibliothèque de documentation internationale contemporaine, and Volkmar Vogt at the Archiv der Sozialen Bewegungen in Baden each helped me establish contact with numerous interviewees. This research would have been much the poorer without their kind assistance.

This book has been a long march through many institutions. I am particularly grateful for the warm welcomes I received at the Institut des sciences sociales du politique of the École normale supérieure de Cachan, at the Wissenschaftszentrum Berlin, at the History Department of the University of Uppsala, at the Centre Marc Bloch in Berlin, and at the Humboldt-Universität zu Berlin. Generous grants from Merton College, the Clarendon Fund, and the Overseas Research Scheme supported me through most of the research, followed by assistance from the Oxford–Uppsala Exchange, the Michael Foster Memorial Scholarship (DAAD), and the Centre Marc Bloch. The Colin Matthew Fund sponsored a trip to the IISG in Amsterdam and the Society for the Study of French History made possible archival and interview visits to Bretagne, Normandie, and the Larzac. Funds from the Exzellenzinitiative des Bundes und der Länder disbursed by the Humboldt-Universität zu Berlin made it possible to turn this thesis into a book manuscript.

I am profoundly grateful to my DPhil supervisors at the University of Oxford, Robert Gildea and Jane Caplan, who repeatedly opened my mind to ideas, methods, and possibilities that I would not have discovered on my own. Their encouragement and constructive criticism have greatly improved this book and its author. I also thank Martin Conway for his help and guidance over many years, as well as Belinda Davis and Holger Nehring for their repeated and consistently helpful feedback on several drafts. Dieter Rucht, Xavier Vigna, Olivier Wieviorka, Michelle Zancarini-Fournel, and Maria Ågren also gave helpful advice at critical junctures in the research. Well before I undertook this project, Lloyd Kramer and Leora Auslander set me on the path to a PhD and encouraged me to keep going. I thank Gabriele Metzler for consistently supporting me as a post-doctoral researcher.

I am grateful to Léa Barbisan, In-Sook Choi, Rebecca Clifford, Torsten Feurstein, Julie le Gaec, Leah Goldman, Anna von der Goltz, Jan Hansen, Lasse Heerten, Tomas Högberg, Chloe Jeffries, Alan Ross, Johannes Schmid, Sinje Schuck, Jake Smith, Milan Terlunen, Simon Teune, Jon Waterlow, and Tom Williams for providing moral support along the way.

This work might never have been brought to completion without the tireless support of Erik Albrecht. His professional advice as a writer and interviewer were consistently on target; his kindness, patience, and generosity are immeasurable. This thesis is dedicated to him and to the rest of my family, all of whom have remained a vital presence in my life even as we have sometimes been separated by great distances.

Contents

List of Figures

List of Tables

List of Abbreviations

Archive abbreviations appear in the bibliography

AD	Action Directe
	French 'armed struggle'/'terrorist' group of the late 1970s and early 1980s
ADLT	Les Amis de la Terre
	French branch of Friends of the Earth
AKPÖ	Arbeitskreis Politische Ökologie
	Political Ecology Working Group within the Hamburg BUU
AKW	*Atomkraftwerk* or *Kernkraftwerk*
(or KKW)	German term for a nuclear power station (regardless of specific technology)
BBU	Bundesverband Bürgerinitiativen Umweltschutz
	Federal Association of Environmental Protection Citizens' Initiatives, a West German environmentalist umbrella organization composed of local BIs
BI	Bürgerinitiative
	'Citizens' Initiative', a general term for local groups organizing to oppose nuclear projects, environmental problems, and so on
BUND	Bund für Umwelt und Naturschutz Deutschland
	Federation for Environment and Nature Protection Germany
BUU	Bürgerinitiative Umweltschutz Unterelbe
	Lower Elbe Environmental Protection Citizens' Initiative, the principal regional organization opposing nuclear power plants in Brokdorf and across northern Germany
CFDT	Confédération Française Démocratique du Travail
	Left-leaning trade union
CNV	*Combat Non-Violent* newspaper (briefly merged with *GO* in 1977)
CRA	Comité Rhône-Alpes
	Coordinating committee for Malville protests
CRILAN	Comité de Réflexion, d'Information et de Lutte Anti-Nucléaire
	Local anti-nuclear organization based in Normandy (near La Hague and Flamanville)
CRS	Compagnie Républicaine de Sécurité
	French riot police unit
CSFR	Comité pour la Sauvegarde de Fessenheim et la plaine du Rhin
	Committee to Save Fessenheim and the Rhine plain, the principal regional organization opposing the construction and operation of Fessenheim and other nuclear power plants in Alsace
EDF	Électricité de France
	French national electricity supplier

EUP	*Enquête d'utilité publique*
	Public utility survey, administrative procedure required for approval
	of infrastructural projects in France
FBR	Fast breeder reactor (*surgénérateur, Schneller Brüter*)
GO	*La Gueule ouverte* newspaper
GWR	*Graswurzelrevolution* newspaper
IAEA	International Atomic Energy Agency
KB	Kommunistischer Bund
	West German radical left group of Maoist inspiration, strongest in
	northern Germany; sister organization of OCT
MEP	Member of the European Parliament
Nimby	'Not in my backyard' (i.e. narrowly self-interested) protest
NSM(s)	New social movement(s)
OCT	Organisation Communiste des Travailleurs
	French radical left group of Maoist inspiration; sister organization of KB
PCF	Parti Communiste Français
	French Moscow-aligned communist party
PWR	Pressurised water reactor
RAF	Rote Armee Fraktion
	Red Army Faction, the best-known of several 1970s West German
	'armed struggle'/'terrorist' groups
RFW	Republik Freies Wendland
	Free Republic of Wendland, name given to camp occupying Tief-
	bohrstelle 1004 (Test Drilling Site number 1004) during May 1980
RG	Renseignements Généraux
	French domestic intelligence service
RZ	Revolutionäre Zellen
	A smaller 'armed struggle'/'terrorist' group active in West Germany
	in the 1970s and early 1980s
VHSWW	Volkshochschule Wyhler Wald
	A programme of informational events organized by nuclear energy
	opponents, initially on the occupied site in Wyhl
WRI	War Resisters' International
WWW	*Was Wir Wollen* newspaper

Note on Spelling and Translations

All translations in the text are my own unless otherwise noted. I have generally translated quotes that appear in the body text, but left the original French or German in footnotes. Where the meaning of a word or phrase was ambiguous or modified through translation, I have indicated the original in brackets. I have also used French or German spelling for place names throughout the text (e.g. 'Hannover' instead of 'Hanover', 'Basse-Normandie' instead of 'Lower Normandy') and maintained language-specific capitalization and punctuation in titles and quotes. French or German terms used in the text are italicized, but proper names are not. The names of organizations have generally been capitalized as in English in order to improve legibility.

1

The Opposition to Nuclear Energy

A Transnational History
of Protest in the 1970s

On 31 July 1977, one man was killed and three others seriously wounded when French police in Creys-Malville (Rhône-Alpes) used stun grenades to quell a violent demonstration of up to 60,000 participants. French politicians and media held hundreds of West German protesters (some of whom had travelled 1,000 kilometres to join the protest) responsible for the bloodshed. Less than two months later, on 24 September 1977, West German authorities tried to prevent similar violence at a related protest in Kalkar (Nordrhein-Westfalen) by setting up checkpoints with armoured vehicles and heavily armed police along roads leading to the demonstration site. Up to 30,000 mostly West German protesters managed to reach the site after long delays, but hundreds of foreigners were reportedly blocked at the border. In response to these and related protests where turnout climbed to 100,000 and more, observers expressed fears that West Germany was becoming 'ungovernable' and that France might be moving towards 'civil war'. Yet the protests in question were not part of a social, political, or cultural revolution in the manner of 1848, 1917, or 1968. In Malville and Kalkar, as at dozens of other sites throughout both countries, concerned citizens were demonstrating against a specialized procedure to generate electricity: these were protests against civil nuclear power.[1]

Only a few short years earlier, no one could have predicted that this issue would provoke such intense protest. When a first demonstration against the nuclear power station in Fessenheim (Alsace) took place on

---

[1] *Aujourd'hui Malville* (1978); Colonel de la Gendarmerie Roy, 'Rapport', summary police report, 5 August 1977, AD Isère, 6857 W 36; Ermittlungsausschuss der Bürgerinitiativen gegen Kernenergie, *Wir, das Volk* (1977); Hans Filbinger, 'Energie für Baden-Württemberg', Regierungserklärung, 27 February 1975, ABEBI, 'Werbung Kernkraftwerk II Wyhl 1977'; 'Irons-nous jusqu'à la guerre civile ?', *GO/CNV*, no. 169 (4 August 1977), p. 1.

12 April 1971, it had been a wholly different affair. About 1,000–1,500 protesters came from France, West Germany, and Switzerland, but mostly from within a 50-kilometre radius of this future borderland power station. Though the local press described the event as an 'impressive mass demonstration' which 'the residents of Fessenheim will not soon forget', the drama was entirely symbolic: protesters marched in silence through town, placed a veil over the sign at the site's entrance, and released balloons before peacefully dispersing. Organizers went out of their way to stress their non-violent intent (distributing flyers in advance advising demonstrators on how they should behave) and their willingness to compromise. Asked on French radio why she had helped organize the protest, Esther Peter-Davis said, 'We would have preferred to discuss things seriously with those responsible', and insisted that 'the current plan does not yet—I repeat, not yet—present the necessary guarantees for the population'.[2]

The opposition to nuclear energy in France and West Germany during the 1970s thus represents something of a riddle. Why did an issue seemingly so narrow and technical come to be perceived as so broadly important? How did individuals with such different approaches work together within this movement? Why did protests in France, West Germany, and elsewhere so closely resemble one another? The answers to all of these questions have as much to do with the informal, decentralized character of this social movement during the 1970s as they do with the specifics of nuclear energy. As a contribution to the social history of transnational protest, this book examines the 1970s anti-nuclear movement as a prism through which to view grassroots extra-parliamentary politics more generally, up to and including the present day. Like the early anti-nuclear movement, recent protests such as those associated with Occupy Wall Street and parts of the Global Justice Movement have also emphasized (and profited from) their resistance to formal organization.[3] Looking at protest from the bottom up, this book will show how anti-nuclear activists[4]

---

[2] 'L'opération « stop—centrale nucléaire » : une impressionnante manifestation de masse', *Dernière nouvelles d'Alsace*, 14 April 1971; 'Manif à Fessenheim (Alsace) contre la construction d'une centrale nucléaire', 13 April 1971, Inter-Actualités de 7 h; Memo, 13 April 1971, AD Bas-Rhin, 1743 W 54.

[3] For a critical evaluation of such claims, see Craig Calhoun, 'OWS in Perspective', *British Journal of Sociology* 64, no. 1 (2013).

[4] Throughout the text, I refer to the individuals under consideration as 'activists' (in most cases used interchangeably with 'protesters'). The term is one of convenience, chosen to highlight a shared characteristic relevant to the purposes of this study; in my use, 'activist' does not indicate an exclusive group, an exceptional level of commitment, or an individual's primary identity.

in the 1970s constructed a movement[5] that crossed national, political, cultural, and social boundaries, and which thus involved a volatile mix of individuals with conflicting interests and approaches. Indeed, the anti-nuclear movement managed to attract attention consistently throughout that decade precisely because its internal diversity made it seem outwardly unpredictable and potentially explosive.

At international demonstrations such as those in Fessenheim, Malville, and Kalkar, participants from France, West Germany, and across Western Europe joined forces, forging a coalition that included tractor-driving farmers, banner-waving communists, middle-aged housewives, radical anarchists, and Gandhian pacifists. These varied protagonists were animated by a range of concerns about nuclear technology: for its potential military use, as a symbol of capitalism or the state, because local communities perceived it as a threat. Remarkably, few if any of these concerns had commanded much attention when the first nuclear power stations were built during the 1950s. It was only with the rapid expansion of nuclear programmes in the 1970s (specifically the construction of new power stations) that the issue attracted the attention of particular groups and, eventually, whole societies. The controversy surrounding nuclear power thus owed more to the timing, scale, and spaces of its expansion than to the relatively unchanged fundamentals of the technology itself.[6]

Though protest against nuclear energy continues today, its rise and exceptional strength during the 1970s merit particular attention. The

---

[5] I use the term 'movement' to refer to a complex, non-unitary social actor consisting of a politically mobilized network of individuals who claim to share a common cause. On networks, see Claire Lemercier, 'Analyse de réseaux', *Revue d'histoire moderne et contemporaine* 52, no. 2 (April–June 2005).

[6] Both the French and West German nuclear programmes were planned before the oil crisis of 1973–4, but their implementation was sped up thereafter. In France, the 'rapid and massive recourse to nucleo-electric energy' was publicly announced as part of the government's upcoming VIIth Economic and Social Development Plan (for 1976–80) in 1972; plans for a new nuclear power plant in Fessenheim (Alsace) had been floated as early as 1964, and land for the project was acquired in 1967. See Robert Hirsch, Letter to Maurice Picard, 19 February 1965, AD Haut-Rhin, 1391 W 17; François-Xavier Ortoli, 'La politique française du nucléaire', *Le Courrier du Parlement*, 30 March 1972. In the early 1970s, nationalist politicians and the Parti communiste français made much of the switch from ('French') gas-graphite technology to ('American') pressurized water reactors (PWRs). However, the distinction was not fundamental to most protesters in France, and the shift from boiling water reactors to PWRs in West Germany did not have the same nationalist connotations. For more on the development and abandonment of gas-graphite reactors in France, see Gabrielle Hecht, *Radiance of France* (1998). The West German government likewise passed its nuclear programme in September 1973 and presented it to the Bundestag shortly before the Yom Kippur War (6–25 October 1973) that triggered the oil crisis. On the development of nuclear technology in West Germany, see Joachim Radkau, *Aufstieg und Krise* (1983). On energy policy cooperation and competition between France and Germany, see Sandra Tauer, *Störfall* (2012).

decade is often seen as a transitional period in Western Europe, sandwiched historically between the upheavals of the late 1960s and the revival of Cold War tensions in the 1980s. Contemporaries described the 1970s in terms of 'crisis' and historians have associated it with the decline of everything from industrial society, the working class, and Marxism to traditional political parties and even optimism itself.[7] Yet the 1970s also brought tremendous gains for women, gays and lesbians, ethnic minorities, and environmentalism, all of which benefited from the spread of protest beyond the realm of the 'usual suspects' on the political left and deep into the lives of 'ordinary citizens'.[8] The anti-nuclear movement of the 1970s was one instance of 'popular politics'—political expressions by broad populations, outside formal (parliamentary) channels, often with a complicated relationship to the political 'left' and 'right'.[9] During that decade, the opposition to nuclear energy was widespread but decentralized, organized informally or semi-formally rather than within professional NGOs of the kind that became so intimately associated with environmentalism from the 1980s onward.[10] Within this movement, individuals from very different backgrounds met for the first time, exchanged ideas, argued with one another, shared experiences, and found themselves working together—for better and for worse.

The emergence and growth of this movement also took place during a decade when processes associated with 'globalization' began to take forms that are familiar today; those years thus in some sense constitute 'the beginnings of our modernity'.[11] The seemingly sudden and rapid expansion of nuclear power generated opposition that was itself 'global' in some sense.[12] By the mid-1970s, communities close to prospective nuclear power stations in Austria, Denmark, France, Italy, Japan, the Netherlands,

---

[7] Niall Ferguson, 'Crisis?', in *The Shock of the Global*, edited by Niall Ferguson et al. (2010); Andreas Wirsching et al., 'Turning Point?', *Journal of Modern European History* 9, no. 1 (March 2011), pp. 10, 15, 18–19. See also Anselm Doering-Manteuffel and Lutz Raphael, *Nach dem Boom* (2008); Konrad Jarausch, ed., *Das Ende der Zuversicht?* (2008).

[8] On these gains, see Wirsching et al., 'Turning Point?', p. 18; Geoff Eley, *Forging Democracy* (2002), pp. 366–83, 457–69.

[9] Belinda Davis, 'What's Left?', *American Historical Review* 113, no. 2 (April 2008).

[10] See Hein-Anton van der Heijden, 'Great Fear', in *A History of Environmentalism*, edited by Marco Armiero and Lise Sedrez (2014), pp. 189–90.

[11] Wirsching et al., 'Turning Point?', p. 20. See also Timothy S. Brown, '"1968" East and West', *American Historical Review* 114, no. 1 (February 2009), p. 69.

[12] It was global not in the sense of being coordinated from upon high nor of 'diffusing' outward from one source. Anti-nuclear protest had no single point of origin and emerged in part through spontaneous reactions in local spaces to the actions of governments; significantly, though, it was repeatedly synchronized across space through the agency of activists who participated in transnational exchanges, debates, and learning processes. A similar sort of 'globality' is described in Michael Geyer and Charles Bright, 'World History', *American Historical Review* 100, no. 4 (October 1995).

Spain, Sweden, Switzerland, the United Kingdom, the United States, and West Germany[13] almost simultaneously found themselves asking very similar questions about the potential impact of nuclear energy on their health, environment, and way of life. Anti-nuclear activists everywhere argued that problems at a nuclear power plant anywhere in the world could have far-reaching repercussions on a regional, continental, and even planetary scale—as accidents in Harrisburg (1979), Chernobyl (1986), and Fukushima (2011) have since repeatedly demonstrated.

Of all the countries where this movement existed, France and West Germany stand out in terms of both their interconnectedness and the different outcomes protest had in each.[14] Despite being near neighbours in Western Europe with similarly advanced economies and highly developed, state-sponsored nuclear industries, France is today more dependent on nuclear energy than any other country in the world, while Germany is in the process of phasing it out entirely.[15] However, as a grassroots movement during the 1970s, anti-nuclear protest in France and West Germany was closely related, involving shared themes, arguments developed in tandem, strategies synchronized (however partially) across borders, and thousands of protesters who moved back and forth between these (and other) countries. This shared history has disappeared from view as different policy outcomes have led to 'the German anti-nuclear movement' being considered a success while 'the French anti-nuclear movement' has come to be seen as a failure. The misleading distinction between the two is reinforced by the very different electoral scores of each country's Green parliamentary party: Die Grünen began to enter West Germany's regional

[13] This is to make no mention of the Soviet Union and its allies, who also continued to build new plants during the 1970s, or of countries like Brazil, Iran, and South Africa, which either purchased or considered purchasing civil nuclear technology from abroad in the same period.

[14] They also stand out in terms of the intensity of protest. See Mario Diani and Hein-Anton van der Heijden, 'Anti-Nuclear Movements across States', in *States and Anti-Nuclear Movements*, edited by Helena Flam (1994), p. 362; Felix Kolb, *Protest and Opportunities* (2007), p. 224. The opposition to nuclear energy in these two countries is thus not necessarily representative of the 'European' or 'global' anti-nuclear movement(s) of which it was a part, though this book argues that these cases can tell us much about the complexity of transnational relationships more generally.

[15] As of 31 December 2014, 76.9 per cent of electricity produced in France was nuclear in origin (418 terawatts in 2014). Only the United States, with a population four times as large, produced more electricity from nuclear sources in absolute terms (799 TW), but this amounted to no more than 19.5 per cent of the total electricity produced in that country. IAEA, *Reactors in the World 2015*, pp. 10–11, 76. In Germany, the coalition between Social Democrats and Greens established an agreement with the nuclear industry in 2000, which was put into law in 2002. In 2010, a coalition of Christian Democrats and Liberals, who had been hostile to the phase-out from the beginning, significantly decelerated the phase-out, but then sped it up again following the Fukushima nuclear accident in 2011.

parliaments in the 1980s, were elected to the Bundestag in 1984, served as the junior partner in national government (with Joschka Fischer occupying the important post of foreign minister) from 1998 to 2005, and even became the strongest party in the federal state of Baden-Württemberg in 2011; in France, Les Verts and their splinter parties won no seats in the Assemblée Nationale until 1997 and have served in government only briefly, always subordinate to the Parti Socialiste, and never outside the environmental ministry.[16] Yet the anti-nuclear movement of the 1970s from which these parties (claim to have) emerged was not particularly interested in parliaments or political power. It was also much more internally diverse and contradictory than the organized groups that have since succeeded it, and therefore needs to be approached differently. Recovering the more ambiguous history of anti-nuclear protest prior to the parliamentarization of the 1980s is thus one of the principal tasks of this book.

Remembering the 1970s anti-nuclear movement also entails questioning national histories and popular perceptions which have read narratives of success and failure backward in time. French environmentalism is commonly assumed to have made a 'late and timid' start and always to have been at a disadvantage compared to its 'Anglo-Saxon, German, and Scandinavian neighbours'.[17] Guillaume Sainteny has argued that ecology is 'elusive' (*introuvable*) in France and implicitly compared it with the shipwreck depicted on his book cover.[18] Environmental historian Michael Bess has argued that radical environmentalism never quite caught on in France because that society's twin longings for *dirigiste* high-technology projects and rural, peasant life led to a 'light-green' compromise.[19] German historians have likewise highlighted national particularities that seem to explain the special resonance of environmentalism there, such as understandings of *Heimat* and national identity, the history of nature protection organizations, or the compatibility of certain ecological ideas with

[16] Both Die Grünen and Les Verts have traditionally done better in European elections. In national politics, French ecologists obtained more than 10 per cent of the vote in 1993, but split their vote among three different parties so that none made it into parliament.

[17] Roger Cans, *Mouvement écolo en France* (2006), p. 9.

[18] Guillaume Sainteny, *L'introuvable écologisme* (2000). The title is reminiscent of Raymond Aron's pessimistic assessment of 1968, *La révolution introuvable* (1968).

[19] Michael Bess, *Light-Green Society* (2003), pp. 11–52, 115–40. France's lacklustre environmental reputation is largely traceable to its nuclear policies: the *force de frappe*, heavy reliance on nuclear energy, the bombing of Greenpeace's *Rainbow Warrior* ship, and authorities' unconvincing dismissals of the dangers presented by the Chernobyl accident. Though Bess attempts to dispel the impression of French environmentalist weakness, his book has been criticized for reinforcing national stereotypes. For a sharp critique, see Geneviève Massard-Guilbaud, 'Une « société vert claire » ?', *Vingtième siècle* 113, no. 1 (2012).

Nazi authoritarianism.[20] In the popular imagination, these arguments have occasionally been distorted into the idea that environmentalism in West Germany is rooted in a specifically 'German angst' with regard to modernity.[21]

The national particularities at the centre of these studies mask a great deal about how the anti-nuclear movement emerged in the first place. During the 1970s, activists in France and West Germany conceived of their opposition to nuclear energy not in national terms, but primarily in local ones. Especially under the presidency of Valéry Giscard d'Estaing (1974–81) and the chancellorship of Helmut Schmidt (1974–82), many protesters felt they had no means of affecting national politics on this issue, and so they turned their energies to undermining it at the local level instead. Things did not improve greatly for the anti-nuclear movement under their successors, François Mitterrand (1981–95) and Helmut Kohl (1982–98), but both the professionalization of protest and increasing national divergence make it difficult to speak of 'popular politics' on this issue in the same transnational sense during the 1980s (especially as the issue of nuclear weapons came to overshadow nuclear energy in West Germany). In the 1970s, activists pulled every lever and pushed every button at their disposal (including some they could only access from abroad) in their attempts to shut down nuclear power. Posing the question in terms of national 'success' or 'failure' thus largely misses the point for a movement that was both very local and transnational, and reduces a complex process to simple outcomes that tell us little about long-term change or about what protest meant to participants and the societies of which they were a part.

This book deliberately eschews any reference to 'the French anti-nuclear movement' or to a separate, West German counterpart, preferring to speak of the anti-nuclear movement *in* France or *in* West Germany. This reflects an understanding of anti-nuclear protest as part of a trans-national network, which may have had an unequal presence in different localities, but within which arguments, strategies, and indeed activists themselves circulated relatively freely. Activism was one transnational activity (like migration, tourism, and so on) which brought people together on the basis of shared experiences that pushed the usual geographic and

---

[20] See Raymond H. Dominick, *Environmental Movement in Germany* (1992), pp. 81–115; Franz-Josef Brüggemeier et al., eds, *How Green Were the Nazis?* (2005); Jonathan Olsen, *Nature and Nationalism* (1999); Willi Oberkrome, *Deutsche Heimat* (2004); Joachim Radkau and Frank Uekötter, eds, *Naturschutz und Nationalsozialismus* (2003). See also J. R. McNeill, *Something New under the Sun* (2000), pp. 329–31.
[21] Joachim Radkau argues against this idea in 'Mythos German Angst', *Blätter für deutsche und internationale Politik*, no. 5 (May 2011), p. 79.

social limits into the background, even if it did not eliminate them entirely. This book therefore examines the anti-nuclear movement in France and West Germany from the perspective of transnational social history in order to explain what brought its participants together, how it worked during its formative phase, and why it developed the way it did.

TRANSNATIONAL SOCIAL HISTORY

As transnational history, one purpose of this book is to draw attention to people and processes that lie outside, between, and across national narratives, or which otherwise cannot be contained fully within them.[22] One method transnational historians often use involves focusing on 'transfer', examining how ideas and practices are diffused between national contexts, whether indirectly (i.e. via media) or through the engagement of 'active transnational' carriers.[23] Unfortunately, 'transfer' tends to imply a unidirectional flow of ideas between supposedly distinct objects, which can obscure ways in which transnational exchange involves complex, multidirectional interactions in which partially overlapping, internally contradictory entities affect one another.[24] For a movement as decentralized and interconnected as anti-nuclear protest in the 1970s, it might be more apt to conceive of such circulations in terms of repeated (attempts at) 'synchronization' between local sites and across national borders.[25] However, some transnational phenomena cannot be grasped by looking only at movement from one context to another (however that is conceived). Postcolonial scholarship has helpfully focused attention on liminal, in-between spaces, and highlighted the 'hybridities' that can emerge even from asymmetrical interactions such as those between England and

---

[22]   Kiran Klaus Patel, *Nach der Nationalfixiertheit* (2004); Patricia Clavin, 'Defining Transnationalism', *Contemporary European History* 14, no. 4 (2005); Jürgen Kocka, 'Comparison and Beyond', *History and Theory* 42, no. 1 (February 2003); Hartmut Kaelble, 'Vergleich und Transfer', *H-Soz-u-Kult* (8 February 2005).

[23]   Timothy Scott Brown, *West Germany and the Global Sixties* (2013), p. 44; Ingrid Gilcher-Holtey, 'Transfer zwischen Studentenbewegungen', in *Transnationale Öffentlichkeiten im 20. Jahrhundert*, edited by Hartmut Kaelble et al. (2002). On the related concept of 'diffusion' in sociology, see Doug McAdam and Dieter Rucht, 'Cross-National Diffusion', *Annals of the American Academy of Political and Social Science* 528 (July 1993).

[24]   Michael Werner and Bénédicte Zimmermann, 'Penser l'histoire croisée', *Annales* 58, no. 1 (2003), pp. 12–15.

[25]   Ingrid Gilcher-Holtey, drawing on Pierre Bourdieu's notion of 'critical events', describes how the Tet Offensive helped synchronize protest in 1968. See Ingrid Gilcher-Holtey, *68er Bewegung* (2001), p. 72.

India or France and Africa.[26] Though relations between protesters in wealthy, allied, European states are not structured by the same inequalities that reign in imperial centre–periphery relations, insights from postcolonial studies can inform work on Western Europe, where transnational interactions are powerful, frequent, and often overlooked in state-centred historiography.[27] Since the 1990s, scholars from France and Germany especially have been engaged in an intense theoretical debate about transnational history, one result of which has been the development of *histoire croisée* as an alternative to comparative and transfer history. Known in English as 'entangled history', this approach insists on recognizing overlap between objects of comparison and examining spaces, moments, and cycles in which they interact.[28] A further advantage of *histoire croisée* is that the entanglements it examines are not defined exclusively in terms of nation states, but can encompass relationships between different kinds of objects at multiple levels of scale.

Yet many studies in transnational history have had problems conceptualizing protest, particularly when the movements in question were not primarily organized at the national level. Most existing scholarship on post-war transnational social movements tends to focus on the themes and sources of diplomatic, intellectual, or organizational history: relations between states and intergovernmental bodies, the ideas of prominent thinkers, and the work of political parties, NGOs, or institutions. These approaches largely obscure interactions among activists, especially at the local level. At their worst, they risk misrepresenting protest as a response by anonymous masses to intellectual 'guides' or high politics, reversing the flow of agency: rather than focusing on the people who actually took to the streets, these studies make Great Men out to be the true instigators of protest.[29] Organizational studies likewise tend to focus on a single group

---

[26] This is especially true in the work of Homi Bhabha, e.g. *Location of Culture* (1994), p. 5. See also Kocka, 'Comparison and Beyond', p. 42.

[27] Indeed, Patricia Clavin has written of the need to open up the study of Europe itself through a closer examination of centripetal and centrifugal transnational ties within and beyond the (shifting) borders of the continent. See 'Time, Manner, Place', *European History Quarterly*, no. 40 (2010), pp. 630–1.

[28] Werner and Zimmermann, 'Penser l'histoire croisée', p. 15.

[29] For example, the diplomatic historian Jeremi Suri argues that protest in 1968 was the result of charismatic leaders like Kennedy and de Gaulle creating high hopes that they could not fulfil, leading disappointed citizens to protest in the idiom of intellectuals such as Herbert Marcuse. He therefore concludes that 'Organizational ties between protesters across different societies were a minimal factor' in 1968, since '[d]omestic conflicts grew from local conditions that, though unique in each case, produced a similar dynamic of rising expectations and attempted repressions'. Note that this view also conceives of *movement* connections among protesters in terms of 'organizational' ties. Jeremi Suri, *Power and Protest* (2003), p. 165.

to the detriment of others, and do not account for the informal participants and committed but non-organized activists who were vital to anti-
nuclear protest.[30] Furthermore, they associate transnational connections
almost exclusively with the prominent leaders of national organizations, an
approach which works poorly for anti-authoritarian activists who rejected
hierarchy. This book focuses instead on grassroots anti-nuclear activists
and the networks they forged within and beyond national borders, often
informally and independent of national organizations.

In doing so, it follows the work of social historians who have examined
other instances of 'popular protest' in post-war Europe.[31] Social history in
this sense is concerned with understanding the agency of individuals,
examining how they resisted, reinforced, and over time altered the structures of politics and society. Recent scholarship has drawn attention to the
importance of low-level interactions to this kind of long-term social
change. For example, Xavier Vigna and Michelle Zancarini-Fournel
have argued that the events of May 1968 led to 'improbable encounters'
within France between students and workers, workers and peasants,
French citizens and immigrants, and others who ordinarily had little or
no contact.[32] The 'de-compartmentalization' that occurred in this
moment was part of an attempt to enact utopian ideals that have had a
long-term impact on social relations (not least on the orientation of
subsequent social movements).[33] In certain instances, contact also led to
forms of 'hybridization', especially within the issue-centred local action
committees which formed in and after '68,[34] and which closely resemble
the *comités anti-nucléaires* and *Bürgerinitiativen* that proliferated across
France and West Germany during the 1970s. Social scientists have also
argued that such encounters have the potential to change political culture,
as Simone Tosi and Tommaso Vitale observe with regard to the Italian

---

[30] Social scientists have recently begun giving more attention to informal participation.
See, for example, Bert Klandermans et al., 'Mobilization without Organization', *European
Sociological Review* 30, no. 6 (2014).

[31] Some of these include Belinda Davis, 'Whole World Opening Up', in *Changing the
World, Changing Oneself*, edited by Belinda Davis et al. (2010); Robert Gildea et al., eds,
Europe's 1968 (2013); Richard I. Jobs, 'Youth Movements', *American Historical Review*
114, no. 2 (2009); Padraic Kenney, *Carnival of Revolution* (2002); Holger Nehring,
'National Internationalists', *Contemporary European History* 14, no. 4 (2005).

[32] Xavier Vigna and Michelle Zancarini-Fournel, 'Rencontres improbables', *Vingtième
siècle* 101, no. 1 (2009). See also Michelle Zancarini-Fournel, *Moment 68* (2008),
pp. 216–23.

[33] Geographers have similarly argued that place-based solidarities and the spaces of social
movement activism facilitate unstructured interactions between diverse individuals. Walter
Nicholls, 'Place, Networks, Space', *Transactions of the Institute of British Geographers* 34,
no. 1 (2009), pp. 79–83.

[34] Vigna and Zancarini-Fournel, 'Rencontres improbables', p. 172.

peace movement. Within the framework of peace activism, Catholics and Marxists had repeated, asymmetrical encounters over the course of several decades. Exchanges shifted over time, such that Catholics imitated Marxists in the 1950s, but later came to *be* imitated by them by the 1980s; interaction between the two led to changes in both that fed into Italian political culture more generally.[35] This argument demonstrates the potential embedded within 'popular politics': informal protest movements that cut across national, class, and other social boundaries bring unpredictable combinations of people together who interact and change one another as they pursue shared goals.[36] Entanglements like these do not, of course, always result in 'happy hybridities'.[37] Vigna and Zancarini-Fournel emphasize the fragmentary nature of such encounters, which can be interrupted by misunderstandings, clashing values, questions of violence, or simply impatience.[38] Yet as this book will seek to demonstrate, even when interrupted, such interactions often had an impact on the lives of individuals. Where they proved more durable, they were capable of bringing about broader political change.

Social history relies on different sources from those found in diplomatic archives, published works, or organizational papers. Newspapers, magazines, and radio and television broadcasts provide a valuable measure of how well protest resonates, but such sources filter out information about small or routine activities, internal disputes among activists, and the meanings participants ascribe to their own actions, because these are deemed too subjective or not publicly relevant. Some of these aspects come through more clearly in activists' own 'counter-media' (including movement newspapers, bulletins, pamphlets, and films), though these tend to reflect consensus views intended for public consumption. At the other end of the spectrum, police reports provide some of the greatest detail about protest activity as seen from outside, but they are heavily skewed by the biases, fears, and projections of officers who are generally more concerned with 'maintaining law and order' than understanding activists.[39] This book triangulates

---

[35] Simone Tosi and Tommaso Vitale, 'Explaining How Political Culture Changes', *Social Movement Studies* 8, no. 2 (2009).

[36] Davis, 'What's Left?'.

[37] Smadar Lavie and Ted Swedenburg, 'Between and Among', *Cultural Studies* 10, no. 1 (1996), p. 167.

[38] Vigna and Zancarini-Fournel, 'Rencontres improbables', pp. 173–7.

[39] Further misunderstandings arise from the tendency of police to regard demonstrators as adversaries (and vice versa) and to associate them with other 'enemies'. For instance, at an early demonstration in Fessenheim in 1971, French domestic intelligence (the Renseignments généraux, RG) described one international environmental organization as a movement that was opposed 'aux techniques avancées, surtout quand elles sont françaises'. Memo, 28 April 1971, AD Bas-Rhin, 1743 W 54. West German police likewise described

among these different sets of sources in order to understand the anti-nuclear movement more comprehensively. However, the movement itself is also only part of the story. Like any other social movement, it was built by its participants; focusing on their life histories provides a different, and often more illuminating, perspective on protest. This book therefore draws extensively on oral history interviews with former activists, including many 'grassroots elites' (local and regional organizers) but also casually or sporadically engaged individuals. Oral history is particularly suited to exploring subjectivity, relationships between the personal and the political, and changes over time in political engagement;[40] such sources allow one to gain access to many unrecorded events—and to better understand the importance that their protagonists did and did not ascribe to them. Used together with other sources, they can provide a valuable corrective to the excessive optimism of some transnational histories, revealing where cross-border links were truly developed and where tenuous connections were exaggerated.

As with any source, some caution is advised. The stories related here are second-hand memories, shared thirty years after the fact, and subject to conscious as well as unconscious distortions: some details have disappeared into the fog of time, certain embarrassments have likewise been 'forgotten', and some narrative embellishments have undoubtedly been made.[41] However, the aim of oral history is not to establish objective 'truth', but to get at the personal truths of the interviewee: as Alessandro Portelli writes, an interview 'tells us less about events as such than about their meaning [. . .], not just what people did, but what they wanted to do, what they believed they were doing, what they now think they did'.[42] In this book, oral history is thus not used to establish facts, but primarily to provide insight into how protagonists subjectively perceived events. Methodologically, oral histories of protest also have the advantage of

one publication as an 'organ of the Red Army Faction', and this in spite of the fact that 'Erkenntnisse über eine Finanzierung [. . .] durch die RAF nicht vorliegen.' Memo, 16 October 1979, Nds, 100 Acc. 2003/116 Nr. 67.

[40] See Robert Gildea and James Mark, 'Voices of Europe's '68', *Cultural and Social History* 8, no. 44 (2011), pp. 442–3; Gildea et al., *Europe's 1968*.

[41] Many written sources are also subject to similar limitations; for example, Alessandro Portelli argues that hardly any written sources are produced in the exact moment they describe. Alessandro Portelli, 'Peculiarities', *History Workshop Journal*, no. 12 (August 1981), p. 101. It would also be a fundamental mistake to regard the ghost-written memoirs and transcribed, edited musings of *grands témoins* as somehow more 'truthful' than the personal narratives of less formally powerful individuals. For examples of the former, see the statements by Helmut Schmidt and Valéry Giscard d'Estaing in Serge Berstein and Jean-François Sirinelli, eds, *Les années Giscard* (2006).

[42] Portelli, 'Peculiarities', pp. 99–100.

placing periods of activism in the contexts of entire lives and bringing into view politicizing and demobilizing perspectives that are not accounted for in other sources. In tandem with the written remnants of protest, this book draws on oral history to reconstruct lived experiences of activism in the 1970s.[43]

SITUATING ANTI-NUCLEAR PROTEST IN TIME AND SPACE

The anti-nuclear movement was at once transnational and deeply local, with the construction of specific nuclear facilities constituting the main flashpoint of protest during the 1970s. The history of anti-nuclear protest in the middle and second half of that decade is thus in many respects a history of those local struggles (see Fig. 1.1), aspects of which can be traced by looking at some of the most important demonstrations that took place.[44] These are held together within a loose narrative (details of which are explored in later chapters) that began in the Franco-German border region.

A nascent anti-nuclear movement first became visible to the media and authorities in 1971 following the protest against the construction of a nuclear power station in Fessenheim (Alsace). Though small by later standards, the demonstration attracted nearly as many participants as the town (population: 1,200) had residents. Moreover, it was the first in a wave of protests throughout the region that would last for a decade or more (see Table 1.1). Only a few weeks later, this demonstration was followed by another in Bugey (Rhône-Alpes) attended by an astounding 15,000 participants, most of whom had come at the call of the nationally circulated satirical paper *Charlie Hebdo*. The protest, though largely a one-off event, appeared to constitute 'a counterculture revival of the themes of May 1968'.[45] These two early demonstrations in France showed the potential for protest against nuclear energy, which

---

[43] For examples, see Gildea et al., *Europe's 1968*; Kenney, *Carnival of Revolution*; Davis, 'Whole World Opening Up'; Studs Terkel, *Division Street* (1968); Nicolas Daum, *Mai 68 raconté par des anonymes* (2008). For more on methods, see Portelli, 'Peculiarities'; Gildea and Mark, 'Voices of Europe's '68'; Alistair Thomson, 'Unreliable Memories?', in *Historical Controversies and Historians*, edited by William M. Lamont (1998); Paul Thompson, *Voice of the Past*, 3rd edn (2000).

[44] Demonstrations serve as milestones to mark a certain development of protest, but, as other chapters will show, they are not the only or even necessarily most important manifestation of activism.

[45] Dorothy Nelkin and Michael Pollak, *Atom Besieged* (1981), p. 58.

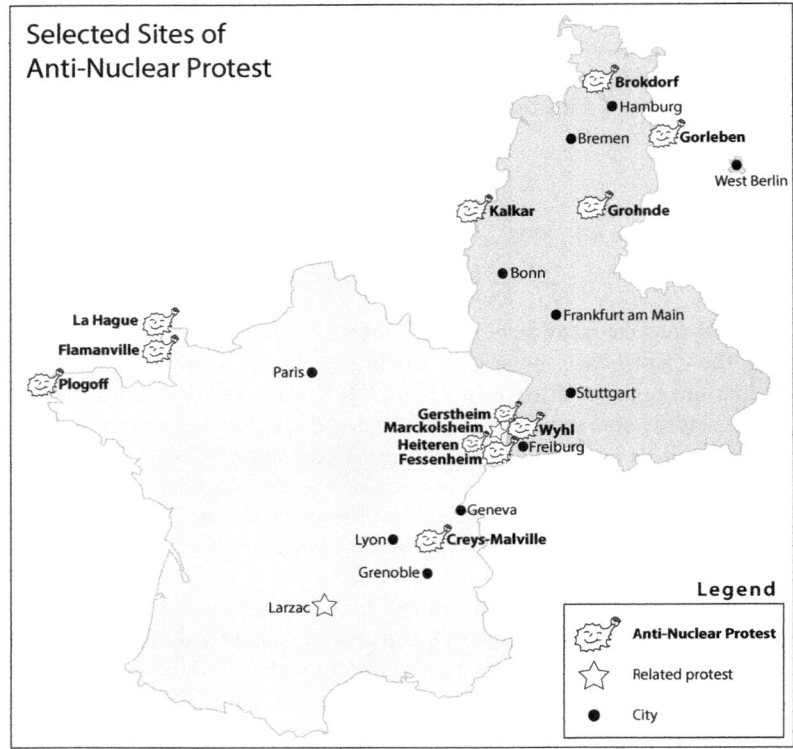

Fig. 1.1. Map of sites considered in this study. Map created by Andrew Tompkins.

would continue to grow, attracting much more attention by the middle of the decade.

The first major breakthrough for anti-nuclear protest in West Germany occurred 30 kilometres north of Fessenheim along the Rhine, in the town of Wyhl (Baden-Württemberg). The proximity of the protests was no accident. On both sides of the border, concern about nuclear plans in the region had been growing quietly since at least 1970.[46] Having been unable to stop construction in Fessenheim from beginning in September 1971, nuclear energy opponents took decisive action when work crews arrived at the (separate) German site in February 1975. After an early protest at the

---

[46] On the German side, protests began in 1971–2 in Breisach, before the project was moved to Wyhl on 19 July 1973. Bernd Nössler and Margret de Witt, eds, *Kein Kernkraftwerk in Wyhl* (1976), pp. 29–44. See also Stephen Milder, *Greening Democracy* (2016).

Table 1.1. Major anti-nuclear and related demonstrations in France and West Germany up to 1981

Country[47]	Location	Date	Estimated number of participants[48]
FR	Fessenheim	12 April 1971	1,000–1,500[P]
FR	Bugey	10 July 1971	15,000[M]
FR	Larzac	25–6 August 1973	80,000[M]
FR	Larzac	17–18 August 1974	23,000[P]–103,000[A]
FR	Marckolsheim	20 September 1974 (site occupied until cancellation of construction plans on 25 February 1975)	4500[A]
DE	Wyhl	18 February 1975 (site occupied until 20 February)	200[P]
DE	Wyhl	23 February 1975 (site occupied until 7 November, then kept 'guarded' by activists thereafter)	7,000[P]–28,000[A]
FR	Across France	26–7 April 1975	15,000–20,000[M] (Paris) + 8,000–10,000[M] (provinces)
FR	Creys-Malville	3–4 July 1976 (site occupied until 8 July)	5,000[P]–20,000[M]; 300–500[P] remain on site
DE	Brokdorf	30 October 1976	5,000[P]–8,000[A]; 800[P]–2,000[A] occupy a portion of the site for about four hours *(760 police)*
DE	Brokdorf	13 November 1976	25,000[P]–30,000[A] *(1,300 police)*
DE	Brokdorf and Itzehoe	19 February 1977	10,000[P] (Brokdorf) + 10,000[P] (Itzehoe) or 50,000[A] (Total) *(7,907 police)*
DE	Grohnde	19 March 1977	6,000[P/A]–20,000[A]
FR	Malville	31 July 1977	20,000[P]–60,000[A]
FR	Larzac	13–14 August 1977	15,000[P]–50,000[M]

(continued)

[47] FR = France, DE = West Germany.
[48] By Source: P = Police, M = Media, A = Activists.

Table 1.1. Continued

Country	Location	Date	Estimated number of participants
DE	Kalkar	24 September 1977	40,000[P]–70,000[A]
DE	Hannover	31 March 1979 (following decentralized protests in mid-March and a tractor journey from Gorleben starting 25 March)	100,000[A]
FR	Plogoff	16 March 1980 (celebrating the end of the 6-week EUP)	50,000[P]–60,000[A]
DE	Gorleben	3 May–4 June 1980 (occupation of Tiefbohrstelle 1004)	5,000[A] initial squatters 2,000[A] squatters evicted *(by 8,000[A/M] police)*
FR	Plogoff	24–5 May 1980	40,000[P]–150,000[A], including Larzac delegation and guest speakers from across Europe
FR	La Hague	28–9 June 1980 (cancelled at last minute due to weather)	7,000[P]–30,000[M]
DE	Brokdorf	28 February 1981 (banned demonstration)	100,000[A/M]

site was quickly repressed by authorities, activists held a demonstration on 23 February attended by 28,000 people, followed immediately by an occupation of the construction site that lasted until 7 November. A major factor in the size and success of the protest was how West German protesters profited from protest experiences across the border. A few months before (and only 10 kilometres from Wyhl across the Rhine) in Marckolsheim, environmental activists (some of whom had been involved in Fessenheim earlier) had occupied the construction site of a planned chemical plant. They in turn had been inspired partly by the highly publicized protests that had taken place on the Larzac plateau (Midi-Pyrénées) in southern France in 1973 and 1974 to oppose a military base.[49] Information and strategies from Fessenheim,

---

[49] See Robert Gildea and Andrew Tompkins, 'The Transnational in the Local', *Journal of Contemporary History* (2015); McAdam and Rucht, 'Cross-National Diffusion'.

Marckolsheim, and the Larzac (all in France all) flowed together in Wyhl, where they provided the spark that ignited a larger anti-nuclear movement.

The site occupation in Wyhl spawned many imitators in West Germany, France, and elsewhere, the most immediately important of which was in Brokdorf (Schleswig-Holstein). In the wake of the Wyhl site occupation, local activists and allies who rushed to their side from Hamburg (about an hour's drive away) borrowed strategies and arguments wholesale from their counterparts along the Franco-German border.[50] However, police too had learned from Wyhl, and went to extremes to prevent a new site occupation. Protest in Brokdorf thus took on a very different dynamic, as police used far greater force to expel the mix of urban and rural protesters who attempted to occupy the site on 30 October 1976 and again on 13 November. Subsequent demonstrations in northern Germany (in Brokdorf on 19 February 1977, in Grohnde one month later, then again in Brokdorf in February 1981 after a pause in construction) would vacillate between non-violence and violence.

The sudden change of course in West Germany had a knock-on effect across the border, inspiring many (and more militant) demonstrators to join an 'international' protest in Creys-Malville (Rhône-Alpes). The construction site there of a fast breeder reactor (FBR) had already been the focus of an attention-getting, peaceful protest by up to 20,000 people in July 1976. The FBR was a special technology supposedly capable of producing more fuel (as plutonium) than it consumed (as uranium), making it central to the fuel cycle of France's nuclear programme. As police and protesters in France prepared for the demonstration that would take place on 31 July 1977, both sides had frequent contact with their counterparts in Germany, and the violence in Brokdorf fed fears of a similar confrontation in Malville. In this tense atmosphere, the protest ended tragically with the death of Vital Michalon, a young physics teacher killed by a police stun grenade exploding at close impact.

Instead of invigorating anti-nuclear protest across France and beyond as activists had hoped, Malville signalled the end of the movement's influence on national politics in France, and set it back in neighbouring West Germany as well.[51] A thousand or more German demonstrators had attended the demonstration in Malville, and many returned home fearful and disappointed.[52] For the rest of West Germany, a similar message

---

[50] Compare Nössler and de Witt, *Kein Kernkraftwerk in Wyhl*, pp. 248–9; BUU, *Brokdorf* (1977), pp. 59–60.

[51] Dieter Rucht, 'Movement and the State in France', in *States and Anti-Nuclear Movements* (1994), p. 136.

[52] No accurate numbers are available, but police counted 800–1,200 people at the main campsite to which Germans were sent before the demonstration. Roy, 'Rapport'.

would be driven home on 24 September 1977, when authorities all but prevented a demonstration against that country's own FBR from taking place in Kalkar. Malville and Kalkar thus represent two closely related protests that took place under the shadow of escalating violence, synchronized across borders. Thereafter, the opposition to nuclear energy fragmented internally, as groups advocating different strategies became much more reluctant to come together for mass demonstrations.

Outcomes in France and West Germany also began to drift apart around the same time, as the crucial matter of nuclear waste disposal showed. In France, the issue had already been raised in late 1976, when the Confédération Française Démocratique du Travail (CFDT) trade union made working conditions at the La Hague nuclear fuel reprocessing centre (Basse-Normandie, not far from another planned power station in Flamanville) the subject of a documentary, and subsequently the focus of a strike.[53] Cooperation between trade unionists and anti-nuclear activists was mutually beneficial (giving the former greater leverage and the latter inside information), but it was necessarily focused on improving safety rather than shutting down the facility. Nuclear waste became central to protest in West Germany after politicians and courts decided that plausible plans for waste disposal would be a precondition for approving new nuclear power stations.[54] On 22 February 1977, the government of Niedersachsen announced that a 'nuclear waste disposal park' (integrating both waste storage and a reprocessing centre modelled on the La Hague facility) would be built near the border with East Germany in Gorleben. Within a couple of years, Gorleben became the focus of revitalized anti-nuclear protest in West Germany, even as French protest continued to be haunted by the legacy of Malville.

Contingency also played a role in reinforcing these developments. Days before the end of a month-long campaign against the Gorleben project, the accident at Three Mile Island nuclear power station near Harrisburg, Pennsylvania (USA) on 28 March 1979 vastly increased concern about the risks of nuclear power—and dramatically increased turnout at the long-planned demonstration in Hannover three days later (to as many as 100,000 demonstrators). This was the beginning of a consolidation of protest in West Germany, cemented by the first major anti-nuclear demonstration in that nation's capital on 22 October (again 100,000).

---

[53] François Jacquemain, *Condamnés à réussir*, 1976, 60 mins. German activists translated the text of the film and printed it with other reports as Arbeitskreis Radioaktive Verseuchung, 'Verdammt zum Erfolg – Filmtext – Bericht über den Streik in der WAA La Hague – Das Geschäft mit dem Atomstrom', brochure, 25 pp., 1977, ASB, 12-A4-89. Originally built in the 1950s under military auspices, La Hague was expanded and turned into a commercial enterprise during the 1970s.

[54] See BUU, *Brokdorf*, p. 67.

If coincidence helped protest in Germany, it dampened it (literally) in France. There, isolated protests against nuclear power stations continued everywhere from Cruas-Meysse (Rhône-Alpes) to Gravelines (Nord) to Le Pellerin (Pays de la Loire), but there was little effective mobilization beyond the local level until a major rally planned for 29–30 June 1980 in La Hague.[55] The movement's flagging fortunes were not helped when a violent storm forced the event's cancellation at the last minute, after some 30,000 demonstrators had already arrived.

Protests that took place in 1980 would become emblematic of the ultimately divergent political outcomes in West Germany and France. Activists achieved a media coup in Gorleben, by then fast becoming the undisputed centre of anti-nuclear protest in West Germany, when they occupied a test drilling site[56] for a month starting on 3 May 1980 and declared it to constitute the territory of an autonomous 'Republik Freies Wendland' (RFW). Though the event went down as a defeat in the short term (squatters were evicted from the site by 8,000 police on 4 June),[57] the protest laid the groundwork for long-term cooperation that has now sustained local protest in Gorleben and national opposition to nuclear energy in Germany for more than thirty-five years. Vociferous protest continued to follow the reprocessing centre throughout the 1980s, as German planners moved it first to Dragahn (Niedersachsen) and then to Wackersdorf (Bayern) before ultimately dropping the idea entirely in favour of a contract with France to process waste at La Hague. However, as local protests oriented themselves increasingly towards a national movement, the transnational connections at the grassroots that had repeatedly synchronized protest in the 1970s became less and less important. The anti-nuclear movement has not been successful everywhere in Germany, but it has remained vibrant enough to keep (re-)mobilizing support nationally, help push through a planned phase-out, and make Germany appear much greener than its neighbour across the Rhine.

France too witnessed dramatic protest around the same time, notably in the remote town of Plogoff in Bretagne. Though protest there remained primarily local and regional (as at most other French sites after 1977), it attracted national and even international attention. Conflict that had been brewing there for several years finally came to a head during a six-week public inquiry starting on 31 January 1980. Local activists fought tooth and nail

[55] See P. H., 'après la hague, un rapide bilan', *Offensives*, no. 8 (July–September 1980), pp. 5–6.
[56] The drilling was undertaken to verify whether underground salt deposits would provide a safe environment for long-term storage of radioactive waste.
[57] 'BRD-Truppen überfallen Freie Republik Wendland', *tageszeitung*, 5 June 1980, p. 1.

against daily incursions by national police and military units, who were tasked with ensuring that the inquiry be held in spite of the local mayor's refusal to cooperate. After the inquiry ended, protesters held two large rallies on 16 March and 24 May 1980 to celebrate, attracting up to 100,000 people from across France and Western Europe. When François Mitterrand was elected the first Socialist president of the Fifth Republic the following year, one of his first actions was to cancel the Plogoff nuclear project (together with the Larzac military camp). However, after a brief moratorium, other components of the national nuclear programme proceeded largely unchanged, in spite of similarly intense local resistance in Chooz (Champagne-Ardenne) and Golfech (Midi-Pyrénées) and despite complaints from neighbouring states near Cattenom (Lorraine, along France's border with Luxembourg and Germany) and Malville (near the Swiss border). As of today, no local struggle in France has achieved the national stature of Gorleben in Germany, and no organization has succeeded in channelling the disparate protests that continue to take place periodically into an effective force at the national level.[58] This has created the appearance of a stable consensus in favour of nuclear power in France, and led to a collective amnesia about the vibrant movement that once opposed it there—and which contributed decisively to the growth of protest in West Germany.

The narrative described above and pursued in greater detail throughout this book is focused first on protest that involved significant cross-border connections between individuals and events, and second on local protests that resonated nationally and transnationally (e.g. Brokdorf, Plogoff). That said, it necessarily excludes several other notable sites: Braud-et-Saint-Louis (Aquitaine), where attention-getting protests (supported by the Larzac farmers) in 1975 failed to stop construction; the aforementioned struggles in Chooz and Golfech, where sometimes violent local protests resembling those in Plogoff occurred in the early 1980s; Cattenom, which continues to attract sporadic protest today; Biblis (Hessen), where anti-nuclear protest became linked with (and ultimately overshadowed by) the struggle against Frankfurt airport's Startbahn West; Grafenrheinfeld, Isar/Ohu, and Rehling (Bayern), where protest was more regional, homogeneous, and smaller than elsewhere in Germany; and Wackersdorf (also Bayern), which continued the protests against a nuclear reprocessing centre that had begun in Gorleben. This book makes occasional reference to Kaiseraugst (Switzerland), which had an important, albeit secondary, influence on protests in the Upper Rhine Valley.[59]

---

[58] Sortir du nucléaire (SDN) has attempted to do so, but the organization has suffered from internal problems in recent years.

[59] See Françoise Lafaye, 'Une centrale pas très nucléaire' (1994); Ute Hasenöhrl, *Zivilgesellschaft und Protest* (2011), pp. 405–71; Alexandre Bardelli, 'L'impact d'une

PROTEST IN HISTORICAL DEBATE

This book contributes to a wider literature on the nature of protest in Europe during the second half of the twentieth century and attempts to situate the anti-nuclear movement within it.[60] It is structured so as to answer a range of questions about protest, some of which have been raised by scholars in other disciplines (chiefly sociologists and political scientists) or by historians examining other social movements. The most directly relevant studies pertain to '1968', the so-called 'new social movements' (NSMs), and the history of environmentalism.

The protests associated with '1968' are among the most frequently studied in twentieth-century Western European history. Most studies of them are focused on the activities of a few student organizations and their leaders in select major cities over the span of a few months in 1967–9. Though the events of those years were perceived to be globally interconnected at the time, the vast majority of existing histories focus on separate national narratives, sometimes presented alongside one another but seldom connected.[61] Commemorations of 1968 (particularly at ten-year anniversaries) have been important in shaping and producing its (frequently

---

centrale électronucléaire' (1997); Tauer, *Störfall*, pp. 261–8, 301–12; Patrick Kupper, *Atomenergie und gespaltene Gesellschaft* (2003). On Braud, see also Xavier Vigna, 'Lip et Larzac', in *68 : une histoire collective*, edited by Philippe Artières and Michelle Zancarini-Fournel (2008). Several of these protests have not yet been closely examined by historians, but there exists extensive documentation produced by activists themselves, including *Nur wer sich bewegt* (1982); Claude Courtes and Jean-Claude Driant, *Golfech* (1999); Roman Arens et al., *Wackersdorf* (1987); Wolfgang Ehmke, *Zwischenschritte* (1987); Michael Schroeren, *Zum Beispiel Kaiseraugst* (1977); *Un récit de lutte de Chooz* (1998).

[60] The most comprehensive existing treatments are found in the work of political scientists and sociologists, including especially Kolb, *Protest and Opportunities*; Nelkin and Pollak, *Atom Besieged*; Wolfgang Rüdig, *Anti-Nuclear Movements* (1990); Christian Joppke, *Mobilizing against Nuclear Energy* (1993). The German case has been examined repeatedly, most notably in Dieter Rucht, *Von Wyhl nach Gorleben* (1980). There are fewer French studies, though a notable exception (from the perspective of Science, Technology, and Society studies) is Sezin Topçu, *La France nucléaire* (2013). Several recent theses have taken an explicitly transnational approach, including Milder, *Greening Democracy* (2016); Karena Kalmbach, 'Meanings of a Disaster' (2014); Emmanuel Rivat, 'La transnationalisation de la cause antinucléaire' (2013).

[61] The work of the 'Around 1968' research group constitutes an important exception in its consistent attention to transnational connections. See Gildea et al., *Europe's 1968*; Robert Gildea et al., 'European Radicals and the "Third World"', *Cultural and Social History* 8, no. 4 (2011). Other transnational histories with a narrower geographic focus include Gilcher-Holtey, *68er Bewegung*; Martin Klimke, *Other Alliance* (2010); Jeremy Varon, *Bringing the War Home* (2004). Among the better books telling national narratives side by side are David Caute, *1968* (1988); Ronald Fraser et al., *1968* (1988); Norbert Frei, *1968* (2008); Barbara Ehrenreich and John Ehrenreich, *Long March* (1969).

nationalized) historiography. They have also contributed to powerful media narratives about '68 that shift with the political winds and the interventions of former protagonists.[62] Because these memories are so contested, it is difficult to specify concrete, long-term legacies of 1968. In terms of individual trajectories, many histories trace only relatively prominent individuals such as Daniel Cohn-Bendit or Joschka Fischer.[63] Historians have also traced multiple movement trajectories, none of which is satisfying on its own. In the short term, various radical left groups (known as *gauchistes* in France and *K-Gruppen* in Germany) responded to perceived failures by advocating organization of the working class in line with Marxist–Leninist, Maoist, or Trotskyist theory. Many authors, however, are quick (arguably too quick) to dismiss such groups as having had little or no long-term impact. Instead, they focus on feminism and/or 'terrorism' as (respectively) positive or negative successors in the 1970s.[64] Finally, there are several studies that have asserted continuity with subsequent protest via concepts such as 'participatory democracy'[65]—which supposedly animated anti-nuclear protest and other so-called NSMs as well.[66]

The term 'new social movements' (NSMs) describes protest on a variety of issues which (though not necessarily new) took on far greater importance in the 1970s than ever before, including women's liberation, anti-nuclear protest, gay rights, peace, and so on. According to contemporary social scientists such as Ronald Inglehart, the common denominator of these diverse protests was their purported anchoring in 'post-materialist'

---

[62] For criticism of this, see especially Kristin Ross, *May 68* (2002).

[63] Among the better such studies is Paul Hockenos, *Joschka Fischer and the Berlin Republic* (2008).

[64] On these trajectories, see Arthur Marwick, *Sixties* (1998); Nick Thomas, *Protest Movements* (2003).

[65] There is a growing literature on democracy and its development in the post-war period, and a tendency, especially in West German historiography, to regard the 1970s as a turning point for 'democratization'. This book takes an agnostic view on whether and how anti-nuclear protest led to 'democracy' for several reasons. First, many narratives of democratic progress tend to be teleological and oriented towards high politics within national political venues, framing arguments in ways that this book's approach aims to avoid. Second, claims to 'democracy' were part of contemporary discourse and, indeed, of the anti-nuclear movement's own rhetorical strategy, and so cannot be taken at face value. Third and most importantly, meanings of 'democracy' were (and remain) highly contested. Anti-nuclear activists understood themselves to be 'democratic', but they did not always agree on what this meant or on how it related to the liberal parliamentary systems that also claimed the label. On the fluidity of this term over time, see Martin Conway and Volker Depkat, 'Discussing Democracy', in *Europeanization in the Twentieth Century*, edited by Martin Conway and Kiran Klaus Patel (2010).

[66] See, for example, Carl Boggs, 'Rethinking the Sixties Legacy', in *Social Movements*, edited by Stanford M. Lyman (1995); Eley, *Forging Democracy*; Gerd-Rainer Horn, *Spirit of '68* (2007).

values such as ecology, to which a young and highly educated generation turned while growing up in the prosperous *trente glorieuses*. Their experiences contrasted with those of prior generations, for whom the Second World War was a living memory, and prior protest movements, the primary concern of which had supposedly been the material well-being of the industrial working class.[67] Alain Touraine even hypothesized that the anti-nuclear movement might, in a post-industrial era, 'take over the central role played by the working-class movement and the labour conflicts of industrial society'.[68] Others, however, used the distinction between 'new' and 'old' values as a means of categorically excluding Marxist groups, reinforcing with theoretical trappings the claims of some anti-nuclear protesters that these groups did not belong (often because they were seen as competition for leadership). The NSM paradigm has fallen into disuse since the 1990s, as subsequent scholars have rightfully questioned the alleged novelty of these movements. However, given that the sociology of protest usually focuses on case studies of supposedly discrete movements, the NSM literature remains valuable for recognizing the simultaneity and compatibility of protest on a range of issues during the 1970s. Anti-nuclear protests were notable for the way in which they combined different groups and agendas, a phenomenon that also characterizes environmentalist movements more broadly.[69]

In the past two decades, a growing literature has developed on environmental history, much of it addressing the history of environmentalism.[70] Though studies have traced 'green' thinking back to Jean-Jacques Rousseau, uncovered ecological problems present during the French Revolution, and found predecessors to today's 'environmentalists' in

---

[67] Ronald Inglehart, *Silent Revolution* (1977).

[68] Alain Touraine et al., *Prophétie anti-nucléaire* (1980), p. 3. The English translation used here is taken from Alain Touraine et al., *Anti-Nuclear Protest*, trans. Peter Fawcett (1983), p. 11. Touraine is unique in speaking of 'the' new social movement; most other authors speak of NSMs in the plural.

[69] For examples, see Karl-Werner Brand et al., *Aufbruch* (1983); Jan Willem Duyvendak, *Power of Politics* (1995); Hanspeter Kriesi et al., *New Social Movements in Western Europe* (1995); Ruud Koopmans, *Democracy from Below* (1995). For criticism of NSM analysis, see Nelson Pichardo, 'New Social Movements: A Critical Review', *Annual Review of Sociology* 23 (1997); David Plotke, 'What's So New?', in *Social Movements*; Lorna Weir, 'Limitations of NSM Analysis', *Studies in Political Economy*, no. 40 (Spring 1993). Weir in particular characterizes old/new distinctions as being based on 'trite binarisms' and argues that 'The critique is aimed against the straw figures which NSM theorists have fashioned with respect to both socialist and social movement history.'

[70] For reviews of environmental history as a field, see Franz-Josef Brüggemeier, 'Umweltgeschichte', *Archiv für Sozialgeschichte* 43 (2003); Fabien Locher and Grégory Quenet, 'L'histoire environnementale', *Revue d'histoire moderne et contemporaine* 56, no. 4 (2009); J. R. McNeill, 'Nature and Culture', *History and Theory* 42, no. 4 (December 2003).

Germany's nature protection societies of the nineteenth century, historians generally agree that the early 1970s constituted a 'turning point' or 'watershed' that ultimately led to an 'ecological revolution'.[71] This sudden growth occurred not because environmental problems were new, but because people began to construct grievances differently, perceiving problems that had once seemed locally isolated in relation to a globally interconnected natural environment.[72] According to some, this consciousness was shaped by landmark publications such as Rachel Carson's *Silent Spring* (1962) or the Club of Rome's *Limits to Growth* study (1972).[73] While one can trace an important evolution in environmentalist thinking by studying canonical texts by critical scientists, protest was the work of people and not of pure ideas.[74] Other authors point to media-savvy organizations and their leaders, such as the activists-turned-politicians Brice Lalonde of Les Amis de la Terre and Petra Kelly of the Bundesverband Bürgerinitiativen Umweltschutz.[75] Professional NGOs have since become so synonymous with environmental protest that it is difficult to conceive of the latter without them.[76] Political parties and professional organizations are an enduring legacy of environmentalism, but it requires some effort to peel back the layers and uncover the informal, decentralized grassroots movements from which they emerged.

Taken together, these different studies point to several problems in explaining the history of anti-nuclear protest. The first, addressed in Chapter 2, relates to its emergence: who protested against nuclear energy and why? Answering this question helps to historicize the movement, showing the kinds of continuities that tend to be marginalized in social scientific studies (particularly on NSMs). However, those continuities

---

[71] On the change around 1970, see Bess, *Light-Green Society*, p. 80; Frank Uekötter, *Am Ende der Gewissheiten* (2011), p. 101; Joachim Radkau, *Ära der Ökologie* (2011), pp. 134–7. On precursors to environmentalism, see Cans, *Mouvement écolo en France*; Thomas Le Roux, *Laboratoire des pollutions industrielles* (2011); Radkau, *Ära der Ökologie*.

[72] Uekötter, *Am Ende der Gewissheiten*, pp. 82–5.

[73] These were supplemented by numerous French and German publications, including Michel Bosquet [pseud. André Gorz], *Écologie et liberté* (1977); Bernard Charbonneau, *Le Jardin de Babylone* (1969); Robert Jungk, *Atomstaat* (1977); Holger Strohm, *Friedlich in die Katastrophe. Eine Dokumentation über Kernkraftwerke* (1973).

[74] Joachim Radkau, *Natur und Macht* (2000), p. 308.

[75] Lalonde was a student protester in May '68 who went on to become a Green politician after founding the French branch of Friends of the Earth International. Kelly worked at the European Commission in the 1970s and served as a leading member of the environmental umbrella organization BBU before becoming known during the 1980s for peace activism within the Green Party. See Brice Lalonde, *Sur la vague verte* (1981); Brice Lalonde, *L'écologie en bleu* (2001); Saskia Richter, *Die Aktivistin* (2010).

[76] Hence Roger Cans's overstatement that French nuclear waste dumping in the Atlantic during the 1960s did not lead to protest 'because Greenpeace didn't exist yet'. Cans, *Mouvement écolo en France*, p. 88.

were not simply a direct inheritance from '1968'; the latter year was an ambiguous point of reference or a bar against which protest was measured rather than a straightforward point of origin for the anti-nuclear movement.[77] The opposition to nuclear energy is often regarded as a 'single-issue movement', the product of a negative coalition that came together to stop a new problem as it emerged supposedly in the wake of the oil crisis. Its participants included 'local' activists who had immediate, material concerns about the location of particular power stations (and who thus poorly fit the NSM thesis), but also 'outsider' activists of many different kinds. Some of these people had been politicized by other struggles, and brought motivations associated with particular protest traditions with them. The myriad constituencies of the anti-nuclear movement initially constructed their grievances against nuclear sites and programmes differently. As Chapter 2 argues, though, their arguments ultimately coalesced into a broad critique of 'nuclear society' which suggested the need for alternatives.

Chapter 3 aims to answer questions about how activists worked together across national borders. Most studies of social movements operate within national or comparative frameworks that, already at the conceptual level, screen out cross-border interactions. Yet such connections are essential to explaining why protest movements so often and so closely resemble one another from one country to the next, from their issues and strategies down to their timing.[78] Existing transnational histories have attempted to address this problem by highlighting instances of transfer, for example by arguing that European student leaders learned new tactics at the International Vietnam Congress in West Berlin in February 1968 which they then applied at home.[79] However, as environmental historians have argued with regard to their own field, transfer histories such as these have focused more on 'emphasizing the existence of transnational connections' than analysing their actual importance.[80] Chapter 3 therefore picks apart the cross-border networks of the anti-nuclear movement, which were based not around national, issue-oriented organizations, but around specific, local struggles and the (sometimes transnational) regions in which they were embedded. Linking these together across borders was no simple

---

[77] Michelle Zancarini-Fournel has argued that such comparisons are one reason why 1968 continues to be such an important (and contested) site of memory. *Moment 68*, p. 257.

[78] Donatella della Porta and Dieter Rucht, 'Left-Libertarian Movements', in *The Politics of Social Protest*, edited by J. Craig Jenkins and Bert Klandermans (1995).

[79] Gilcher-Holtey, 'Transfer zwischen Studentenbewegungen'.

[80] Astrid Kirchhof and Jan-Henrik Meyer, 'Global Protest against Nuclear Power', *Historical Social Research* 39, no. 1 (2014), p. 168.

task. Cooperation between French and West Germans was often plagued by misunderstandings and projections, but differences could also be turned to productive use, and activists proved especially creative at overcoming difficulties. Even for those who related to protest abroad in a more casual and limited way, transnational contact could have a dramatic impact on their lives.

If interactions across national borders were complex, so too were those that crossed the city limits: to many urban activists, the countryside could feel like a foreign country. Though contemporary observers were acutely aware of how urban–rural relationships were changing in the 1970s, subsequent research has tended to overlook how this affected protest specifically. Histories of '1968' are focused almost exclusively on major cities such as Paris and West Berlin; though recent research has broadened the view to include smaller towns, protest events and effects in the countryside are rarely considered.[81] Arguments about NSMs are likewise implicitly focused on the urban, 'post-materialist' component of anti-nuclear protest.[82] Chapter 4 thus explores how changing urban–rural relations in the 1970s, particularly the growing nostalgia for rural environments that appeared to be rapidly disappearing, were caught up in the growth of the anti-nuclear and environmental movements. At the same time, it looks at how protesters made use of rural space. Sociologists have studied how protest is affected by the arrangement of space within the built environment, but political demonstrations in the 'unbuilt' environment of the countryside were likewise profoundly shaped by their surroundings.[83]

Chapter 5 explores one of the greatest controversies within any protest movement, the question of violent versus non-violent strategy. Narratives of violence and protest in the 1970s mostly revolve around the history of 'terrorism' or 'armed struggle'[84] connected with groups like the Rote Armee Fraktion (RAF) or Action Directe. Some histories of '1968' in West Germany hold that the wave of student protests unleashed on 2 June 1967[85] inaugurated

---

[81] Zancarini-Fournel, *Moment 68*, p. 11.

[82] Inglehart, *Silent Revolution*, pp. 284–90.

[83] Dingxin Zhao, *Power of Tiananmen* (2001), pp. 239–66.

[84] Such groups are conventionally described as 'terrorists', though they saw themselves engaged in an anti-imperialist 'armed struggle' to bring about revolution. This book uses both terms within quotation marks so as to avoid condemning, valorizing, or otherwise passing judgement on the motivations behind their actions. See also Varon, *Bringing the War Home*, p. 3.

[85] Following a protest against the Shah of Iran's state visit to West Berlin on 2 June 1967, police chased students through the streets and beat them. In the midst of this repression, police officer Karl-Heinz Kurras shot dead Benno Ohnesorg, an unarmed demonstrator.

a decade of left-wing political violence that culminated in the so-called 'German autumn' of 1977.[86] For a handful of individuals, connections between events in 1968 and 'terrorism' or 'armed struggle' during the 1970s are easy to demonstrate, and facile analyses condemning 'the student movement' for sins retroactively imputed to it abound.[87] This unsympathetic view of '1968' casting a long shadow of violence contrasts with the counter-narrative that some historians propose, which holds up NSMs such as the anti-nuclear movement as exemplars of 1968's positive, non-violent legacy. Indeed, the NSM and environmental history literature characterizes such movements generally as non-violent, often failing to note that anti-nuclear protest was an exception. Ignoring violence is problematic because, as Kristin Ross has written with regard to the 'forgotten' deaths at protests during May 1968, doing so marginalizes real conflict, making protest appear harmless and contributing to the idea that 'nothing happened'.[88] The violence that occurred in Malville in 1977 played an important role in shaping the anti-nuclear movement, but this was not 'terroristic' violence of the kind that dominates histories of the 1970s. Indeed, the emphasis on either terroristic violence or principled non-violence in the literature obscures the vast grey area in between, in which a great deal of anti-nuclear protest is to be located. Though mutually exclusive in theory, violence (towards police and property) and non-violence (principled or tactical) co-existed in practice, sometimes even resembling, enabling, and complementing one another.

Chapter 6 returns to the question of continuity evoked in Chapter 2 by examining anti-nuclear protest's continued impact on political and personal trajectories since the 1970s. Stories of parliamentarization and professionalization (a 'long march through the institutions' which lost its radical edge along the way) loom large in the existing literature on '1968', NSMs, and environmentalism.[89] As noted above, Green parties are often

[86] The *Deutscher Herbst* began on 5 September 1977 with the kidnapping of Hanns Martin Schleyer by members of the RAF, who demanded the release of imprisoned comrades. A Lufthansa flight was also hijacked to increase pressure on the West German state. The conflict ended on 18 October, when West German special operations troops stormed the airplane; Schleyer's kidnappers then murdered him and RAF members in Stammheim prison died the same day in an apparent collective suicide.

[87] Certain actions by the RAF appear to draw inspiration from student movement pamphlets, though these advocated sabotage, not murder. See Stefan Aust, *Baader-Meinhof-Komplex*, 3rd edn (2008).

[88] Ross, *May 68*, pp. 19, 152. That said, it would be false to assume that violence is the best indication of the seriousness of political conflict.

[89] Christopher Rootes notes that the institutionalization of protest in professionalized organizations has been a major source of discontent among activists. 'Environmental Movements', in *The Blackwell Companion to Social Movements*, edited by David A. Snow et al. (2004), pp. 624–7.

seen as a measure of the anti-nuclear movement's supposed 'success' in West Germany and its alleged 'failure' in France. However, notions of 'success' and 'failure' are too simplistic to capture the kinds of changes that anti-nuclear protest brought about in *both* countries (albeit to different degrees), particularly if one looks beyond high politics and official policy. Chapter 6 thus explores not only parliamentary changes, but also the impact of the anti-nuclear movement on subsequent protest and within society. Alongside these political legacies are also vitally important personal ones. Family, friendships, and careers could suffer as a result of time lost to activism, and many people eventually adjusted or abandoned their commitment to protest as a result. In other cases, though, protest was precisely what opened people up to new relationships and communities, ones which might put their entire lives on a different path. These personal and political legacies were interwoven: by changing their own lives, protesters changed political culture more broadly.

As this implies, the anti-nuclear movement of the 1970s was not simply a successor to '1968', nor does its importance lie primarily in prefiguring Green parties. Many different paths led into, through, and sometimes back out of this movement. Yet the 1970s were a moment when those paths intersected, often crossing ideological, social, and national borders as they did so. The resulting 'improbable encounters' that occurred within the space of the anti-nuclear movement reconfigured understandings of 'politics' and reshaped the lives of the activists who participated in it. Who they were and why they became involved will be addressed in the next chapter.

2

Anti-Nuclear Fusion

Protesters, Motivations, and Traditions

At first glance, the opposition to nuclear power appears to be a classic 'single-issue movement'. The very term 'anti-nuclear' seems to limit the horizons of protest to the sole question of nuclear safety risks, fears of which have been used to explain both the intensity of protest and its appeal to wildly different constituencies. Indeed, contemporary critics tended to characterize the movement in one-dimensional terms, cultivating stereotypes of farmers with 'not-in-my-backyard' attitudes on the one hand and professional protesters seeking to re-enact May '68 on the other. For such observers, the emergence of anti-nuclear protest in the 1970s was an almost automatic response to the construction of new power stations, a major wave of which took place as national governments expanded existing programmes in the wake of the so-called 'energy crisis'.

Yet even pro-nuclear forces were occasionally forced to admit that something more than this was at stake. In 1980, for example, authorities in France expressed alarm that nuclear energy seemed to be 'the theme of choice for an amalgam of protests' that were converging to form an 'ecological *Internationale*' and thereby bringing together 'an informal mass, sometimes divided into contradictory tendencies and therefore of unstable behaviour from the point of view of public order'.[1] The caricature outlined above is thus problematic for several reasons. The stereotypes of anti-nuclear activists suggest misleading answers to the question of where anti-nuclear protest came from, in the sense of both its immediate causes and its long-term continuity. The single-minded focus on fear as a motivating factor is in many respects a retroactive reading influenced by (activists' responses to) the serious nuclear accidents of Chernobyl and Fukushima, which have pushed questions of risk and danger so far into the foreground that they now obscure other motivations and issues. The

---

[1] 'Le Mouvement écologique : internationalisation—doctrine anti-énergétique—amalgame des contestations', AN, 19850718, art. 25.

anti-nuclear movement also drew on existing protest traditions, but it was no straightforward continuation of the revolts of the previous decade.

This chapter examines who protested and why in order to better understand where anti-nuclear protest came from and why it occurred with such intensity when it did. It does so by first examining the conventional categories into which different protesters were placed and certain motivations associated with them. The most salient division within the anti-nuclear movement was usually between 'local' protesters on the one hand and 'outsiders' to the affected communities on the other, though both categories were constructed (by activists as well as their opponents) around vague stereotypes and generalized characteristics. The boundaries of local belonging were particularly difficult to define, sometimes encompassing an entire region (such as Alsace or Wendland), but often excluding larger cities within it. Among those typically regarded as locals, material interests could be as important a motivation as fear, but it was frustration with authorities that most powerfully spurred them to action, often in spite of deep reservations about protest. As they faced down the combined forces of state and industry to oppose nuclear power stations near their homes, these local activists found themselves standing side by side with 'outsiders' whose 'political' motives they often regarded with suspicion. Cast in a supporting role in spite of their greater number, outsiders came in many varieties, but the most visible clusters formed around ideals connected with non-violence, the radical left, and countercultural 'environmentalism'.[2] Each looked back on different protest traditions that furnished them with particular arguments: nuclear energy could be about the ills of industrialization, the wastefulness of consumer society, the dangers of a creeping police state, war and violence on a planetary scale, threats to one's personal health, or the demise of democracy at the hands of technocrats.

Over time, it increasingly came to mean all of these things at once. Though certain reasons were more important to certain kinds of people, almost no one committed herself to anti-nuclear protest for only one reason, and no group had a monopoly on any particular flavour of 'concern'. As activists from very different walks of life interacted throughout the 1970s, they built an encompassing movement that constructed a shared vision of what kind of society was desirable and what kind was not. What appeared on the surface to be a 'single-issue movement' was actually, during the 1970s, a vehicle for much greater aspirations.

---

[2] The anti-nuclear movement also included some outsiders on the right and even far right. They are not discussed in detail here, but more information on the West German case can be found in Silke Mende, *Nicht rechts, nicht links* (2011), pp. 72–134.

LOCAL PROTESTERS

At the local level, several factors combined to produce (and quickly intensify) protest. Wherever nuclear power stations were sited, residents had to confront the real possibility that these facilities would transform their way of life, perhaps for the worse. Local nuclear energy opponents may have feared vague risks and invisible radioactivity, but they were also angry that, in their view, they would bear risks while others benefited. They perceived nuclear power stations as an injustice imposed on them by outside powers whose intervention in local affairs might harm residents and their material interests.[3] Even the criteria by which sites were chosen, though in some ways conceived to avoid controversy, frequently exacerbated conflict rather than defusing it. In certain places, local defiance dovetailed with environmentalist or regionalist protest traditions that furnished nuclear energy opponents with additional arguments. However, for most local opponents, political activism was something new, which they took up only reluctantly and with ambivalent feelings. Many (though not all) locals initially denied any 'political' motivation behind their actions and preferred to describe themselves neutrally as 'concerned citizens'. More than anything else, it was their negative encounters with representatives of state and industry, who struck them as condescending and even violently confrontational, that propelled initially hesitant critics and loyal government supporters to protest. Immediate concerns, protest traditions, and building frustrations thus all contributed to the development of local anti-nuclear protest.

It is often assumed that local opponents of nuclear power were primarily motivated by fear of the risks associated with it, be they the potential dangers of explosion, radioactive contamination, or pollution.[4] The precise role that fear played is hard to pin down: activists clearly recognized its mobilizing potential, but sometimes downplayed it in order to counter charges that their opposition was 'irrational' or 'emotional' (potentially damaging claims given the scientific language in which pro-nuclear

---

[3] In this sense, nuclear power represents a late but very visible example of the difficulty that national (and federal) state structures had 'regain[ing]' precedent over the local' after the Second World War, during which many communities had been forced to fend for themselves. See Martin Conway, 'Western Europe's Democratic Age', *Contemporary European History* 13, no. 1 (2004), p. 75.

[4] There is an extensive literature on 'fear' related to anti-nuclear and environmental protest, much of it pertaining to West Germany in the 1980s. See, for example, Annekatrin Gebauer, 'Apokalyptik und Eschatologie', *Archiv für Sozialgeschichte* 43 (2003). See also Dorothy Nelkin and Michael Pollak, *Atom Besieged* (1981), pp. 141–3.

arguments were usually formulated).[5] However, concern and even 'fear' regarding potential dangers to human health were not necessarily 'irrational'. Even pro-nuclear politicians and industry spokespeople acknowledged that nuclear power was not entirely risk-free. The scientific community was itself divided on whether recent advances in fundamental research were ready to be exploited on the massive, industrial scale that power companies wanted.[6] Those living near nuclear installations were confronted with wildly contradictory arguments about potential dangers, and had to choose whom to believe. According to the sociologist Alain Touraine, fear within the anti-nuclear movement was 'denied by some, stressed by others, accepted or rejected by the same activists according to the precise state of the debate'.[7] The early work of the anti-nuclear Comité pour la Sauvegarde de Fessenheim et de la plaine du Rhin (CSFR) in Alsace typifies the movement's ambivalent attitude and calls into question the supposed incompatibility of fear and scientific rationality. One flyer depicts a stork (a symbol of Alsace) delivering a baby with three webbed hands and four club feet under the headline 'Alsace must not die!' (see Fig. 2.1). This kind of blunt imagery had clear potential to mobilize protest in the early 1970s, when memories of the Second World War and the atomic destruction of Hiroshima and Nagasaki (not to mention more recent threats to peace such as the Cuban Missile Crisis or the Vietnam War) were still very much alive. However, CSFR also made dramatic appeals on the basis of scientific arguments, which its members took as evidence that nuclear power was a life-and-death issue. One of the group's first steps was the publication, in 1970, of an informational booklet about the dangers of radiation, pollution, and accidents at nuclear power plants which culled information from American, British, German, Swiss, and French articles, studies, and reports.[8] Whether irrational and

---

[5] Indeed, the accusation of irrationality was levelled so often that protesters occasionally appropriated it ironically for themselves: mocking their own supposed backwardness, activists in Malville printed flyers proclaiming, 'on July 31, we're going to stop progress'—meaning not only nuclear technology but also the discourse of rationality they took it to represent. See 'Le 30 juillet à Malville, on va arrêter le progrès', envelope with artwork, 1977, PA Putinier.

[6] Scientists critical of nuclear energy made important interventions in the public debate, including through books like Groupement des scientifiques pour l'information sur l'énergie nucléaire, *Électronucléaire, danger* (1977); Arbeitsgruppe Schadstoffbelastung am Arbeitsplatz und in der Industrieregion Unterweser, *Zum richtigen Verständnis* (1975). For more on the scientific debate (not treated here in detail), see Sezin Topçu, 'De l'engagement « savant »', *Natures Sciences Sociétés* 14 (2006); Nelkin and Pollak, *Atom Besieged*, pp. 89–101.

[7] Alain Touraine et al., *Prophétie anti-nucléaire* (1980), p. 57.

[8] CSFR, 'Fessenheim : vie ou mort de l'Alsace', brochure, 69 pp., February 1971, PA Tompkins.

Fig. 2.1. 'Alsace must not die!' This flyer by CSFR opposes plans for both a chemical plant in Marckolsheim ('first step on the Alsatian Ruhr') and the nuclear power station in Fessenheim ('nuclear power is not the solution of the future!'). Reproduced by permission of Jean-Jacques Rettig.[9]

[9] CSFR, 'L'Alsace ne doit pas mourir', flyer, 2 pp., undated [1974?], AA, 'Ökologiebewegung im Elsass'.

exaggerated or rationally commensurate to the risks involved, fear was a flexible motivation that anti-nuclear activists could draw upon to mobilize protest.

However, fear does not by itself explain the force behind anti-nuclear protest. Significantly, the risks associated with nuclear projects would not be borne by the bureaucrats in capital cities who planned them or by the managers of energy companies that profited from them, but rather by those living close to the sites in question.[10] In such communities, initial concerns (which authorities hoped could be addressed by scientific arguments) mixed readily with resentment against perceived incursions on local life by the rich and powerful. The resulting sense of injustice served as a major spur to action. Speaking at a rally in Wyhl, the local woman Anne-Marie Sacherer reportedly argued that 'Politicians in Stuttgart wish to impose on us, by law, an atomic cuckoo's egg, knowing full well that they will not have to bear the consequences of their actions. They are defending the interests of big business.'[11] A statement like this one might have appealed to the residents of nearby small towns because it expressed local citizens' anger at outside intervention in their communities. It also rang true for left-wing activists who saw it as an expression of anti-capitalism. The concerns at the heart of such statements could also be pitched to an entirely different audience, such as when a religious group in Freiburg wrote that 'The suffering of a stillborn or crippled child is not borne by the government in Bonn or Stuttgart, nor by the Badenwerk [power company]—but rather by its parents.'[12] Within affected communities, concerns about risk quickly spilled over into anger at its unjust distribution, and this anger could be used to mobilize different supporters depending on how it was articulated.

For a variety of reasons, potential nuclear sites tended to be located in certain kinds of areas. Because water access was crucial to supplying reactor cooling systems, locations near rivers, lakes, and the sea were in greatest

---

[10] Ulrich Beck argued in his book *Risikogesellschaft* (1986) that this disconnect between risk and profit was a distinctive marker of a contemporary phase of modernity, though Jens Ivo Engels argues that this and other contemporary terms (*Problemdruck*, *Postmaterialismus*) do little to explain the rise of environmentalism. Jens Ivo Engels, *Naturpolitik* (2006), p. 405. See also the summary of Beck's arguments in Anselm Doering-Manteuffel and Lutz Raphael, *Nach dem Boom* (2008), pp. 68–9.

[11] The term 'cuckoo's egg' describes a burden foisted off on others. (It refers to the parasitic brooding practice of cuckoo birds, which lay their eggs in the nests of other species; upon hatching, cuckoo chicks then expel the eggs of the host species so as to monopolize food resources.) This English translation of Sacherer's speech appears in Solange Fernex, 'Non-violence Triumphant', *The Ecologist*, vol. 5, no. 10 (December 1975), pp. 372–85 (p. 384). The original speech (in local dialect) is recorded in Nina Gladitz, *Lieber heute aktiv als morgen radioaktiv*, 1976, 63 mins.

[12] 'Schützt das ungeborene Leben!', flyer, 1975, ASB, 12.1.7.

demand.[13] Since major waterways often formed 'natural' borders, many potential sites were to be found along national borders, such as on France's Atlantic coast, certain parts of the Elbe valley in West Germany, and along the Rhine.[14] Borderland nuclear facilities were common enough to prompt international cooperation among activists in places like Fessenheim and Wyhl (or later Cattenom and Chooz), all of whom felt their towns had been 'consciously chosen according to the principle of "divide and rule"', as national borders would presumably fragment resistance and its impact.[15] From a planning perspective, out-of-the-way regions in the countryside were vastly preferable to urban ones, as low population density (at least of one's own citizens) helped minimize the risk exposure that had to be accounted for.[16] The preferences of residents near potential sites were rarely, if ever, surveyed in advance, though nuclear projects were occasionally put to a vote. Local referenda on nuclear power were usually limited to the single closest town, which could be expected to receive a tax windfall from the nuclear facility.[17] The most intense opposition therefore often formed in neighbouring towns and the surrounding region, whose residents were not consulted (Weisweil near Wyhl, Wewelsfleth near

---

[13] For some illustrative maps, see Ministère de l'Industrie et de la Recherche, 'Localisation des centrales nucléaires', dossier, 40 pp., November 1974, BDIC, F Δ 1190; BBU, 'Standorte für Kernkraftwerke', flyer, 4 pp., undated [1975?], StAF, W 100/1 Nr. 97.

[14] Sites in these areas included Plogoff (Bretagne), Flamanville and La Hague (Basse-Normandie), and Fessenheim (Alsace) in France as well as Wyhl (Baden-Württemberg) and Gorleben (Niedersachsen). Another major cluster of potential reactor sites in France existed along the (inland) Rhône River. In West Germany, prospective sites were scattered throughout the country, though inland portions of the Elbe and Rhine tributaries were most affected.

[15] 'Internationale Zusammenarbeit gegen grenznahe Atomanlagen', flyer, 6 pp., undated [1981], PapierTiger, 'AKW – Westeuropa'.

[16] The principle of placing nuclear power plants away from major population centres was first established by the US Atomic Energy Commission. In West Germany and France, conflict avoidance was often the reason for the choice of thinly populated areas. See Joachim Radkau, *Aufstieg und Krise* (1983), pp. 371–84; Gabrielle Hecht, *Radiance of France* (1998), p. 166. However, nuclear power stations in or near major cities were considered. Plans were even drawn up in the early 1960s for a commercial reactor in West Berlin, but were dropped when it became apparent that residents would have to be evacuated to East Germany in the event of a disaster. Radkau, *Aufstieg und Krise*, pp. 373–6. Even in the late 1970s, French planners considered building a small-scale reactor in Grenoble for heating purposes. 'THERMOS : une mini-centrale nucléaire pour le chauffage urbain', *Le Monde*, 12 October 1977; 'Kraftwerk im Keller', *Spiegel*, no. 51 (15 December 1980).

[17] Nuclear energy opponents also denounced the way authorities offered perks and exerted pressure in the communities in question. Not every site was put to a vote, and outcomes varied. For example, two simultaneous referenda on 6 April 1975 ended with Port-la-Nouvelle (Languedoc-Roussillon) voting solidly against a reactor (1,250 against, 385 for) and Flamanville in favour (248 against, 428 for). In Wyhl, activists lost a referendum (55 per cent in favour) on 12 January 1975. See 'Pour ou contre les centrales ?', *Le Monde*, 8 April 1975; Bernd Nössler and Margret de Witt, eds., *Kein Kernkraftwerk in Wyhl* (1976), pp. 66–76.

Brokdorf, Bouvesse near Malville, and so on). If local acceptance was not necessarily taken into account, policy planners did endeavour to choose, when possible, areas considered less likely to rebel against state authority. For example, the choice of Gorleben for West Germany's nuclear waste site was grounded in part in the conservative Niedersachsen government's belief that it disposed of greater trust (*Vertrauenskapital*) among voters there than elsewhere.[18] Planners also saw nuclear power plants as a fast track to economic prosperity in 'showcase' border regions such as Alsace or in areas in need of development and employment. The lure of jobs, tax revenue, and infrastructure (almost always in the form of swimming pools and sports facilities) helped win over many local officials. A mix of geographic, demographic, and political considerations was thus ultimately responsible for which sites were chosen.

However, the logic of nuclear geography had a number of unintended consequences that ironically made it more, not less difficult to pacify the 'natives'. Most important was the discrepancy between existing ways of life and the ultra-modernity of which nuclear power was a symbol. Farmers, fishermen, and winegrowers were not always eager to give up their livelihoods for the chance to work in a new, nuclear factory. Contrary to common assumptions about anti-nuclear activism, these protesters initially perceived nuclear power as more of a threat to their material interests than to their health. For example, the fisherman Balthasar Ehret from Weisweil, a member of the (pro-Soviet) Communist Party, opposed the nuclear project in nearby Wyhl in part because he believed the plant would worsen pollution in the Rhine, just as other industrial installations previously had. Stories of fish with genetic mutations near an existing power plant in Obrigheim worried him, but primarily for economic reasons, since, he wrote, 'Experts have confirmed that such fish cannot be sold and no one wants to eat them.'[19] Even if pollution and radioactivity could be kept at bay, fishermen like Ehret worried that using the Rhine, Rhône, or Elbe to cool nuclear reactors would raise water temperatures and upset the delicate ecological balance required for fish spawning.[20] When cooling towers were proposed instead, farmers and especially winegrowers worried that the steam clouds they released would blot out the sun and ruin crops. It was concrete, material concerns like these, rather than fear or 'post-materialist values', which initially provoked much of the opposition at the local level. Ehret's neighbours also became engaged in

[18] 'Druck abgeschüttelt', *Spiegel*, no. 12 (14 March 1977), pp. 35–6 (p. 36). See also '(nicht nur) Gorleben will weiterleben', *Wendblatt*, no. 2 (March 1977), p. 3.
[19] Nössler and de Witt, *Kein Kernkraftwerk in Wyhl*.
[20] See also BUU, *Brokdorf* (1977), pp. 95–6.

anti-nuclear protest because of the harm they perceived it would inflict on their business. Siegfried Göpper, the politically right-wing owner of a large and successful grain mill, raised a legal objection to the Wyhl plant and demanded financial compensation on the basis that the removal of water from the Rhine would cause groundwater levels to sink, thereby rendering his mill stream unusable.[21] When authorities ignored his objections, he and other neighbours sued, launching a long legal battle that would contribute to the eventual abandonment of the Wyhl project.[22] Within local communities, shared material concerns helped bridge the political chasm separating people like Göpper and Ehret, whose politics were diametrically opposed.

Affected communities also drew together out of concern that their local environment would be irreversibly transformed by the rampant industrialization that some expected to follow nuclear facilities. This argument was frequently invoked even in regions that had some experience of industrialization. In partly urbanized areas between Bremen and Hamburg in northern Germany, nuclear energy opponents were concerned that industrialization was spreading beyond the planned industrial zone in Brunsbüttel and into the greenbelt (*Naherholungsgebiet*) near Brokdorf.[23] In Alsace, one of France's more economically developed regions, nuclear energy opponents expressed alarm at the scale of new industrial projects, asking, 'Where will our children play? In a real country landscape or between concrete and asphalt?'[24] Across France and West Germany, anti-nuclear activists referred to the heavily industrialized Ruhr as an example of what they did *not* want their own region to become (see Fig. 2.1). A typical flyer from Brokdorf asked, 'Does the increasing pollution of the Elbe—SWIMMING BAN!—[. . .] not show that we're closer to the "second Ruhrgebiet" than we think? Do we even have to outdo the Ruhrgebiet and build NUCLEAR POWER PLANT after NUCLEAR POWER PLANT [. . .]?'[25] Affected towns expected (further) industrialization to change not

---

[21] Siegfried Göpper, 'Einspruch gegen das KKW Wyhl', letter of objection, StAF, F 23/23 Nr. 8.

[22] Badisch-Elsässische Bürgerinitiativen, 'Der Wyhl-Prozess', brochure, 24 pp., 1977, DfuL, D 0250; Nelkin and Pollak, *Atom Besieged*, pp. 155–66.

[23] Helmut Häuser and BUU, 'Brokdorf. Macht den Bauplatz zur Wiese!', November 1976, PA Tompkins, p. 3. See also Markus Mohr, *Alles wie geplant. Die katastrophale Industrialisierung von Brunsbüttel/Unterelbe* (1985). (The book was followed up a year later by another volume, entitled *Anders als geplant*.)

[24] 'Plus d'énergie, encore plus d'industrie, notre milieu de vie est en danger', *Ionix*, no. 6 (January 1974).

[25] See BUU, 'Liebe Mitbürger', flyer, 1 p., 25 July 1975, AA, Brokdorf 76/77 JS. Original emphasis. See also CSFR, 'L'Alsace ne doit pas mourir'; 'Was hat der Arbeiter vom KKW?', *WWW*, no. 2 (10 November 1977), p. 9; Yves Lenoir, 'Une Rhur [sic] française en Saône et Loire avec une centrale nucléaire', *Libération*, 6–7 November 1976.

only the landscape, but also their own social and economic make-up. In the Upper Rhine Valley, nuclear energy opponents argued that land would shift from farms and forests to large companies, production would become decoupled from local needs, and the employment of 'foreign workers' would 'create social problems', uprooting the existing population.[26] This last argument had clearly racist undertones that made many anti-nuclear activists, especially those from outside these communities, deeply uncomfortable. The spectre of industrialization, with all its (imagined) concomitant economic and social transformations, was thus initially perceived as a greater threat to small towns than radioactivity or nuclear accidents.

If radioactivity was not the primary concern in early conflicts like the one in Wyhl, this was at least in part because it 'cannot be seen, heard, or smelled'; in fact, an environmental group at the University of Freiburg was among the first to bring concern about radioactivity to the attention of local citizens.[27] In the early 1970s, the environmental networks that reached into local communities tended to be associated with birdwatchers, hunters, and traditional nature protection societies in the vein of the Fédération Française des Sociétés de Protection de la Nature or the German Naturschutzbund rather than post-1968 'political ecology' groups like Les Amis de la Terre (ADLT) or the Bund für Umwelt und Naturschutz Deutschland (BUND). Classic, 'bourgeois' organizations were initially hesitant to involve themselves directly in controversial matters, but, starting in the late 1960s, became more and more politicized. Raymond Schirmer, an environmental activist who grew up near Marckolsheim and became involved in protests there and elsewhere, remembers that he experienced 1968 'as an environmentalist' and 'via nature protection', as tensions brewed within his own traditional group over whether and how to engage in politics. By 1974, the debate had been resolved in favour of more overt, even confrontational protest, with respected university scientists backing calls to occupy the site of the lead processing plant in Marckolsheim.[28] In argument and deed, nature protection groups and their allies connected the opposition to nuclear power with struggles against more conventional threats to nature, such as the

---

[26] 'Bericht über die Versammlung am 27.10.1974', *WWW*, no. 1 (1974), pp. 2–3. In West Germany, themes like *Überindustrialisierung* and *Überfremdung* were also picked up by the far right. See Solidarische Volksbewegung, 'Es ist etwas faul in unserem Staat...', flyer, 2 pp., undated [1976?], HIS, SBE 731 Box 02, 'Rechte Anti-AKW-Bewegung'.

[27] Arbeitskreis Umweltschutz, 'Gefährdung durch Kernkraftwerke. Kein KKW in Wyhl!', brochure, 36 pp., January 1975, ASB, 00004308, p. 13. See also Engels, *Naturpolitik*, p. 359.

[28] RS in Marie-Reine Haug and Raymond Schirmer, joint interview with the author, Rammersmatt, 17 April 2010. On nature protection societies in the case of Bavaria, see Ute Hasenöhrl, *Zivilgesellschaft und Protest* (2011).

planned expansion of the Rhine–Rhône canal (which further fuelled protest in Alsace), the Naussac dam project (linked to the Malville protests in 1977), or the Amoco Cadiz oil spill (which affected the Breton coast near Plogoff in 1978). Though the nuclear issue was in many respects abstract, relating it to other environmental issues made it more tangible and gave anti-nuclear activists further networks—and outrage—into which they could tap.[29]

Another unintended consequence of nuclear geography was that the isolated areas chosen might be much more resentful of outside authority than planners expected. Gorleben, for example, was surrounded on three sides by the East German border and many local citizens were strongly anti-communist. Yet rather than being grateful to West German leaders for nuclear-led economic development, some argued that the state was ready to sacrifice their community in an emergency: Gorleben could be easily sealed off, but not evacuated (unless hostile East Germany opened its borders to fleeing Westerners).[30] Near Wyhl, residents of South Baden revived (and reinvented) traditions of rebellion going back to the German Peasants' War of the 1500s and directed their purportedly centuries-old rage against the 'Herren in Stuttgart' (the regional government) who were responsible for the nuclear plans.[31] Much of that anger was, however, far more recent, stoked by the clumsy post-war merger of Baden and Württemberg (not confirmed until 1970, long after the referenda of 1950 and 1951 in which a majority in South Baden had rejected it). South Badeners were thus happy to join Alsatians in proclaiming opposition to the 'centralism' of both Paris and Stuttgart, in spite of fundamental differences between the state structures in question.[32]

---

[29] Sociologists and political scientists refer to these networks as 'pre-existing mobilization structures'. See, for example, Donatella della Porta et al., *Globalizing World* (1999), p. 9. French anti-nuclear protesters also argued that the nuclear programme and infrastructure projects like the Naussac dam were mutually reinforcing. See Henry Chevalier, 'Les barrages-réservoirs liés aux centrales nucléaires', *La gazette nucléaire*, no. 127/128 (1993), p. 6; Catherine Decouan, 'Naussac : les bonnes raisons', *GO*, no. 117 (4 August 1976), p. 2.

[30] '(nicht nur) Gorleben will weiterleben', *Wendblatt*, no. 2; BI Lebensschutz Uelzen, 'Atommüll-Anlage', flyer, 1 p., 14 January 1977, HIS, SBe 731 Box 01, Mappe 'Gorleben'. In January 1982, activists in Gorleben briefly occupied a space on the East German side of the border (but in front of perimeter defences) in order to draw attention to their lack of escape routes. See the extensive documentation by GDR border troops. 'Handlungen der "Demonstranten"', report, 27 January 1982, BArch, DVH 48/138758.

[31] Engels, *Naturpolitik*, pp. 357–8.

[32] VHSWW, '31. Programm', schedule flyer, 2 pp., January 1978, ASB, 12.1.11.I. Some of this animosity stemmed from confessional differences, with Catholic South Baden opposing Protestant Württemberg (of which Stuttgart was the historic capital). See Reinhold Weber and Hans-Georg Wehling, *Geschichte Baden-Württembergs* (2007), pp. 110–16.

In France, regional identities were much stronger than in West Germany, and their proponents much better organized. Paris planners were thwarted again and again in their attempts to place a nuclear power plant in Bretagne, not least because anti-nuclear activists and regionalists made common cause opposing them. The Front de Libération de la Bretagne-Armée Révolutionnaire Bretonne (FLB-ARB) even issued a 'declaration of war' against the French state (along with its 'Breton collaborators and irresponsible local elected officials') over the nuclear site at Plogoff, claiming responsibility for numerous arson attacks against suppliers of construction materials for the site.[33] Violence of this kind was unknown among Alsatian regionalists, who in the 1970s were more focused on cultural revival and limited political autonomy than on seceding from France (having only recently experienced violent annexation by Germany during the Second World War). Yet there too, opposition to nuclear power and to the central state that imposed it were mutually reinforcing. As home to the first reactor of France's new nuclear programme, Alsace provided especially fertile soil for cultivating opposition to nuclear power in both France *and* West Germany. By the 1970s, the region had accumulated a century's worth of grievances against (and experience of opposing) various incarnations of the French and German states.[34] Bi- or trilingual (including their shared Alemannic dialect), with family members on both sides of the border, many Alsatians were also in a unique position to compare the situations in France and West Germany and to denounce what they saw as the pollute-thy-neighbour policy of both states placing nuclear and industrial plants along their shared border. Opposition to nuclear energy was at its most ardent in places like these, where it was perceived as yet another affront to an aggrieved region.

Ordinary citizens in rural communities began to protest against nuclear energy because they felt personally affected in some way by nearby nuclear sites. However, their responses were also shaped by the political climate of the 1970s, and particularly by enduring images of '1968'. Local activists' memories of that earlier year illustrate the very divided stance towards 'political' activism that reigned in many of the affected small towns. Some anti-nuclear activists, like the Alsatian organizer Jean-Jacques Rettig (b. 1939), remembered '68 as something that created possibilities even for people utterly disconnected from the left-wing protests of Paris and West Berlin.

---

[33] Note, 6 July 1976, AD Finistère, 1235 W 24.

[34] One Alsatian woman claims to have crossed the border illegally as part of anti-nuclear protest using the same routes her father had employed as a member of the Resistance during the Second World War. Ginette Skandrani, interview with the author, Paris, 11 January 2010.

JJR: We didn't participate in what was brewing in the cities—we didn't
       pull up paving stones in the Quartier Latin, but we followed it on
       the radio. We were . . . enthusiastic about what people dared to
       do. And the difference between before '68 and after '68—well,
       after '68 came the idea of ecology. [. . .] Before, we loved nature,
       we loved the milieu of our life. But now, we dared to say it and
       stand in the way, with our bodies in the street, in public. We said
       to ourselves, 'Those people high up, how are they [better] than us?'
       [. . .] We [*on*] felt mentally equipped [*armé* . . .] to go to the
       minister, to the general in the army—these are real things we
       experienced that I'm citing—to the bishop of Strasbourg.[35]

Jean-Jacques himself lived in northern Alsace, more than an hour and a
half by car from Fessenheim. Nevertheless, his Alsatian identity (and
mastery of dialect) frequently allowed him to blend in and be perceived
as a local activist. His integration was also helped by his involvement in
numerous regional associations that promoted gardening, organic food,
opposition to vivisection, and other causes prior to the 1970s. Like nature
protection, these issues were not necessarily 'left-wing' or even 'political' at
the outset, but for people like Jean-Jacques, they proved increasingly
compatible with the changing left of the 1970s.

   However, others were suspicious of activism because they considered
themselves to be 'directly concerned' as 'citizens' by nuclear power, a
problem that they initially deemed not to be political in nature. This
was one reason for the popularity of the term *Bürgerinitiative* ('Citizens'
Initiative') throughout West Germany. Gottfried Mahlke (b. 1947)
worked as a Protestant pastor in Gorleben in the late 1970s, and it was
his role within the church that firmly anchored him within that local
community. He described himself as having not been very political,
'because when it started in Gorleben in 1977, that was a dimension that
I wasn't prepared for. And '68 went right past me.' Back then, he had been
a university student in theology, but he could not understand 'why the
students in the cafeteria always stood around with placards instead of
studying properly'. However, as he engaged in anti-nuclear protest, he also
began to stake out more progressive positions within his church and his
community.[36] For many local activists like Gottfried, anti-nuclear protest

[35] Jean-Jacques Rettig, interview with the author, Fréconrupt, 19 April 2010.
[36] Gottfried Mahlke, interview with the author, Luckau, 24 August 2010. See also
Gottfried Mahlke, 'Einstellungen zu Homosexualität und Kirche', presentation to Kirchenkreis
Dannenberg, 9 pp. text, 21 September 2000, http://www.zentrum-seelsorge.de/dms/zentrum-
seelsorge/arbeitsbereiche/pastoralklinikum/downloads/15_06_10_homosexualitaet_mahlke/
15_06_10_homosexualitaet_mahlke.pdf (accessed 4 December 2015).

was politicizing, but that politicization was a long-term process that they embarked upon only reluctantly.

Some local activists were openly hostile to '1968' and the tradition of left-wing protest they associated with it. On the Larzac plateau, which became a transnational hub for various protest movements during the 1970s, Jean-Marie Burguière (b. 1938) remembers being 'strongly against' those who protested in 1968, finding them 'disgusting' at the time.[37] His brother Pierre (b. 1943) saw things similarly, only calling that view into question when he and his neighbours found their own opposition to the local military camp expansion grossly distorted by politicians and the media: 'we discovered at that moment that they had lied to us in May '68.'[38] Among local activists in West Germany, the antipathy towards 'politics' (and the left) sometimes had much deeper roots. For example, Siegfried Göpper (b. 1929) spoke of 'marching in one direction' with fellow anti-nuclear protester Lore Haag, 'not just since '68. Since '38!' Both were in Nazi youth organizations and Siegfried claims to recall experiencing 'how enthusiastic people [*das Volk*] could be' when listening to Hitler speak on the radio. When asked if he had been politically engaged after the war, he responded that he 'was never again politically organized. [...] Based on experience, I was never ready to join a party.'[39] The rhetoric of rejecting 'politics' was for him, as for many of his generation in post-war West Germany, a way of distancing himself from a tainted national (and personal) past. However, it also reflects the way many rural residents continued to operate in the 1970s with an understanding of 'politics' inherited from an earlier time, when the term was narrowly associated with parliamentary parties and grand ideologies.[40] Local protesters of all kinds (including some on the far right but many more without strong political preferences or interests) preferred to regard their protest as 'non-political', in part because they did not want to be associated with left-wing '68ers.

Resentments old and new prepared the terrain for protest, but not everyone was eager to engage in it; what ultimately provoked local opponents to protest was their frustration with officials, which increased sharply over time. This began with the basic information supplied to local communities, which sometimes came across as so misleading or implausible that it stretched the patience of those trying to develop an informed opinion. Albert

[37] Jean-Marie Burguière, interview with Robert Gildea, 21 May 2008, http://around1968.modhist.ox.ac.uk/ (accessed 5 June 2009).

[38] Pierre Burguière and Christiane Burguière, joint interview with Robert Gildea, 22 May 2008, http://around1968.modhist.ox.ac.uk/ (accessed 5 June 2009).

[39] Siegfried Göpper, interview with the author, Weisweil, 18 April 2010.

[40] William Marotti, 'Japan 1968', *American Historical Review* (February 2009), pp. 98–9; Engels, *Naturpolitik*, pp. 192–6.

Reimers (b. 1936), a farmer from the town of Wewelsfleth, remembers being angry and incredulous after receiving an 'informational' brochure from the electricity company promoting plans for Brokdorf nuclear power plant. Under the heading 'Why must we build it?' was a graph comparing household and industrial energy consumption, drawn in such a way that the former appeared to reach levels four to five times higher than the latter by 1980. Only upon further inspection did it become clear that household consumption would remain around half that of industry in absolute terms (and this according to the power company's own self-serving projections). Anti-nuclear activists interpreted this to mean that, counter to what the graph seemed to imply, industry would incontestably be the prime beneficiary of the power station, and that households, which did not receive the bulk rebates given to large companies, would foot the bill.[41] Next to the graph, cartoon drawings of happy fish explained that pumping water from the Elbe through the reactor's cooling system would actually make it cleaner, 'thereby greatly improving biological conditions in the river'.[42] Albert Reimers found this unconvincing, but was frustrated when he tried to take action:

> AR: And I thought, no, if that were true—60 m³ [of water] per second [...] used for cooling—if that came out into the Elbe cleaner than when it was taken out, and only one gram of dirt was sifted out, then they would have [...] five tons of dirt accumulating daily. And that would have to pile up somewhere, since it 'comes out cleaner than it was taken out'. It would have to pile up somewhere! We never heard that anywhere. And I ... I went to the police and—yeah *[AR laughs]*, that's the way it was—I reported it as false advertising. And the prosecutor wrote me back later that they [the power company] can do what they want, one doesn't have to believe it, it's not a punishable offence. And so we had to defend ourselves some other way.[43]

Reimers later had 1,000 copies printed of a flyer comparing the fence around the future Brokdorf nuclear power station with the Berlin Wall (see Fig. 2.2). Visually, this played on the similarity between images of barbed wire, used in Brokdorf to protect the private property of a powerful industry just as the East German 'enemy' used it to defend a border that many West Germans considered illegitimate. In this manner, he connected

---

[41] See also Häuser and BUU, 'Brokdorf', pp. 48–51.
[42] Nordwestdeutsche Kraftwerke, 'Kernkraftwerk Brokdorf', foldout brochure, undated, PA Reimers.
[43] Albert Reimers and Marlene Reimers, joint interview with the author, Wewelsfleth, 21 August 2010.

Wo Macht mißbraucht wird, sieht man Stacheldraht.

PRIVATEIGENTUM
BETRETEN VERBOTEN
Der Eigentümer
Nordwestdeutsche Kraftwerke AG

Hier entsteht unser
Kraftwerk Brokdorf
Auf dem Gelände befinden sich wertvolle
Anlagen und Baumaschinen.
Bitte haben Sie Verständnis
für unsere Schutz- und
Bewachungsmaßnahmen

„Die Pflicht jedes einzelnen ist es, laut zu rufen, wenn
Ungerechtigkeit sich ausbreiten sollte, und spätestens
jedenfalls dann handelnd einzugreifen, wenn die Regie-
renden Gebot und Gesetz verletzen sollten!"

Helmut Schmidt, Bundeskanzler,

in seinem Buch:
„Als Christ in der politischen Entscheidung"
1976

**Zum Jahrestag der Nacht- und Nebel-Aktion
25./26. Oktober 1976**

Bewohner der Wilster Marsch forderten:
Kein Baubeginn am AKW Brokdorf
vor Gerichtsentscheid!
Vor der Wahl haben 'unsere Politiker'
das akzeptiert.So sagten sie.
Bis zum 25.10.76.
15 Jahre nach dem Mauerbau in Berlin
wurden mit der Mauer in Brokdorf
vollendete Tatsachen geschaffen.

Jahr für Jahr beklagen diese Heuchler
den Machtmißbrauch in Berlin.

Von Brokdorf reden sie nicht!

Wir haben unser Recht erzwungen.
die ersten Prozesse bestätigen das.Aber
politische Erfüllungsgehilfen
terrorisieren uns weiter.
Wie lange noch?
Sie verstoßen gegen das Grundgesetz.

Wer nicht aktiv gegen die Brokdorfer
Mauer vorgeht,hat keinen Anspruch auf
unser Vertrauen.
Die Alternative ist nicht:
Kohle oder Atom.
Die Mauer muß weg!

Stacheldrahtpolitiker
können wir nicht wählen!

V.i.S.d.P.:Albert Reimers,Wewelsfleth   Auflage=1000

BERLIN   BROKDORF

Fig. 2.2. 'Where power is abused, one sees barbed wire.' Reproduced by permission of Albert Reimers.

a conservative narrative about communism with a local narrative of victimization to argue that, in Berlin and Brokdorf, 'The wall must go!'

The way authorities promoted nuclear projects was one problem, but the way they reacted to local citizens' concerns was another. Rural populations especially resented the implication that they were backward or ignorant, and prickled at the condescension they sensed when dealing with official experts. Chantal and Maurice François (b. 1932 and 1929, respectively), whose farmland stretches up to the edge of the Malville plant, invested considerable time and effort educating themselves about nuclear issues and were frustrated that it earned them so little respect. Chantal described her irritation when, during one visit to the site, the director of the plant expressed surprise at Maurice's mastery of the technical details:

CF: The director was talking to my husband and [Maurice] said 'Yes, but there's this, there's that, and so on.' Well, the director said, 'And on top of everything, he's—'

MF: 'He's competent!'

CF: Like that: [*incredulously*] 'He's competent?!' And I said, 'Sir, if you think that we do this to amuse ourselves, well not at all!' [...] Because he thought he was dealing with some local peasant who had read *Science et vie* [a popular science magazine] and that was it! [...] This local peasant had arguments that made sense and—

MF: Yeah, to take a position like that, after all, I wouldn't have taken it lightly![44]

In addition to whatever concerns they may have had about nuclear technology or the social, political, and economic implications of its introduction into their communities, many local opponents were angry because they felt misled, insulted, and not taken seriously by officials.

In cases where locals remained unconvinced by pro-nuclear arguments, the nuclear industry and its allies in government often pushed ahead, even using force where they deemed it necessary. Local communities across West Germany and France repeatedly complained that construction was proceeding on sites that had not yet received full administrative approval. Earlier power stations such as those built during the 1950s and 1960s had been accepted without great controversy, and authorities had occasionally looked the other way to facilitate rapid construction of facilities they regarded as a public good.[45] As nuclear energy became more controversial in the

[44] Maurice and Chantal François, joint interview with the author, Creys-Mépieu, 25 January 2010.
[45] See the Bavarian examples described in Hasenöhrl, *Zivilgesellschaft und Protest*, pp. 209–10, 215–16.

1970s, opponents saw this (rightly or wrongly) as the deliberate creation of irreversible facts on the ground. In West Germany, construction of basic infrastructure (roads, fences, etc.) and even particular buildings could and usually did proceed as soon as partial authorizations for land and water use were given—even when no decision had officially been made as to whether this purpose-built infrastructure would belong to a nuclear power plant or some unspecified alternative. Local opponents quickly lost faith in consultative procedures (whose piecemeal nature led them to accuse authorities of 'salami tactics'[46]) and began turning every administrative step into an opportunity to protest and vent frustration. In France too, local opponents were angered by public utility surveys (*enquêtes d'utilité publique*, EUP) that seemed to be a mere formality and by construction that often began before authorization was granted.[47] One activist from Normandie became so fed up with how authorities tolerated construction in Flamanville—in violation of their own procedures—that he reportedly told activists in Plogoff not to bother trying to influence the EUP but to focus on direct action instead.[48] At sites where plans were announced later, local opponents reacted not only to their own personal frustrations with authorities but to expectations created by an entire history of similar experiences elsewhere.

The French and West German states saw energy production by means of nuclear technology as so important, so prestigious, and so economically vital that they were also willing to use coercion. In West Germany, mass demonstrations regularly met with shows of overwhelming force by authorities (especially, but not exclusively, in 1976–7). The most glaring example of this occurred at the 1977 protest in Kalkar, when busloads of outside supporters were blocked or remained stuck for hours on the highway by a series of checkpoints. A convoy carrying 2,000 demonstrators from Stuttgart was searched no less than six times, stretching a 500-kilometre journey out over a period of eighteen hours.[49] On this and numerous other occasions, the West German state treated nuclear energy opponents like 'terrorists' and brought out heavy military equipment to intimidate protesters.[50] The French government was equally willing go to extremes, as it showed in Le Pellerin and Cheix-en-Retz in 1977, in Golfech in 1979, and most famously in Plogoff in 1980. When the mayors of these small towns closed their offices in defiance of laws requiring

---

[46] Christoph Büchele et al., *Der Widerstand* (1982), p. 161.

[47] Construction without permission was also apparently tolerated in Malville and Cruas-Meysse. 'A Creys-Malville, les travaux ont commencé sans les autorisations officielles', *Le Monde*, 29 April 1977; 'L'EDF a commencé les travaux sans autorisation', *Libération*, 20 October 1977.

[48] Memo, 17 February 1980, AD Finistère, 1347 W 164-2.

[49] *Kalkar. Ein Schritt auf dem Weg zum Polizeistaat*, 1977, 45 mins.

[50] See Karrin Hanshew, *Terror and Democracy* (2012), pp. 173–4.

them to display construction blueprints, Paris literally sent in the army: central authorities arranged for vans marked 'Town Hall Annex' (*Mairie annexe*) to be escorted into and out of town every weekday in order to display and solicit public comment on planning documents during ordinary working hours.[51] When such procedures were repeated in Plogoff, the local community established daily rituals of resistance to oppose what it regarded as a regular 'invasion' by the central state, barricading roads at night, verbally assaulting police in the afternoon, and pelting gendarmes with projectiles in the afternoon. By the end of the consultation, the Renseignements Généraux (RG, domestic intelligence service) conceded that 'there are many—even of moderate opinion—who feel keeping up appearances at all costs can be dangerous'.[52] Shows of force like this made people feel that their legitimate concerns were being ignored. When authorities who behaved this way still claimed to be 'democratic', protesters appropriated 'democracy' for themselves and redefined it in opposition to politicians, parliaments, and police.[53]

Already at the level of local communities, individuals with very different concerns forged coalitions to fight against what they perceived as a common threat. That threat was defined not primarily in terms of radioactive dangers to be feared, but immediate concerns about the impact of nuclear-led industrialization on their jobs, communities, and surroundings. Local opposition included some who connected with environmentalist or regionalist traditions or who were otherwise receptive to the political left, but also others who were conservative in outlook as well as many more who considered themselves 'apolitical'. However, even those who were hesitant to associate themselves with protest grew increasingly angry over time with authorities who they felt condescended to them, trampled their wishes, and attacked their communities. These experiences pushed them to take up protest, even in spite of themselves, and to forge an alliance with outsiders willing to help.

OUTSIDERS

Away from the directly affected communities, people opposed nuclear power for additional reasons which were sometimes very different. Though there are no reliable statistics on the composition of the anti-nuclear

[51] The police strategy in Plogoff was modelled on similar procedures first tried in Le Pellerin. See Memo, 13 July 1977, AD Finistère, 1347 W 164-2.

[52] RG, 'Réflexions sur l'Enquête d'Utilité Publique', March 1980, AD Finistère, 1235 W 24, p. 17.

[53] See '"... mehr Demokratie überhaupt". Ein Bericht von den Bürgerinitiativen um Wyhl', brochure, 68 pp., January 1977, IISG, Bro 2188/16.

movement, outsiders clearly outnumbered locals. This is one reason why their perspectives are the focus of most sociological literature about the movement and its supposedly 'post-materialist' values. Ironically, the contributions of these same people are understated within the movement's own propaganda, which emphasized the concerns and agency of 'authentic', directly affected locals in order to appeal to a wider public. Many outsiders came from cities or university towns with vibrant alternative milieus.[54] Their ranks included not only the students who captured most media attention, but also vocational apprentices, high-school pupils, and other youth as well as the unemployed and people of different ages who mingled together within 'scenes'. During the occupation of the construction site in Wyhl, dozens of them made nightly or weekly trips from Freiburg, and thousands came for rallies and demonstrations; protest in Creys-Malville in the Rhône-Alpes region of France attracted activists from the nearby cities of Grenoble, Lyon, and Geneva; in Brokdorf, the Hamburg political scene in many respects dominated the terrain; and even Gorleben, where protest was perhaps most firmly anchored in the local community, owed much of the attention it received to its status as a weekend retreat for residents of West Berlin and Hamburg. Not all outside activists were from urban areas though. The anti-nuclear movement also profited from the same impulses that led some to move 'back to the land', creating rural communes (*communautés* or *Landkommunen*) across France and West Germany during the 1970s. Outsiders of every flavour contributed to the anti-nuclear movement, bringing with them motivations, arguments, and networks that might be specific to their particular group, but which were often broadly shared. Though the boundaries between groups were never absolute, outsiders tended to be associated with three large categories of protesters (whether or not they identified themselves as such): advocates of non-violence, left-wing radicals, and 'environmentalists' associated with a growing alternative milieu. These partially overlapping groups were stitched together not only within anti-nuclear networks, but also within other contemporary protest movements.

Some of the most influential outsiders to become involved in anti-nuclear protest defined themselves by their adherence to principles of non-violence.[55] Characterized by a plurality of motivations, they often

[54] On the concept of 'milieu', see Sven Reichardt, *Authentizität und Gemeinschaft* (2014), pp. 38–41.
[55] The term 'non-violent' here denotes not merely a shared strategy employed for tactical purposes, but the defining principle around which the individuals in question organized. It is distinct from 'pacifist', which denotes specifically the opposition to war.

belonged to networks of the Christian left and/or of conscientious object-ors. Within many 'non-violent action groups',[56] the border between secular and religious activism could be blurry, with anarchists and Christians (and more than a few Christian anarchists) working together. Though local activists still usually regarded them as outsiders, non-violent groups generally enjoyed good relations with local anti-nuclear protesters in rural areas, in part because they could communicate using a shared Christian vocabulary. In West Germany, Protestants were generally more engaged in anti-nuclear activism than Catholics, and church groups provided one space in which anti-nuclear protest grew and developed.[57] French Protestants such as Solange Fernex in Alsace or Hervé Ott on the Larzac were also prominent in certain non-violent struggles and were able to establish contact with counterparts in Germany in part through cross-border religious ties. Even if the hierarchy of the Catholic Church gener-ally opposed its representatives taking a public stance on the issue of nuclear power, dissenting Catholics also grounded their opposition to nuclear energy in their faith.[58] There was significant dialogue between Catholics and Protestants within magazines like *Témoignage chrétien* and interfaith organizations such as the International Fellowship of Reconciliation.[59]

Remarkably few of the nuclear energy opponents of the 1970s had been involved in the large-scale West German protests against nuclear weapons or the (much smaller) French protests against nuclear technology that had taken place two decades earlier.[60] For a younger generation of action-oriented non-violent activists, '1968' was a more important point of reference—though they connected it less with *pavé*-wielding Parisian students or the *Osterunruhen* in West Germany than with Czechoslovak resistance to the Soviet invasion and the tragic assassination of Martin

---

Gene Sharp, 'Meanings of Non-Violence', *Journal of Conflict Resolution* 3, no. 1 (March 1959), pp. 42, 44.

[56] In West Germany, the term *Gewaltfreie Aktionsgruppen* is used to designate precisely these groups. Their French counterparts do not share one specific epithet, but the most prominent such group is the Mouvement pour une alternative non-violente.

[57] Nelkin and Pollak, *Atom Besieged*, pp. 65–6, 109.

[58] Peter Modler, 'Was können Christen jetzt noch tun? Theologisches Gutachten über den Handlungsfreiraum für Christen im Widerstand gegen das Atomkraftwerk Wyhl nach dem Mannheimer Urteil', 1983, DfuL, D 03382.

[59] IFOR is known as Mouvement international de la réconciliation in France and Internationaler Versöhnungsbund in Germany. See http://ifor-mir.org/.

[60] On the early movement against nuclear weapons, see Holger Nehring, *Politics of Security* (2013). Those activists who had been involved in the 1950s were just as likely to be radical leftists with whom most non-violent activists did not identify; among those inter-viewed for this project, Ginette Skandrani and Günter Hopfenmüller would fit this description.

Luther King.[61] Nevertheless, non-violent groups drew on long-standing traditions of religious activism for peace and the civil disobedience practices associated with figures like Mahatma Gandhi. Lanza del Vasto, one of the non-violent movement's leading figures in France, effectively personified this fusion of Christian and Gandhian non-violent traditions as well as their continuity over time. A dissenting Catholic, del Vasto had gone to India in 1936 to meet Gandhi, who rebaptized him Shantidas ('servant of peace'). Upon returning to Europe, he founded the Communauté de l'Arche, establishing a farming settlement in La Borie Noble modelled on Gandhi's own Sabarmati ashram. The settlement became a site of pilgrimage for some non-violent (and anti-nuclear) activists, though del Vasto's patriarchal style and the Arche group's cultish asceticism were not to everyone's taste.[62] In post-war France, del Vasto became well known for his fasts against the Algerian War (1957), at the Second Vatican Council (1963), and especially on behalf of the farmers of the Larzac (1972), the latter being located only a short drive from La Borie Noble. He was also one of the few to have protested against nuclear energy well before the 1970s, having organized a fast before the gates of France's research reactor in Marcoule as early as 1958.[63] Though del Vasto was much better known in France, his books circulated in West Germany as well.[64] Despite being much older than most 1970s nuclear energy opponents, Lanza del Vasto epitomizes the internationality of non-violent anti-nuclear activists as well as the mixture of direct action and religious inspiration that characterized many of them.

Younger activists who became involved in non-violent action groups had grown up watching Martin Luther King on television and many were eager to employ civil disobedience against injustice. They focused their energies not (exclusively) on spiritual dimensions of non-violence, but on the theory and practice of non-violent direct action. Indeed, several groups were founded out of a desire to create a more action-oriented alternative to

---

[61] Wolfgang Hertle, interview with the author, Hamburg, 22 July 2010; Bernd Nössler, interview with the author, Freiburg, 14 April 2010. Activists like these were strongly opposed to the Vietnam War, but did not join their radical left peers in cheering for a North Vietnamese victory that would bring about a communist revolution. On the complicated relationship between the New Left (including its radical offshoots) and non-violent movements, see Andrew Oppenheimer, 'Conflicts of Solidarity' (2010).

[62] Yves Hardy and Emmanuel Gabey, *L . . . comme Larzac* (1974), pp. 76–9.

[63] 'Le jeûne de Marcoule et de Genève', *Nouvelles de l'Arche* (October 1958), pp. 1–6; Lanza del Vasto, *Technique de la non-violence* (1978), pp. 81–97.

[64] In French, del Vasto's books included *Le pèlerinage aux sources* (1943) and *Technique de la non-violence* (1978). Books by and about the Arche were published repeatedly in German, including one edition by anti-nuclear activists: *Die Arche stellt sich vor* (1980).

traditional pacifist organizations.[65] These activists might read about non-violent theory in magazines such as *Alternatives non-violentes* or *Gewaltfreie Aktion*; other nationally distributed newspapers such as *Graswurzelrevolution* (*GWR*) and *Combat non-violent* (*CNV*) spread news of civil disobedience actions at home and abroad to a less theoretically inclined audience.[66] Through these publications and international organizations such as War Resisters' International (WRI), some non-violent activists were closely networked across borders.[67] The WRI's triennial meetings were one important site of exchange among non-violent activists; together with IFOR, WRI also hosted a women's meeting in 1976 in Les Circauds, France (home of *CNV*), providing an opportunity for the many girlfriends, wives, and other women involved in the male-dominated conscientious objection movement to develop their own international perspective on anti-militarism.[68] Activists from West Germany and France also repeatedly crossed paths on the Larzac plateau in southern France, which, though not related to nuclear power, became a cause célèbre of the post-1968 period and later a hub for many non-violent activists involved in the anti-nuclear movement.[69]

Owing to the composition and intellectual heritage of these non-violent groups, one element of their critique of nuclear energy focused on the potential military uses of 'civil' nuclear power. France's nuclear energy programme had incubated under military auspices and projects like the commercial, plutonium-producing fast breeder reactor (FBR) at Malville seemed destined for 'dual use'.[70] After the Second World War, few were willing to believe in the supposedly peaceful intentions of West Germany's nuclear programme, least of all Germans themselves. Some non-violent advocates actively linked their struggles against the civil and

[65] Hertle, interview; 'La révolution au ras du sol', *S!lence*, no. 370 (July 2009).

[66] Each of these publications was founded after 1968: *Gewaltfreie Aktion* in 1969, *CNV* in 1971, *Alternatives Non-Violentes* and *GWR* in 1972.

[67] Bernadette Ridard, interview with the author, Hamburg, 25 August 2010; Hertle, interview; Haug and Schirmer, interview. On this more generally, see Oppenheimer, 'Conflicts of Solidarity', pp. 279–347; Holger Nehring, 'National Internationalists', *Contemporary European History* 14, no. 4 (2005), pp. 572–6.

[68] Ridard, interview; WRI, 'Erstellung stärkerer transnationaler Verbindungen und Kooperationsnetz für fortschrittliche Kräfte', report on workshop in Noordwijkerhout, 1–6 July 1975, HIS, no call number.

[69] Robert Gildea and Andrew Tompkins, 'The Transnational in the Local', *Journal of Contemporary History* (2015); Wolfgang Hertle, *Larzac 1971–81* (1982).

[70] Anti-nuclear protesters felt their worst fears were confirmed when, in 1978, General Thiry told *Le Monde* that 'La France sait faire des armes atomiques de tout modèle et de toute puissance. Elle pourra en fabriquer en grandes quantités dès que les surgénérateurs lui fourniront en abondance le plutonium nécessaire.' *Le Monde*, 19 January 1978, cited in Chaïm Nissim, *L'amour et le monstre* (2004), pp. 73–4.

military uses of nuclear technology together. For example, in Alsace in 1976, conscientious objectors and their partners organized an 'international march for de-militarization' across the Franco-German border that included, on the anniversary of the Hiroshima bombing, speeches by activist friends who were involved in struggles against nuclear power plants in Wyhl, Fessenheim, and Malville.[71] The next year, approximately eighty of them followed up their anti-militarist march with participation in the anti-nuclear energy protest in Malville and other protests in Naussac and the Larzac.[72] The struggles between military and civilian use of nuclear technology were also linked together in the biographies of individual activists. For example, *GWR* editor and founder Wolfgang Hertle began his activist career supporting conscientious objection, then campaigned against French atmospheric nuclear tests in the Pacific in 1973 before becoming deeply involved in protests in and around Hamburg against nuclear power; for many years after that, he lived in the Wendland region near Gorleben.[73] For other activists, it was nuclear energy that led to nuclear weapons: protests during the 1980s against West German acquiescence to stationing American missiles in Europe and against continued French nuclear weapons testing could be a logical continuation of prior activism against nuclear power in the 1970s.[74] For non-violent activists especially, nuclear power was a force to oppose in part because of its 'dual use' nature.

A second pole around which outside anti-nuclear protesters gravitated was the radical left (though its orbit contained spaces of overlap with non-violent and 'environmentalist' activism). In the early 1970s, the radical left was dominated by the kinds of Marxist groups that had experienced a resurgence around 1968, known collectively as *gauchistes* in France and *K-Gruppen*[75] in West Germany; later in the decade, they were partially

---

[71] See 'Internationaler gewaltloser Marsch für Entmilitarisierung. Teilnehmer-Information', brochure, 8 pp., 4–10 August 1976, AA, Internationaler Gewaltloser Marsch 1976–80.

[72] 'La « descente » vers Malville : un certain désenchantement', *Le Monde*, 27 July 1977; Isabelle Cabut, 'serpent des luttes, premier anneau : haguenau-la frontière allemande', *GO/CNV*, no. 167 (21 July 1977), pp. 3–4.

[73] Hertle, interview. See also 'Stoppt die franz. Atom-tests!', *GWR*, no. 4/5 ([June] 1973), p. 1; Green Peace [sic], 'Vive la France ! Vive la bombe !', various flyers, 1973, APO, S 46.

[74] Dominique Lalanne, interview with the author, Orsay, 25 February 2010; Patrice Bouveret, interview with the author, Lyon, 23 January 2010.

[75] Hereafter, the terms *gauchiste* and *K-Gruppe* are used more or less interchangeably. The 'K' refers to the *Kader*, or cadres, that they trained. On such groups generally, see Roland Biard, *Dictionnaire de l'extrême-gauche* (1978); Isabel Sommier, 'Gauchismes', in *Mai–Juin 68*, edited by Dominique Damamme et al. (2008); Gerd Koenen, *Das rote Jahrzehnt* (2001).

supplanted by anarchist 'autonomists' (see below).[76] The *gauchistes* were
generally centralized, hierarchical organizations of Maoist or Trotskyist
inspiration that competed with one another and particularly with the
official, Soviet-aligned parties that they most despised (the Parti Communiste Français and Deutsche Kommunistische Partei). They began to
decline earlier in France than in West Germany (around 1973–4 as opposed
to after 1977),[77] but the more flexible among them survived until the end of
the decade or beyond (the Trotskyist Ligue Communiste Révolutionnaire
and post-Maoist Organisation Communiste des Travailleurs in France,
the ever-less-Maoist Kommunistischer Bund and Kommunistische Partei
Deutschlands in West Germany). In most cases (Hamburg being a notable
exception), these groups were not *the* driving force behind anti-nuclear
protest.[78] Yet even when they were not in control, they dominated the
'revolutionary' sector of the protest movement and constituted a foil for
other activists.

It is often argued that *gauchistes* entered the movement late and with
dubious motivations, but the situation was neither as simple nor as sinister
as many critics saw it: these organizations were also changing at the time
and, in any case, individual members were more dynamic than the
organizations themselves.[79] Though structured by top-down hierarchies,
these groups also came into the anti-nuclear movement in part through
the bottom-up initiative of individuals within them. For example, members of the Hamburg-based KB 'voted with their feet' for change before
the leadership took up the anti-nuclear protests in Brokdorf and pushed

[76] *Autonomen* or *les autonomes* are often referred to simply as 'anarchists' in English,
though the more specific term 'autonomist' denotes a form of revolutionary, radical left
politics that emerged in the 1970s. The anarchist tradition of the late nineteenth and early
twentieth centuries was not a significant point of reference for most such activists. Those
who are referred to here as 'autonomists' are not to be confused with activists seeking
regional autonomy and independence (e.g. in Bretagne), who are described throughout this
book as 'regionalists' for the sake of simplicity. See also George N. Katsiaficas, *Subversion of
Politics*, updated edn (2006), pp. 6–9.
[77] The demise of French *gauchistes* is conventionally dated to the decision by Gauche
prolétarienne (far and away the best-known such group) to dissolve itself in late 1973 and
(less convincingly) to the publication of Solzhenitsyn's *Gulag Archipelago* in French in early
1974. However, other groups (and many former GP members) continued with radical left
activism for many years thereafter. In West Germany, the demise of the *K-Gruppen* is
usually seen as a response to the 'terrorism' of the *Deutscher Herbst* in September–October
1977, though the death of Mao in 1976 was a more important factor for some. Around the
same time, the rise of NSMs detracted from the ability of some *K-Gruppen* to attract new
members. See Chapter 6.
[78] Dieter Rucht, *Von Wyhl nach Gorleben* (1980), p. 91.
[79] See Philippe Buton, 'Extrême-gauche et écologie', *Vingtième siècle*, no. 113 (2012),
p. 203; Michael Steffen, *Geschichten vom Trüffelschwein* (2002), pp. 175–268.

the entire organization to get involved.[80] OCT, the KB's French sister organization, also joined the anti-nuclear movement out of a desire on the part of its *mouvementiste* militants to go where the action was and work with the people they found there.[81] None of these groups was devoted exclusively or (with the possible exception of KB in 1976–7) even primarily to the anti-nuclear movement. Indeed, they participated in it in part out of a desire 'to see to it that this movement was linked to other societal struggles'.[82] The negative side of this was that they were often accused (and often enough, rightly so) of opportunistically trying to take over the anti-nuclear movement and lead it in their own direction.[83] Some groups' anti-nuclear credentials were also questionable, since they equivocated about the safety of nuclear power in socialist countries; different organizations were not equally guilty in this regard, but it was difficult for the uninitiated to distinguish between them.[84] For all of these reasons, their contributions have largely been written out of most histories of the anti-nuclear movement.

Nevertheless, *gauchistes* and *K-Gruppen* participated actively and constructively in anti-nuclear protest. Some of the cadres trained by these professional and highly politicized groups included nuclear physicists such as Patrick Petitjean (Révolution !) and Jens Scheer (KPD), who lent their expertise to other anti-nuclear activists regardless of ideological affiliation. Scheer, a professor at the University of Bremen, aroused enough attention through anti-nuclear protest that he briefly found himself disqualified from public service (allowing him to claim to be the first anti-nuclear opponent to fall victim to *Berufsverbot*, the West German state's policy of excluding avowed communists from public service).[85] Even apparently

---

[80] Steffen, *Geschichten vom Trüffelschwein*, p. 150. This did not, however, stop the leadership from chastising some members for not taking anti-nuclear protest seriously enough. KB, 'Rundbrief des Leitenden Gremiums', 4 January 1977, StHH, 136–3, Nr. 653.

[81] Bernard Dréano and Suzanne d'Hernies, joint interview with the author, Paris, 20 January 2010.

[82] Atom Express, *Und auch nicht anderswo!* (1997), p. 23.

[83] KB, 'Rundbrief LG'.

[84] As late as 1977, the KBW argued that 'Nicht die Technik ist gefährlich, sondern ihre Anwendung durch die Kapitalistenklasse' and 'Die Arbeiterklasse kann die Technik zum Nutzen des Volkes entwickeln [...] Dazu zwei Beispiele aus der Volksrepublik China.' KBW, 'Dat Ding kummt hier nicht her', brochure, 50 pp., February 1977, HIS, unsorted brochures, pp. 25, 28–30. Whatever the merits of such arguments, they were more off-putting than attractive to most in the anti-nuclear movement.

[85] Jens Scheer, letter to World Information Service on Energy, 1 May 1980, IISG, WISE 7. Patrick Petitjean was involved in anti-Vietnam War groups in the 1960s and worked with the group Révolution ! and leftist unions for much of the 1970s. Upon moving to Strasbourg in 1977, he became involved with CSFR, editing its paper *Ionix*. Patrick Petitjean, interview with the author, Paris, 23 February 2010. Referring to Jens Scheer, the editors of an activist history of the West German anti-nuclear movement wrote that 'Sein

self-interested actions by *gauchiste* groups could have a positive impact on the overall movement. Jan Stehn (b. 1957), an activist from near Hamburg who later worked with non-violent activists, remembers how the *K-Gruppen* tried to 'obtain influence' over his high school student group, but he also remembers their involvement as something 'which we actually at that time felt to be supportive, that they—even though we didn't belong to them—supported us too'.[86] *Gauchistes* and *K-Gruppen* also brought their large publishing resources to bear in an effort to spread anti-nuclear protest to a wider audience. The KB newspaper *Arbeiterkampf* reported so extensively on anti-nuclear protest that even bourgeois activists valued it as a sort of 'intelligence service' for the movement.[87] Communists also produced anti-nuclear propaganda targeted specifically at the working class, challenging the pro-nuclear argument that 'energy equals job creation'.[88] Criticizing technological progress in this way did not always come easily to historical materialists, especially when trade unions placed themselves strongly behind the nuclear industry.[89] Rather than being simple opportunists, many Marxists were willing to challenge certain of their own orthodoxies in order to participate in the anti-nuclear movement.

Befitting their protest tradition, communist groups such as these elaborated a critique of nuclear power focused on anti-imperialism and anti-capitalism. In both France and West Germany, proponents of nuclear power argued that it would assure energy independence in the aftermath of the oil crisis. *Gauchistes* countered this by arguing that government nuclear programmes would merely shift dependence from oil to uranium; the difference would be that, instead of relying on Middle Eastern dictatorships, French and German industry would depend on the exploitation of African uranium mines (notably in Niger, a former French colony) to

uneitles, engagiertes und fachkundiges Auftreten beeindruckte auf zahllosen Treffen, Konferenzen und Demonstrationen auch jene AKW-GegnerInnen, die seine politischen Überzeugungen eher skeptisch beurteilten.' Atom Express, *Und auch nicht anderswo!*, p. 173.

[86] Jan Stehn, interview with the author, Blütlingen, 24 August 2010.

[87] Rudolf van Hüllen, *Ideologie und Machtkampf* (1990), p. 111.

[88] See KB, 'Atomenergie und Arbeitsplätze', brochure, 64 pp., 2nd edition, 1977, AK.

[89] See Markus Mohr, *Gewerkschaften im Atomkonflikt* (2001). In France, anti-nuclear activists worked closely with trade union allies, especially CFDT members who took part in a 1976 strike at the La Hague nuclear fuel reprocessing centre. See especially François Jacquemain, *Condamnés à réussir*, 1976, 60 mins; Michel Bosquet [pseud. André Gorz], 'Les damnés de l'atome', *Nouvel Observateur*, no. 621 (4 October 1976), p. 42. Bernard Laponche, the CFDT's leading expert on nuclear power, continues to consult internationally on energy issues today. Bernard Laponche, interview with the author, Paris, 11 March 2010; Charlotte Nordmann and Bernard Laponche, 'Entre silence et mensonge : le nucléaire, de la raison d'État au recyclage « écologique »', *La Revue internationale des livres et des idées* (November–December 2009), pp. 6–13.

keep their machines running.[90] They also heavily criticized the 'imperialist competition' between the French and West German nuclear industries, which fought one another for contracts to build nuclear installations for the dictatorial Shah in Iran, for the racist regime in South Africa, and for developing countries like Brazil and Pakistan that could ill afford to squander their resources on such an expensive technology.[91] The KB in particular cast doubt on the wisdom of exporting nuclear material and technology to countries like these whose commitments to peace were questionable—an argument that they also extended to West Germany itself.[92] Within their own national contexts, these groups criticized nuclear power as merely the latest scheme to further enrich the wealthy, as the French group OCT argued:

> The French nuclear programme was not decided by the 'inevitability' of scientific and technical 'progress'. It is a class-based choice, desired by the government in order to assure substantial profits for a few large trusts, with complete disrespect for the working, health, and living conditions of the greatest number.[93]

Communist groups found ways to match their core tenets to the reality of anti-nuclear protest. In their critique of nuclear power, Maoists, Trotskyists, and the 'undogmatic' left thus assured continuity with one legacy of '1968', refitting their analyses to the concerns of NSMs like the opposition to nuclear energy. The fact that Marxist perspectives like these could coexist, however uncomfortably, alongside those of apolitical and even right-wing country folk is indicative of the breadth of opposition to nuclear power in this time period.

Another strand of the radical left was drawn to the anti-nuclear movement primarily by an anti-authoritarian narrative of nuclear power. Autonomists became a visible force in anti-nuclear protest towards the end of the 1970s, as more traditional *gauchiste* groups were declining. A different, often younger cohort of protesters than Marxist '68ers, they strongly resented the hierarchy and 'dogmatism' of *gauchistes* and *K-Gruppen*,

---

[90] 'Le Gouvernement persiste dans son programme nucléaire', *Quotidien du Peuple*, 30 June 1977.

[91] KB, 'Warum kämpfen wir gegen Atomkraftwerke?', brochure, 2nd edn, 48 pp., 1977, AK, pp. 40–6. For an academic treatment of the Iranian case, see Daniel Poneman, *Developing World* (1982), pp. 85–92.

[92] Of the aforementioned countries, only Iran had then signed the Non-Proliferation Treaty. With regard to West Germany, the KB argued that 'The development of the Federal Republic of Germany into a leading power in the domain the nuclear industry' would provide 'the prerequisites for a comprehensive armament with nuclear weapons.' KB, 'Warum kämpfen wir?', p. 4.

[93] OCT, 'L'après-Malville', *l'étincelle*, 5 July 1977, p. 2.

criticizing them from the left and developing their own, independent groups in response. Autonomists usually participated in the anti-nuclear movement within ad hoc structures or working groups, such as the Arbeitskreis Politische Ökologie (AKPÖ) in Hamburg. As repression of the anti-nuclear movement increased dramatically in 1976 and 1977, AKPÖ and other groups focused on the 'criminalization' of protest, supporting imprisoned demonstrators who had been arrested at protests. In the view of many autonomists, the state's heavy-handed repression of protest was a sign of the 'police state' that nuclear power necessarily entailed.[94] For them, it was no accident when anti-nuclear protesters were confronted with water cannon (at sites across Germany, starting from the earliest protests in Wyhl), grenades (Malville, Plogoff), or machine guns (Kalkar). There was a certain perverse logic to the way protesters were increasingly treated like terrorists: because sensitive nuclear technology had to be kept out of the wrong hands, everything connected to it was militarized in the extreme. They predicted that more nuclear power plants would bring with them more intrusive, police-escorted waste transports, constant surveillance, and the further criminalization of dissent. According to them, the security apparatus necessitated by nuclear power was a means by which the state would extend its power over citizens. Some autonomists thus saw nuclear power as 'the perfect symbol of a new order', one that would be based on the 'technocratic power of the state, military-police power'.[95]

Autonomists were also distinguished from other radical left activists by their greater willingness to employ violent protest tactics. Given the dystopian terms in which they viewed nuclear power, some saw violence as a form of 'legitimate self-defence'.[96] Occasionally, this view carried over into hyperbolic comparisons with fascism and the Nazi period. One group in northern Germany styled itself after the anti-Nazi resistance during the Second World War, calling itself the 're-founded White Rose' and claiming to fight against 'the nuclear concentration camp Brokdorf'. The group's newsletter, *1984*, reported on acts of sabotage that were committed in solidarity with imprisoned anti-nuclear protesters.[97] Sabotage

---

[94] 'Bullen-Terror gegen AKW-Gegner', flyer, 1977, HIS, SBe 731 Box 02, 'Kriminalisierung'; 'Freiheit für alle inhaftierten AKW-Gegner!', flyer, 4 pp., 24 March 1981, RF, 15.230 'Kriminalisierung 70er Jahre'; AKPÖ, *Bilanz und Perspektiven* (1978), pp. 9–11; 'Contre l'électro-fascisme', *Casse-Noix*, no. 6 (July 1977), p. 2.

[95] Cited in 'Violence Politique—Thèmes d'actions des « autonomes »', police report, 2 February 1978, PPP, B^A 2332.

[96] Yannick, 'Légitime défense', *Casse-Noix*, no. 4 (July 1976), p. 6.

[97] weiße Rose, 'Verhindert den totalen Staat', *1984* no. 1, undated, APO, S 37; weiße Rose, 'wie war es wirklich?', *1984* no. 5, undated, APO, S 37.

was far more common (and far more serious) in France than in West
Germany, where it took off in 1975 and remained frequent even well
after 1981.[98] Such actions reached a climax after the violent repression of
the anti-nuclear demonstration in Malville in July 1977, culminating in a
nuit bleue anti-nucléaire on 19–20 November 1977. The next day, a group
calling itself the Coordination Autonome des Révoltés en Lutte Ouverte
contre la Société (CARLOS—a tongue-in-cheek reference to the terrorist
'Carlos the Jackal') claimed responsibility for the seventeen arson and
bombing attacks that had taken place against nuclear-related installations
in nine different cities across France.[99] Towards the end of the 1970s, the
question of violence came to overshadow all other debates within the anti-
nuclear movement.

The last and probably largest contingent of outsiders who participated
in the anti-nuclear movement consisted of people who were referred to as
écologistes in French and *Ökos* in German. In both countries, these terms
are associated with a 'hippie' legacy of the late 1960s. The nearest English
equivalents, 'environmentalist' (used hereafter) and 'ecologist',[100] do not
convey the breadth of this group, which was defined as much by 'countercultural' values as by concern for the environment. While some environmentalists were members of new political ecology associations such as
ADLT and BUND, the appeal of special-interest NGOs like these was, on
the whole, limited.[101] Indeed, many environmentalists were suspicious of
organizations generally, just as they were wary of being associated with any
particular ideology. Though emanating from the political left, they were
also repulsed by many of the groups within it and (like older, local
activists) preferred not to identify themselves in political terms.[102] The
answers French *écologistes* gave reporters when asked to describe themselves are illustrative: 'I don't talk about either the left or the right—I'm

---

[98] Nelkin and Pollak, *Atom Besieged*, p. 74. See 'Actions directes contre le nucléaire,
1973–96', 2008, http://infokiosques.net/spip.php?article553 (accessed 6 Feb 2010). The
document is based on Claude Courtes and Jean-Claude Driant, *Golfech* (1999).
[99] See Courtes and Driant, *Golfech*, pp. 84–5.
[100] In English, the term 'ecologist' is often narrowly associated with scientific opposition
to environmental problems and is therefore either eschewed or referred to in quotation
marks throughout this book. See Peder Anker, review of Michael Bess, *The Light-Green
Society, Isis* 95, no. 4 (2004).
[101] Nelkin and Pollak, *Atom Besieged*, p. 128.
[102] 'This utopia, this desire for a less hierarchical, more open, more just society, this
force growing out of socialism, is today invested in ecology. There is no future on the
right . . . but neither do we consider ourselves part of a symmetric left. Certainly the
historical failure of the left accounts for our existence . . . It would be dangerous to consider
the ecological movement as an heir of [*gauchisme*].' Interview with Serge Moscovici in Jean-
Paul Ribes, *Pourquoi les écologistes font-ils de la politique?* (1978), p. 138, cited in Nelkin and
Pollak, *Atom Besieged*, pp. 128–9.

not interested in that'; 'I'm not *just* an environmentalist'; 'I have lots of [*vachement de*] motivations.'[103] Because they often rejected structured organizations, environmentalist networks were much looser than those of the radical left or non-violent groups. In France, the national publication *La Gueule ouverte* (*GO*) was a hub of information and activity, linking activist journalists together and consolidating a readership that occasionally came together at demonstrations. Indeed, one of the first major demonstrations to take place, in Bugey in 1971, was assembled at the call of *Charlie Hebdo*, a forerunner of *GO*.[104] In West Germany, there was no comparable national organ of *Ökos*, but they were also far more embedded in the greater alternative infrastructure of that country.[105] Environmentalists were overwhelmingly non-organized (*inorganisés, Nichtorganisierte*) and usually became involved in protest on an individual basis or together with small groups of friends rather than through involvement in formal associations. This meant that they seldom spoke with a unified voice and often found themselves caught in the middle of the debates that raged between (organized) non-violent activists and the radical left. A flyer from Hamburg complaining about in-fighting within the local anti-nuclear initiative is a testament to the frustration many environmentalists felt:

> No [more] leadership struggles! We non-organized [activists] are here too! In terms of numbers, we more than match the total count of organized activists in Hamburg. We need the organized activists, but what would you all be, what would the entire anti-nuclear movement be without us, the non-organized?[106]

For better or for worse, environmentalists constituted that majority of anti-nuclear activists who 'did not and do not want to be counted as part of any particular current' within the movement.[107]

The environmentalist opposition to nuclear power was much more 'nebulous'[108] than other anti-nuclear factions, but some of the impulses

---

[103] 'Qui sont les écologistes ?', 13 August 1977, Antenne 2.
[104] *La Gueule ouverte* (literally 'The Open Beak', i.e. a mouth shouting) was the brainchild of Pierre Fournier, who had previously written for the satirical weeklies *Hara-Kiri* and *Charlie Hebdo*. His experiences there convinced him that 'Shouting [*gueuler*] was not enough'. The demonstration in Bugey helped give him the idea for a new journal that would get out the 'urgent' message that 'l'homme est en train, à force d'exploitation technologique incontrôlée, de rendre la terre inhabitable', [Pierre] Fournier, 'Premier et dernier éditorial', *GO*, no. 1 (November 1972). In 1977–8, *GO* merged briefly with the pacifist journal *CNV* (as *GO/CNV*). It ceased publication in 1980.
[105] Pierre Jacquiot, 'Comparaison des processus', *Cahiers internationaux de sociologie* 123, no. 2 (2007).
[106] See 'Nichtorganisierte! Laßt Euch Eure BUU nicht kaputtmachen', flyer, 2 pp., 3 March 1977, HIS, SBe 731, Box 2/2.
[107] Atom Express, *Und auch nicht anderswo!*, p. 22.
[108] Nelkin and Pollak, *Atom Besieged*, p. 140.

that inspired it are clear. The most important element was criticism of consumption, as nuclear power was a symbol of the potential dangers of unrestrained economic growth. Odile Wieder (b. 1947), a close friend of several journalists from *GO*, was one of the organizers of the anti-nuclear demonstrations in Malville in 1976 and 1977. She described her views on nuclear power as such:

> OW: For me, nuclear [power] was—and is—a symbol of something that goes against individual autonomy. It leads to a society that resolves all problems and incites people to consume more and more, etc. I don't say we need to go back to using candles, that wasn't at all my perspective, but it was this symbolic side [...]. I wasn't like 'I'm afraid, I'm afraid of nuclear [power]!' because there are plenty of other dangers out there everywhere, all the time. Although I do think that it's dangerous nevertheless.[109]

For many environmentalists, criticism of consumption went hand in hand with a desire to live life differently, more in accord with their own principles than with the rules of society. Sometimes, this manifested itself as a movement 'back to the land' that could overlap politically with anti-nuclear activism, as in the case of Mireille Caselli (b. 1948). French by birth, she married a German man as she was finishing her studies and moved with him to Freiburg, where she immediately entered professional life as a university lecturer. However, within a few years, she felt alienated by her job, her marriage, and bourgeois life in general:

> MC: And all at once, I had a need to explode all of that. [...] The movement, everything that was going on politically, was very important because I was living a life that didn't correspond to my ideas or my needs. [...] I quit working and entered the alternative scene. [...] In Freiburg, there was a group of people who were looking for a farm to start a commune in the wild, so I joined up with that group.[110]

Like many other environmentalists, Mireille was also motivated by the desire to live life simply, according to the principle that 'small is beautiful'.[111] Nuclear power, by contrast, seemed to represent a centralizing force on an impossible, inhuman scale. When French officials first announced the massive expansion of their nuclear programme in 1974, they happily boasted that construction costs would constitute 'the largest contract ever

[109] Odile Wieder, interview with the author, Annecy, 29 April 2010.
[110] Mireille Caselli, interview with the author, Freiburg, 12 April 2010.
[111] E. F. Schumacher, *Small is Beautiful: A Study of Economics as if People Mattered* (1973).

signed in the world', one that would make Électricité de France the world's largest electricity supplier and necessitate so much capital that not even the French state could provide the loans by itself.[112] This gigantism was precisely the sort of thing that Mireille and others rejected:

> MC: It's really the refusal of that which is done on too great a scale—whatever it is. [. . .] The more something is done on a higher level, the more dangerous it is politically. That's what's going on now with all these stories of virtual money.[113] [. . .] There's no more true democracy. There are no means of action. [. . .] My opinion on nuclear power is that there should be a bit of solar, a bit of wind, a bit of water [. . .] the greatest possible diversity.[114]

Among environmentalists, opposition to nuclear energy was part of a perspective that criticized mainstream society and sought to propose simpler, feasible alternatives to it.

A final factor contributing to anti-nuclear protest was the way it was enmeshed within the broader web of activism associated with the left in the 1970s.[115] Many anti-nuclear activists were not *only* opposed to nuclear energy; they also attended demonstrations, signed petitions, and participated in boycotts addressing other specific issues, all of which called society into question in interrelated ways. For example, at a 1975 protest against Fessenheim, there were stands for gay activists and Alsatian regionalists as well as *gauchistes* and environmental groups.[116] Protest, for whatever cause, was in the air throughout the decade.[117] A certain left way of thinking was common at the time, even among people who did not identify with left-wing organizations: Christine Scheer (b. 1953), an architect and the wife of a farmer from Brokdorf, remembers participating in protests sponsored by the *K-Gruppen* during her university studies, though she says the groups themselves were 'not my thing [. . .] To be

---

[112] 'Les commandes de chaudières nucléaires par EDF constituent le plus grand contrat du monde', *Le Monde*, 28 March 1974.

[113] Other interviewees also compared nuclear energy in the 1970s to the financial crisis that began in 2008. On parallels and connections between anti-nuclear and anti-neoliberal globalization protests, see Emmanuel Rivat, 'Continuity of Transnational Protest', in *Understanding European Movements*, edited by Cristina Flesher Fominaya and Laurence Cox (2013).

[114] Caselli, interview.

[115] 'Die linksradikalen Subkulturen waren auch deshalb so relevant, weil ein Charakteristikum der 1970er Jahre darin bestand, dass, pointiert gesprochen, jung und intellektuell gleich links war.' Detlef Siegfried, 'Einstürzende Neubauten', *Archiv für Sozialgeschichte*, no. 44 (2004), p. 44.

[116] '2 000 Polizisten für 20 000 Demonstranten', *National-Zeitung Basel*, 26 May 1975.

[117] Conny Baade and Christian Petty, joint interview with the author, St-Jean-de-Buèges, 19 September 2010.

sure, after '68, we all [shared in] a left-wing spectrum, a left-wing thought [*Gedankengut*], but for me that [the *K-Gruppen*] went right past reality.'[118]

If the NSMs constitute a 'movement family',[119] it is in part because they all tapped into the same pool of mobilizing potential created by the upsurge of the left in and after '1968'. During the 1970s, the 'left' was a major point of reference, with individuals and ideas aligned to it that in retrospect might appear more ambiguous. Asked in 1975 why the Paris branch of ADLT considered itself 'left' or even 'far left', its speaker (and future left-wing, then right-wing politician) Brice Lalonde declared:

> First, because a certain number of ideals to which we lay claim are ordinarily considered 'left'. Because we have the same adversaries as the classic left: large 'managers', big capitalist property owners who, by their power and their activities, are responsible for the ecological crisis, responsible for exploitation in the third world, for the living conditions of immigrants and many other people. Next, because ecology, like part of the left, asserts the principle of [*pose en postulat*] self-management [*autogestion*]. And then [there is] the clear convergence between ecological struggle, the struggle for regional autonomy, or the women's struggle.[120]

Intersections between anti-nuclear and other activism were especially productive when it came to the women's movement. Radical feminists objected to nuclear energy as the fuel for household appliances, which perpetuated the 'transformed, converted [*aménagé*] slavery' of domestic work. Françoise d'Eaubonne even conceived of a hybrid struggle for 'eco-feminism' and called for an 'end of separations' between these and other post-'68 struggles. Other women, including housewives, elaborated their own criticisms of nuclear power, arguing on the basis of their roles as mothers that it presented a danger to future generations.[121]

Organizing amongst themselves, women also discussed and sought to address the inequalities within the anti-nuclear movement, arguing that

---

[118] CS in Heinrich Voß and Christine Scheer, joint interview with the author, Wewelsfleth, 21 August 2010.

[119] Donatella della Porta and Dieter Rucht, 'Left-Libertarian Movements', in *The Politics of Social Protest*, edited by J. Craig Jenkins and Bert Klandermans (1995).

[120] '« L'énergie nucléaire débouche sur l'état policier » nous déclare Brice Lalonde, président des « Amis de la Terre »', *Quotidien de Paris*, 14 January 1975.

[121] Frauenarbeitskreis der BI Barmbek, 'Frauen gegen Atomkraftwerke', brochure, 8 pp., 1977, APO, S 39; OCT, 'les femmes dans la lutte contre le nucléaire', *l'étincelle*, no. 31 (29 September 1977), p. 22; Françoise d'Eaubonne, *Écologie/féminisme : révolution ou mutation ?* (1978), p. 180; Mouvement écologie féministe, 'Nous nous joignons à la manifestation anti-nucléaire . . .', flyer, 26 April 1975, BnF, FOL-WZ-1588; Kaiserstühler Frauen, 'Presseerklärung', press release, 1 p., 15 October 1974, ASB, 00002872. For a look at feminist opposition to nuclear power in the United States, see also Dorothy Nelkin, 'L'énergie nucléaire', *Sociologie et sociétés* 13, no. 1 (1981).

politics and science were not merely 'men's work'. There were separate women's anti-nuclear demonstrations, such as a 'go-in' by fifty pregnant women and recent mothers into the Baden-Württemberg state parliament in Stuttgart; women marched in their own blocs at mass protests near nuclear sites, even at violent ones (in Grohnde, 600 women marching together proved, according to one militant activist, that women could demonstrate 'without having to be protected'); and numerous women's meetings within the anti-nuclear movement discussed everything from 'procreation strikes' to day-to-day energy conservation, female scientists, and women in the church. Dialogue among women provided part of the glue that held the anti-nuclear movement together. Urban feminists were inspired by their sisters in the countryside and, in return, supported their organizing efforts, making women some of the most important intermediaries between locals and outsiders. In all of these ways, the anti-nuclear movement was informed by the specific concerns of women and those engaged in other, contemporary protest movements, who greatly broadened the opposition to nuclear energy and contributed their own ideas to it.[122]

FLUID BOUNDARIES

Outside activists of various stripes—principally non-violent activists, radical leftists, and environmentalists—all brought their own arguments and protest traditions to the table when they joined locals in opposing individual nuclear power plants. Non-violent activists drew particular attention to the thin line between civil and military use of the atom; the radical left concerned itself with anti-capitalism, anti-imperialism, and anti-authoritarianism; and environmentalists were motivated by a desire to escape consumerism and refashion their lives in harmony with nature and their own ideals. The actions of all of these groups were reinforced by support from other contemporary protest movements like feminism, whose members linked the nuclear issue to their own primary concerns.

These categories are useful for understanding the anti-nuclear movement in a broad sense, but it is important to remember that none of these motivations was exclusive to a single group or faction, and multiple

---

[122] Ulla Bonczek, 'Go-in im Landtag', 2 July 1980, IISG, WISE 8; OCT, 'femmes dans la lutte', *l'étincelle*, no. 31; Mouvement écologie féminisme, 'manifestation anti-nucléaire'; Gorlebenfrauen, 'Frauen treffen Frauen in Gorleben', flyer, 1 p., 1980, APO, S 42. The *Gebärstreik* session at the Gorleben women's meeting was one of the best-attended, with 300 participants. 'betr.: internationales frauentreffen zu ostern 1980 in gorleben', report, 7 April 1980, Nds, 100 Acc. 2003/116 Nr. 67; Gorlebenfrauen, 'Frauen treffen Frauen in Gorleben'; 'Chères femmes de Malville', open letter, 5 pp., 1977, PA Putinier.

motivations or even belongings were common. For example, the KB elaborated a broad critique of the potential military uses to the West German government of nuclear power that converged with non-violent analyses, even if its origins were very different.[123] Environmentalists and religious non-violent activists were just as likely to voice concern for the Third World as communists, and they criticized the same nuclear contracts that attracted the anti-imperialist ire of *gauchistes*.[124] Anti-authoritarianism was present among all but the most Leninist of activists, enough so that autonomists and non-violent activists, despite fundamental differences over strategy, could agree that they opposed nuclear power because of the concentration of political and financial power that it represented. The language of resisting the police state, usually a marker of radical left protest, was also occasionally uttered by non-violent activists, religious protesters, and mainstream environmentalists—not to mention local activists who were fed up with the way authorities treated them.[125] From the start of the 1970s, nuclear power attracted a heterogeneous mix of criticism from opponents of different kinds. The borders between these groups, though real, were highly permeable, and motivations like anti-capitalism, criticism of consumption, anti-authoritarianism, and anti-militarism were never far apart.

Even the boundary between locals and outsiders was fluid, with motivations overlapping across the spatial divide. For instance, local activists such as Bernd Nössler had become interested in non-violence through personal experiences and readings of Martin Luther King and Gandhi before they encountered the organized groups of non-violent activists with whom they worked together within the anti-nuclear movement.[126] There were also local activists with left-wing views who found that contact with outside activists strengthened them in positions that would otherwise have been marginal in their own rural communities. This was the case for Heinrich Voß and Paul Lepoittevin, two then-young farmers from Brokdorf and La Hague (b. 1951 and 1945, respectively), both of whom

---

[123] The KB's arguments rested on the thesis that West Germany was on the path to becoming fascist again. See Atom Express, *Und auch nicht anderswo!*, p. 23.

[124] For example, a secondary focus of the prominent Alsatian environmentalist Solange Fernex was on the Third World. See Élisabeth Schulthess, *Solange, l'insoumise* (2004).

[125] Büchele et al., *Der Widerstand*, p. 28; 'malville n'est pas brokdorf', *GO/CNV*, no. 163 (23 June 1977), p. 9; Hans-Jürgen Benedict, 'Staatsgewalt oder Protest "gewalt" in Brokdorf. Hat die gewaltfreie Bewegung noch eine Chance?', no. 1/77 Beiheft 'Von Wyhl nach Brokdorf' (1977); Evangelische Akademie, 'Widerstand – damals und heute. Vom Nationalsozialismus zum Atomstaat?', poster for events at Gemeindehaus Dahlem, 18–19 July 1981, APO, S 42; Solange Fernex, 'Profession de foi', election campaign materials, March 1976, AA, 'Ökologiebewegung im Elsass'; 'Plogoff–Larzac solidarité', flyer, 4 pp., 24–5 May 1980, BM, IZ 65.

[126] Nössler, interview; Rettig, interview.

were attracted to radical left ideas and who found a new outlet for their energies in opposition to nuclear projects near their homes.[127] For others, the path connecting rural to urban activism could lead in the other direction: Dieter Halbach (b. 1953) was an environmental activist from West Berlin whose involvement in the anti-nuclear movement led him to move to the countryside near Gorleben.[128] Within the space of this broad-based movement, political labels never fully lost their meaning, though they did lose much of their precision. Terms like 'left' and 'right'—not to mention 'revolution', 'democracy', and 'Europe'—became more context-dependent than ever before.[129] The non-violent activist Wolfgang Hertle (b. 1946), who (reluctantly) described his own political perspective as *libertär* (libertarian anarchist), added that 'I'm no dogmatic anarchist. These terms often [...] do more harm than good. [...] I would understand the Larzac farmers as libertarian, at least in terms of their development, even though they would certainly never have called themselves anarchists.'[130] Even if locals and outsiders had different interests in the aggregate, the distinction between them frequently broke down at the individual level.

As this melting pot of activism was stirred over the course of the 1970s, anti-nuclear activists came to formulate their aspirations in shared, over-arching terms. In France, everyone from Alsace to Bretagne, from non-violent environmentalists to their militant detractors, spoke of nuclear power as a *choix de société*.[131] In West Germany, opposition to the *Atomstaat* similarly extended from the radical left to traditional nature protectionists to the 'Gorleben women' and, above all, to the overwhelming majority of activists whose views cannot be precisely pinned down.[132] The anti-nuclear movement was held together by shared perceptions of what nuclear power itself represented and how opposing it could potentially lead to the creation

---

[127] Voß and Scheer, joint interview; Paul Lepoittevin, interview with the author, Tollevast, 23 September 2010.

[128] Dieter Halbach, interview with the author, via telephone, 23 August 2010.

[129] Belinda Davis, 'What's Left?', *American Historical Review* 113, no. 2 (April 2008); Martin Conway and Volker Depkat, 'Discussing Democracy', in *Europeanization in the Twentieth Century*, edited by Martin Conway and Kiran Klaus Patel (2010).

[130] Hertle, interview.

[131] Thierry Jund, *Le nucléaire contre l'Alsace* (1977), p. 104; FLB-ARB, 'Gens de Plogoff et de Brennilis', flyer, 7 February 1979, AD Finistère, 1235 W 24; Jean-Michel Asselin, 'Malville', *GO/CNV*, no. 160 (2 June 1977); 'Contre l'électro-fascisme', *Casse-Noix*, no. 6.

[132] KB, 'Kalkar am 24.9.', brochure, 64 pp., 1977, IISG, Bro 537/10 fol, p. 5; Gorlebenfrauen, 'Frauen treffen Frauen in Gorleben'; Robert Jungk, *Atomstaat* (1977); Günter Zint et al., eds, *Gegen den Atomstaat* (1979); 'Atomstaat – Polizeistaat. Der plötzliche Tod der Republik Wendland', *Atom Express*, no. 21 (July/August 1980). Hans-Helmuth Wüstenhagen, involved in local struggles in Wyhl and elsewhere as the president of the national BBU, was loudly booed by the radical left at a demonstration in Gorleben before being applauded all around upon speaking about *Elektro-Faschismus*, the *Atomstaat*, and *Polizeistaat*. Report, 16 March 1977, Nds, 100 Acc. 2003/116 Nr. 71.

of a better society. During the 1970s, a critical mass of people would have agreed with the following (present-day) assessment by Jean-Luc Pasquinet (b. 1953), who was at that time an autonomist demonstrator:

> JLP: In case of accident or nuclear war, we have the capacity to destroy, well, everything [. . .]. And nuclear [technology] is also symbolic of the way the world is run [. . .]. The atom has structured diplomatic and international relations [. . .]. It's also part of an economic mode of thinking, where one does 'cost-benefit' analyses. We consider human beings like accounting units [. . .], we weigh things against one another that have no business being compared: health, the life of a person against the cost that that will entail for society [. . .]. Nuclear technology is really in a class of its own [. . .]. To abandon nuclear [power], we'd certainly have to change our way of life [. . . and] our civilization.[133]

For many, it was precisely this desire to change society that animated their own opposition to nuclear energy. The anti-nuclear movement was always about preventing (particular) power stations from being built, but it was never *only* about that. Nuclear energy meant many things to its opponents, but in the 1970s those meanings readily cross-fertilized into an encompassing discourse that went well beyond the concerns of a straightforward 'single-issue movement'.[134]

Nevertheless, unity among anti-nuclear activists was not absolute, and tensions were simmering just below the surface. The motivations of all these protesters might be broadly compatible, but their cultural and political backgrounds—not to mention the contradictory protest strategies they pursued—contained the potential for serious misunderstandings, bitter disagreements, and sometimes open conflict. The next three chapters will explore three sets of relationships within the anti-nuclear movement that demonstrate both how well and how badly protesters worked together across various divides: first, the transnational cooperation between French and West German activists, who had to overcome practical problems and historic hostilities in order to work together (Chapter 3); second, the tense alliance between rural activists and their urban allies, which was plagued by misperceptions and mutual misunderstandings (Chapter 4); and finally, the conflict over violent versus non-violent strategy, which most seriously threatened the cohesion of the anti-nuclear movement (Chapter 5).

---

[133] Jean-Luc Pasquinet, interview with the author, Paris, 17 November 2009.

[134] The same could certainly be argued about 'globalization' and the so-called Global Justice Movement. Jens Ivo Engels likewise argues that environmental protest has always been about more than single issues. *Naturpolitik*, pp. 408–9, 416–17.

3

'Radioactivity Doesn't Stop at the Border—and Neither Do We!'

Transnational Networks, Protest, and People

In late August 1974, local citizens and environmental activists from both France and West Germany came together to oppose two industrial projects along their shared border. Twenty-one groups from Alsace and Baden jointly declared their intent to occupy the site of a chemical plant in Marckolsheim (being built by a German company just inside French territory) and a nuclear power plant in Wyhl (the planned German counterpart to a French nuclear project already under construction in Fessenheim, just 30 kilometres to the south).[1] Looking back a few weeks later, the protesters argued that direct action in the form of a site occupation had been necessary because, up to that point, no one had taken any responsibility or shown any concern for the problems these projects would generate:

> Only through this declaration did [we] manage to force the governments of Baden-Württemberg and Alsace, as well as the governments in Bonn and Paris, to discuss with one another the transnational [*grenzüberschreitenden*] problems. [. . .] Without the site occupation [in Marckolsheim], there would already be a lead processing plant that would lethally endanger 20,000 people in this region. And no members of parliament or governments would have concerned themselves with our problems.

Taken together, they claimed, all of these facts proved that 'our struggle is an international struggle!!'.[2] The site occupation in Marckolsheim laid

---

[1] Solange Fernex, 'Non-Violence Triumphant', *The Ecologist*, vol. 5, no. 10 (December 1975), pp. 372–85 (p. 374); Badisch-Elsässische Bürgerinitiativen, 'Erklärung der 21 Bürger-initiativen an die badisch-elsässische Bevölkerung / Déclaration des 21 organismes de sauve-garde de l'environnement aux populations Badoises et Alsaciennes', poster, August 1974, ASB, 00017652. Some information used in this chapter also appears (in different form) in Andrew Tompkins, 'Grassroots Transnationalism(s): Franco-German Opposition to Nuclear Energy in the 1970s', *Contemporary European History* 25, no. 1 (2016), p. 117–42.

[2] 'Seit acht Wochen [. . .]', *WWW*, no. 3 (17 November 1974), p. 9. 'International' was the contemporary term for what this book refers to as 'transnational' phenomena—that is to say, those involving people in two or more countries, but not necessarily involving

the groundwork for subsequent occupations in Wyhl (Germany, 1975) and Kaiseraugst (Switzerland, 1975) as well as Heiteren and Gerstheim (both in France, 1977), eventually leading to the cancellation of all new nuclear projects in the Upper Rhine Valley. In the course of these struggles, French and German activists fashioned a collective identity distinguished by its firm anchoring in this region, which they conceived in transnational terms. The narrative of protest that they crafted around this identity conferred legendary status on these anti-nuclear protests and made the region a model for protest elsewhere—even in places where conditions were radically different.

During the 1970s, opposition to nuclear power was 'international' or even 'global' in other ways as well: across the capitalist, industrialized world, from the United States to Japan, France, and West Germany, people were concerned about nuclear power as an issue of global importance. Contemporaries characterized its transnational nature in terms of the structural changes of 'post-industrialization', the parallel development of nuclear technology in multiple states, or international catalysts such as the so-called energy crisis. The broader environmental consciousness on which it fed has also been explained in terms of internationally circulated ecological texts such as the Club of Rome's *Limits to Growth* (1972) and the activities of the United Nations and various NGOs.[3] Yet, as the Alsatian example illustrates, there is more to the story. Beyond top-down processes such as those emanating from national politics or international problems, individual activists forged myriad bottom-up connections that synchronized protest across borders, connecting disparate struggles within regional, European, and global networks.

Links such as these were subject to important limitations, making it hard to speak of a 'global movement' unified in much more than aspirations or symbolism; the kind of transnational consciousness present in the Upper Rhine Valley was not always felt to the same extent elsewhere. Most protesters regarded regional electricity suppliers or national governments as their opponents, and their own political engagement usually

macro-economic changes, international organizations, or relations between states (all of which are here referred to as 'international').

[3] See John McCormick, *The Global Environmental Movement*, 2nd edn (1995); J. R. McNeill, 'Environment, Environmentalism', in *The Shock of the Global*, edited by Niall Ferguson et al. (2010), pp. 269–72; Jan-Henrik Meyer, 'Challenging the Atomic Community', in *Societal Actors in European Integration*, edited by Wolfram Kaiser and Jan-Henrik Meyer (2013), esp. pp. 201–2; 'Transformations of the Ecology Movement: From the "Limits to Growth" to the Rio Conference', Berlin, Heinrich-Böll-Stiftung, 14–15 November 2014, http://www.boell.de/en/2014/04/29/transformations-ecology-movement-limits-growth-rio-conference (accessed 14 May 2015); Nils Freytag, '"Eine Bombe im Taschenbuchformat"', *Zeithistorische Forschungen*, no. 3 (2006).

remained confined to a particular local struggle that was representative of the larger issues (as indeed it did in Alsace and Baden). As a popular slogan held, anti-nuclear protesters saw themselves as acting at a local level (where nuclear energy facilities were concrete, tangible, and affected real people) to fight a global problem (one which touched on universal concerns and transcended the parochial interests of any one person, community, or nation).

Even at times and in places where the transnational and the global were not at the centre of activists' consciousness, protesters were affected by the actions and ideas of colleagues abroad. Numerous (sometimes tenuous) links across borders, at multiple levels, helped synchronize the content, forms, and timing of protest internationally such that it would be difficult, at best, to explain the history of the anti-nuclear movement in either France or West Germany without reference to connections between these two, and with other countries. If the anti-nuclear movement was perhaps not global in the sense of being common to all states and planetary in scale,[4] it was certainly transnational: cross-border links changed protest in ways that could be dramatic, banal, or (quite often) both at once. This chapter seeks to elucidate what transnational protest meant for the anti-nuclear movement and its participants by examining how transnational links structured activist networks, altered patterns of protest, and shaped the lives of individuals.

A GLOBAL NETWORK OF LOCAL STRUGGLES

In a 1980 Interior Ministry report on the environmental movement, French authorities noted what appeared from the perspective of the nation state to be an anomaly, even an absurdity of anti-nuclear activism:

> It is not the smallest paradox of the nuclear debate that it often starts with the critique of a site (which sensitizes a whole region) then of the [national] programme and once underway leads to a total rejection of nuclear [technology], whereas a true debate should follow the inverse order: [national] energy balance, examination of the programme, and a choice of sites.[5]

---

[4] This chapter primarily uses the term 'global' in a different sense, implying either a relationship to broader processes of integration (a 'global movement') or transnational connections extending beyond a single continent (the 'global level').

[5] The word 'national' does not appear in the text, but can be inferred from the exclusively national framework in which discussions of energy balances and programmes took place. 'Le Mouvement écologique : internationalisation—doctrine anti-énergétique—amalgame des contestations', AN, 19850718, art. 25.

Its normative assumptions aside, the assessment is surprisingly accurate: anti-nuclear protest during the 1970s and early 1980s sprang up where local communities faced the possibility of having a nuclear power plant built near them, and protest from these local communities formed the foundation of networks that could be regional, national, and even trans-national. Anti-nuclear activists from outside these communities often became involved in particular struggles near them or travelled from site to site to participate in different protest actions. Near each potential site, local activists saw themselves as fighting their own battle against a power-ful outside enemy. A common analogy was to the popular comic book hero Astérix, whose unnamed Gallic village relentlessly (and usually single-handedly) fought off repeated attempts at conquest by the Romans.[6] Though attitudes usually changed over time, local activists initially focused their energies exclusively on the fight for their own community, sometimes to the detriment of wider struggle. Didier Anger (b. 1939), who became an anti-nuclear activist when a power plant was built in Flamanville near his own home in Normandie, felt that solidarity was not always self-evident at protests he attended against the Plogoff power station in Bretagne: 'During the demonstrations, they would cry "No to nuclear power...in Bretagne!" And we would add "...or any-where else!"'[7]

Nevertheless, activists from different communities established contact with one another in various ways. For example, local groups might relate to one another within loose confederations (such as the network of Comités Malville) or umbrella organizations (such as the Bundesverband Bürgerinitiativen Umweltschutz, BBU). The links between people and places could just as easily be informal, as was often the case in France. According to one Alsatian activist, 'organization [between sites] was from person to person. Certain leaders moved about, [but] the internet didn't exist. There was the post [...] and sometimes people who travelled for discussions. But it was principally attempts at local mobilization around a site.'[8] The 'grassroots elites' behind such exchanges were at the core of anti-nuclear networks in West Germany as well, though regional (and eventually national) conferences allowed them to come together more

---

[6] 'Asterix und das Atomkraftwerk', brochure, 46 pp., 1980, IISG, Bro 565/1 fol, p. 2; 'Eine Einführung in die Guerillataktik des bretonischen Dorfes Plogoff im Widerstand gegen den Atomwahn', brochure, 43 pp., 1981, PA Tompkins, p. 3; 'Astérix antinvcléaire', February 1979, BnF, 4°WZ-13630.

[7] Didier Anger, interview with the author, Les Pieux, 22 September 2010.

[8] RS in Marie-Reine Haug and Raymond Schirmer, joint interview with the author, Rammersmatt, 17 April 2010.

frequently than in France.[9] Other activists created complementary (if usually less durable) links through shorter-term forms of engagement such as 'social tourism', participating in demonstrations at multiple sites and bringing their experiences from elsewhere with them.[10] Still others engaged with activists away from home in a more limited manner, imagining themselves as parts of a much broader, potentially worldwide movement. Disparate local struggles were thus networked in different ways and to varying degrees: asymmetrically or reciprocally, with many or few participants, briefly or sustained over many years (see Fig. 3.1). Anti-nuclear networks also existed at multiple levels of scale, connecting people and protest at the regional, national, European, and global levels. The rest of this section will explore the structures and frames associated with each of these different levels.

Though local sites constituted the basic nodes of anti-nuclear networks, they often clustered together within a wider geographic area, giving protest a regional character. For example, the concentration of nuclear reactors along the Elbe River helped forge an activist link between various country towns in northern Germany and the historically autonomous, administratively independent city of Hamburg. Anti-nuclear activists pointed out that the city drew energy from nuclear power stations in Brunsbüttel, Stade, and Krümmel, but might also face evacuation in the event of an accident at these or one of the new nuclear facilities in Brokdorf, Grohnde, or Gorleben. They drove this point home by drawing maps showing the relative distances to each site, captioned 'Hamburg, you're surrounded!'[11] This regional relationship between town and country was given organizational form and strength within the Bürgerinitiative Umweltschutz Unterelbe (BUU[12]), which held regional conferences bringing local groups out in the country together with neighbourhood-based anti-nuclear committees in the city (*Stadtteilgruppen*).[13]

---

[9] See 'Bundeskonferenz Bremen', document collection in brochure format, 160+ pp., 29–30 November 1980, RF, misc. brochures; BUU, 'Erklärungen der Delegierten der Landeskonferenz', collection of resolutions, 3 September 1977, HIS, V. Tonnätt. The Coordination nationale antinucléaire (CNAN) attempted to play a similar role in France from 1976 to 1984, but it was far less visible. See Claude Courtes and Jean-Claude Driant, *Golfech* (1999), pp. 231, 287.

[10] 'malville, naussac, larzac : le tourisme social marque des points', *GO/CNV*, no. 171 (18 August 1977), p. 1.

[11] 'Dezentraler Widerstand', *GWR*, no. 38 (October 1978), pp. 2, 4 (p. 4); 'Ich schließe mich hiermit den Klagen an [. . .]', flyer, undated, APO, S 37.

[12] Not to be confused with the Bundesverband Bürgerinitiativen Umweltschutz (BBU).

[13] The votes of delegates from various local groups are tallied by region (Hamburg, Marschen, Ostküste, Westküste, etc.) in BUU, 'Erklärungen', p. 7.

Translocal and Transnational Anti-Nuclear Networks (A Selection)

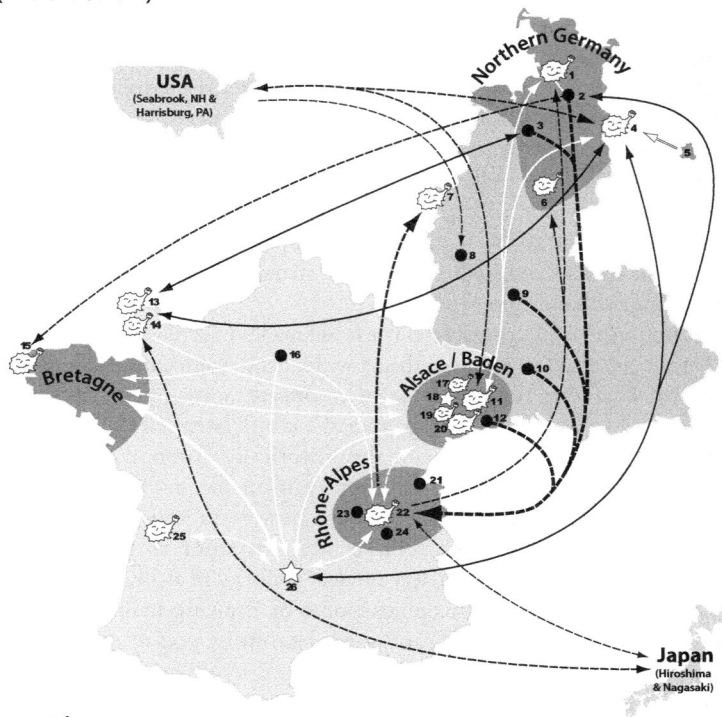

Legend

| Anti-Nuclear Protest | ☆ Related protest | ● City | | Regional network (all sites in close contact) |

→ Cross-border contact	
⇨ Domestic contact	
◆→ Mutual exchange	
→ Asymmetrical	
➤ Many participants	
→ Fewer participants	
→ Frequent contact	
--→ Infrequent contact	

West Germany	France
1 Brokdorf	13 La Hague
2 Hamburg	14 Flamanville
3 Bremen	15 Plogoff
4 Gorleben	16 Paris
5 West Berlin	17 Gerstein-Erstein
6 Grohnde	18 Marckolsheim
7 Kalkar	19 Heiteren
8 Bonn	20 Fessenheim
9 Frankfurt am Main	21 Geneva (Switzerland)
10 Stuttgart	22 Creys-Malville
11 Wyhl	23 Lyon
12 Freiburg	24 Grenoble
	25 Braud-et-St-Louis
	26 Larzac

Fig. 3.1. Translocal and Transnational Anti-Nuclear Networks (A Selection). Map created by Andrew Tompkins.

Structures like these were vastly more effective where they coincided with pre-existing regional identities. Though important regional identities existed in South Baden and Wendland, they tended to be far more developed and combative in centralist France than in federal West Germany. In Bretagne, a dispersed network of Comités Locaux (et Régionaux) d'Information Nucléaire (CLINs and CRINs) kept protest alive throughout the region as planners repeatedly shifted between possible sites in Erdeven, Beg-an-Fry, and Ploumoguer before finally settling on Plogoff. Though the townspeople of Plogoff were always presented in the media as being at the forefront of the intense protests that occurred there, support from throughout the region was critical to its success.[14] In Bretagne, Alsace, and even Occitanie, anti-nuclear activists presented their regions as the victims of 'internal colonization' by the Bonapartist central state.[15] With pointed irony, Bretons suggested that central planners build a nuclear power plant in downtown Paris to supply the countryside with electricity.[16] Similarly, Alsatians argued that their region had 'always produced more energy than it consumes' and that the reactor in Fessenheim could therefore only serve to supply Paris, not Alsace, with electricity; electricity projects in Alsace were dismissed as 'the solution by Paris for Paris'.[17] In this way, regional identity and anti-nuclear struggle reinforced one another. As the anonymous author of the book *Elsaß: Kolonie in Europa* argued, environmental and anti-nuclear activists were 'not primarily regionalists, but their engagement has regionalist consequences'.[18] Regional networks brought structures and identities into play that complemented local anti-nuclear struggles.

[14] Police reports noted that the Plogoff protests attracted financial support from Breton expatriate communities as far away as New York, Canada, and Australia. However, they estimated that only 20–25 per cent of demonstrators at a major 1979 protest came from outside Finistère *département*, and then mostly from surrounding areas within Bretagne (support from Paris was deemed 'insignificant'). Memo, 23 October 1978, AD Finistère, 1235 W 24; Memo, 5 June 1979, AD Finistère, 1347 W 164-2. Support within Bretagne was, however, both intense and widespread, especially at protests in Quimper and during the EUP in 1980. One local woman interviewed on film specifically thanked the 'many, many' people who came 'from outside' Plogoff. Nicole Le Garrec, *Plogoff : des pierres contre des fusils*, 1980, 90 mins.
[15] Robert Gildea, *Past in French History* (1994), pp. 188–9.
[16] 'Par solidarité les Parisiens ont décidé d'implanter une centrale nucléaire dans le trou des Halles pour alimenter Plogoff en électricité', CRILAN, *140 dessins contre le nucléaire* (1980).
[17] Thierry Jund, *Le nucléaire contre l'Alsace* (1977), p. 32; Union alsacienne pour les solutions de remplacement à l'énergienucléaire, 'La solution de Paris pour Paris', flyer, 2 pp., 1981, BnF, 4°WZ-13629.
[18] Jean [pseud.], *Elsaß: Kolonie in Europa* (1976), p. 95.

Because the anti-nuclear movement so passionately valorized the 'local', activists frequently behaved as though national politics were unimportant or irrelevant to their cause. One indicator of this is the fact that demonstrations in national capitals were rare: aside from a 1975 march in Paris and a 1979 demonstration in Bonn,[19] nearly all major anti-nuclear demonstrations took place directly at nuclear sites themselves or in nearby towns. Much like the movement against nuclear weapons in the 1950s, opponents of nuclear energy 'chose a method which highlighted their commitment to the cause [...] [r]ather than protesting at the heart of political decision-making'.[20] In West Germany, activists even went so far as to argue, 'We cannot take our resistance to Bonn or somewhere else in order to demonstrate there. We must go to the construction site and show that we are determined to realize our demands ourselves.'[21] This attitude reflected the constraints of nuclear policy as much as the preferences of anti-nuclear activists. State nuclear policies were difficult to change, and the governments of Helmut Schmidt and Valéry Giscard d'Estaing proved singularly unresponsive on the issue of nuclear energy. Nor was any political party able or willing to represent the opposition to nuclear power at the national level until well into the 1980s. It seemed more effective—not to mention more in line with anti-nuclear activists' ideals— to obstruct nuclear power locally.

The few national organizations capable of bringing local struggles together were also of secondary importance, serving mostly as points of contact for the media and/or liaison offices for networking. In France, Les Amis de la Terre (ADLT) began as a Parisian import of the Anglo-Saxon group Friends of the Earth. Within the capital, well-connected ADLT

[19] The march on 27 April 1975 in Paris (approximately 15,000 participants) was part of a series of actions throughout the country in the week prior to debate in the Assemblée nationale about France's nuclear programme. The Paris demonstration was in part intended to show 'that the capital isn't to be outdone, [even] if the regions have so far furnished the bulk of the troops'. Parisian demonstrators were nevertheless dismissed as insincere ('des ralliés de dernière heure, des politicards') and less diverse than their provincial cousins: 'Triste à dire quand on revient d'Erdeven [en Bretagne], où les réunions rassemblent régulièrement et sans exclusives, ni anathèmes, un public de convictions politiques et d'origines sociales très variées . . .' 'Aujourd'hui s'ouvre à Paris la semaine anti-nucléaire', *Libération* (21 April 1975). The October 1979 demonstration in Bonn (up to 100,000 participants) took place several months after the Harrisburg nuclear accident, which led to a resurgence of anti-nuclear protest at the national level in West Germany. See BBU, 'Reden der Großdemonstration gegen die Atomenergie', brochure, 20 pp., 14 October 1979, AGG, A Petra Kelly Nr 2874. Further demonstrations on an even larger scale took place in Bonn in 1981 and 1983, but these were connected primarily with opposition to nuclear *weapons* rather than civil nuclear energy.
[20] Holger Nehring, 'National Internationalists', *Contemporary European History* 14, no. 4 (2005), p. 579.
[21] *Wehrt Euch. Brokdorf 19.2.1977*, 1977, 40 mins.

members like Brice Lalonde quickly established themselves as ambassadors of ecology for the national media.[22] Nevertheless, most protests by Paris ADLT were events for Parisians rather than properly national demonstrations.[23] Other branches throughout France used ADLT as a network to exchange information with one another, but each branch operated independently, and some had completely different understandings of what ADLT represented. For example, when Brice Lalonde announced that ADLT (meaning the Paris group) would not attend the 1977 Malville demonstration unless the organizers met certain conditions, the more radical Grenoble and Marseille branches reproached Lalonde for speaking in 'their' name and demonstratively declared their solidarity with local organizers.[24] In West Germany, the BBU performed a similar function, with prominent members of its steering committee such as Petra Kelly and Jo Leinen attracting and channelling media attention, particularly during the 1980s. Like ADLT though, the BBU functioned more as a network than as a formal association. As an umbrella group of local citizens' initiatives, it lobbied on behalf of member organizations and facilitated communication among them, but it was not an outlet for the passions of individual activists (other than perhaps its own small staff). Only late in the decade (at the aforementioned Bonn demonstration) did the BBU function as the national organizer of a national demonstration. Otherwise, it supported and facilitated the actions of local groups (though not always modestly).[25] National associations like ADLT and BBU provided additional channels for communication among the protagonists of local anti-nuclear struggles, but they neither directed nor were themselves the key protagonists.

---

[22] Lalonde went on to become an environmentalist presidential candidate in 1981 and later Minister of the Environment under Mitterrand (1991–2). Other prominent members of the Paris ADLT include the journalist Alain Hervé, the mathematician Pierre Samuel, and the physicist Yves Lenoir.

[23] This is apparent from the approximate size of most of ADLT's demonstrations, estimated by police as follows: 10 June 1972, demonstration against the Rive Gauche expressway—2,500 participants; 6 May 1973, demonstration on the Champ de Mars against radioactive pollution—2,000 participants; 16 March 1974, bicycle demonstration on Place de la Concorde—4,000 participants. PPP, Série F^D.

[24] *Aujourd'hui Malville* (1978), pp. 42–5. ADLT-Marseille wrote, 'Une fois encore le « leader » des Amis de la Terre engage l'ensemble des groupes existants en France sans les avoir consultés. Peu importe qu'il signe sous l'étiquette des Amis de la Terre de Paris, c'est le leader fabriqué par les média[s] qui parle.'

[25] Dorothy Nelkin and Michael Pollak, *Atom Besieged* (1981), p. 129. According to Jens Ivo Engels, the BBU (and especially its leading personalities) occasionally threatened to overshadow local groups in places like Wyhl and Gorleben. Jens Ivo Engels, *Naturpolitik* (2006), p. 338. However, the BBU saw its mission as supporting and advising local initiatives and committed itself to a decentralized organizational model. See Wolfgang Sternstein, *Mein Weg zwischen Gewalt und Gewaltfreiheit* (2005), pp. 194–6.

If protest was seldom organized through national organizations, this does not mean that the stakes were exclusively local. Indeed, certain local struggles had unquestionably national importance on account of their centrality to the French and West German nuclear programmes. The fast breeder reactor (FBR) Super-Phénix in Malville became a flashpoint in France because this particular technology would produce plutonium as a by-product of its operation. Activists feared this could be used for nuclear weapons, but they were no less suspicious of the official explanation: the high-yield plutonium could be used to resupply other reactors in the future, giving the French nuclear programme a vastly extended lease on life.[26] In West Germany, initial plans for the nuclear waste disposal site in Gorleben included a nuclear fuel reprocessing centre (like the French one in La Hague) that would have performed a similar function, extracting plutonium that could be mixed again with uranium to create new (mixed oxide, or MOX) fuel for reactors.[27]

To counter perceived national and international threats emanating from these specific local battles, activists created structures that placed the local at the heart of contestation. In preparation for the large-scale demonstration in Malville in 1977, they designed a system of concentric pairings (*jumelages*) to link supportive Comités Malville together. Representatives of local committees in the twenty to twenty-five small towns closest to the planned nuclear power station were paired with urban groups from the surrounding region, who were in turn paired with anti-nuclear groups in other parts of France or Europe: activists from the hamlet of Lhuis, the nearby city of Grenoble, and various towns in more distant Alsace were all linked together in this way.[28] Via the same system, German activists were connected to a group in Geneva, which made arrangements for the camping site in the local partner town Morestel during the week of the demonstration.[29] Gorleben activists in West Germany tried something similar, creating a network of Gorleben-Freundeskreise and conceiving a three-phase plan of local, regional, and national mobilization that emphasized the role of local activists as the 'centre of resistance'.[30] The idea was even reflected in seating at meetings:

[26] Chaïm Nissim, interview with the author, Geneva, 28 January 2010.
[27] Even when the retreatment centre plans were dropped, Gorleben retained its significance as a result of changes that made construction of new nuclear power plants contingent on waste disposal plans.
[28] 'Groupes jumelés', *Super-Pholix*, no. 13 ([June/July] 1977), p. 11; 'Malville : une organisation horizontale par jumelage', *Libération*, 25 July 1977.
[29] 'Malville—Ziel: 100.000 Demonstranten', A4 flyer, 2 pp., 1977, AA, Ordner 'AKW+Widerstand', 'Malville 77'.
[30] BI Lüneburg, 'Stellungnahme der BI Lüneburg gegen Atomenergie zum 3-Phasenmodell', flyer, 2 pp., undated [1978], HIS, V. Tonnätt (AKW).

activists from Gorleben and the surrounding towns sat in the inner circle while outside supporters were relegated to the backbenches.[31] Though neither the *jumelages* in Malville nor the three-phase model in Gorleben were implemented as fully or effectively as intended,[32] each communicated the anti-nuclear movement's view of itself as being first and foremost local, then regional, and only thereafter national or international.

Appropriate to the way anti-nuclear activists understood themselves, they developed many and varied transnational connections between specific local struggles. Sometimes, such connections were purely symbolic, as when the Wyhl squatters' paper *Was Wir Wollen* listed the names of ongoing anti-nuclear struggles in its masthead, always showing 'Marckolsheim—Wyhl—Kaiseraugst' first, then adding and dropping references to Brokdorf, Malville, Grohnde, and others as they saw fit.[33] These communicated an imagined solidarity among activists sharing similar circumstances, even when communication between them was limited or non-existent.[34] When it came to concrete cooperation, the strongest cross-border links were usually between geographically close sites. For example, local French and German environmental groups in the Upper Rhine Valley regularly worked together within the Badisch-Elsässische Bürgerinitiativen, which opposed both the chemical plant in Marckolsheim and the nuclear power plant in Wyhl—two major industrial projects that were only 10 kilometres apart, but on opposite sides of the Franco-German border. The fact that the polluting chemical plant was to be built so close to the border, on French territory, and by a West German company that had been unable to obtain permits at home made it easier for activists from the two countries to come together.[35] In a similar

---

[31] 'Bericht über die Veranstaltung in Gorleben', flyer, 2 pp., 21 October 1978, HIS, V. Tonnätt (AKW).

[32] Georges David describes the *jumelages* as 'Une très bonne idée ! [. . .] Le problème c'est que ça n'a pas suffi à mobiliser suffisamment de monde au niveau local pour contrebalancer la force extérieur.' Georges David, interview with the author, Lhuis, 27 January 2010. The Gorleben-Freundeskreise fizzled out in late 1978, but fed into a series of meetings in Trebel that paved the way for subsequent actions (including the 1980 'Anti-Atom-Dorf' at Tiefbohrstelle 1004). Dieter Halbach and Gerd Panzer, *Zwischen Gorleben & Stadtleben* (1980), p. 114.

[33] The masthead changed in this fashion with almost every new edition during the year 1977. See also the article 'Marckolsheim → Wyhl → Kaiseraugst → und jetzt auch Malville', *WWW*, no. 9 (24 June 1976), p. 5.

[34] Robert Gildea et al., 'European Radicals and the "Third World"', *Cultural and Social History* 8, no. 4 (2011).

[35] Axel Mayer, interview with the author, Freiburg, 12 April 2010. See also Peter Brügge, '"Da werden sich die Neger freuen"', *Spiegel*, no. 34 (18 August 1975), pp. 46–8. (The article title is a quote from the head of the chemical company, suggesting that Africans will be happy to welcome the kinds of polluting industry that Western Europeans reject.)

manner, the proximity of the FBR Super-Phénix in Malville to the Swiss border made possible substantial cooperation between French activists and members of an existing anti-nuclear committee in Geneva, the Comité Contre le Verbois Nucléaire (CCVN). Chaïm Nissim, a member of CCVN, became one of the leading members of the Coordination Rhône-Alpes (CRA), which laid the groundwork for the large protests in Malville in 1976 and 1977.

Transnational protest links could also come about between struggles that were not geographically adjacent through the work of individual activists.[36] For example, West Germans who closely followed the struggle of farmers on the Larzac plateau in southern France tried to cultivate links between it and the opposition to the nuclear waste site in Gorleben (even though the former struggle was unrelated to nuclear power). In fact, this connection was forged by two distinct, competing networks. One was associated with the anarcho-pacifist journal *Graswurzelrevolution* (*GWR*) and its editor Wolfgang Hertle.[37] Inspired by the non-violent methods of the French struggle, Hertle set up a training centre for direct action in Gorleben, the Kurve Wustrow, modelled directly on the Cun du Larzac, a similar centre established by his friend Hervé Ott.[38] A separate Larzac-Freundeskreis in Hamburg also existed, under the leadership of Volker Tonnätt and Heidi Burmeister. More closely associated with radical left-wing anti-militarism, this group also promoted the cause by inviting a delegation from the Larzac to speak in Hamburg and in Gorleben.[39] In combination, both (competing) networks kept Gorleben and Larzac supporters informed about one another's activities, publishing news in West Germany about both struggles, writing articles about Gorleben for the *Gardarem lo Larzac* newsletter, and publishing German-language books about the Larzac struggle.[40] The importance activists attached to political engagement at the local level meant that 'transnational' protest

[36] Sociologists describe the spread of protest forms and content via diffusion as being most likely when activists are spatially or culturally close. See Hanspeter Kriesi et al., *New Social Movements in Western Europe* (1995), pp. 189–90.

[37] See, for example, *Graswurzelrevolution* no. 40 (March/April 1979), pp. 20–1, 26–9 and no. 44 (October/November 1979), pp. 9–11, 36.

[38] Wolfgang Hertle, interview with the author, Hamburg, 22 July 2010; Hervé Ott, interview with the author, St-Martin-du-Larzac, 18 September 2010.

[39] Larzac-Freundeskreis, 'Larzac: Neun Jahre Kampf um das Überleben einer Region!', poster for event in Trebel, 1 p., 26 September 1979, PA Pineau, 'Larzac en RFA'; 'Gorleben–Larzac même combat', flyer for event at l'Hôpital du Larzac, 1 p., 10 September 1979, BM, IZ 62.

[40] Wolfgang Hertle, *Larzac 1971–81* (1982); Heidi Burmeister and Volker Tonnätt, *Zu kämpfen* (1981); Larzac-Freundeskreis, 'Neun Jahre Kampf'; 'Gorleben–Larzac même combat'. See also Robert Gildea and Andrew Tompkins, 'The Transnational in the Local', *Journal of Contemporary History* (2015).

networks were usually between specific sites, connected by geography or personal links.

Despite the many connections that existed between activists in France and West Germany, opponents of nuclear power in each country had to confront serious contextual differences that shaped the possibilities of protest. Some of the most critical differences were related to national legacies of the Second World War. In many ways, efforts to distance West Germany from the Nazi state that preceded it made formal conditions for protest easier there than in France. As the leading Alsatian activist Jean-Jacques Rettig (b. 1939) succinctly puts it, 'Germany had the luck to lose the last world war. The luck! That led to at least a minimum of self-criticism.'[41] Above all, it led to a retreat from the centralization of power that had occurred under the Nazis. In France, by contrast, the centralist tradition has been more or less unbroken since 1789. Social scientists argue that this centralism makes France a much more closed political system than (West) Germany,[42] causing citizens to resort more readily to street protest tactics that may quickly radicalize. In federal Germany, citizens can in certain cases bring grievances against national policies to regional authorities and vice versa. Indeed, West German courts frequently mandated changes to nuclear plans that were unheard of in France.[43] Another critical difference was that West Germany did not possess its own nuclear weapons, whereas French politicians, supposedly haunted by memories of the country's capitulation in 1940, regarded their independent nuclear capabilities (the so-called *force de frappe*) as an essential guarantor of French sovereignty. Even the PCF, fiercely critical of the country's right-wing and liberal leadership but patriotic to the bitter end, rallied to the military use of nuclear technology in 1977 (it had long supported civil nuclear energy).[44] Opponents of nuclear power in France thus found themselves at odds with French patriotism, sometimes in the guise of an established force on the political left—one which had no equivalent in West Germany. Indeed, anti-communism in West Germany

---

[41] Jean-Jacques Rettig, interview with the author, Fréconrupt, 19 April 2010. On the 'trial-and-error' nature of liberalization of post-war West Germany, see Ulrich Herbert, 'Liberalisierung als Lernprozeß', in *Wandlungsprozesse in Westdeutschland*, edited by Ulrich Herbert (2002).

[42] See, for example, Nelkin and Pollak, *Atom Besieged*; Kriesi et al., *New Social Movements in Western Europe*; Felix Kolb, *Protest and Opportunities* (2007); Herbert Kitschelt, 'Political Opportunity Structures', *British Journal of Political Science* 16, no. 1 (1986).

[43] Nelkin and Pollak, *Atom Besieged*, pp. 155–66. See also Badisch-Elsässische Bürgerinitiativen, 'Der Wyhl-Prozess', brochure, 24 pp., 1977, DfuL, D 0250.

[44] On the PCF's early opposition to nuclear weapons, see Gabrielle Hecht, *Radiance of France* (1998), pp. 139–45. On its turnaround on nuclear weapons, see Maud Bracke, *Which Socialism?* (2007), pp. 333–41.

was another significant variable affecting protest: anti-nuclear activists there constantly had to contend with accusations of infiltration from the East, even though Maoist, Trotskyist, and undogmatic Marxists in West Germany generally despised Moscow and its German satellite.[45] (At the same time, the relative weakness of Moscow-aligned Communists created an opening to the left of the Social Democrats, into which the Greens were eventually able to place themselves.) All of these factors shaped protest in each country.

The numerous connections that existed between France and West Germany (as well as with their other near neighbours) were sometimes discussed together in terms of a 'European' anti-nuclear movement. 'Europe' thereby functioned as an intermediate space between the intimate local and the boundless global, one that was associated with ideals, interests, and institutions that were larger than any one state. For French and West German citizens, 'Europe' most often meant specifically Franco-German reconciliation, which had been an official policy of both states since the early 1950s.[46] Institutionalized forms of cooperation established after the Second World War sometimes fed indirectly into later anti-nuclear protest (much in the way that US government-sponsored student exchanges inadvertently fed European anti-Vietnam War protests).[47] For example, the Frenchwoman Mireille Caselli (b. 1948) remembers her youth as 'the era when one wanted Franco-German reconciliation at any cost'. She learned fluent German in part through teacher and pupil exchange programmes, and later put it to use translating for Radio Verte Fessenheim, a trilingual (German–French–Alemannic) pirate radio project of anti-nuclear activists.[48] On rare occasions, there was even direct, institutional support for protest-related activities, such as when the

---

[45] See Komitee für Grundrechte und Demokratie, 'Bericht über den Verlauf der Demonstration am 12. Oktober 1985 in München: Wider den Bau einer atomaren Wiederaufarbeitungsanlage bei Wackersdorf/Oberpfalz', demonstration observation report, 19 pp., November 1985, PA Tompkins, pp. 6–7; Nelkin and Pollak, *Atom Besieged*, p. 127.

[46] See Rod Kedward, *Vie en Bleu* (2006), p. 475. In the Upper Rhine Valley, 'Europe' was also sometimes invoked to include Switzerland, but the Swiss connection was weaker than the one between France and West Germany (perhaps due to the greater economic disparities). Axel Mayer, who grew up in the Kaiserstuhl region near Wyhl, remembers that local farmers felt a greater affinity towards Alsace than Switzerland: 'Vom Kaiserstuhl aus gesehen, ist die Schweiz einfach mehr Ausland als Elsass. [... Elsass] ist ja irgendwie nicht Ausland, das ist schon Nachbarschaft.' Mayer, interview.

[47] See Doug McAdam and Dieter Rucht, 'Cross-National Diffusion', *Annals of the American Academy of Political and Social Science* 528 (July 1993), p. 70; Martin Klimke, *Other Alliance* (2010). On exchanges more generally, see Richard I. Jobs, 'Youth Movements', *American Historical Review* 114, no. 2 (2009).

[48] Mireille Caselli, interview with the author, Freiburg, 12 April 2010.

Franco-German Youth Office (OFAJ/DFJW) provided funding for an environmental youth camp in Wyhl in 1979.[49]

However, anti-nuclear activists emphasized that 'Europe' was not about these institutions or their official representatives.[50] Indeed, along the Franco-German border, activists argued that they 'have not the slightest need to be represented by delegations in order to understand one another'.[51] As the Alsatian anti-nuclear organizer Jean-Jacques Rettig put it, 'it wasn't just De Gaulle and Adenauer who shook hands, but the grassroots as well!'[52] Their anti-nuclear 'Europe from below' was directed against the 'Europe from above' constituted by the institutions and member states of what was then the European Economic Community.[53] Sometimes, activists made this explicit, as when peasants from the Larzac visiting Gorleben concluded their report with a call for more exchange and network-building between the two sites: 'After the Europe of parliamentarians, it is time to make the Europe of struggles and the Europe of peoples.'[54] Critical appeals to 'Europe' were also a way of attacking one's own government. In 1977, the OCT and its sister organization KB jointly published a Mayday edition of their respective party organs, *L'étincelle* and *Arbeiterkampf*, with a bilingual title page that cried out, 'Down with the Europe of Schmidt and Giscard!'[55] A few months later, KB and OCT members attempted to realize Europe on their own terms by demonstrating together—along with thousands of other French and German activists—against the FBRs in Malville and Kalkar.[56] Other groups also framed nuclear power as an issue for all of Europe. Non-communist ecologists from Freiburg wrote that Super-Phénix was 'a European Community project' in which German and Italian electricity

---

[49] Internationale Jugendgemeinschaftsdienste (AG Umwelt), 'Industriealisierung [sic] — Kernkraftwerke — Umweltgefährdung', brochure, approx. 80 pp., 1979, PapierTiger, Wyhl-Broschüren.

[50] Historians too have argued against a too narrowly institutional focus in studies of 'Europeanization'. See Ulrike von Hirschhausen and Kiran Klaus Patel, 'Europeanization in History', in *Europeanization in the Twentieth Century*, edited by Martin Conway and Kiran Klaus Patel (2010).

[51] F. H., 'Die Wacht am Rhein', *Ionix*, no. 10 (March 1975), pp. 7–9.

[52] Rettig, interview.

[53] Bernd-A. Rusinek, 'Wyhl', in *Deutsche Erinnerungsorte*, edited by Etienne François and Hagen Schulze (2001), p. 656.

[54] Pierre-Yves [de Boissieu] and Joseph [Pineau], 'Durant l'été [. . .]', [October] 1979, PA Pineau, dossier 'Larzac en RFA'.

[55] 'Nieder mit dem Europa von Schmidt und Giscard! À bas l'Europe des Schmidt et des Giscard !', *Arbeiterkampf/l'étincelle* (29 April 1977), p. 1.

[56] 'Contre l'Europe du nucléaire, la solidarité des antinucléaires, des révolutionnaires, est une nécessité politique impérieuse. Réalisée à Malville, elle se poursuivra avec la manifestation de Kalkar le 24 septembre.' 'De Malville à Kalkar', *l'étincelle*, no. 29 (15 September 1977), p. 14.

concerns had a financial stake and which 'all European nuclear energy opponents' therefore needed to oppose.[57]

Anti-nuclear activists saw themselves as bringing about Europe through protest, breaking down national borders with solidarity. For example, during a protest on 7 August 1977, they claimed that 'for two hours, the Franco-German border did not exist'. Alsatian activists crossed over the Rhine from the town of Neuf-Brisach to 'pick up' their German (and Swiss) comrades in Breisach and accompany them across the border into France. 'None of the demonstrators were checked, it was as if there were no border, as if Europe had, for a short time, become reality.'[58] Reflecting today on the large, international turnout at the 1977 Malville protest, CRA member Georges David (b. 1943) says, 'When you think about it, in some way that paved the way for Europe, this solidarity that we were able to set in motion with a process like Malville.'[59] Today, French and German anti-nuclear activists retrospectively regard themselves as having had some of the first grassroots visions of Europe.[60] Their references to 'Europe'—like those to 'democracy'—contested official understandings and invested these terms with new meanings.[61] However, building 'Europe from below' appears to have been less a conscious goal than a happy by-product of their activism, and one which became more important after the fact. During the 1970s and early 1980s, associating anti-nuclear protest with 'Europe' and its possible alternatives was primarily a means of positioning protest above and beyond the power of states, allowing activists to claim to transcend parochial, national interests.

Transnational connections were, of course, not isolated to Europe and they occasionally connected two or more struggles over very great distances. Among industrialized, capitalist countries, Japan was about as far from Europe as one could get. When, in 1977, members of the Japanese Congress

[57] 'Sommer 1977 nach Malville', flyer, 13 July 1977, ASB, 12.1.9.II/00024359. The industrial consortium behind the project received loans through the European Investment Bank and EURATOM. See Boris Saitcevsky, 'Accords de coopération', *Revue générale nucléaire*, no. 6 (November–December 1979). On the complications of technical cooperation between France and West Germany, see Joachim Radkau, *Aufstieg und Krise* (1983), pp. 340–3; Sandra Tauer, *Störfall* (2012), pp. 206–20.
[58] 'Französische Chauvinisten gegen deutsche KKW-Gegner', flyer, 3 pp., 1977, ASB, 12.1.7/00024377.
[59] Indeed, Georges argues that if he and other organizers had, at the time, more consciously framed Super-Phénix in terms of its danger to people across Europe rather than to the 'directly affected' local communities near the site, the 1977 protest there might have had better chances of success. David, interview.
[60] Mayer, interview.
[61] On the early construction of, subsequent modifications to, and associations forged between the terms 'Europe' and 'democracy', see Martin Conway and Volker Depkat, 'Discussing Democracy', in *Europeanization in the Twentieth Century*, p. 151.

against A- and H-Bombs (known abroad by the abbreviation Gensuikin) invited European activists to join them at their conference in Izu-Nagaoka, Didier Anger and Chantal François (b. 1932) jumped at the chance to go for their respective groups: this was an excellent opportunity to link their local struggles to victims of nuclear and environmental devastation on the opposite end of the earth.[62] During their three-week trip, Didier and Chantal visited the bombed sites of Hiroshima and Nagasaki as well as the polluted Minamata region, where industrial waste had poisoned the local environment with mercury.[63] Afterwards, Didier maintained contact with some of the Japanese activists he had met, inviting several of them to La Hague (including the artists Iri and Toshi Maruki, who displayed their Hiroshima-related art at the Salle des fêtes in Cherbourg).[64] When, in the late 1970s, nuclear waste from Japan was shipped to France for reprocessing in La Hague, Didier and his Japanese friends organized protests to block the transports at their point of departure in Japan and upon arrival in Cherbourg. Perhaps surprisingly, this collaboration began earlier—and more to Didier's satisfaction as a French activist—than the repeated, famous 'Tag X' protests against transports bringing reprocessed, German nuclear waste from La Hague back to Gorleben between 1996 and 2011.[65]

> DA: My contacts with Japan . . . went a bit faster than with Germany. [. . .] There were some pretty strong [protests] related to Japan. [. . .] We were always opposed to the arrival [of nuclear waste] and not necessarily its return [and . . .] sometimes that provoked some difficulties with our German friends. [. . .] Their demonstrations usually take place on the other side of the border, and we're sometimes on the rails [to block the return] but it's more to attract attention than to block it really. We would have liked blockades that went in the opposite direction, like we had with Japan.[66]

---

[62] The conference was also attended by Lore Haag from Wyhl. See Christoph Büchele et al., *Der Widerstand* (1982), pp. 127–32.

[63] Anger, interview.

[64] Anger himself also paints as a hobby, and considers this artistic engagement a typical example of the entanglement of the personal and the political: 'on était à la fois sur le militantisme, sur le culturel, etc.' Anger, interview.

[65] The earliest 'Tag X' protests in Gorleben occurred in 1984, but the first transport of highly radioactive waste from La Hague did not take place until May 1996. Further transports of low- and intermediate-level waste from La Hague as well as high-level waste from Sellafield are expected, but the last high-level waste from La Hague arrived in Gorleben in November 2011. See Bundesamt für Strahlenschutz, 'Rückführung und Rücktransport aus der Wiederaufarbeitung abgebrannter Brennelemente', 2014, http://www.bfs.de/DE/themen/ne/abfaelle/rueckfuehrung/rueckfuehrung.html (accessed 8 December 2015); Wikipedia, 'Atommülltransporte in Deutschland', 2014, http://de.wikipedia.org/wiki/Atomm%C3%BClltransporte_in_Deutschland#.C3.9Cbersicht (accessed 22 February 2015).

[66] Anger, interview.

Global solidarity depended not only on what sort of partners one had abroad, but on the local context in which it was exercised. For Chantal François, the trip to Japan had a completely different impact because of the way the local situation in Malville changed during her absence. Only a week into her visit, the demonstration in Malville on 31 July 1977 ended with the death of Vital Michalon, an innocent demonstrator fatally wounded by a police stun grenade; his body was initially brought to the François farm, which stood closest to the site. For Chantal, it was 'agonizing' to learn of this tragedy while so far away from her home and family. Upon returning to Malville, Chantal tried to encourage her friends with messages of solidarity, with the knowledge that people on the other side of the world were thinking about them and carrying on a similar struggle. However, she found her neighbours 'so flattened, so emptied after everything that had happened that I couldn't even get across the message that we're not alone. [...] I tried to talk to them about it, but they were immediately taken back to the things they had experienced on the ground.'[67] The actions of individuals working transnationally against nuclear power could only go so far. In the end, anti-nuclear protest was seen in terms of struggles that were fundamentally local in nature, even if these were linked together within global networks.

PATTERNS OF TRANSNATIONAL PROTEST

Yet if anti-nuclear protest was primarily local, it could nevertheless be powerfully affected by connections to the wider world. This was so even when the links between sites were mostly imaginary, when the signals activists transmitted were vague to start with, refracted through the prism of the news media, and misinterpreted at the point of reception abroad. Transnational contact relied more on the laborious (mis-)translation of half-understood ideas than on clear communication within stable channels. Nor were cross-border connections only about 'transfer' and adaptation: often enough, innovative strategies emerged through interactions among people from different (if perhaps partially overlapping) backgrounds or developed within transnational learning processes. The synchronization of protest across borders, though always incomplete, rested on both imagination and interaction. These chaotic transnational connections brought with them considerable advantages, but also certain critical limitations. Protest was most effective in those situations where activists

---

[67] CF in Maurice and Chantal François, joint interview with the author, Creys-Mépieu, 25 January 2010.

could symbolically and practically turn such disadvantages on their heads. Transnational connections thus changed protest in important ways, for better and for worse.

Transnational networks made possible forms of international solidarity that were especially helpful to anti-nuclear activists engaged in local struggles. Sometimes, allies and audiences abroad were able to help activists directly circumvent channels that were closed at home.[68] In Plogoff, for example, international news crews from Germany, Denmark, Belgium, Britain, Sweden, and Switzerland provided more (and more sympathetic) coverage to protesters than French media.[69] International solidarity also increased turnout at demonstrations, with a concomitant boost to the perceived importance of a given local struggle. However, as 'Arthur'[70] from *GO/CNV* wrote with regard to the 1977 Malville protest, 'The number of demonstrators is less important than the symbolism.' Referring to a few dozen international demonstrators marching from the German border down to Malville, Naussac, and the Larzac, he added, 'It's one thing to demonstrate in your own area against "your" [*sa*] power station and for "your" bike lanes, it's something else to participate in a month-long march. [. . .] Better still: the participation of Germans and Italians will give an international dimension that the local revolts lack.'[71] Transnational solidarity was all the more important *because* protest was so intensely local: what better way to dispel the accusation that protesters were self-interested Nimbys (i.e. 'Not-in-my-backyard' opponents of nuclear power) than to point to the presence of foreign demonstrators, who had presumably travelled great distances in the name of shared principles? And what better way to show one's own principled concern than to forge links with those struggling in other countries? After hundreds of West Germans came to Malville from cities as distant as Frankfurt, Freiburg, Hamburg, Hannover, and West Berlin in 1977, activists from the region around Malville made a point of attending the next major West German demonstration, in the town of Kalkar. By doing so, they asserted that, because 'electro-fascism' did not stop at the border, 'neither do we!' (see Fig. 3.2).

---

[68] Keck and Sikkink have described how solidarity can have a 'boomerang effect', with movements in one country calling on allies from abroad to exert outside pressure on the offending state. Margaret E. Keck and Kathryn Sikkink, *Activists beyond Borders* (1998).

[69] Théo Le Diournon et al., 'Plogoff-la-Révolte', brochure, 87 pp., 1980, PA Le Garrec, p. 70.

[70] Pseudonym of the satirist Henri Montant.

[71] Arthur [pseud.], 'Haguenau-Larzac, via Malville : la racaille écologique est en marche', *GO/CNV*, no. 160 (2 June 1977), pp. 7–10 (p. 7). The protest in Naussac was in opposition to a dam project.

Fig. 3.2. *Casse-Noix* no. 8. Reproduced by permission.

As the geographic distance between activists increased, transnational contact usually diminished in frequency and depth, but increased exponentially in importance. Simple messages from abroad showed how far and wide support reached and how important a particular local struggle was perceived to be. In Brokdorf, the BUU reprinted messages of solidarity it had received from groups in Denmark and Ireland, noting that it generated 'a feeling of great security and certainty' to know that 'tens of thousands stand behind us and actively support our work'.[72] When the Larzac farmers camped out under the Eiffel Tower in 1980, German activists (mostly anti-nuclear groups) separately left at least seven telegrams of support addressed to 'Paysans du Larzac, Champ de Mars'.[73] Sometimes, foreign assistance was explicitly solicited, as when German activists claimed (accurately or not) that 'in our experience, protest from abroad makes the greatest impression on German authorities'.[74] As suggested by the aforementioned connections between French activists and Japanese victims of the Bomb, solidarity with the victims of nuclear technology was of particularly great symbolic importance. When West Germans held their 1979 demonstration in Bonn, they pointedly invited Cathy McCaughin from Harrisburg, Pennsylvania (USA) to speak to the crowd of nearly 150,000 about the recent accident at Three Mile Island nuclear power plant. McCaughin told her audience that 'What happened to us can happen to you! [. . .] The nuclear lobby is organized worldwide. The nuclear threat knows no borders. We will therefore resist worldwide and stand together.'[75] Statements like this, though largely symbolic, encouraged the perception that anti-nuclear protest was not about the limited concerns of only one community or one nation, but tied to something global.

The most common way in which transnational connections created advantages for protest was by inspiring activists abroad.[76] Precisely because activism was so local and each struggle in many respects different,

[72] BUU, *Brokdorf* (1977), p. 137. The BUU also distributed a flyer listing a selection of the messages of support that it received. BUU, 'Uns erreichten in den letzten Tagen [. . .]', flyer, 1976, HIS, SBe 731 Box 02 (1/2) Brokdorf.
[73] 'Wir denken an euch [. . .]', telegrams of solidarity, 1980, BM, Larzac IZ 63 (1980). Three were from local anti-nuclear groups (in Hamburg, Gorleben, and Wyhl) and one from the BBU; one came from a non-nuclear citizens' initiative and two others from private individuals.
[74] Jens Scheer, letter to World Information Service on Energy, 1 May 1980, IISG, WISE 7.
[75] BBU, 'Reden der Großdemo', pp. 14–15. This quote has been translated back into English from the available German source.
[76] In such instances, 'communication mostly took the form of mutual observation', as it did for 1950s anti-nuclear weapons protesters. Nehring, 'National Internationalists', pp. 561–2.

networks connecting disparate sites had great potential benefits. By linking themselves together, anti-nuclear activists could draw on ideas developed in different contexts (local as well as national), fine-tuning protest strategies that worked elsewhere to suit their own (perceived) conditions.[77] Activists thus developed ideas in discussion and in parallel, adapting (rather than merely adopting) strategies for their own purposes.

Within the anti-nuclear movement, the site occupation was one form of protest that evolved considerably as it moved across time and space. When Alsatian activists first occupied the chemical plant in Marckolsheim in 1974, one of their inspirations was the nationally known struggle of the Larzac farmers, who had managed to constructively channel the energies of a broad base of supporters through non-violence and local leadership.[78] The site occupation in Marckolsheim took the idea of locally controlled, peaceful protest a step further to encompass site occupation, a direct action response to the inaction of the centralized French administration. Six months later, some of the same activists participated in the occupation of the nuclear power plant construction site just across the Rhine in Wyhl. Here, their ranks were considerably reinforced by supporters drawn from the local left-wing scene in nearby Freiburg and the network of the BBU. In a twist on previous strategy, Wyhl activists occupied the site en masse during a rally attended by 28,000 people. Direct action on this kind of scale inspired activists across the ocean in turn. A pair of American activists came to Wyhl in the summer of 1975 to study its example, and German activists also travelled to visit anti-nuclear protesters in the United States.[79] In a series of actions partly inspired by those in Wyhl, thousands of American anti-nuclear protesters repeatedly occupied the construction site of a nuclear power plant in Seabrook, New Hampshire in 1976–7. They organized themselves into small-scale affinity groups that were capable of acting independently but which coordinated their actions on the basis of consensus decision-making. The affinity group idea then journeyed back to West Germany. In Gorleben, the organizers of a large-scale site occupation in 1980, referring explicitly to Seabrook as one of their models, encouraged the formation of such groups, proposing that their

---

[77] Nehring, 'National Internationalists', p. 573.

[78] 'Le Larzac rencontre l'Alsace à Marckolsheim', flyer, 1974, ASB, 24416.

[79] Joanne Sheehan and Eric Bachman, 'Seabrook—Wyhl—Marckolsheim: Transnational Links in a Chain of Campaigns', 2008, http://wri-irg.org/de/node/5182 (accessed 20 Febuary 2012). American activists made a return visit in 1977 to report back to the Volkshochschule Wyhler Wald about their experiences occupying the site 'nach dem Vorbild von Wyhl'. VHSWW, '27. Programm', schedule flyer, 2 pp., 15 July–18 August 1977, ASB, 12.1.11.I.

actions be coordinated through a 'speaker's council'.[80] The Gorleben activists also drew on other transnational learning processes that had led to increasingly sophisticated occupation practices and different experiments in non-violent (and violent) strategy.[81] At every step along the way, activists established cross-border connections, drew on the resources of local and transnational networks to implement them, and innovated by de- and recontextualizing ideas—usually amplifying protest in the process. In this way, the consequences of protest at any one site escaped the confines of national borders, sometimes making themselves most strongly felt in places very far from their supposed point of origin.

Protest in one country could inspire activists in another, but that inspiration frequently rested on selective interpretation. One of the common ways that the world abroad intervened in local anti-nuclear protest was when particular factions seized upon developments elsewhere as evidence of the way forward. In 1980, West German radicals watched from afar as the local struggle over a planned nuclear power station in Plogoff developed into an intense (and heavily media-driven) conflict involving regular skirmishes between townspeople and police. Some in Hamburg were convinced that Plogoff represented a new model of local uprising that needed to be tried at home, and propagated the legend of the town's militancy with a brochure entitled 'An Introduction to the Guerrilla Tactics of the Breton Village Plogoff'. Accordingly, the bulk of the German brochure is devoted to questions of repression and resistance, including a lengthy, blow-by-blow retelling of the battles that took place during the six-week public enquiry. However, the French brochure on which it was based, 'Plogoff-la-Révolte', makes for tamer reading. The work of eight area journalists, it balances the story of epic combat with information about everyday life in the region, emphasizing the importance of Breton identity and local demands for greater democracy—all elements which receive short shrift in the German version. Viewed from abroad (or even from outside Bretagne), the nuances and complexities of the struggle in Plogoff fell away, making it into a symbol of militancy that was useful to a certain constituency.[82]

---

[80] Trainingskollektive für Gewaltfreie Aktion, 'Handbuch zur Durchführung von Aktionstrainings', brochure, 46 pp., 4th edition, October 1983, HIS, SBe 731 Gorleben (A5-Broschüren), pp. 13, 23.

[81] See Chapters 4 and 5.

[82] 'Einführung in die Guerillataktik'. Plogoff was frequently invoked as a symbol of militancy in both France and West Germany. See the chapter 'Plogoff occupé' in Gérard Borvon, *Plogoff* (2004). For other West German references to Plogoff militancy, see autonome anti-akw-gegner der initiative 'plogoff ist überall', 'Wir verbinden mit den folgenden Thesen [...]', *Radikal* (September 1982), p. 18; Essener Initiative gegen Atomanlagen, 'Kalkar. Die Interessen der Brütertechnologen und Betreiber', photocopied article, 2 pp., 1981, PapierTiger, 'Kalkar Presse 81 Doppelt'.

However, the grass was almost always greener on the other side, and the same kinds of imaginings travelled in the opposite direction. In the run-up to the 1977 protest in Malville, many a French anti-nuclear activist looked towards West Germany, where protesters in Brokdorf had responded violently to a dramatic, militarized escalation initiated by authorities. Demonstrator violence provoked heated discussion in Germany, but also cast a long shadow that reached into France, where the upcoming protest in Malville was already shaping up to be 'the major event of anti-nuclear contestation'[83] for the year. For militant French activists, Brokdorf exemplified the repression and police state tactics that nuclear energy would entail wherever it was implemented.[84] Certain groups therefore concluded that it was necessary to fight nuclear power at home with the same vigour that Germans had shown in Brokdorf. According to them, 'the Germans know what it's about when they attack nuclear power', and 'they knew you don't attack Super-Phénix with flowers'.[85] Against arguments like these, other activists found themselves fighting an uphill battle. Advocates of non-violent strategy argued in *La Gueule ouverte/Combat non-violent* that 'Malville is not Brokdorf' and asked, 'Do we not have our own protest experiences (with non-violence and using our imagination)?'[86] Yet in other instances, non-violent protesters were themselves more than happy to point to foreign examples. In 1975, a *GO* report on Wyhl asked rhetorically, 'And if the watchword came from Germany? Systematic occupation.' It went on to suggest that protesters 'in Fessenheim, and especially in Malville' might consider similar tactics.[87] No matter where one stood, protest abroad served as a foil to action at home, capable of revealing the deficiencies and desires of the local movement or some part of it. On all sides and from all directions, activists selectively interpreted events abroad, using them as resources for their own (factional) purposes.

Cross-border activism was subject to a variety of problems and limitations that did not affect networks within the same country. Between France and Germany, the difficulties began with communication itself, which usually necessitated translation. Even along the Franco-German border, where multilingualism was more common than elsewhere, activists complained of the 'difficulté à faire des traduction exact' [sic] in

---

[83] 'Manifestation contre la centrale nucléaire de Creys-Malville des 30 et 31 juillet', police report, 7 pp., 1977, AD Isère, 6857 W 36, p. 2.

[84] See, for example, 'La guerre de l'atome « pacifique »', *GO*, no. 152 (6 April 1977), p. 1.

[85] 'J'ai eu honte. Quand on invite un copain à dîner, on ne lui fait pas faire la cuisine et laver la vaisselle. . .', *Casse-Noix*, no. 7 (August 1977), p. 6.

[86] 'malville n'est pas brokdorf', *GO/CNV*, no. 163 (23 June 1977), p. 9.

[87] Monique Gironde, 'Le printemps atomique', *GO*, no. 42 (26 February 1975), p. 7.

meetings (due in part to the 'tendency of the translator to give his own interpretation of the text that he is translating').[88] The act of translation itself could be wearisome, making already tedious procedural meetings in particular drag on for hours.[89] When ideas or concrete plans of action were at stake, transnational communication posed the problem of how to 'include foreigners in our discussions without causing these to lose some of their spontaneity'.[90] Accuracy as well as spontaneity could suffer, creating misunderstandings of greater or lesser importance. For example, French- and German-language reports on a meeting about protests in Alsace and Baden in late 1974 both state that further mobilization depended on activists disseminating more information about nuclear power (and 'the industrialization of Alsace [sic]'). However, this conclusion was connected to opposite understandings of prior protest: according to the French minutes, 'in Marckolsheim, the site occupation permitted consciousness-raising among the population' whereas in the German version, it was 'the population's consciousness [that] made the site occupation in Marckolsheim possible'.[91] Friendly advice in the other direction came across similarly mangled. Elsewhere in the German version of the minutes, Alsatian women are encouraged to learn from their German sisters that the problems of a site occupation concern 'not only' men; however, most *Alsaciennes* would probably have found the matter even more dire, as men (in the French version) were 'not especially' concerned.[92] Different linguistic connotations could also sow ideological confusion, as when peaceful German sit-down strikes (*Sitzblockaden*) were understood as a peculiar form of *barricades* or when ordinary, rank-and-file activists (*militants* in French) suddenly turned out to be their most radical comrades-in-arms (*Militante* in German).[93] Yet mistranslation was not always strictly a disadvantage, and protest could even profit from it. Robert Joachim (b. 1948), an Alsatian regionalist who was involved in the occupation of an electricity tower in Heiteren, remembers his own group engaging in what might be termed

---

[88] See 'Problèmes divers' (no page number) in 'bilan marche été 76', *CRAN*, no. 4 (1976).

[89] Internationale Jugendgemeinschaftsdienste (AG Umwelt), 'Industriealisierung', p. 42.

[90] Internationale Jugendgemeinschaftsdienste (AG Umwelt), 'Industriealisierung', p. 47.

[91] 'Alors qu'à Marckolsheim l'occupation du terrain a permis la conscientisation des populations, à Wyhl c'est l'information préalable qui mobilise les populations.' 'Compte-rendu de la réunion du 27.10.74', *Le « Que Voulons Nous » !*, no. 1 (1974), pp. 2–3. 'Das Bewußtsein der Bevölkerung hat die Platzbesetzung in Marckolsheim ermöglicht, jetzt muß die Information über Wyhl die Bevölkerung weiter mobilisieren.' 'Bericht über die Versammlung am 27.10.1974', *WWW*, no. 1 (1974), pp. 2–3.

[92] 'Das Problem der Besetzung betrifft nicht nur die Männer.' 'Le problème de l'occupation ne concerne pas spécialement les hommes.'

[93] Wolfgang Hertle, 'Stärke durch Vielfalt—Einheit durch Klarheit', 2011, http://divergences.be/spip.php?article2346 (accessed 11 March 2012).

'value-added' translation: 'We never "translated" our texts. We always took advantage of the second language to say something else, so as not to waste space.'[94] His group's very name was ambiguously translated in such a way as to enhance its appeal to different constituencies: German speakers might sympathize with the explicitly political, 'federalist' goals of the Elsass-Lothringen föderalistische Bewegung whereas the Mouvement Régionaliste Alsace-Lorraine resonated with French 'regionalism' that had cultural as well as political valences. Sometimes deliberate, often not, miscommunication along these lines was endemic to transnational protest.[95] However, the fact that activists did not always fully understand the nuances of the ideas being shared with them was less important than their ability to successfully apply whatever they (mis-)understood to their own situation.

The greatest practical problem of transnational protest therefore occurred when protesters misunderstood the situation in which they found themselves, such as when demonstrating abroad. German activists discovered this in the worst possible way when they travelled in large numbers to Malville in July 1977, thereby inserting themselves into an already high-stakes, potentially violent conflict between French demonstrators and French police.[96] Transcultural misunderstandings began well before the demonstration. Vague calls by the protest organizers for autonomy and self-organization among protesters went largely unheeded in France, but West Germans were given more detailed instructions to form 'maximally independent' groups with their own food, water, tents, and first aid supplies.[97] Though Germans were encouraged to 'mingle among French activists', the Malville organizers themselves undermined this by setting up a separate campsite for foreigners in Morestel (ostensibly in order to facilitate 'self-organization' among non-French speakers).[98] Consequently, foreign and especially West German protesters appeared to constitute an organized group distinct from their French allies, making it easier for authorities to exploit supposed national differences. Flyers distributed in West Germany had also warned activists not to forget

[94] Robert Joachim, interview with the author, Haguenau, 23 April 2010.
[95] For a discussion of cultural misunderstandings within the 1950s movement against nuclear weapons, see Nehring, 'National Internationalists', pp. 564–5, 570.
[96] This case is dealt with in greater detail in Andrew Tompkins, 'Transnationality as a Liability?', *Revue Belge de Philologie et d'Histoire* 89, no. 3/4 (2011).
[97] 'Sommer 1977 nach Malville'.
[98] 'Sommer 1977 nach Malville'; David, interview. There was even confusion about where this camping site was. Most German flyers correctly told foreign demonstrators to report in Morestel, but one got it doubly wrong, announcing that 'Alle Deutschen treffen sich bis zum 30.7. in POLERIEN (Nähe Malville)'; no such place exists, but they likely meant Poleyrieu. 'Wer Malville vergisst macht Mist!!', clipping from unidentified source, 2 pp., 1977, AA, Ordner 'AKW+Widerstand', 'Malville 77'.

their 'personal defensive equipment',[99] such as helmets and gas masks, when going to Malville. However, French police were much less accustomed to seeing such items at demonstrations, and interpreted them as a provocation, to which they (over-)reacted accordingly.[100] Whether German activists in fact behaved more aggressively than their French counterparts remains a matter of dispute today. West Germans probably made some assumptions about the rules of engagement in Malville based on their experiences in Brokdorf and Grohnde, but they were also conscious that they were not on their own terrain.[101] In any case, French police did not react to protesters in the same ways that their West German colleagues did, and the clash of protest 'choreographies'[102] led to dangerous misjudgements. For example, one nineteen-year-old from Bremen attempted to pick up a tear gas grenade and throw it back towards police lines, a relatively common practice in West Germany. However, French police weaponry was of different manufacture, and this one, rather than simply releasing smoke, exploded in his hand.[103] Experiences and expectations from one context could depart greatly from foreign realities, sometimes with serious consequences.

A further difficulty of cross-border activism was that it could make protest more susceptible to disruption by the state. For example, when Alsatian activists held their first protest in Fessenheim in 1971, French border guards were advised to search German and Swiss cars for 'improvised weapons (axe handles, parts of placards, etc.) [sic]' and, if found, to conduct a further search for drugs, 'the verifications possibly lasting until the scheduled end of the protest at 5:30 p.m.'.[104] Harassment of foreign protesters was even greater at the 1977 demonstration in Malville. On the weekend of the protest, French police repeatedly visited the so-called 'German camp' in Morestel before conducting a massive raid there at

---

[99] 'Sommer 1977 nach Malville'.

[100] This was the impression of demonstrators like CP in Conny Baade and Christian Petty, joint interview with the author, St-Jean-de-Buèges, 19 September 2010; Hans-Hermann Teichler, interview with the author, Hamburg, 20 August 2010. Police reports more or less confirm that police associated helmets with 'hostility' (and with Germans). 'Manifestation des 30 et 31 juillet', p. 3.

[101] 'Malville. Erfahrungsbericht von 7 Hannoveranern', brochure, 40 pp., 1977, DfuL, D 1450, pp. 6–7; Teichler, interview.

[102] BD in Bernard Dréano and Suzanne d'Hernies, joint interview with the author, Paris, 20 January 2010.

[103] Gewerkschaft Erziehung und Wissenschaft, *Kriminalisierung* (1977), p. 15. Some West German demonstrators blamed the French organizers for this incident, arguing that the latter should have communicated more about their 'experiences with French cops, both about their tactics and their weapons'. 'Petra' and 'Hardi', 'Diskussionspapier zu Malville', flyer, 3 pp., 13 August 1977, ASB, 12.1.9.II/00024357, p. 2.

[104] Memo, 7 April 1971, AD Haut-Rhin, 1391 W 17.

6:00 a.m. the day before the march. In addition to confiscating everything from Molotov cocktails (not yet assembled) to pocketknives, gloves, and '1 black flag', they seized and deported Chaïm Nissim, the Swiss CRA member responsible for the organizers' walkie-talkie communications system.[105] After the demonstration itself, police arrested eleven Germans and two Swiss along with six French citizens. Charges were brought against twelve, half of whom (five Germans and one Frenchman) were given prison sentences; all arrested foreigners were reportedly barred re-entry into France for ten years or more (as was Chaïm Nissim, who was expelled by administrative decree, without trial).[106]

Protesters' opponents were also able to exploit nationalism to turn the public against them. In France, authorities and the media tapped into stereotypes old and new in order to defame German demonstrators. Even before the protest, the far-right newspaper *L'Aurore* wrote of 'columns' of Germans entering the region, and quoted an anonymous CRS officer as saying, 'It seems that among them are fanatics from the Baader gang[107] flanking veritable commandos trained in hand-to-hand combat, who proved themselves [*qui ont fait leur preuves*] last year under similar circumstances in the Federal Republic of Germany.'[108] Closely echoing this sentiment, Interior Minister Christian Bonnet later announced on television that violence at the protest was the work of 'action groups of anarchist inspiration[109] who ignore borders, who moreover have "drilled" [*qui se sont déjà fait la main*] elsewhere—notably in West Germany—and who we are beginning to track down through the cooperation that has been put

[105] Colonel de la Gendarmerie Roy, 'Rapport', summary police report, with appendices, 5 August 1977, AD Isère, 6857 W 36, Annexe II. Activists assembled in Grenoble later cited the lack of radio communication among demonstrators as one of the problems that overwhelmed the organizers. Participants de l'usine de Sogreah, 'Échos et réactions', *Super-Pholix*, no. 14 ([August] 1977).

[106] A further three French and four West German citizens were detained but not charged. Of the twelve charged, four were acquitted (two German, one French, one Swiss) and two subsequently had their convictions overturned (one French, one Swiss). Of those receiving prison terms, one (German) had his sentence fully suspended; the remaining five received sentences of three to six months that were partly suspended, though each spent one to three months in prison. See Roy, 'Rapport', Annexe III; 'Le tribunal de Bourgoin-Jallieu prononce huit peines d'emprisonnement [. . .]', *Le Monde*, 9 August 1977, p. 6; *Aujourd'hui Malville*, p. 200; Gewerkschaft Erziehung und Wissenschaft, *Kriminalisierung*, p. 17.

[107] The Rote Armee Fraktion was also referred to as the 'Baader-Meinhof-Gruppe' (after two prominent members, Andreas Baader and Ulrike Meinhof).

[108] 'Malville : le sang après la boue', *L'Aurore*, 1 August 1977.

[109] The related term *anarchistes allemands* was commonly used at the time as a euphemism for the Rote Armee Fraktion. See, for example, 'Les influences anarchistes en milieu étranger', report, 38 pp., [1 July] 1977, PPP, B^A 2330.

in place among the different countries of the [European] Community'.[110] Europe was, here again, a contested and ambiguous symbol. Activists constantly emphasized that they had come 'from across Europe' to demonstrate against a 'europeanizing' nuclear industry.[111] Their state opponents, however, were equally capable of using 'European' cooperation within institutions to crack down on protest, even as they mobilized national enmities. At a press conference the night before the demonstration, René Jannin, prefect of Isère, announced that the town of Morestel, where foreign protesters had been instructed to camp, 'has been occupied by the Germans for a second time.'[112] In response, French and German protesters pointedly argued that it was the police, not the overwhelmingly peaceful protesters, who deserved to be compared to Nazis (see Fig. 3.3). French authorities were more consistently arbitrary in dealing with German protesters than was true in reverse, yet the Federal Republic of Germany also used its powers to shut out foreign demonstrators when it wanted to. When French and Dutch protesters attempted to join the demonstration in Kalkar on 24 September 1977 (two months after the debacle in Malville), activists claimed that as many as 800 of them were blocked at the border for hours or denied entry completely.[113] Despite official rhetoric about European cooperation, protesters from neighbouring countries were more likely to find themselves at the mercy of hostile states than those who remained in their own country to protest.

Though transnational protest was subject to a variety of limitations, its greatest strengths lay in the symbolic possibilities that emerged from efforts to overcome such difficulties. Nowhere was this more evident than along the Franco-German border, where protesters outwardly claimed to have moved beyond national, linguistic, and cultural differences. Taken together, Alsace and Baden formed a region that was at once 'local' to its inhabitants, arguably at the centre of 'Europe' (understood as Western Europe) and indisputably 'international'. By emphasizing cross-border cooperation (sometimes to the point of exaggerating it), activists wrote a potent protest narrative of local people overcoming national resentments in order to fight together against nuclear power. They portrayed civil nuclear energy as a danger imposed upon their region by outside powers, a danger they explicitly compared with local memories

[110] 'Journal de 20 h', 31 July 1977, TF1.
[111] BI gegen Atomkraftwerke Freiburg, 'Kein Schneller Brüter in Malville!', flyer, 1977, ASB, 00024372; participants de l'usine de Sogreah, 'Échos et réactions', *Super-Pholix*, no. 14.
[112] 'Un débat sans frontière', *Le Monde*, 1 August 1977, p. 1.
[113] Ermittlungsausschuss der Bürgerinitiativen gegen Kernenergie, *Wir, das Volk* (1977), p. 4.

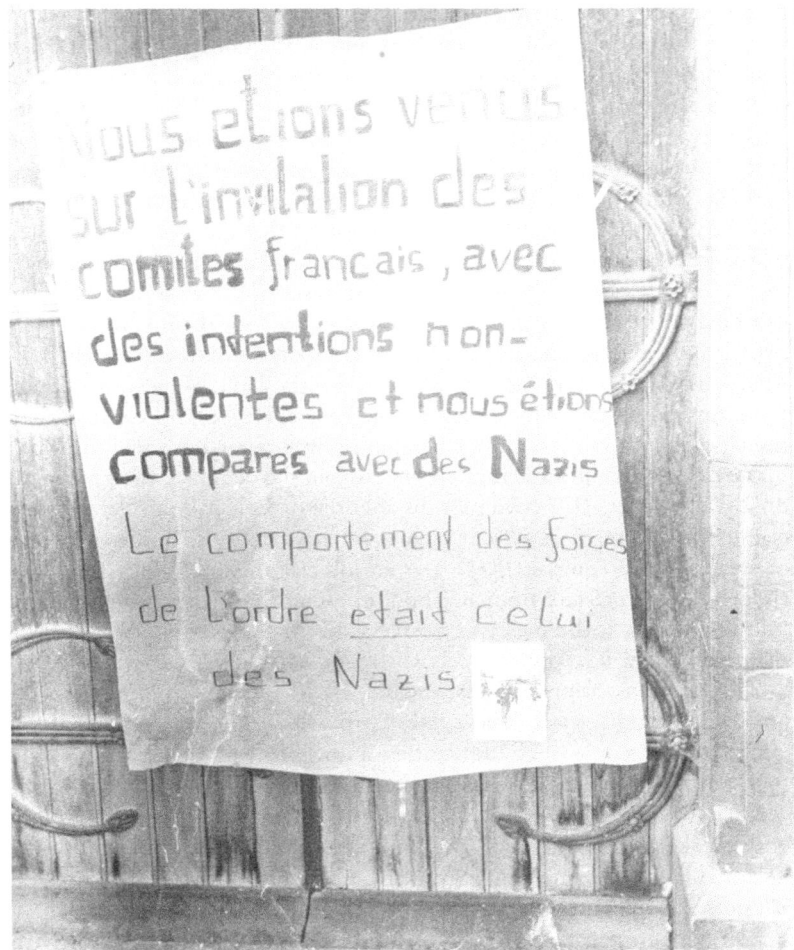

Fig. 3.3. 'Le comportement des forces de l'ordre était celui des Nazis' ('We had come at the invitation of the French committees, with non-violent intentions and we were compared with the Nazis. The behaviour of the police forces was that of the Nazis.') Below the text is taped a photo of a policeman carrying a grenade launcher. Reproduced by permission of Georges David.

of war. For example, the Freiburg-based journalist and protest singer Walter Moßmann (1941–2015) wrote a song turning the century-old, anti-French hymn 'Die Wacht am Rhein' into an anthem celebrating a new and different 'watch along the Rhine', kept by local citizens of Alsace and Baden together:

> Im Elsaß und in Baden war lange große Not
> Da schossen wir für unsre Herrn im Krieg einander tot
> Jetzt kämpfen wir für uns selber in Wyhl und Marckolsheim
> Wir halten hier gemeinsam eine andere Wacht am Rhein[114]
>
> (In Alsace and in Baden there was ever great distress
> In war, for our masters, we shot each other dead
> Now we fight for ourselves in Wyhl and Marckolsheim
> Here, together, we keep a different watch along the Rhine)

Cultural production like this, often presented in the Alemannic dialect common to Alsace and Baden, provided an anchor for the 'rebel identity'[115] that anti-nuclear protesters fashioned for the region. In poems like 'Rhingold' by André Weckmann (about exploitation of the Rhine by outside powers from France and Germany) and songs like 'Die Grenz esch a Bleedsinn' by François Brumbt ('The border is rubbish'), activists articulated a transnational opposition to nuclear power and everything they associated with it. Another Brumbt song, 'Dreyeckland',[116] succinctly described how activists reconceptualized their region: through a clever twist on the term *Dreiländereck* (the point where the 'corners' of France, West Germany, and Switzerland met), they declared solidarity among 'Three corners that already had a history, a culture, a language in common. Three regions that suffer from centralism, [. . .] invaded by multinationals.'[117] Dreyeckland was largely symbolic, and its supporters openly admitted that its unity was marred by historic, national animosities.[118] They nevertheless held it up as the idea of an a- or anti-national utopia, 'in which there is no above and no below, nothing foreign, nothing oppressive, nothing contradictory, nothing contaminated, nothing poisoned'.[119] Because protest

---

[114] Reproduced by permission of Beate Riess (for the estate of Walter Moßmann). These lyrics appear in Badisch-Elsässische Bürgerinitiativen, ed., *Lieder aus Wyhl* (1975), pp. 10–12.

[115] Engels, *Naturpolitik*, p. 357.

[116] The text of this song is reprinted in Jean [pseud.], *Elsass. Kolonie in Europa*, p. 137.

[117] Daniel Coche, *Écoutez RVF vous écoute*, 1978, 30 mins.

[118] Roland ['Buki'] Burkhart, 'Dreyeckland. Wo liegt das? Was soll das? Wer will das?', *WWW*, no. 15/16 (1 December 1977), pp. 2–4.

[119] Burkhart, 'Dreyeckland', *WWW*, no. 15/16, p. 2.

in Dreyeckland could take place directly along state borders, activists from the region could use the space to symbolically negate not just the politics of particular governments, but the very idea of the nation state itself. Ginette Skandrani (b. 1938), an Alsatian member of the Fédération Anti-Nucléaire des Environs de Fessenheim,[120] claims to have participated in a protest where she and a German friend each burned their respective national flags in the middle of a bridge over the Rhine before hoisting an anti-nuclear banner over the ashes.[121] Her story illustrates the symbolism into which the region's protesters readily tapped. The same holds for the greatly celebrated use of Alemannic dialect, though it did not magically obviate translation and eliminate communication problems between French and German activists, as is sometimes claimed.[122] As Walter Moßmann points out, the use of dialect served an important symbolic purpose.

> WM: The shared dialect, that wasn't the basis. It was [. . .] a twist
>   [*Pointe*]. Because this story was, in and of itself, trilingual—
>   German, French, and dialect—and we would have excluded
>   countless people if the dialect had dominated everything. It was
>   important for people in the villages and because dialect was
>   frowned upon. Then we naturally leveraged that and said, 'No,
>   that's the twist, that it's transnational [*grenzüberschreitend*]. Here
>   in Marckolsheim and in Sasbach on the other side, they belong
>   together, [they] speak [the same] dialect.' But of course it was in
>   part an assertion. It was a poetic model.[123]

Anti-nuclear protesters along the Franco-German border claimed to imagine their differences away. Even if the reality remained more complicated, behaving 'as if'[124] they were united gave their struggle a powerful narrative, rich with symbolism, which attracted support from far and wide.

At the border between France and West Germany, activists were able to take advantage of the possibilities of transnational protest in other, more practical ways as well. States could use their borders to block out foreign

---

[120] FANEF was similar in purpose to the CSFR, but based in Haut-Rhin instead of Bas-Rhin.

[121] Ginette Skandrani, interview with the author, Paris, 11 January 2010.

[122] It probably was easier, as Roland Burkhart argues, for certain local activists from Alsace and Baden (especially older ones) to communicate in their shared dialect than to go 'via Hannover' and speak *Hochdeutsch*. Roland Burkhart, interview with the author, Freiburg, 22 April 2010. However, by the 1970s, even many Alsatians no longer spoke dialect. Haug and Schirmer, interview.

[123] Walter Moßmann, interview with the author, Freiburg, 1 April 2010.

[124] This is in some ways comparable to Padraic Kenney's argument (based on Václav Havel's notion of 'living in truth') that Eastern European dissidents behaving 'as if in Europe' took some of the first steps towards revolution, imagining their way into a better situation. Padraic Kenney, *Carnival of Revolution* (2002), pp. 91–120.

protesters, but activists found ways to turn the situation around. During the site occupation in Marckolsheim, French officials effectively closed the border to all German protesters; in response, activists swarmed the nearest border crossings and sent friends in cars to block bridges up and down the Rhine, creating tremendous traffic snarls and a massive headache for authorities. (The next day, the border was open again.) Ginette Skandrani, who described the border as *un sacré avantage* for protesters, recalls employing this strategy on several occasions in the late 1970s and early 1980s, helping create traffic jams that (she claims) forced authorities to reroute vehicles as far north as the Netherlands.[125] The fact that the border separated different state jurisdictions from one another was also something that activists could and did exploit. This was particularly true for the pirate radio station Radio Verte Fessenheim (later renamed Radio Dreyeckland). Mireille Caselli, a (non-Alsatian) Frenchwoman who lived in Freiburg and worked with RVF, explains that she and her friends 'learned to play with the border'.[126]

> MC: Playing with the borders at the time, that meant [. . .] it was better to broadcast our programmes for France from Germany, since the French police didn't have the right to act here and vice versa [. . .] The borders really existed back then. It's not the case anymore. And instead of dividing us, on the contrary, it was an asset for us.[127]

Being along a border also gave anti-nuclear activists in Alsace and Baden access to multiple channels of information. Residents on both sides of the Rhine frequently complained that they received insufficient information from their respective governments about plans for evacuation in the event of an emergency at Fessenheim. Taken together, though, two sets of incomplete information might prove complementary or contain revealing gaps.[128] Furthermore, actions on one side of the border could force the hand of authorities on the other. In October 1976, French authorities in the Haut-Rhin *département* deemed that 'It is becoming urgent that we rapidly mount a counter-campaign, all the more so since West German authorities have proceeded with the publication of certain elements of the

---

[125] Skandrani, interview. See also Büchele et al., *Der Widerstand*, pp. 124–6. Activists in Freiburg, West Berlin, and on the northern border with Denmark also proposed border blockades in connection with a national day of action for Gorleben in 1979. 'Police telex, 15 March 1979, Nds, 100 Acc. 2003/116 Nr. 66.

[126] Büchele et al., *Der Widerstand*, p. 54.

[127] Caselli, interview. See also Claude Collin, *Écoutez* (1979), p. 48.

[128] Arbeitsgruppe 'Katastrophenplan', 'Fessenheim Katastrophenplan', brochure, 78 pp., 1977, ASB, 12-A4-45; Écologie et survie, 'Plan ORSEC allemand traduit — commenté — édité', brochure, 40 pp., 1977, PA Skandrani.

German Civil Protection Plan. This publicity accentuates again the gap on the French side between the population and public authorities.'[129] In all of these different ways, transnational activists were able to turn the disadvantages of transnational protest into advantages. As Ginette summarizes it, 'the fact that we worked across borders and that we mastered French, German, and Alsatian' meant that 'we were able to play all of them [against one another]—to make fun of power in fact'.[130]

BORDER CROSSERS

It should not be forgotten that transnational protest never happened automatically—it was the work of people who found (or placed) themselves at the intersections of different countries, cultures, and languages. People became transnational activists for a variety of different reasons: because they possessed the necessary skills for it, because their interests led them to do so, or simply by accident. Activism was often not the only aspect of their lives that involved border-crossing, but it interacted with their identities in sometimes decisive ways. For many of them, the border-crossing they engaged in as activists was closely connected to how they saw themselves and who they were as individuals. This section looks at how different people experienced transnational activism.

Jean-Jacques Rettig (b. 1939) is an Alsatian for whom environmental activism is firmly anchored in the history of his home region and his own family.[131] As he explains it, his transnational commitment to anti-nuclear activism stems directly from his identity as an Alsatian. The region's historic victimization during centuries of Franco-German rivalry made him a convinced internationalist, sceptical of nation states and the militarism he associates with them. He thus continues a long Alsatian tradition of 'national indifference', which resents and resists outside claims on the region, its inhabitants, and their identities.[132] Jean-Jacques feels that his family has often been caught between France and Germany. His

---

[129] 'Contre-campagne antinucléaire', note de dossier, 1 October 1976, AD Haut-Rhin, 1391 W 18.

[130] Skandrani, interview.

[131] Jean-Jacques Rettig, 'Alsace & le Rhin supérieur : une région-phare du mouvement écologique', 2007, http://vorort.bund.net/suedlicher-oberrhein/rettig-umweltgeschichte-fr.html(accessed 30 May 2011). The idea of this entanglement is communicated clearly in the German-language translation of this speech, Jean-Jacques Rettig, 'Elsass. Umweltgeschichte, Familiengeschichte und Regionalgeschichte', 2007, http://vorort.bund.net/suedlicher-oberrhein/rettig-umweltgeschichte.html (accessed 2 May 2011).

[132] On the concept of national indifference, see Tara Zahra, 'Imagined Noncommunities', *Slavic Review* 69, no. 1 (2010).

grandfather fought for Germany in the First World War, but received his disability pension from France after it retook Alsace; Jean-Jacques's brother was forcibly conscripted into the German army during the Second World War (a *malgré-nous*[133]), and Jean-Jacques himself was drafted by the French into the Algerian War. (According to him, both fought against their will and sabotaged the respective war efforts.) The arbitrariness, compulsion, and injustice of these conflicts propelled Jean-Jacques towards pacifism, which placed him further outside the categories of the nation state. Upon returning to Alsace from Algeria, Jean-Jacques became increasingly committed to non-violence, reading the works of leaders such as Mahatma Gandhi, Martin Luther King, Dom Hélder Câmara, and Lanza del Vasto.[134] The military utility of 'civilian' nuclear technology was thus one reason for his opposition to the nuclear power plant in Fessenheim.

Like many Alsatians, Jean-Jacques has family on both sides of the Rhine. (His wife, Inge, was born in Germany but subsequently naturalized as a French citizen.) It was thus natural for him to work closely with German activists, which he did in several capacities. As early as 1972, he helped found Rheintal-Aktion/SOS Plaine du Rhin, which served as one channel through which CSFR worked together with local groups in Baden, the BBU, and additional allies from Switzerland and the Netherlands. Among its earliest activities, Rheintal-Aktion sent letters of protest to Willy Brandt and Georges Pompidou, set up a Franco-German meeting of winegrowers potentially affected by nuclear facilities, and registered French complaints against the initial West German nuclear project in Breisach (later moved to Wyhl).[135] To underscore the lack of democratic consultation on nuclear energy issues, Jean-Jacques made a point of personally speaking at an official meeting about the Breisach/Wyhl nuclear project, where he stressed his Alsatian identity and his fondness for life on both sides of the Rhine. The West German audience energetically applauded him as a symbol of both grassroots reconciliation and anti-nuclear protest, while German pro-nuclear representatives greeted him with perceptible impatience.[136] During the site occupations in both Marckolsheim and Wyhl, he was a regular fixture and one of the leading organizers. According to Jean-Jacques, ecology is by definition a transnational struggle, since environmental and radioactive pollution do not stop at the border.[137] Indeed, in the case of the Rhine, they seemed to start there.

---

[133] See Geneviève Herberich-Marx and Freddy Raphaël, 'Les incorporés de force alsaciens', *Vingtième siècle*, no. 6 (1985).
[134] Rettig, interview.
[135] 'après la marche du 7 mai 72', *Ionix* (November 1972), p. 4.
[136] *s' Weschpenäscht. Die Chronik von Wyhl (1972–1982)*, 1982, 111 mins.
[137] Rettig, 'Umweltgeschichte'.

If transnational activism came naturally to Jean-Jacques as a result of his Alsatian identity, for others, crossing borders could be a way of challenging identities with which they were uncomfortable. Conny Baade (b. 1948) was a student in Freiburg during the 1970s who took part in the Wyhl protests. She remembers the confrontation with German history during her youth as part of what awakened her political consciousness. Like many other Germans born after the war, she associated a certain personal and political alienation with Germany itself.[138] She vehemently rejected the politics of her parents, who were not Nazis but had supported the *völkisch* and anti-Semitic Ludendorffer movement. As a university student, she became involved with the Bund kommunistischer Arbeiter (BKA), 'a quite friendly group' that operated a theatre for working-class apprentices with which Conny enjoyed working. From 1971 to 1972, Conny studied abroad in southern France; during her absence, the BKA was taken over by the Kommunistischer Bund Westdeutschland (KBW), which, among other things, shut down the apprentices' theatre. The changes that had occurred in Freiburg while Conny was away made her experience in France seem all the more important.

> CB: France was refreshing for me, because, among the Trotskyists [from the Ligue Communiste], the right to factions was practically sacred. [...] When you come back after that and all your friends are in the Organization, you feel completely alien [*arg fremd*] and don't know where to go.

Repulsed by what she considered the 'dogmatism' of the KBW, Conny found a new home for herself in the nascent anti-nuclear movement. During the protests in Wyhl, she was one of those who translated between speakers of German, French, and the local Alemannic dialect. The close work with Alsatian activists in particular strengthened her positive feelings toward France.

> CB: The cooperation with the Alsatians [...] led me to be more starry-eyed [*blauäugiger*] towards France. Because it was from them that the ideas came. They were more awake [*munterer*] and they didn't have so many inhibitions. They [...] weren't always driven by this feeling of guilt. And that was very attractive.

Conny now looks back on her early attitude towards France with scepticism, saying she and others misread French street protest as a sign of heightened political awareness, overlooking the lack of other opportunities to influence the

---

[138] This seems to have been common among West Germans of her generation. See Belinda Davis, 'Whole World Opening Up', in *Changing the World, Changing Oneself*, edited by Belinda Davis et al. (2010).

political process. In the 1970s, though, France still seemed like a democratic foil to Germany's historic authoritarianism. Transnational activism further 'nourished my illusions' about France, she says, playing some role in her decision to move there permanently in 1981. Equally important were her feelings towards Germany and the political culture she associated with it.

CB: I was in a pretty bad way in Germany. I had difficulties as a schoolteacher, I was in an area that was really decidedly reactionary. [...] It got more and more cramped [...] and then, in the alternative movement—it too became so stupidly dogmatic. And afterwards, that was for me something that had to do with Germany.

Confrontation with German history was central to Conny's political identity and something that propelled her towards anti-nuclear and other protest. Yet to her, activism in Germany seemed doomed to descend again and again into disappointment. When Conny ultimately decided to leave Germany, contacts and experiences from her prior stay in France made it seem like an attractive alternative to Germany.[139] For Conny Baade, the door opened by transnational activism was thus an exit leading out of Germany.

Though Conny found her own national identity uncomfortable in many respects, the transnational identities of some anti-nuclear activists were not necessarily more comfortable. This is certainly true for her partner, Christian Petty (b. 1947). The son of a British agent and a German heiress who had met during the final days of the Second World War, Christian was raised in West Germany and Austria, but carries a British passport. After his father returned to Yorkshire in 1948, Christian had a very difficult upbringing in his mother's wealthy family. He reacted very strongly against them and their lifestyle and today says that he is 'disgusted [by] all that is wealthy, from perfume to jewellery and everything else. I'd rather go around in ragged trousers.' Until Christian was sent to a boarding school at the age of thirteen, he was privately tutored at home and isolated from other children. Whenever he could, he took refuge from his family in nature. When he moved to Freiburg as a young adult and became involved in environmental activism there, it was, he says, 'a liberation from my parents' home', something that gave him 'a certain security'. After being disowned by his mother, he sued the family for inheritance and received a large settlement, which he used to fund activist groups and alternative projects in Freiburg. He spent most of his own time working for a printing press that produced leaflets for such groups, including many from Alsace. During the 1970s, Christian

---

[139] CB in Baade and Petty, joint interview.

attended protests in France, but, unlike his Alsatian friends, he saw the border 'more as an obstacle' than as an advantage. 'I'm always a bit nervous when I go over borders,' he says. 'And I have my British passport, and that's another thing that's always a little different.'[140] In the pre-Schengen era of the 1970s, Christian's very appearance—a young man with a beard in ragged clothes, driving a VW bus with an *Atomkraft—Nein Danke!* sticker—seemed to invite harassment by French customs officials.

CP: Have you ever met a French customs agent?
AT: No.
CP: They're real assholes. *[CP, CB, and AT laugh.]*
CB: They don't exist in that form anymore.
CP: It was a real nightmare, when you crossed over the border, you were confronted with these guys who immediately smelled that you're not from their tribe. And then you're told to pull over to the right and then [...] they'd take you completely apart for 6–7 hours. They'd look up your ass! [...] It was like barbed wire. [...] You could go over to the others, but there were these customs agents in between. I'm not upset that they've been put out of business, but I sometimes worry about where they might be today.

Protesters did, however, adapt to the more predictable forms of harassment at the border. As Christian puts it, 'it was kind of a game to trick them'. Before heading to Malville, Christian says he packed gas masks into the trunk of a rented BMW instead of his own car, and a female friend drove the BMW over the border minutes after Christian reached the same checkpoint. While several customs agents searched his vehicle, another officer waved the BMW through without inspection. Nevertheless, it was Alsatians and not Germans who were best able to exploit the border. 'The Alsatians were a lot more flexible, [...] more agile. They had more experience with these French *flics* [...] and more *esprit* in these matters.' Christian and Conny became a pair around 1977–8, around the time when his financial support within the Freiburg scene was becoming a psychological burden.[141] In 1981, the two of them moved to France, where Christian's transnational identity took on a new meaning.

CP: In Germany, I was British. In Austria, I was German. Here I'm a *boche*—also German. It's incredibly irritating—you aren't seen in terms of what you present, the ideas that you have, what you try

¹⁴⁰ CP in Baade and Petty, joint interview.
¹⁴¹ Christian says that, within the alternative scene, he came to be seen 'nicht mehr als Gründer [...] sondern als Bank [...] Ich wollte nicht der Übervater sein, aber ich war automatisch das.'

to do. You're constantly confronted with these stories from the Second World War and so on. I find that a bit irritating. [...] There isn't any nation that—I'd like to live in a sort of environmental refuge, without political borders and without this whole history, which is important but gets overemphasized [*überbewertet*].

For most of the last thirty years, Christian has effectively found security in just such an anational, environmental refuge. With money from his inheritance settlement, he purchased land in the mountains near his and Conny's new home in southern France. There, he raises sheep, keeps border collies, and fights for the legal protection of a small population of endangered golden eagles that live there. Christian is an activist for whom nature and ecology have enabled him to partially escape the complications of his own difficult, transnational identity.[142]

Transnational identities and activism also came together in dramatic ways outside the borderland space of Alsace and Baden. Bernadette Ridard (b. 1947) is the daughter of a military officer. Her family moved around a great deal in her youth between France, its (soon-to-be-former) African colonies, and the French-occupied zone of Germany. Bernadette continued along this peripatetic trajectory in early adulthood, moving from Grenoble to Kuala Lumpur for a year in 1967, then to Canada, England, Brussels, and the French countryside before finally settling in Hamburg almost a decade later. These repeated reorientations were not always easy: 'When you move all the time, you don't really belong to anything,' she says today. In all this turbulence, activism became something that helped Bernadette find her footing. Her first direct political engagement came while she was in England in the early 1970s, where she responded to an advertisement by the Peace Pledge Union (PPU) in the *Sunday Observer* and quickly found herself picketing and distributing leaflets to promote desertion among British troops bound for Northern Ireland. The work with PPU brought her into contact with Greenpeace London (then campaigning against French nuclear testing in the Pacific) and War Resisters International (WRI), where she met a German man to whom she took a liking. She moved with him to the Brussels WRI office, then later followed him to Hamburg after a short stint with *Combat non-violent* in southern France. Bernadette arrived in Hamburg in October 1976, just as anti-nuclear protests in Brokdorf were beginning to take off. Despite her many transnational connections, she knew few people in Germany other than her boyfriend. When he chose to participate in the first illegal site

---

[142] CP in Baade and Petty, joint interview.

occupation at Brokdorf, she felt uncomfortable because of her vulnerability as a foreigner:

> BR: It was getting dark, I didn't speak a word of German, I didn't know anyone other than [him . . . I] didn't know where [I] was [. . .]. I was very worried because I said to myself, if I get checked [by the police], I'll be in an illegal situation. I had just arrived in Germany [. . . Back then,] you still had to get a residency permit.

Nevertheless, activism made it possible 'to meet lots of people very quickly', and she attended the next demonstration two weeks later with a large group of new friends. Activism could be an entire social world of its own and, in the 1970s, anti-nuclear protest was but one element in a larger web of activism. Feminism was centrally important; Bernadette's first experiences with activism had involved showing that women too had an important role to play in the opposition to conscription, the army, and militarism. For Bernadette, anti-nuclear protest was always part of a 'global perspective' that involved challenging exploitation, poverty, and injustice. 'One day it was nuclear power, the next it was violence against women, then it was peace, etc. We were active night and day and it was really a period when we didn't do anything else.' Reflecting back on this period of her life today, Bernadette in some ways feels like she drifted from place to place and from passion to passion without a firm anchoring.

> BR: I've never learned, as a result of my biography, to arrive somewhere. You have to sort things out [*se débrouiller*] very quickly, but in any case you'll also leave again quickly. So, you know, you remain at the margins. [. . .] Like I often said later: As soon as I could have said 'we', I left, I was going.[143]

Bernadette nevertheless carried skills and knowledge culled from trans-national protest with her wherever she went. In Germany, this travelling Frenchwoman brought her experiences in England to bear, participating in efforts to start a centre for battered women (*Frauenhaus*) modelled on the one in Chiswick described in Erin Pizzey's book *Scream Quietly or the Neighbours Will Hear*. Her language skills in English, German, and her native French consistently proved to be an asset professionally and for protest (the two most often in combination), even well after she stopped moving around. In Hamburg since 1976, she served for a time on the staff of *GWR* and worked for the Lutheran church when Hamburg hosted

---

[143] 'Comme j'ai dit souvent après, „*Sobald ich wir*"—« Dès que j'aurais pu dire 'nous', je suis partie », je partais.' Bernadette Ridard, interview with the author, Hamburg, 25 August 2010.

the 1981 Kirchentag;[144] more recently, she has offered adult education French language classes and continues to write letters for Amnesty International.[145] For Bernadette, political engagement is something that has helped channel valuable aspects of her transnational identity.

In Hamburg, one of the people with whom Bernadette worked closely was Wolfgang Hertle (b. 1946), founder and longtime editor of *GWR*. Transnational activity was not necessarily something that came naturally for Wolfgang in the way that it did for Bernadette or Christian; it was something he actively sought as a result of his political engagement. Wolfgang developed an interest in non-violence at an early age, inspired in part by readings of Gandhi and Martin Luther King. Together with like-minded individuals, he looked for other examples of what non-violent action could be.

> WH: For a while at first, I found nothing except for examples from abroad and in the past. [...] We knew very little about what there was [in the way of activism] in Germany before us and we didn't find the few things that we did know particularly attractive. So we looked more abroad. In retrospect, it turns out there were others before us, people who were also searching, but there wasn't such a stunning tradition as the [American] Civil Rights movement or [movements] in other countries.

He and his friends explored the options available to them in existing peace organizations in West Germany, but Wolfgang felt that 'something was missing' for him in them. In his view, non-violence (*Gewaltfreiheit*[146]) and civil disobedience were underdeveloped in German protest traditions. Looking abroad, Wolfgang found that the more difficult legal framework for conscientious objection in France had shaped a more appealing tradition of firm, disciplined non-violence.

> WH: In France, they had a completely different understanding of legality and action than was common in Germany. [...] There were very few conscientious objectors and the law [establishing conscientious objection] was practically forced through in 1968 by an unlimited hunger strike. Most people who worked toward

---

[144] The Lutheran church holds its Kirchentag conference every two years in a different location. In 1981, it was the occasion for a large demonstration against nuclear weapons with the motto *Fürchtet euch!* ('Be afraid!'), playing on that year's Kirchentag theme, *Fürchtet euch nicht.*

[145] Bernadette Ridard, 'Français Compact Sprachtraining', http://www.brfc.de/ ubermich.html (accessed 30 May 2012).

[146] In German, this term is used in contrast to *Gewaltlosigkeit* to indicate a fundamental principle rather than the mere absence of violence.

anti-militarism there were already outside the law from the beginning, whereas in Germany, this right was acknowledged as a
matter of principle in 1949 in the Basic Law—even if it was
very difficult to get it [recognized . . .] That has a different quality
from [going] to jail for it.[147]

Wolfgang read widely, first in English then in French, and developed a
relationship to events and places abroad without direct contact, through
texts.[148] In 1967, he went on holiday to France, seeing the country for the
first time and meeting a French woman who he later married. When she
joined him back in Germany, they subscribed to French magazines,
including *Témoignage chrétien*, where he first read about the struggle of
the Larzac farmers. Wolfgang visited the Larzac for the first time in 1973,
becoming so fascinated with the creative, non-violent action strategies
developed there that he later wrote his doctoral thesis about it.[149] Like
many others, he found foreign protest more attractive. In his case, it was
because non-violence seemed to be practised more resolutely there: 'Even
if not everyone on the Larzac believed 100 per cent in non-violent
ideology, they had agreed on a shared way forward [*ein gemeinsames
Verhalten*], they stuck with it and had success with it.' At struggles in
Germany, he says, such a decision 'never took place' and local activists
blamed either police or outside activists for violence, but failed to
unequivocally denounce it themselves. Wolfgang also worked actively to
bring lessons from France to bear in the anti-nuclear struggle in Gorleben,
setting up the aforementioned Kurve Wustrow, hosting Franco-German
seminars, and inviting his friend Hervé Ott (b. 1949) to speak about the
Larzac in West Germany.[150] Wolfgang has lived most of his life in
Germany, but his strong commitment to non-violence led him to search
for inspiration abroad, visit and connect with activists there, and foster
long-term, transnational exchange among French and German activists.

Activism and activist identities themselves were of course not always
transnational. Yet even local activism could lead to unforeseen connections with very distant people and places, as it did for Yves François
(b. 1956). Yves grew up directly next to what became the Malville
FBR. Today, he is the third generation of the François family to farm

---

[147] Hertle, interview.
[148] Though the texts in question are different, this is similar to Jeremy Varon's argument
that worldwide opposition to the Vietnam War was built on 'an international protest
culture organized around master texts'. Jeremy Varon, *Bringing the War Home* (2004), p. 1.
[149] Hertle, *Larzac 1971–81*.
[150] See, for example, 'Zur Initiative für einen Kontakt und besseren Austausch zwischen
Gruppen der deutschen und französischen Friedensbewegung', letter, 2 pp., 15 October
1983, AA, 'Le Cun du Larzac'.

this land. As Yves and his family describe it, their home is a quiet, isolated place, a 'sheltered milieu' approximately one kilometre from the nearest village.[151] Nevertheless, during the 1970s, the wave of protest that washed over the area around Malville brought the François family into close contact with anti-nuclear activists from far and wide. The visitors were, first and foremost, French *écologistes*, but also some Swiss, German, and Italian activists. As a young adult at the time, Yves found these people 'fantastic', but sometimes also 'very bizarre'.[152] His father, Maurice (b. 1929), reaches a similar verdict: shared opposition to nuclear power brought people 'with their feet on the ground' together with others 'with their heads in the clouds'. However, even those with 'unrealistic' perspectives posed thought-provoking and eye-opening questions.[153] During the years of intense protest against Super-Phénix (especially 1975–7), the François family opened its home to these people, consistently offering food and shelter to activists from near and far who came for anti-nuclear information sessions, planning meetings, and protests.[154] Maurice François also built a device to trap methane gas from the farm that could be used as an alternative source of energy, something that was exceedingly rare at the time. The stark contrast between this simple, renewable form of energy and the high-tech, industrial nuclear plant next door garnered even more attention. In addition to schoolchildren whose teachers brought them to see the methane installation while on class trips to Super-Phénix, there were visitors from Romania, Chad, and Kazakhstan who examined it as a model for similar projects at home. The family was repeatedly interviewed by French and foreign media about both the local anti-nuclear struggle and alternative energy. In 1980, Yves and his family received a visit from a Japanese journalist preparing a report on nuclear energy politics in Europe; he had received their contact information from anti-nuclear activists that Yves's mother, Chantal, had met during her 1977 trip to Japan. After staying for a night, the journalist moved on, but the woman who worked as his interpreter returned two weeks later. Intending to stay only a week, she and Yves soon began (as Yves puts it) to *approfondir certaines relations*; she extended her stay, remaining for another two months. After Yves visited her in Japan the following year, they married in August 1981. Since that time, Kuniko François has lived in the French countryside, where she and

---

[151] François and François, joint interview; Yves François, interview with the author, Creys-Mépieu, 24 January 2010.
[152] Y. François, interview.
[153] MF in François and François, joint interview.
[154] Chantal speaks of a tradition of hospitality in her family; having grown up herself near the Saint Curé d'Ars, she was accustomed to accommodating pilgrims, be they religious, political, or otherwise. CF in François and François, joint interview.

Yves have raised three children in their farmhouse a stone's throw away from Super-Phénix. Though the François family have been vigorous opponents of the FBR since its early development, Yves is fond of saying today that nuclear power isn't all bad: had it not been for the power plant, he is certain he would never have met his wife.[155] Anti-nuclear protest brought the world to Malville, and the François family (like many others) welcomed it into their home.

CONCLUSION

The anti-nuclear movement was at once deeply local and broadly global in scope. The critical nodes of its networks were the local communities struggling at the sites of existing or potential nuclear power installations. Regional protest might be seen as an extension of the local, but national organizations were generally less important. Even when protesters did not consciously imagine themselves in relation to a global movement, they were nevertheless affected by events beyond the borders of their own country. Transnational connections carried great symbolic value, making the local seem less provincial and the anti-nuclear movement seem greater than its (national) opponents. For French and West German activists in the 1970s, 'Europe' was an ideal intermediary space, one in which they could position themselves above the nation state while still remaining (literally and figuratively) close to home.

Connections between local sites, though they tended to weaken as distance increased, provided channels of communication between different spaces of possibility. Transnational networks thus allowed for a particular ferment of ideas. Legal, linguistic, and cultural differences pulled protesters in particular directions, making French street protest appear more democratic or West Germans seem more effectively organized. Though such assessments rest in part on stereotypes, they also reflect activists' desires and the weaknesses they perceived in protest movements in their own country. Yet transnational networks and imaginings meant that characteristics of protest in one country could spill over into the other—or, more accurately, that interested parties could actively import those aspects of foreign protest that appealed to them in order to adapt them for their own purposes. When French and German activists learned from one another (and from their peers elsewhere), protest tended to increase in intensity and sophistication. Indeed, the dramatic progression

---

[155] Y. François, interview.

of protest from Fessenheim and Marckolsheim (1971–4) to Wyhl and Brokdorf (1975–6), then on to Malville and Kalkar (1977) and back to Gorleben (1977–80) gave the anti-nuclear movement much of its trans-national character and a certain Franco-German hue. Nevertheless, unity across borders was usually more imagined than real, and transnational protest was at least as symbolic as it was concrete. In practice, transnational activism was subject to important constraints, such as those posed by translation, political or cultural misunderstandings, and the very real power of nation states themselves.

Operating at the junctures of French and German protest was thus not always easy or pleasant. Those who naturally found themselves between spaces could feel fragmented and tentative about their identities (as did Christian and Bernadette). Yet cross-border environmental activism could also provide such people with a sense of continuity, a place to go to, even an escape. For others, crossing borders could be the natural, logical consequence of who they were (as it was for Jean-Jacques in Alsace) or something that they actively sought to do for personal and/or political reasons (as was the case, in different ways, for Wolfgang and Conny). Though transnational protest remained purely symbolic for the over-whelming majority of anti-nuclear activists, those who worked across borders, even to a limited extent, could find their lives transformed in unforeseen ways (as Yves and Kuniko François did). At the same time, foreign countries were not the only places where transformative, 'improb-able' encounters occurred. Urban and rural opponents of nuclear power within the same country could often seem just as foreign to one another as did French and West German citizens. As the next chapter will show, activism across the urban–rural divide also had to contend with clashes between imaginings and reality as well as with shocks that could be life-changing for those involved.

4

'Power to the Bauer!'

Local Protest in the Rural World

The town of Morestel in the Rhône-Alpes region of southern France was unaccustomed to the amount of attention it received during the last week of July 1977. Throngs of anti-nuclear activists from across France, West Germany, Switzerland, Italy, and elsewhere descended upon Morestel and neighbouring villages that week, setting up camp in advance of the protest that was to take place against the fast breeder reactor (FBR) in nearby Malville on Sunday, 31 July. Photos from the time show Morestel's few main streets clogged with bumper-to-bumper traffic, moving at a crawl between columns of parked cars lining both sides of the road. The human traffic was no less formidable: film footage from the night of 30 July shows the town's central square teeming with protesters gathered together to hold their last preparatory meeting for the march the next day.[1]

By virtue of their numbers, their appearance, and their transience, the demonstrators turned life in the region upside down for several days. The mayor of the neighbouring *commune* Saint-Victor-de-Morestel (1975 population: 525) was alarmed upon visiting the so-called 'German camp' set up in his village, where protest organizers sent most foreign demonstrators. If police estimates are accurate, the population of this temporary camp—one of several scattered throughout the region—outnumbered that of tiny Saint-Victor-de-Morestel by almost two to one. Shortly before the protest, the prefect of Isère held a press conference at which he declared that 'Morestel has been occupied for a second time by the Germans.'[2] Though his words were calculated to exploit national

---

[1] PA Maryse Budin, Georges David, and Marie-Jo Putinier; *Weil ich das Leben liebe*, 1977, 34 mins.

[2] INSEE, 'Statistiques locales : Saint-Victor-de-Morestel (commune)', 2011, http://www.statistiques-locales.insee.fr/FICHES/DL/DEP/38/COM/DL_COM38465.pdf (accessed 26 April 2011); 'Manifestation contre la centrale nucléaire de Creys-Malville des 30 et 31 juillet', police report, 7 pp., 1977, AD Isère, 6857 W 36; Colonel de la Gendarmerie Roy, 'Rapport', summary police report, with appendices, 5 August 1977, AD Isère, 6857 W 36;

Fig. 4.1. Demonstrators marching along country roads near Malville. Reproduced by permission of Günter Zint.

enmities, residents may indeed have felt that their local community was being subjected to a full-scale invasion by protesters—French and foreign.

However, for the local anti-nuclear activists who had helped organize the event, this was a moment of incomparable excitement. So many people arrived for the march that they decided to start from three separate locations (Courtenay, Montalieu, and Poleyrieu, between 6 and 15 kilometres apart), with the processions converging in the tiny hamlet of Faverges.[3] Marie-Jo Putinier (b. 1937), a local anti-nuclear activist, was at the head of the second-largest group, which left from Montalieu. She described the scene as 'a serpent of people [. . .] a continuous crowd. We couldn't believe our eyes when we saw that. We were almost swept away to see all those people who were there for that.' (See Fig. 4.1.) The organizers later claimed that up to 60,000 people came together for the march in support of their cause on 31 July. The much lower estimate by police put

Marc Ambroise-Rendu and Bernard Elie, 'La non-violence en échec à Creys-Malville', *Le Monde*, 2 August 1977.

[3] Similar plans were originally floated in May and confirmed on 27 July, when four starting points were designated. However, following police raids on 30 July, the planned march from Morestel was integrated into the one starting from Courtenay. See 'Compte-rendu de la Coordination du 21 Mai', *Super-Pholix*, no. 12 ([June] 1977), p. 1; 'Le film des évènements', *Super-Pholix*, no. 14 ([August] 1977), pp. 2–7.

the count at only 20,000, but even this was more than the population of all the surrounding towns put together. According to Marie-Jo, 'It was our very own May '68.' Maryse Budin (1944–2013), another activist from the local community, remembered it as 'the Revolution in Morestel'.[4]

During the second half of the 1970s, scenes like the one in Morestel repeated themselves in provincial towns across France and West Germany. As politicians and planners built nuclear facilities in remote, rural areas, outside activists concerned about nuclear power flocked to the countryside to demonstrate in solidarity with the affected local communities. This chapter will explore the ways in which anti-nuclear protesters imagined, interacted within, and used the rural environment during the 1970s. The rural setting in which many demonstrations took place enhanced the appeal of anti-nuclear protest, as the movement fed on, and fed back into, a diffuse nostalgia for rural life that was especially pronounced in the 1970s. Rural people in general, and farmers in particular, were the awe of outside protesters, who placed these authentic, local activists on a pedestal and vied for their affections. Outsiders' imaginings of the rural world were part of the appeal of anti-nuclear protest, even if the realities of the countryside were far more complex. As local activists from rural communities interacted with outsiders from more urban environments, both sides changed one another in lasting ways. However, the rural space in which they encountered one another also affected the kinds of protest that could take place.

IMAGINING THE RURAL AND
THE LOCAL IN THE 1970S

The countryside has historically been imagined in deeply contradictory ways. For most of the modern era, the political left especially has tended to regard the 'provincial' with hostility. In France, the countryside has long been seen through the prism of the French Revolution, which made local particularisms out to be vestiges of the Ancien régime and the rural world a bastion of counter-revolution, filled with backward peasants under the sway of monarchy, clergy, and aristocracy. The Vendée insurrection of 1793–6 was a powerful source of such stereotypes, not least because

---

[4] Marie-Jo Putinier, interview with the author, Bourgoin-Jallieu, 26 January 2010; Maryse Budin, interview with the author, Vézeronce, 27 January 2010. 1975 population for the *canton* of Morestel: 16,178. INSEE, 'Statistiques locales : Morestel (canton)', 2011, http://www.statistiques-locales.insee.fr/FICHES/DL/DEP/38/CV/DL_CV3819.pdf (accessed 26 April 2011).

various right-wing political forces have cultivated local myths of resistance to Revolutionary excess ever since.[5] A century after the French Revolution, Karl Marx elaborated a specifically socialist scorn for the peasantry in *The 18th of Brumaire*, arguing that peasant communities were devoid of class consciousness and therefore pawns of more powerful social groups ('They cannot represent themselves, they must be represented. Their representative must at the same time appear as their master, as an authority over them').[6] Even before Marx, farmers (*Bauern*) in German-speaking lands were generally associated with 'god-given order' and seen as anti-revolutionary. By the second half of the twentieth century, rural people and spaces in both France and West Germany were also tainted by association with the discredited ideologies of *Blut und Boden* and *retour à la terre* that had been promoted by the Nazis and their collaborators in Vichy.[7]

Yet the symbols of the rural world were also highly ambiguous, and there existed other traditions which imbued peasants and the countryside with more positive connotations. In complete contradiction to the image of the farmer as a god-fearing counter-revolutionary, there also existed the idea of farmers as a revolutionary force that could, if angered, unleash a pitchfork-wielding mob against the sources of tyranny and injustice. Medieval *jacqueries* in France and the *Bauernkrieg* in the German lands provided historical precedents for possibilities of revolution 'from below', memories of which were celebrated whenever the contemporary context was opportune (such as during the revolutions of 1848).[8] In the socialist tradition, even Marx's negative view of the peasantry was not absolute, since he too was fascinated for a time with peasant communities as a model of communal ownership.[9] Rousseauist and Romantic traditions associated the countryside with natural living and egalitarian democracy rather than with backwardness. As industrialization accelerated in the late nineteenth and early twentieth centuries, large cities (often described in terms of a *ville dévoratrice* or *Moloch Großstadt*) increasingly became the undesirable foil to such idyllic refuges.[10] In the post-war period, nostalgia

---

[5] Thierry Gasnier, 'Le Local', in *Les Lieux de mémoire*, edited by Pierre Nora (1992); Robert Gildea, *Past in French History* (1994), pp. 26–31.

[6] Karl Marx, *The Eighteenth Brumaire of Louis Bonaparte*, trans. Saul K. Padover (1999).

[7] Werner Conze, 'Bauer', in *Geschichtliche Grundbegriffe*, edited by Otto Brunner et al. (1972), pp. 421–2, 436–7; Anna Bramwell, 'Blut und Boden', in *Deutsche Erinnerungsorte*, edited by Etienne François and Hagen Schulze (2001), pp. 380–3.

[8] Conze, 'Bauer', pp. 411–12, 420. See also Rolf Kießling, 'Der Bauernkrieg', in *Deutsche Erinnerungsorte* (2001).

[9] Conze, 'Bauer', p. 431; Gareth Stedman Jones, 'Marx and the Village Community', Oxford, Examination Schools, 22 October 2012.

[10] Alain Corbin, 'Paris-Province', in *Les Lieux de mémoire* (1992), p. 785; Hildegard Châtellier, 'Moloch Großstadt', in *Deutsche Erinnerungsorte* (2002).

grew for rural ways of life that appeared to be on the brink of extinction. In 1967, the sociologist Henri Mendras wrote that 'In contrast with the fever of industry, peasant wisdom seemed eternal: the city and industry attracted all the energy, but the countryside always supplied the bucolic dreams of peaceful happiness, of security, and of eternity.'[11] By the 1970s, anti-nuclear activists could draw on a variety of tropes, both negative and positive, to interpret the rural world.

Remarkably though, activists in that decade consistently chose to read the rural in a positive light and to prioritize the interests of 'local' activists in small towns over those of their outside counterparts in larger cities. Anti-nuclear activists imagined rural people and spaces to be somehow exceptional: revolutionary, authentic, and special by virtue of their local environment or history. That left-wing activists in particular came to see the rural world predominantly in such terms by the 1970s was related to changes that had occurred during the previous decade. Already in the mid- to late 1960s, the notion that the rural and the revolutionary were intimately linked gained currency, inspired by revolutions in the mostly agrarian 'Third World'.

Though such a view was not uncommon on the left generally, it was most clearly articulated by the Maoist groups that flourished in the immediate aftermath of May 1968; it was especially pronounced in France, where the agricultural sector remained substantially larger (in both absolute and relative terms) than in West Germany.[12] As early as June 1968, announcements were posted at the Sorbonne inviting students to spend their summer break working alongside peasants in the fields, based on the view that 'student youth [. . .] is only a small part of the revolutionary forces and [. . .] it must fuse with the principal forces'.[13] These rural apprenticeships, repeated in subsequent years, took their name and inspiration from Mao Zedong's 'long march' during the Chinese Civil War, when intellectuals went to the countryside to learn the art of revolution from the peasantry.[14] One anonymous group of later 'long marchers' argued that peasants were 'if not openly in revolt against the bourgeois system, at least sceptical' in a way that was 'a mass phenomenon, objectively

---

[11] Henri Mendras, *Fin des paysans* (1967), p. 13.

[12] 3.4 million people were employed in the agricultural sector in France in 1968, making up 15.6 per cent of the civilian workforce. In more populous West Germany, the sector employed only 2.5 million people (9.9 per cent). OECD, 'ALFS Summary Tables', http://stats.oecd.org/ (accessed May 2011).

[13] 'Etudiants, travailleurs, chômeurs', June 1968, CHS-XXe, Fonds Mai 68, F Δ 1190.

[14] See Mao Zedong, *Peasant Movement in Hunan* (1953). Excerpts from this are included in chapters 2 and 11 of the widely distributed 'Little Red Book' of *Quotations from Chairman Mao Tse-tung* (1966).

revolutionary'. Another group argued that it was in the rural world 'more than elsewhere' that Maoists had to test their mettle, because 'in the country, revolutionary phraseology fizzles out. There is no thought but of the Marxist kind, that which precisely articulates in a rigorous fashion the material conditions of existence and the forms of social consciousness.'[15]

The idea that peasants had mystical powers of clairvoyance was perhaps best summed up by the French Maoist slogan *L'œil du paysan voit juste !* ('The peasant's eye sees clearly!'), though the sentiment behind it was by no means isolated to France.[16] 'Long marches' did not take place in the same, organized way in West Germany, but Maoists there too saw farmers as revolutionary insofar as they perceived them in relation to the working class or 'the masses'. As anti-nuclear protest started up in Wyhl, members of the Kommunistischer Bund Westdeutschland (KBW) in nearby Freiburg wrote reports describing the town (not without justification) as populated by 'workers and worker-farmers [*Arbeiterbauern*]' who had been forced into low-wage factory labour when finance capital and bourgeois industrialists drove local agriculture into the ground.[17] The local Kommunistische Partei Deutschlands (KPD) group described the site occupation in Wyhl as 'the masses taking their matters into their own hands', an instance of 'revolutionary violence' that 'radiated from the masses'.[18] During the 1970s, radical left ideology associated the rural with revolt in a way that enhanced the appeal of the former for many outsiders.

Other constituencies on the political left also came to admire the countryside and its inhabitants in the same period. Among young people especially, even those who felt repelled by the style or substance of organized, communist groups had been socialized (and politicized) in the same post-1968 environment. Indeed, according to the contemporary sociologists Léger and Hervieu, May 1968 was also the 'decisive turning point' for a movement 'back to nature' that propagated its own myths

[15] Centre d'action paysanne, *Mouvement de la jeunesse* (1970), pp. 20–1; Union des communistes de France marxiste-léniniste, *Le livre des paysans pauvres* (1976), p. 16.

[16] Indeed, this phrase itself originally appeared in Mao Zedong, *Peasant Movement in Hunan* (1953). However, it does not appear to have been widely adopted as a slogan in other countries, perhaps owing to less dramatic translations produced by China's Foreign Languages Press (the English version states simply that 'The peasants are clear-sighted').

[17] In 1974, the town's largest employer was a cigar factory whose workforce had been halved in recent years. [KBW], 'Vorläufiger Bericht der Untersuchungsgruppe Wyhl', report, 5 pp., 10 September 1974, ASB, 00024351 and KBW (Ortsgruppen Freiburg und Emmendingen), 'Kein Bleiwerk in Marckolsheim — Kein Kernkraftwerk in Wyhl', 1975, ASB, 12-A5-163, pp. 3–7.

[18] KPD, 'Kein Kernkraftwerk in Wyhl! Arbeitereinheit, Volkseinheit — im Kampf für den Sozialismus!', 1975, DfuL, D01215, pp. 6, 33.

about the rural world and which especially appealed to environmentalists. In their view, the dramatic events of May '68 gave rise to a 'revolutionary immediatism' that encouraged the search for alternatives to a capitalist, consumerist society that appeared to be on its last legs (a sentiment later powerfully confirmed by the oil crisis). For those wanting to change the world by changing themselves, the rural environment held a particular attraction: the countryside seemed to be a space outside civilization, at the margins of (post-)industrial society and beyond the direct control of the state. Léger and Hervieu describe neo-ruralists in France as 'not leav[ing] for "the countryside" so much as for the "desert", for "non-civilization"'; by their own description, many left in search of a life that was '"more full", "more coherent", "more authentic"'.[19]

Authenticity[20] was thus to be found in marginality: in remote regions 'at the ends of the earth' such as Bretagne (with its aptly named *département* Finistère) or parts of Normandie, in mountain communes in the Vosges or the Jura, and especially in impoverished areas of southern France such as the Cévennes. Southern France constituted a sort of international capital of rurality that attracted West Germans as well, who found there the kinds of marginal, rural spaces that seemed to be missing in their own, relatively urban country (with the notable exception of the Wendland region along the German–German border). Germans frequently expressed their desire for a 'return to nature' in terms of rejecting a kind of city life that was seen as inauthentic, segmented, and complex. Perhaps typical of this mindset is the story related in a West German alternative magazine about Dietlinde, a woman who left her home in Hamburg to make pottery in a small town near Nice.

> I found the entire world divided up [. . .] And within the different groups, between the different places, there were hardly any possibilities for contact [. . .] Every group, every area was isolated, there was insufficient—usually artificial—communication between them all. [. . .] There is perfection only in nature [. . .] I myself have to try to live and work in harmony with nature, so I can [. . .] achieve satisfying results, satisfying in the fullest human sense.[21]

Nature and the countryside were a kind of marginal Other, a more authentic place to which to escape from contemporary life. This 'return to nature' drew freely on the aforementioned traditions that had valorized the countryside in similar terms during previous centuries. However, in

---

[19] Danièle Léger and Bertrand Hervieu, *Retour à la nature* (1979), pp. 10, 31–2, 48–51. See also Sven Reichardt, *Authentizität und Gemeinschaft* (2014), pp. 459–98.
[20] On this term, see Reichardt, *Authentizität und Gemeinschaft*, pp. 57–60.
[21] Gurda Wirschun, 'Dietlinde', *Ulcus Molle Info*, no. 11/12 (1980).

the decade or so after 1968, positive perceptions of the rural world resonated particularly well because the 'return to nature' became bound up with a rejection of capitalism, consumption, and the complications of an emerging post-industrial world—all concerns that were central to the anti-nuclear movement.

Local activists in rural communities also helped construct the positive image of the countryside that prevailed in the 1970s by playing up local particularities. The specific characteristics of a given community were nearly always posited as unique, though they contributed to a general perception of rural distinctiveness. In Alsace, anti-nuclear activists argued that the 'unique environment' constituted by 'the last strip of the primitive Rhine forest' in their midst was threatened by a 'concentration, unique in the world, of nuclear power plants'.[22] On the Larzac as well, it was in the name of the rocky plateau's exceptionally rich environment that locals and outsiders were initially asked to support protests against the expansion of the military camp there—even though officials described the region as a 'desert'.[23] The relatively common frame of a 'unique' local environment hinted that the real appeal of such arguments lay in the defence of something special that was not, and could not be, part of city life.

At many sites, anti-nuclear activists also celebrated local traditions of protest that were imagined to be continuous over centuries. For instance, a book about the anti-nuclear struggle in Brokdorf (written jointly by rural activists and their allies in Hamburg and Bremen) opens with a local history of the region. Its protagonists, 'the farmers of the marsh', are shown to have successively resisted serfdom, aristocratic dominance, and the city of Hamburg for centuries—often through extra-legal means. Naturally, the struggles of the past culminated in the contemporary one against nuclear power: 'As so often in its 800-year history, now too it is a question of defending the right to health and a healthy environment [*Lebensraum*] through personal action.'[24] The emphasis on a farmer-driven, hyper-local history even in Brokdorf (where activists from Hamburg sometimes dominated) is indicative of the almost universal appeal of such particularist narratives.

At certain sites, especially in the rebellious regions of provincial France, usable histories and ready-made regional identities that activists could turn to anti-nuclear ends were even closer to hand. In Plogoff, the rejection of

---

[22] Solange Fernex, 'Non-Violence Triumphant', *The Ecologist*, vol. 5, no. 10 (December 1975), pp. 372–85 (p. 373); CSFR, 'En Allemagne, conscience et civisme ont encore un sens !', *Ionix*, no. 1 (February 1972), p. 20.
[23] Comité départemental de sauvegarde du Larzac, 'Le Larzac', brochure, 27 pp., 1973, BnF, 4°Lo10-3143, p. 11.
[24] BUU, *Brokdorf* (1977), pp. 17–20.

nuclear power was connected to a Breton identity 'forged over the course of centuries' in a community supposedly knitted together by 'the difficulty of their existence' in a region with minimal infrastructure and little industry beyond fishing.[25] Perhaps the place where local history and identities were most dramatically put at the service of the anti-nuclear cause was along the border between Alsace and Baden, where the 450th anniversary of the German Peasants' War of 1525 (*Deutscher Bauernkrieg*) propitiously coincided with the site occupations in Marckolsheim (France) and Wyhl (West Germany). Joß Fritz, who in the early sixteenth century had been the leader of numerous *Bundschuh* conspiracies along the Upper Rhine region, was resurrected in the 1970s as a left-wing saint, whose image adorned the banners of Alsatian regionalists, students from Freiburg, and anti-nuclear activists in Baden, Alsace, and the area around Swiss Basel alike.[26] Stories of the *Bauernkrieg* helped forge an 'Alemannic' identity, shared by anti-nuclear activists throughout the region, which gave their protest a special appeal that contributed to the mythical status that it attained for many opponents of nuclear power. The 'rediscovery' of these revolutionary traditions was, however, often the work of students and other community outsiders,[27] for whom the tropes of *jacquerie* had a special attraction. Unique local environments and (invented) traditions of revolt contributed to the perception that rural spaces were special and distinctive.

In the urbanizing, globalizing 1970s, these new imaginings of the 'rural' likewise affected understandings of the 'local'.[28] Indeed, the two were frequently conflated. As the political scientist Hélène Hatzfeld puts it, the 1970s witnessed the celebration and invention of 'the local' as a phenomenon that 'valoriz[ed] rural roots, the truth of the earth, and traditions'— all things that had previously been associated with the reactionary right, but which now became 'anchored on the left'.[29] *Rural* authenticity became intimately associated with the authenticity of the *local* within the anti-nuclear movement. This is clear, for example, in a 1977 article by the Freiburg-based activist Walter Moßmann that appeared in the left-wing journal *Kursbuch*. In it, Moßmann pokes fun at his fellow urban leftists' fetish for the rural symbol of the tractor, while at the same time

[25] Théo Le Diournon et al., 'Plogoff-la-Révolte', brochure, 87 pp., 1980, PA Le Garrec, pp. 60–1.

[26] This history provides the namesakes for the Jos Fritz bookstore and Bundschuh printing press in Freiburg, both established in the 1970s.

[27] Jens Ivo Engels, *Naturpolitik* (2006), p. 357.

[28] On the growing importance of place to identity in France, see Rod Kedward, *Vie en Bleu* (2006), pp. 470–5.

[29] Hélène Hatzfeld, *La politique autrement* (2005), pp. 185, 181.

emphasizing the importance of its owner as a directly affected, local stakeholder:

> In the eyes of city-dwellers, the symbol for militancy in the countryside is the tractor: like a tank, it moves not tamely through the streets but rolls unstoppably over rough and smooth [*über Stock und Stein*]. The vehicle isn't squeaky clean like an Opel Kadett [car], but coarse and dangerous, with rear wheels that seem violent. Several tractors in a row look like the movement's cavalry.
>
> But the tractor, it doesn't belong to us. We haven't bought it for our work. We aren't the ones in debt if it hasn't yet been paid off. [...] When a tractor comes to the site, its owner shows that he takes the cause seriously, it is his cause, he risks something for it. He doesn't drive to the site if he sees that it is not his cause, but rather that of students, the left, or travelling protesters.[30]

Though local farmers were seen in terms of their 'ruralness', Moßmann holds that their 'localness' was what made their participation in the movement so important: when they demonstrated, they took risks and accepted responsibility. In the long term, they alone could sustain protest, as struggle became part of their everyday lives. Such views were widely held: an article in *La Gueule ouverte* argued (apparently without irony) that 'ten resolute peasants are worth more than one hundred politically conscious students who return on Monday to their families. On that, everyone agrees.'[31] Adorning the cover of the same issue was a photo of farmers driving equipment at a protest in Malville (see Fig. 4.2).

Anti-nuclear activists' valorization of the local went hand in hand with an emphasis on 'personal' politics that found expression elsewhere in the 1970s, such as in women's movements and in calls for workers' self-management. This was clearest in the pervasive preoccupation with 'concerned' citizens and those who were 'directly affected' by the construction of nuclear power plants (*les concernés, die Betroffenen*). Anti-nuclear activists even argued that the value of an individual's protest was measured in inverse proportion to the distance between her home and the nearest nuclear power plant: 'The closer the geographic vicinity [...], the less moralistic and the more unambiguously existential the concern'.[32] Outsiders struggled to frame their own protest in similar terms.[33] One young participant in a

---

[30] Walter Moßmann, 'Der lange Marsch', *Kursbuch*, no. 50 (1977), p. 10.

[31] Chaïm ['Caïm'] Nissim, 'Malville : les paysans prennent la relève', *GO*, no. 114 (14 July 1976), pp. 3–4 (p. 4).

[32] '"... mehr Demokratie überhaupt". Ein Bericht von den Bürgerinitiativen um Wyhl', brochure, 68 pp., January 1977, IISG, Bro 2188/16, pp. 22–3.

[33] Expressions of *Betroffenheit* by non-local citizens are sometimes taken as evidence for the social construction of environmental grievances. Frank Uekötter, 'Wie neu sind die NSB?', *Mitteilungsblatt des Instituts für soziale Bewegungen* 31 (2004), p. 136.

Fig. 4.2. Title page of *La Gueule ouverte* featuring photo from a tractor demonstration. Reproduced by permission of Jean-Louis Soulié. Photo on cover credited to 'Treillard'.

summer camp near Wyhl felt that his visit to the area under threat had endowed him with some of the same sacrosanct 'concern':

> On the Kaiserstuhl, I felt for the first time an inkling of the 'direct concern' that is so beautifully and at the same time so lifelessly described in all the books. As I went with the farmers I had worked with for a few days through

the vineyards [...] something decisive changed for me too. Here, I was no longer someone who had read [about it...], no, here I myself had become (to some extent) an affected person.[34]

The rhetoric of spreading 'concern' was more pronounced in West Germany than in France (perhaps foreshadowing the preoccupations of the West German peace movement of the 1980s).[35] Nevertheless, French activists also took up this language when it suited them. Indeed, radical leftists from Grenoble who took the rare step of disputing the authority of local activists did so by referring to their own 'concern'. Accusing others of small-minded *comitélocalisme*, they wrote:

> At every meeting of the Coordination of Malville Committees, it's the same thing: the local committees are the first ones concerned, it's up to the local committees to judge, the local committees must decide, the local committees have the righteous eye of the peasant [*l'œil du paysan qui voit juste*]! [...] And we, the residents of Grenoble, we live 60 kilometres from Malville. That's not local?! We too are afraid of the cops but we're even more afraid of the electro-fascism and fast breeder reactors that may extend over all of France up to the point that humanity will be one big local committee![36]

Insistence on one's own 'concern' was part of a transnational discourse that valorized 'localness' within anti-nuclear struggle.

The fact (or perception) of being directly affected made local protest seem more authentic, more important, and above all more legitimate. The most salient division within the anti-nuclear movement was almost always between locals and outsiders, but it was often understood misleadingly in terms of the rural versus non-rural backgrounds of different activists. The 'local' commanded such respect because it was where protest was seen as most vital and most effective, but also because it was nearly always exotically rural. Local sites of anti-nuclear protest out in the countryside were thus attractive to different kinds of (post-1968) activists because they could be imagined as unique places, peopled by 'authentic' and 'revolutionary' folk.

INTERACTIONS BETWEEN TOWN AND COUNTRY

Activists' imaginings made the countryside seem like a natural home for protest, but the reality of life in the rural world was often different. The

---

[34] '[...] zu einem (ansatzweise) Betroffenen'. Internationale Jugendgemeinschaftsdienste (AG Umwelt), 'Industriealisierung [sic] — Kernkraftwerke — Umweltgefährdung', brochure, approx. 80 pp., 1979, PapierTiger, Wyhl-Broschüren, p. 3.

[35] See Susanne Schregel, *Atomkrieg vor der Wohnungstür* (2011), pp. 61–7.

[36] [Eric] 'Kid' Marty, 'L'évolutionnisme selon la zone', *Casse-Noix*, no. 6 (July 1977), p. 3.

one-sided, positive image activists constructed of the countryside frequently gave rise to misunderstandings and problems. It nevertheless persisted because it served the ends of both locals and outsiders, who played up the rurality of protest for the respective purposes of asserting control within the movement and harnessing the legitimacy of perceived 'localness'. Images of tractor demonstrations and country women knitting on illegally occupied land aroused far more sympathy than the by then hackneyed image of 'student protesters' rioting in the streets.[37] In their actual interactions, anti-nuclear activists from small country towns and big cities sometimes found it difficult to get along, though when they did cooperate successfully, it could have a powerful, mutual impact. This section will identify some of the difficulties that arose when activists from these different backgrounds worked together, how they overcame them, and how their interactions changed them.

A rural world that outsiders saw exclusively in positive terms was clearly not one that they understood well. Those who expected peasants to be ripe for a *jacquerie* were often surprised to find them fulfilling the old stereotype of the god-fearing farmer instead. According to the anonymous group of 'long marchers' who went to Bretagne in 1970, religion was 'a problem revelatory of many others' because it demonstrated a mismatch of expectations. Communist and other left-wing militants were inclined to dismiss religion as an obstacle to protest organizing, which blinded them to the ways in which it structured local identities, daily life, and social activity in rural communities. For example, 'long marchers' were surprised to discover that it was an arm of the church, the Jeunesse Agricole Catholique (JAC), that had provided left-wing peasants with their first experiences of organization and activism. This was the case, for example, for Paul Lepoittevin (b. 1945), a farmer from Normandie who says the JAC was 'what politicized me' (even though he eventually broke with the church). Paul went on to serve as a representative of the Marxist-friendly Paysans-Travailleurs (PT) trade union on various organizing committees for protests against the nuclear power plant in Flamanville.[38]

Even outside activists who were themselves religious sometimes failed to understand religion's centrality in village life. Peter Modler (b. 1955)

---

[37] The label 'student protesters' itself is grossly misleading, as several historians of May '68 have argued. See Érik Neveu, 'Trajectoires', in *Mai–Juin 68*, edited by Dominique Damamme et al. (2008), p. 307; Xavier Vigna and Michelle Zancarini-Fournel, 'Rencontres improbables', *Vingtième siècle* 101, no. 1 (2009), p. 164; Michelle Zancarini-Fournel, *Moment 68* (2008), p. 202.

[38] Centre d'action paysanne, *Mouvement de la jeunesse*, pp. 15–16; Paul Lepoittevin, interview with the author, Tollevast, 23 September 2010. On religion in rural life, see Mendras, *Fin des paysans*, p. 79; Alain Corbin, *Les Cloches de la terre* (1994).

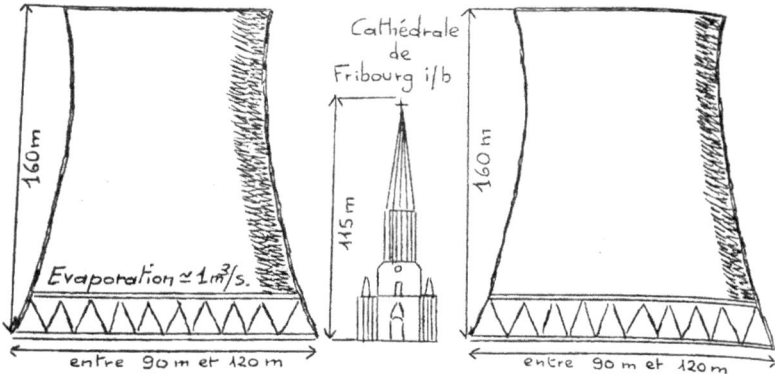

Fig. 4.3. Comparison of the respective heights of the Freiburg cathedral and cooling towers for the planned nuclear power station in Breisach (here in French translation). Reproduced by permission of Jean-Jacques Rettig.[39]

was a member of the non-violent action group Gewaltfreie Aktion Freiburg (GAF) who studied theology and met with local activists from Wyhl for Bible study sessions. He remembers his epiphany at learning that rural anti-nuclear activists did not hold formal meetings every Thursday night like the GAF: they simply met informally after church on Sunday, where the whole town would see each other anyway. (Since members of these small-town groups ran into each other and chatted throughout the week, major decisions could be finalized in a short meeting that took place between the time that church services ended and lunch began.)[40] Underestimating the importance of religion in rural communities could also deprive outside activists of a powerful mobilizing tool. In Breisach along the Franco-German border, rural activists gathering signatures for a petition against a nuclear project appealed to their neighbours' religious sensibilities with a drawn-to-scale diagram that showed the future cooling towers dwarfing a nearby church tower (see Fig. 4.3); they eventually collected more than 65,000 signatures. As construction began on the Marckolsheim chemical plant in late 1974, the local parish drummed up support for the site occupation, condemning environmental pollution in the church bulletin. However, more traditional condemnations still applied: subsequent issues addressed abortion as a symptom of 'pollution of the soul' and

---

[39] 'Pollution provoquée par les tours de refroidissement', *Ionix*, no. 5 (June 1973), p. 14.

[40] Peter Modler, interview with the author, Amoltern, 21 April 2010.

presented a side-by-side comparison of Jesus Christ and Karl Marx, predictably unflattering to the latter.[41] Religion could be mobilized for protest, but its adherents might remain hostile towards, and alien to, many left-wing activists who rejected it as the opiate of the masses.

At every site, local activists were treated as the driving force, the authentic salt of the earth who knew instinctively how to rebel. Peter Modler felt that local activists had a 'much more practical intelligence' than any of the outsiders. Whereas members of his own non-violent group risked life and limb blocking construction equipment in Wyhl with their bodies, the locals simply offered the construction workers a drink (of alcohol) and used the opportunity to discreetly remove the keys from bulldozers and cranes.[42] The legend of peasant wisdom in matters of protest was not isolated to any one site. In Gorleben too, stories were told of hard-drinking farmers 'doing it right' by playing cards in a bar to wait out a police ultimatum instead of debating the appropriate action strategy in the freezing cold as their camping supporters did.[43] Whatever fundamental differences were generally imputed to country folk and their outside supporters, Walter Moßmann argues that protest was one activity capable of bringing out the 'natural talents' of individual participants, especially housewives who had not previously been active in the public sphere.[44]

However, the high esteem in which urban activists held their rural comrades could also be misleading. Exceptionally clever or not, the farmers and rural people who became engaged in anti-nuclear protest generally had no special training for activism.[45] For the most part, they were ordinary people who invested time and energy as they could to understand a difficult issue that affected them personally. Protest calendars did not necessarily align well with the schedule of everyday, rural life. Marlene Reimers (b. 1938), a farmer's wife in Brokdorf, recalled how anti-nuclear activists from Hamburg would come to her home and discuss strategy the entire night, 'and then I had to get up at five o'clock!'[46] Things were similar for Paul Lepoittevin, whose JAC and PT trade union experience might have made him seem like an ideal protester in the struggle against the Flamanville reactor, located a mere 20 kilometres from his home. Yet he was unable to take part in either the site occupation

---

[41] *Le Lien du Ried* (October 1974–February 1975).   [42] Modler, interview.

[43] Wolfgang Ehmke, *Zwischenschritte* (1987), p. 51.

[44] Walter Moßmann, interview with the author, Freiburg, 1 April 2010.

[45] Gilles Simon has developed this argument more fully in his book on the political *apprentissage* that locals underwent. *Plogoff* (2010), p. 17.

[46] Albert Reimers and Marlene Reimers, joint interview with the author, Wewelsfleth, 21 August 2010.

there or any of the major national anti-nuclear protests that took place outside his home region. His work schedule simply did not permit it:

PL: Me, as a peasant . . . my job kept me busy and it's true that I didn't have that much availability. [. . .] But all the peasants were like me. [. . .] Work, you have to do it, you've got no choice. [. . .] I was never able to continuously participate in the occupation, but when [. . .] the police arrived [. . .] they called us for reinforcements to block [the site]. So I did dozens of trips to Flamanville like that, in emergencies. The people who had free time, a little more free time, they did the occupations. Then when there was a ruckus, they would call us.[47]

The belief in rural authenticity masked many of the strains that activism placed on rural communities, not to mention the extent to which local protest depended on outside support for success.

The mutual dependency of locals and outsiders could itself be a source of considerable tension, with each side feeling used by the other.[48] This problem was particularly acute during site occupations, such as the one that took place in Wyhl over a period of seven months. Most of the long-term occupants (*Dauerplatzbesetzer*) came from outside the local community and nearly all were students or unemployed youth. They thus had few resources of their own other than time, which they were free to devote to continuously occupying space. Many were 'long-haired and unwashed' (after a couple of nights of camping—at the latest), characteristics which did not endear them to a relatively closed rural community with its own sense of order.[49] On the occupied site, local women stepped in to establish 'a more ordered life for the site occupants', keeping things clean, preparing and distributing food, and giving the occupation some semblance of respectability in the eyes of the town population and the media. Their intervention was as much an assertion of local control over the protest's image as it was a kindly gesture of solidarity.[50] Nevertheless, the squatters were dependent on these provisions and could offer nothing concrete in return, only their time, labour, and gratitude. As a result, local opinion was divided over the site occupation: 'some explain that the occupants

[47] Lepoittevin, interview.
[48] Fritz Storim, 'Hoffnung auf ein anderes Leben. Eine Bilanz des Widerstandes', in . . . *Und auch nicht anderswo!*, edited by Atom Express (1997), pp. 263–4.
[49] Wolfgang Sternstein, 'Alltag des Widerstands', in *Ökologiebewegung und ziviler Widerstand*, edited by Theodor Ebert et al. (1978), p. 42.
[50] Bernd Nössler and Margret de Witt, eds, *Kein Kernkraftwerk in Wyhl* (1976), p. 202. These ideas are further developed, and some closely related quotes cited, in Jens Ivo Engels, 'Women of Wyhl', in *Le démon moderne*, edited by Christoph Bernhardt and Geneviève Massard-Guilbaud (2002).

helped them with the harvest, others [tell] much more that they had women from the area cook for them in the camp and generally were catered to by the people from the initiatives'.[51] The squatters resented the notion that they were layabouts (*Gammler*) sponging off the community's generosity, especially given that townspeople, busy with their own jobs, were in no position to assure a round-the-clock occupation themselves. One edition of the squatter-produced newspaper *Was Wir Wollen* attempted to dispel this negative image by describing squatters' daily routines on the site: they staffed German- and French-language information stands, built and repaired huts, occasionally worked as farmhands, and performed night watch duty. The authors concluded by saying, 'We hope now that the population has a picture of the site occupants and [recognizes] that we don't just eat and loaf around on the site, but that we really do [our part] so that the nuclear power plant in Wyhl will not be built.'[52] Even outside the context of site occupations, rural activists needed committed outsiders in order to attract attention to their issues, and outsiders needed support from the local community to make protest work. The extent to which they established a symbiotic relationship or saw one another as parasites could decide how effective protest was at a given site.

How well locals and outsiders got along with one another often depended heavily on how outside activists approached the rural community. Earlier in the decade, 'long marchers' seeking to revolutionize the countryside had noted the importance of 'starting from the questions that the masses pose and not from the answers we have already found'.[53] If contact between urban and rural activists was to have any impact, outsiders would have to see the rural world as it really was and not how they imagined it to be. The peasant founder of the PT trade union, Bernard Lambert, addressed such issues in his 1970 book, *Les Paysans dans la lutte des classes*.[54] Lambert's deliberate use of Marxist language to describe the problems of small farmers earned him the respect of the radical left and helped mobilize their support for PT. He wrote that contact between 'students' and peasants was 'necessary [...,] desirable, useful' but also added that 'if students seek, via these contacts, to teach peasants the brand

[51] 'Mehr Demokratie überhaupt', p. 16.
[52] 'Tagesablauf der ständigen Platzbesetzer', *WWW*, no. 5 (undated [1975]), p. 9.
[53] Centre d'action paysanne, *Mouvement de la jeunesse*, pp. 23–4.
[54] Bernard Lambert helped organize the first major rally on the Larzac in 1973 and arranged the symbolic union of that struggle with that of the striking workers of the LIP watch factory in Besançon. The Paysans-Travailleurs were a predecessor to the present-day Confédération paysanne, whose well-known former speaker José Bové ran for president in 2007 (unsuccessfully) and for the European Parliament in 2009 (successfully). See also Jean-Philippe Martin, *Nouvelle gauche paysanne* (2005); Robert Gildea and Andrew Tompkins, 'The Transnational in the Local', *Journal of Contemporary History* (2015).

new theories they've just discovered to direct popular, mass struggle, it would be better for them to stay home'.[55] Criticisms like this were especially directed at *K-Gruppen* and *gauchistes*, whose trained cadres had little difficulty dominating discussions with rural people who were completely new to activism.[56] However, another problem of approach lurked just below the surface. Both for practical reasons and as a consequence of the positive, media-resonant construction of the 'rural' in this time period, it became an unwritten rule of the anti-nuclear movement that authority emanated from the locals and that other anti-nuclear activists should (at least outwardly) submit to their will.

In a decade when anti-authoritarianism ran high, certain activists committed to the anti-nuclear cause chafed under this restriction and it could be difficult to find a balance. However, even radical activists found local participation too important to go without. For example, autonomist activists from Hamburg and Bremen were frequently frustrated by the Brokdorf population's unwillingness to take a radical stance. When a sign saying 'Here the population blocks Brokdorf power plant' had to be replaced,[57] locals rejected autonomist proposals for a sign stressing illegal struggle (an idea they felt unable to sell to their neighbours) or showing a fist raised in anger (one farmer claimed this was 'an international symbol of communists'). Autonomist activists later wrote that 'Some of us were rather disappointed by this development, but in the end found that shared action was too important to fail because of the difficulties described.'[58] This cooperation formed the basis of the movement and had a number of benefits. Indeed, the need to convince authoritative, authentic locals to go along with a particular protest strategy even provided fertilizer for what activists often described as 'grassroots democracy'. When they discussed 'oppositions of opinion and differences in lifestyle (for example city and country)' openly, it was possible for activists to reduce the 'prejudices [...] and unconscious fears of "conservatives" and "liberals" towards "leftists" and "communists", of "moderates" towards "radicals" and vice versa'.[59] For left-leaning outsiders, such open discussions showed that 'one could talk to CDU people, one could have a different opinion—we also

[55] Bernard Lambert, *Paysans dans la lutte* (1970), p. 160. This text was also published in German as Bernard Lambert, *Bauern im Klassenkampf* (1971).

[56] Sternstein, 'Alltag des Widerstands', p. 42.

[57] Being made of sturdy wood, demonstrators had taken the sign down in February 1981 and used it as a plank to cross the ditch in front of the site's perimeter fence.

[58] 'Das Schild am Bauplatz in Brokdorf. Zur Auseinandersitzung mit den AKW-Gegnern vor Ort', *Anti-AKW-Telegramm*, no. 24 (September 1981), pp. 5–6.

[59] Christoph Büchele et al., *Der Widerstand* (1982), pp. 49–50.

had fights!—but we were together in this struggle'.[60] By approaching rural people in the right way, outsiders could not only overcome tensions within the movement, they could construct their movement in line with their ideals.

A further factor fostering cooperation within the movement was the presence of intermediaries. Often, these were rural individuals who connected with outsiders on account of their similar age, political perspective, or marginal status. In Wyhl, Roland Burkhart (b. 1956) was able to play such a role because he was both a native of the Kaiserstuhl region and a student in Freiburg. Annemarie Sacherer (1943–93), a young housewife at the time of the Wyhl protests, connected particularly well with feminist students.[61] In France, PT members had a reputation for radicalism, making them a magnet for some outside activists: the farmer Paul Lepoittevin near Flamanville welcomed Maoist 'long marchers' in the early 1970s and anti-nuclear activists later in the decade.[62] The young farmer Heinrich Voß (b. 1951) played a similar role in Brokdorf, facilitating communication between his neighbours and their radical supporters— and changing his community in the process. During the late 1960s, Heinrich (like Jean-Jacques Rettig in Alsace[63]) had felt an emotional affinity with the student movement, but did not follow it closely. He remembers his own small town at the time as 'a narrow, peasant society with strict control' that he experienced as 'cramped and oppressive'. Perhaps because of this, he connected well with many of the young, left-leaning activists who came to Brokdorf from Hamburg and Bremen. Reflecting on the protests that took place in Brokdorf in the late 1970s, Heinrich says the result is positive. 'It forced open a lot of the confinement [*Enge*] here.'[64] By bridging the divide between his own community and outside activists, Heinrich was able to create a more conducive social environment for himself at home.

At other sites, outsiders themselves played a bridging role between rural anti-nuclear activists and their supporters. At the protests in Marckolsheim (Alsace) and Wyhl (Baden), speaking ability in the region's local dialect became a major marker of inclusion or exclusion in the local movement, and further knowledge of both French and German could

---

[60] CP in Conny Baade and Christian Petty, joint interview with the author, St-Jean-de-Buèges, 19 September 2010. See also Storim, 'Hoffnung auf ein anderes Leben. Eine Bilanz des Widerstandes', pp. 261–4.

[61] Ulla Bonczek, interview with the author, Freiburg, 26 April 2010; Nina Gladitz, interview with the author, Berlin, 2 June 2010.

[62] Lepoittevin, interview.   [63] See Chapter 2.

[64] Heinrich Voß and Christine Scheer, joint interview with the author, Wewelsfleth, 21 August 2010.

be a major asset. On the basis of their trilingual backgrounds, several students and other residents of the city of Freiburg like Walter Moßmann, Conny Baade, and Peter Modler were able to gain the respect of the rural Kaiserstuhl residents and negotiate between town and country. Certain Alsatian activists like Marie-Reine Haug, Raymond Schirmer, and Jean-Jacques Rettig played an even more important role: their language skills and non-violent political orientation earned them acceptance among rural activists on the German side of the border; as French citizens (for whom the Communist Party was a fixture of the establishment), they also had a more relaxed relationship to the political left and were thus well positioned to mediate between different political constituencies.[65] As so often within this broad-based social movement, individuals in liminal positions played a critical role in shaping the interactions between city and country.

Sometimes, the interactions between rural protesters and their outside counterparts had lasting consequences. In many cases, they strengthened activists' desires to escape the confines of their own ways of life—be they urban *or* rural. As with activists' comparisons between France and West Germany, the grass was usually greener on the other side. A flyer inviting activists to a 'city–country meeting' in 'Rest-Berlin' (i.e. West Berlin) amply demonstrates this. One section of the flyer is written from the perspective of an urban activist who wants to get 'out of the scene, out of the big city, out into the country!' Protest in the city has become frustrating to the point where she says 'there's nothing that can be done against the repression here anyway, politically we can't gain a foothold'. Her counterpart in the countryside sees things from the exact opposite perspective and wants to get away 'from the isolation, from the small-town stuffiness, into the city!' The way she sees it, 'there's nothing that can be done against reaction[aries] here anyway, the ruling power is firmly cemented in people's behaviour'. Placed alongside one another, the activist 'scene' in the city and the atmosphere of a small town could seem, in spite of fundamental differences, equally narrow.[66]

Moving across the divide between them allowed some people to find a personal equilibrium, as in the case of Dieter Halbach. Born in West Berlin in 1953, he describes his home city as 'a kind of ghetto, so to speak, where individual scenes were in turn separated from one another'. The special status of West Berlin as an 'island' surrounded by East Germany,

---

[65] Jean-Jacques Rettig, interview with the author, Fréconrupt, 19 April 2010; Sternstein, 'Alltag des Widerstands', p. 44.

[66] Stadt-Land-Büro, 'Stadt-Land-Treffen in Berlin', IISG, World Information Service on Energy Amsterdam, WISE 7.

linked to West Germany but not subject to its military service require-
ments, made the city a magnet for young people who felt marginal in one
way or another and who found like-minded others within urban subcul-
tures. Dieter became involved in anti-nuclear activism in West Berlin and
frequently travelled to West Germany to attend protests in Brokdorf,
Grohnde, and elsewhere. He also felt drawn to the hippie scene and
hitchhiked around Europe, staying in rural communes in southern
France, Denmark, the Netherlands, and elsewhere.[67] Over the course of
the decade, he became increasingly dissatisfied both with life in the city
and with the 'nuclear battle tourism' of the movement. After attending the
disastrous 1977 Malville protest, Dieter went to Gorleben, where he felt
'like a refugee in search of a home [*Heimat*]'.[68]

> DH: I experienced [. . .] the feeling of home, attachment [. . .] that
> people [there had], and also the social organism of village life [. . .]
> As a sort of escaped big city kid from Berlin, [. . .] I valued this
> home, even though it wasn't mine. And here, I met people who had
> a home, and who simultaneously opened up because of the [nuclear]
> threat [. . .] I was invited into bourgeois houses and [. . . we] had
> tools from the local carpenter's workshop practically put in front of
> us and were instructed on how one [builds] a hut, which we then
> built on the playground. The handicraft work, that was always an
> [. . .] important thing for me as a child of intellectuals, so to speak.

In Gorleben, Dieter was able not only to find the 'natural space and
mixing of scenes' that he felt West Berlin lacked, he worked to foster ties
between the city and the countryside.[69] He helped found a cooperative in
Berlin which purchased food from communes in the Wendland, and
contributed to the proliferation of Gorleben-Freundeskreise in cities
across Germany. Similar to the network of Comités Larzac in France,
these allowed local and outside activists to build trust in one another and
develop creative, new action strategies like the ones that culminated in the
spectacular non-violent occupation of Tiefbohrstelle 1004 in 1980.[70]
Since 1977, he has lived in various places, but always with a 'second
residence in Gorleben'.[71] Anti-nuclear activism was thus something that
helped Dieter transform himself and find a place of his own somewhere
between the urban and the rural.

---

[67] Dieter Halbach, interview with the author, via telephone, 23 August 2010.
[68] Dieter Halbach and Gerd Panzer, *Zwischen Gorleben & Stadtleben* (1980), p. 58.
[69] Halbach, interview.   [70] See Chapter 5.
[71] Dieter Halbach, 'Hand in Hand', http://gemeinschaftsberatung.de/dieter-halbach/
(accessed 9 December 2015).

Markus Mohr's activist experiences led him to move in the opposite direction. Born in 1962 in a small town in Schleswig-Holstein, he has felt close to the radical left since adolescence. In the late 1970s, he was thus naturally drawn to the local anti-nuclear initiative, the Bürgerinitiative Umweltschutz Unterelbe (BUU), which served as 'a repository [*Sammelbecken*] of all possible left radicals' at the time. The outward signs and styles of rural and urban radicalism were different, though, or they were at least perceived to be so. Markus recalls growing his hair long, which was 'a kind of protest in the country, but already over with in the cities'.[72] Around the same time, urban activists from Hamburg who set up an 'anti-nuclear village' on land destined for the Grohnde nuclear power plant made a point of installing a 'village barbershop' on the site, where they demonstratively cut their hair 'in order to reduce the local citizens' fears of "long-haired" types'.[73] There were also other differences between rural and urban activism that were more significant, especially insofar as they affected how activism worked. In the countryside, Markus says, the distinctions between various left-wing tendencies meant little:

MM: In provincial areas, that is [outside] big cities, you're happy to [find] any kind of group. And that means you gather everyone you can. In the big cities, you have more separation because the possibilities are completely different. So you can do more to support your [particular] position [. . .] As a leftist in the country, you had—and have even today—[. . .] to survive somehow. And you're happy to find any kind of like-minded people at all, so you don't meticulously ask what position they exactly represent.[74]

What seemed to Dieter Halbach to be a positive, rustic spirit of cooperation could in fact feel like a necessity born of desperation. For someone who grew up in the country, the urban political scene could seem more attractive by contrast. Markus himself eventually left the countryside for the city. After participating in a 1981 demonstration in Brokdorf where violence occurred, Markus was accused of attacking a policeman. Though some in his hometown supported him, Markus was vilified in the national and regional press and felt increasingly stigmatized. During the ensuing legal battle, autonomist protesters from Hamburg and Bremen, who did

---

[72] Markus Mohr, interview with the author, Hamburg, 19 August 2010.
[73] Günter Zint et al., *Atomkraft*, 2nd edn (1979). The 'Anti-Atom-Dorf Grohnde' lasted from 13 June to 22 August 1977. See Ermittlungsausschuss BBA Bremen, „"Den Wurfanker werfen wir in die Zukunft und Zukunft heißt nie wieder Zäune"', brochure, 210 pp., 1978, PapierTiger, 'Grohnde, Gronau, Euko [. . .]' Binder, pp. 21–30.
[74] Mohr, interview.

prison solidarity work as part of their campaign against the criminalization of anti-nuclear protest, stepped in to help, donating to his legal fight, publishing flyers with information about his trial, and organizing protests to support him. After his trial, Markus moved to Bremen, where he participated in the local protest scene. In the mid-1980s, he moved to West Berlin, where he 'noticed that all sorts of things were going on' politically, things he 'hadn't known on that scale' during his previous life in the countryside. A self-described 'critical academic', he now lives in Hamburg and publishes on left-wing politics.[75]

Interactions between urban and rural anti-nuclear activists had perhaps the greatest impact on local activists who continued to live in the countryside. Marie-Jo Putinier recalls how participation in the anti-nuclear movement transformed her politics, her relationships, and her life. Born in 1937, she grew up in the small town of Bouvesse-Quirieu near Malville, an isolated community with 'no distractions' where she lived 'a very narrow life'. As the oldest daughter in a farming family, she was 'the maid for everything and for everyone', a role that her parents continued to impose on her even after she had married and moved in with her husband, whose family lived next door.[76] Describing the political climate in Bouvesse, she compared it to the fictional 'Little World of Don Camillo', a small, provincial town where the arch-conservative Catholic priest and his nemesis, the Communist mayor, constantly undermined one another as they vied for the village's sympathies.[77] Marie-Jo's parents were 'almost far right' in their politics and she claims to have followed their lead until well into adulthood. 'And then', she says, 'I turned around. [I] changed sides.' This did not mean a dramatic leap from Catholicism to Communism, but rather a more modest (yet still significant) repositioning toward centre-left politics. Today, Marie-Jo is a member of the Parti Socialiste, the CFDT trade union, and various local environmental groups. Unlike for many of her urban counterparts, her political awakening was unconnected to May 1968, which more or less passed her (and Bouvesse) by. 'I did my '68 in

---

[75] Mohr, interview. See Markus Mohr, *Alles wie geplant. Die katastrophale Industrialisierung von Brunsbüttel/Unterelbe* (1985); Markus Mohr, *Gewerkschaften im Atomkonflikt* (2001); Sebastian Haunss and Markus Mohr, 'Autonomen und die anti-deutsche Frage', in *„Sie warn die Antideutschesten der deutschen Linken"*, edited by Gerhard Hanloser (2004); Markus Mohr and Hartmut Rübner, *Gegnerbestimmung* (2010). He has also published numerous articles and books pseudonymously.

[76] Putinier, interview.

[77] Several of the novels by Giovanni Guareschi about these two characters were made into films starring the French actor Fernandel. Julien Duvivier et al., *Le petit monde de don Camillo*, 1952, Italy/France, 102 mins. Jean-Jacques Rettig also referred to these two characters (in positive terms) to describe the communist Balthasar Ehret and the wealthy miller Siegfried Göpper in Wyhl.

'76, in '77', when the major protests against the FBR at Malville took place. Her first encounter, in July 1976, with the outside anti-nuclear activists who sought to raise local consciousness through a peaceful site occupation was perhaps more disruptive than anything else.[78]

> MJP: In this area, in these small towns where people had never seen anything but their next-door neighbour, all of a sudden, this mass of people arrived—young people with long hair [. . .] like Wood-stock, but people [here] didn't know that even existed! Naked breasts, living in the wild, and all that. [. . .] It was shocking! It was really destabilizing [. . .] but it was nice! [. . .] It was like a spectacle.

Through these people, Marie-Jo says she discovered new things, opened herself up, and broke with the closed-mindedness of her parents. After being sensitized to the issue of nuclear power, she became involved with the local Comité Malville. As its secretary, she took on political responsibilities that were new for her and which placed her at the centre of a major conflict within the local community. The experience changed her life, in ways that were both positive and negative:

> MJP: Well, we had to create an association, I was the secretary. I had the telephone, it never stopped ringing at home. We had to travel to go see lawyers [. . .] It was kind of hell. *[Pointing to her husband]* Him, he had a hard time of it. [. . .] It was invasive. But on the other hand, I met so many interesting people. Including locally, with our own neighbours [. . .] the neighbours who got involved like me [. . .] the bonds really strengthened between people.

In the face of all of these changes, Marie-Jo began to pose fundamental questions about her role as a woman in her family and community. Activism brought rural women like her into the public spotlight for the first time. Many responded by remaining very much within traditional women's spheres, even consciously exploiting perceptions of female respectability in order to assert local control or to advance the anti-nuclear cause.[79] In this sense, they were like women in earlier decades of the post-war period, who did not necessarily contest traditional gendered divisions of labour, but who nevertheless asserted themselves in new ways within them.[80] This was not feminism, but for women like Marie-Jo, it was a step towards personal emancipation. In her case, protest also brought her into

---

[78] Putinier, interview.   [79] Engels, 'Women of Wyhl'.
[80] Martin Conway, 'Western Europe's Democratic Age', *Contemporary European History* 13, no. 1 (2004), pp. 84–5.

contact with feminists from Geneva and other nearby cities, who helped her go a step further.

> MJP: And the feminist movement made me understand that every-
> thing I had in me that revolted but [where] I just said 'Oh, well'
> and went along with it—that I was right. [...] I had to bring
> out what was inside of me! I didn't have to be led around like
> that. [I needed] to be myself! Whereas before, my religious and
> family culture had been to serve others. But me, I didn't exist.
> [...] So that comforted me and [... enabled] the stands that
> I dared to take afterward. Without being a feminist to the
> extreme I'd say, but still quite a step.

Anti-nuclear activism shook up life in the countryside. Even in a place like Malville, which is remembered primarily for the tragic violence that occurred there in 1977, local participants found their lives transformed in positive ways. Marie-Jo Putinier does not regret her involvement in activism, even if it was sometimes very difficult.

> MJP: And afterward, I met people—really, nuclear [power] has
> been the main thread running through my life [*le fil con-
> ducteur de ma vie*], I tell you—afterward, I met people who
> I had put up who introduced me to other people. [...]
> AT: When you think back on this period [...] how do you assess it?
> MJP: It was the chance of my life. And that's what I always say
> [...] It allowed me to open up to a lot of—to open up to
> myself too! If that hadn't happened [...] what would my life
> have been? I have a hard time answering. *[MJP laughs.]* No,
> no, it was the chance of my life [...] I can't say that to
> everyone, not everyone understands. I think the best friends
> that we've kept [...] are the friends who come from that
> [... sometimes] in indirect ways. They've all been wonderful
> friends—who we wouldn't have found in the nearby area.
> Who we wouldn't have discovered.[81]

Anti-nuclear activism was a venue for interactions between people from very different backgrounds. Such encounters could be powerful, opening up new perspectives to individuals from the city or the country and even to whole communities. For Marie-Jo and others like her, the changes that activism induced in her have long outlived the period of active protest.

---

[81] Putinier, interview.

RURAL SPACE AND THE
POSSIBILITIES OF PROTEST

A defining characteristic of the anti-nuclear movement was that the inter-actions that it fostered between city and country people mostly took place on the home turf of the latter. Protest in the countryside presented different opportunities by virtue of the composition of rural space, allowing activists to use the rural environment and its symbols to amplify the resonance of their protest. However, while rural people were able to exploit the nature of their space with relative ease, outside activists were not always as comfort-able within it. This section will explore the use of rural space by activists in terms of both the advantages and disadvantages it created.

The rural environment presented a number of possibilities for anti-nuclear activists to take advantage of rustic symbols in order to increase the resonance of their protest. Perhaps some of the most original examples of this were the boat protests that took place from time to time along rivers such as the Elbe and Rhine. On one occasion, fishermen concerned about the nuclear power plant at Brokdorf organized a protest in which they painted the sails of their fishing trawlers with anti-nuclear slogans ('Elbe fishers' existence threatened by nuclear power and its industry') and sailed up and down the river.[82] By hitching protest to the tools of their trade, they asserted unmistakeably their authenticity as directly affected locals. Near Wyhl, fishermen from Weisweil hosted a similar protest in the middle of the Rhine forest, floating downstream in a dozen small, flat boats with anti-nuclear banners held aloft. By virtue of their location in rural space, protests like this one were held for a relatively small audience. Their impact derived not from the number of demonstrators or onlookers they attracted (as a typical march through an urban population centre might[83]), but rather from the resonance of their symbolism. It should thus come as no surprise that pictures of the small-scale Wyhl boat demonstration were reprinted in numerous anti-nuclear publications throughout the 1970s.[84]

The same was true, to an even larger extent, for the semi-ceremonial rolling of tractors through towns near new nuclear sites. As Walter Moßmann's ironic comments about this 'symbol for militancy in the countryside' suggest, outside anti-nuclear activists greeted news of tractor demonstrations with particular enthusiasm. Activist media of

---

[82] Zint et al., *Atomkraft* (no page numbers).

[83] See Dieter Rucht, 'Sociology of Protest Marches', in *The Street as Stage*, edited by Matthias Reiss (2007).

[84] See Nössler and de Witt, *Kein Kernkraftwerk in Wyhl*, p. 39; Badisch-Elsässische Bürgerinitiativen, ed. *Die Lieder aus Wyhl* (1975), p. 1.

every political orientation consistently printed photos from tractor demonstrations next to anti-nuclear articles. However, such demonstrations
also served a function within the local community. Heinrich Voß
describes how one tractor demonstration in 1976, coming after several
months of protests in Brokdorf dominated by activists from outside the
community, was meant to bring local farmers together.

> HV: At the beginning of December, we had, for the first time, a real
> tractor demonstration—with only farmers, maybe even to give all
> the farmers here a chance to join in, without people from Hamburg
> being there [..., as] a kind of process of self-discovery. And
> we had a hundred tractors. It was winter, there was snow [...]
> And the day before this demonstration [...] the administrative
> court in Schleswig announced the construction halt. They said it
> [the nuclear power plant] couldn't be built any further. And—it's
> revealing—my first thought was, 'Shit, they want to ruin our
> tractor demonstration!' *[HV and AT laugh.]* Even though that
> was really a victory! [...] But it's true too, it was a reason. Because
> this tractor demonstration, they probably couldn't guess how it
> would turn out. So that was the final trigger, that they—with
> grounded arguments—imposed a halt on construction.[85]

Whether they had a direct impact on policy or not, tractor demonstrations
in the countryside were used for their potential to foster unity locally as
well as for their symbolic effect on audiences further afield.

Of course, tractor demonstrations did not take place only in the
small towns where their owners lived. These symbols of the rural world
were most powerful when placed in an incongruous, urban context. The
French farmers who fought against the expansion of a military camp on
the Larzac were masters of this kind of protest: in January 1973, they went
on their own 'long march' all the way from their homes in southern France
up to Paris, travelling most of the way in tractors; in 1978, they made the
same trip on foot and, in 1980, they came again, bringing sheep with
them and camping out under the Eiffel Tower. (*Libération* described the
1978 march, which was forced to march along the *Périphérique* ring road
without entering central Paris, as 'The Commune de Paris, but in reverse:
the *Versaillais* are inside and the people outside.'[86]) These Larzac actions

---

[85] HV in Voß and Scheer, joint interview.
[86] '« C'est la Commune de Paris, mais à l'envers »', *Libération*, 1 December 1978, p. 4.
This echoed Bernard Lambert's declaration on the Larzac in 1973: 'Jamais plus les paysans
ne seront des Versaillais. Jamais plus ils ne s'opposeront à ceux qui veulent changer cette
société.' *Larzac 73*, 1973, 48 mins (audio).

directly inspired anti-nuclear protests, such as the tractor journey that opponents of the planned nuclear waste disposal centre in Gorleben made in 1979 from Lüchow-Dannenberg to the federal state capital of Hannover.[87] Like the Larzac farmers before them, they built up momentum by going slowly, holding mini-demonstrations and information sessions in towns along the way.[88] Their arrival in Hannover—only days after the Three Mile Island nuclear accident in the United States—included a triumphal procession of tractors rolling behind a banner celebrating solidarity between anti-nuclear protesters in northern and southern Germany (see Fig. 4.4). By using urban space and rural symbols together to express the solidarity between local people from different protest sites, anti-nuclear activists highlighted the broad base of their movement and made it appear capable of transcending the differences between city and country, between different regions, and ultimately between different political perspectives.

The rural world also lent itself to more direct, practical use by activists. Indeed, rural space critically shaped the dominant form of anti-nuclear protest during the 1970s: the site occupation. A kind of extension of the sit-ins and go-ins of the 1960s and a rural adaptation of urban squatting (which ascended in parallel as a protest tactic), site occupations were a form of direct action that seemed uniquely effective in preventing the construction of unwanted nuclear sites. As the title of one book put it, occupation was appropriate, even necessary, 'because wishing didn't help'.[89] The phenomenal success of the early occupations in Marckolsheim (Alsace) and Wyhl (Baden) fuelled the use of this strategy elsewhere, though it became less effective as authorities adjusted their reactions. With various adaptations, activists attempted to copy the famous Marckolsheim/Wyhl model at almost every nuclear energy site. In France alone, occupations were planned, announced, or carried out at Braud-et-Saint-Louis, Cattenom, Creys-Malville, Flamanville, Gersteim, Gravelines, Heiteren, La Hague, and Paluel.[90] In Germany, major occupations were attempted at Brokdorf and Gorleben, with smaller ones in Grohnde, Kalkar, and numerous other places.

The strategy became more sophisticated over time. In Marckolsheim, a wooden 'Frendschaftshüs' ('friendship house' in local dialect) was hastily

---

[87] 'Gorleben–Larzac même combat', flyer for event at l'Hôpital du Larzac, 1 p., 10 September 1979, BM, IZ 62; Wolfgang Hertle, interview with the author, Hamburg, 22 July 2010.

[88] See, for example, *Albrecht, wir kommen*, 1979, 45 mins; Wendländische Filmkooperative, *Die Herren machen das selber, dass ihnen der arme Mann Feyndt wird*, 1979, 126 mins.

[89] Ingrid Müller-Münch et al., *Besetzung* (1981). The book includes an article on the Gorleben site occupation along with stories about urban squatting in Freiburg, Köln, Berlin, and Zürich.

[90] Based on a review of FNSP, 'L'énergie nucléaire en France de 1974 à mai 1981', collection of press clippings, 1972–81, Sciences Po, France 535/Archive 695–8.

Fig. 4.4. 'Wyhl greets Gorleben'. Reproduced by permission of Martin Schulte-Kellinghaus.[91]

constructed to host occasional meetings and serve as a symbol of the occupation. When many of the same activists travelled across the Rhine to protest in Wyhl, they built a more robust venue where concerts and information sessions could be held. The log cabin in Wyhl served as the

[91] Büchele et al., *Der Widerstand*, p. 134.

first home of the Volkshochschule Wyhler Wald, whose programme of educational and cultural events regularly brought locals and outsiders to the site.[92] Alsatian protesters who participated in both the Marckolsheim and Wyhl protests became increasingly professional in managing the logistics of a site occupation, erecting a new 'friendship house' within days of the installation of a weather observation tower at Gerstheim-Erstein and building another such cabin in front of an electricity tower in Heiteren (while the Gerstheim occupation was still ongoing).[93] West German activists expanded on this idea by setting up an 'anti-nuclear village' in Grohnde, which included several other temporary structures. The experience taught them lessons that would later prove valuable in Gorleben.[94] In 1977, activists there illegally built a playground on land earmarked for the planned 'nuclear park'. When the playground was threatened with demolition, an anti-authoritarian parenting group drew attention to it by awarding the playground its 'Red Elephant' prize for the year.[95] Three years later, a much larger protest took place in which Gorleben supporters (connected by a network that had grown out of the Gorleben-Freundeskreise) descended on the site as test drilling was about to take place. Over the course of several weeks, they set up a spectacular 'village' with dozens of buildings and towers, each constructed by groups that used the architecture and arrangement of space as a means of political expression. For example, a 'women's house' was built with outside walls made of empty glass bottles that helped regulate the temperature; coloured and clear bottles were arranged to form the female gender symbol (♀).[96] The squatters in Gorleben also openly mocked the West German state and humorously exploited the proximity to the East German border by setting up checkpoints at the entrance to the site and distributing 'passports' for their own 'Republik Freies Wendland'. (Activists in cities like West Berlin participated by setting up 'embassies' for the 'Republic'.[97]) On rural land in remote places, site occupation proved a wildly popular strategy because it subverted the spaces of protesters' political opponents

[92] Büchele et al., *Der Widerstand*, pp. 48–52.

[93] As Gerstheim had been indicated on a 1974 map of possible nuclear sites, the weather tower built by the French power company EDF was plausibly interpreted as a precursor to a potential nuclear power plant. In Wyhl as well, a weather observation tower was installed prior to construction. Nössler and de Witt, *Kein Kernkraftwerk in Wyhl*, p. 41; 'Mast-Besetzung in Heiteren', *WWW*, no. 5 (14 April 1977), p. 2.

[94] Günter Zint, ed., *RFW* (1980), pp. 138–9.

[95] 'gorleben. verleihung des roten elefanten', *Anti-AKW-Telegramm*, no. 10 (9 January 1978), p. 7.

[96] Zint, *RFW*, p. 124.

[97] 'besetzung der geplanten tiefbohrstelle „1004"', police telex, undated 1980, Bundesarchiv, B 106/107375.

while simultaneously providing a physical space for the representation of activists' own ideas.

One of the reasons such occupations were possible was because nuclear sites in the countryside naturally covered a large area and had many open spaces that made them difficult for police to defend. Taking over and holding onto such sites presented further opportunities for protesters to exploit characteristics of the rural world. Local populations usually knew the lie of the land better than police (and better than outside protesters). In Wyhl, participants at the 28,000-strong public rally in front of the construction site on 23 February 1975 were able to enter and occupy the power company's land because police were distracted by one hundred other anti-nuclear activists who had sneaked up behind the site through the forest.[98] Once the protesters had successfully occupied the space, local activists set up sentries on the borders of their town and barricaded the few streets leading to the construction site using their own farming tools, to powerful symbolic effect. According to Walter Moßmann, local farmers at the barricades stood ready to defend their land with manure spray hoses (a 'parody' of police water cannon), which dramatically exemplified the nature of their struggle: 'The farmers deal with the smell every day. It belongs to their work. It only bothers strangers who have no business here.'[99] In Wyhl, the olfactory assault remained hypothetical, as these 'weapons' were never put to use. In Plogoff on the other hand, the local population deployed an arsenal of filth to oppose the police presence in their town during the six-week EUP. At night, before police escorted the *Mairies annexes* into town on weekdays, protesters built barricades and dumped 'car frames, rocks, human and animal excrement, dead animals, domestic waste, etc.' on the positions police would take up the following morning.[100] In doing so, local protesters asserted control over 'their' space. The Plogoff protesters also employed pastoral symbolism as they laid claim to the power company's land. Copying an idea that had already been tried out on the Larzac, they built a barn illegally (without a permit) on the site and then stocked it with sheep on loan from the farmers of the Larzac. Like the Wyhl–Gorleben link, the demonstrative solidarity between Plogoff and the Larzac created the impression of a unified opposition to state projects in the rural world.

In spite of these advantages, the countryside as a space of protest was not one to which everyone adapted easily; the different structure of rural

---

[98] Nössler and de Witt, *Kein Kernkraftwerk in Wyhl*, pp. 110–11.

[99] Moßmann, 'Der lange Marsch', p. 9. Hamburg activists who sabotaged offices to the local power company likewise dumped manure there 'to express the relationship between resistance in the city and in the country'. AKPÖ, *Bilanz und Perspektiven* (1978), pp. 114–15.

[100] RG, 'Réflexions sur l'Enquête d'Utilité Publique', March 1980, AD Finistère, 1235 W 24.

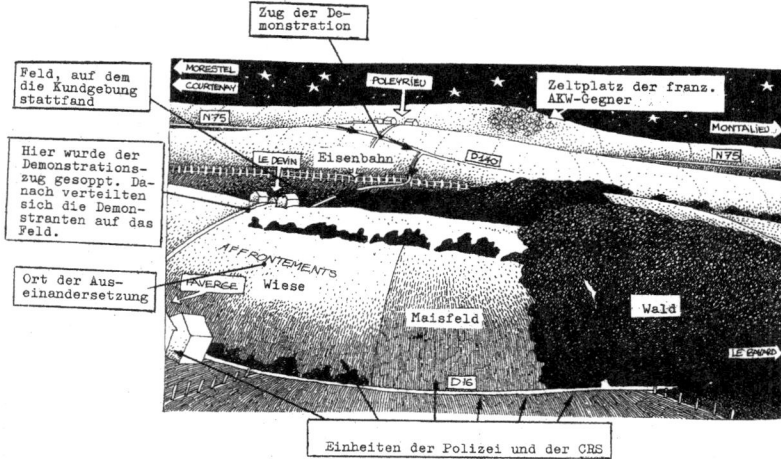

Fig. 4.5. Area of the 1977 Malville demonstration.[101] This drawing shows (with arrows) the last segment of the long route demonstrators followed toward Malville before they encountered heavily armed police (lined up along the D16) near the hamlet of Faverges. Unable to continue marching along the roads, demonstrators spread out onto neighbouring fields (marked 'Affrontements'/'Wiese'), where violent altercations with authorities ensued. Those fleeing could not turn back along the road and were forced to climb up hills or trample through the swampy forest ('Wald'). Reproduced by permission of Jean Caillon, Jean-Louis Soulié, and Georges Didier.

space could work to the disadvantage of protesters as well as police. This was especially true at the international demonstration against the FBR in Malville. Though some local activists were present, the vast majority of demonstrators came from outside the region, including from urban centres near and far (Lyon, Grenoble, Paris), from other protest sites (the Larzac as well as sites in Alsace, Bretagne, Bourgogne, etc.), and from outside the country (nearby Geneva or more distant West German cities such as Frankfurt, Hamburg, or West Berlin). The small size of the towns near the site meant that there was little infrastructure to welcome the droves of protesters who came for the event. The march itself was particularly arduous, winding through miles of country roads, past fields and swamps, across a terrain that only a small fraction of the tens of thousands present would have known well. (See Fig. 4.5.) To make matters worse, the demonstration occurred in the midst of a torrential

---

[101] Original artwork created by Jean Caillon and printed alongside the article 'Malville : hiver précoce', *GO/CNV*, no. 169 (4 August 1977), p. 2. This modified version taken from Gewerkschaft Erziehung und Wissenschaft, *Kriminalisierung* (1977), p. 31.

downpour that lasted for days and which transformed the terrain into a quagmire.[102] Authorities did what they could to exacerbate demonstrators' difficulties. For the weekend of the protest, the prefect of Isère banned all automobile traffic and parking within a 6-kilometre radius of the site, thereby 'obliging the aggressors to undertake long marches on foot in the rain, transporting their equipment'.[103] Anyone who wanted to engage in street fighting in the fields would find himself or herself at a sore disadvantage against the heavily armed police that had been stationed at the site for days. So too would all those who came only to protest against an expensive, plutonium-producing facility that they considered the central and most dangerous element of an undesirable 'nuclear society'.

The rural milieu of the Malville protest contributed a great deal to the reigning atmosphere of confusion. Suzanne d'Hernies and Bernard Dréano were two experienced demonstrators from Paris who attended the protest in Malville. Suzanne described how the practice of protest could be bewilderingly different out in the countryside.

> SDH: When you're at a demonstration in Paris, you've got the street, which is like a corridor. You know you have a goal there, you know that you've got fifteen, ten, three, two blocks of houses and you know that the goal is at this one here. But when you're in the countryside, on a sunken lane, with mud up to here [...] you have no realization that the target is there. It was a different context. Malville was a demonstration of urban people in the countryside—lost in the countryside—with unorganized [activists]. And the worst thing is that neither the place, nor the weather, nor the people help you.[104]

Suzanne and Bernard were members of the Organisation Communiste des Travailleurs (OCT), which shared the difficult task of crowd control with the Ligue Communiste Révolutionnaire and other radical left organizations that were experienced in the art of protest. However, anti-nuclear protest and the rural milieu in which it took place appealed most strongly to environmentalists, who were often distrustful of such organizations and certainly not prepared for the kind of firm, disciplined protest to which communist demonstrators were accustomed.

---

[102] 'C'est très important : il pleuvait. S'il n'avait pas plu, l'histoire aurait été différente.' BD in Bernard Dréano and Suzanne d'Hernies, joint interview with the author, Paris, 20 January 2010. See also Commandant CRS de Lyon, 'Rapport technique de fin de service', 1977, AN, 19850718 art. 25.

[103] 'Rapport d'analyse', 1977, AD Isère, 6857 W 36.

[104] Dréano and d'Hernies, interview. On meanings and practices of protest in Paris, see Danielle Tartakowsky, *Manifester à Paris* (2010).

SDH: We found ourselves with people who had no idea [...]
       you're in the middle of a field with the police charging at
       you, so you're not in your element, and furthermore you're
       in the middle of teaching people: 'This is how you hold on in
       a chain, we're together, we march together, you listen to the
       people in front, [...] you don't let go of the chain.' [...]
       You have genuinely unorganized people [*inorganisés*]. We
       found ourselves actually in situations that I never saw again.
BD: You haven't done any other demonstrations in a cornfield in
       the rain. [...]
SDH: What you can manage in the city, well, it's more complicated
       in the country.
BD: In the rain too.[105]

Suzanne and Bernard were not the only ones who were out of their element,
and certain others were far worse off. According to Bernard, the West
German demonstrators (including many from OCT's sister organization,
the Hamburg-based KB) were caught in a 'German logic' of protest that was
slightly different from the one that applied in France, leading to confusion
and dangerous missteps. The police too were confused by the situation. In
keeping with the 'revolutionary' reading of the rural that held currency in
the 1970s, Suzanne interprets this as a result of police fears of peasants.

SDH: It was utter confusion and you could really tell that the cops
       were completely lost. [...] We weren't doing well ourselves,
       clearly, but you kind of count on the state to structure things
       and the Police nationale had absolutely no idea where they
       were [...] and [if] there's one thing the cops are scared stiff of,
       it's peasants.
BD: Yes, peasant demonstrations are often very violent.
SDH: All of French history is marked by that.[106]

One might be tempted to dismiss this interpretation, given how closely it
hews to left-wing imaginings of the countryside that police presumably did
not share. However, the Renseignements Généraux reached a very similar
conclusion about the police operation in Malville, noting that 'the work
[...] was strongly complicated by the very specific character of this rural
region and the very difficult milieu constituted by a distrustful, frightened

---

[105] Dréano and d'Hernies, interview.
[106] Dréano and d'Hernies, interview. In 1977, memories of violent conflict between
winegrowers and police in Aléria (Corsica) and Montredon (Aude) would still have been
very fresh. Michelle Zancarini-Fournel, 'Aléria et Montredon', in *68 : une histoire collective*,
edited by Philippe Artières and Michelle Zancarini-Fournel (2008).

peasant population'. Though the police considered the operation against the protest to be a success, they noted that 'the lessons that it would be proper to draw from this operation are not automatically applicable to other demonstrations in view of the fact that the events took place in the middle of the countryside or in very small villages of an isolated rural region'. And because of the 'exceptional [. . .] atmospheric circumstances'.[107]

CONCLUSION

The anti-nuclear movement celebrated rurality, sometimes to the point of exoticizing it. In the post-1968 period, activists selectively reinterpreted ambiguous or even negative tropes of the rural world so as to create a positive image that was conducive to protest. Activists' dreams of revolutionary peasants, authentic people, and special places were more legend than reality and often led to serious misunderstandings. Yet such imaginings persisted because they served the purposes of participants on both sides of the urban/rural divide. Outsiders usually went along with the principle that authority rested with directly affected, local activists in part because they hoped that the respect accorded to the latter would rub off on them. Though sometimes overwhelmed by the ensuing responsibilities, local activists accepted this role as a means of maintaining control over the meaning of their protest. The mutual dependence of locals and outsiders was one source of tension among many within the movement, but activists learned that most problems could be smoothed over if people simply approached one another openly and connected with certain natural allies who could serve as intermediaries. Even when problems persisted, the miscommunications, shocks, and surprises that contact between the city and the country elicited could also be productive and life-changing, as the stories of Dieter, Markus, and Marie-Jo demonstrate. Rural space presented a similarly ambiguous constraint on protest and one which shaped the forms that demonstrations could take. Site occupations and rural symbolism considerably enhanced the efficacy and appeal of anti-nuclear protest, but the countryside proved less suited for mass protest of the kind that normally worked so well in the city. Cooperation between activists from the cities and their counterparts out in the countryside could be confusing, tense, and problematic, but in most cases, it ultimately worked. The matter where differences proved most intractable was on the question of violence and non-violence, which will be examined in the next chapter.

---

[107] 'Rapport d'analyse'.

5

'Peaceful but Offensive' Protest

Violence and Non-Violence in the Anti-Nuclear Movement

Around 11.30 p.m. on 18 January 1982, a farmer from the small town of Flévieu near Creys-Malville was awakened by the sound of a detonation. At first, he thought that 'a power tower had been blown up, like in 1979'. (Multiple anonymous groups, acting independently, had regularly bombed electricity pylons throughout the region since the violent 1977 demonstration.) As the farmer looked outside, he saw a ball of flame fly across the river toward the Super-Phénix construction site, where work was nearing completion; this time, the nuclear power plant itself was under attack. Five rockets in total hit the building, launched from a Soviet RPG-7 rocket launcher with filed-off identification numbers that police discovered abandoned in the bushes across from the power station. Two missiles entered the reactor building through an opening in its outer walls, damaging equipment inside, though not to the extent the attackers had hoped.[1]

No one was harmed during the attack, although Électricité de France (EDF) claimed that twenty workers had been in the building at the time.[2] In a statement claiming responsibility, anonymous 'peaceful ecologists' declared that 'every precaution' had been taken to ensure that there would be no injuries. More than twenty years later, the Swiss anti-nuclear activist Chaïm Nissim (b. 1949) admitted that he had been part of the international group of activists behind the bazooka attack.[3] The admission was all the more surprising given that Chaïm had been a member of the Coordination Rhône-Alpes and one of the leading advocates of non-violent protest in

---

[1] Jacques Lesinge, 'Contestation au bazooka', *Le Figaro*, 20 January 1982, p. 13; Claude Francillon and Claude Régent, 'Des roquettes ont été tirées contre le chantier du réacteur Super-Phénix', *Le Monde*, 20 January 1982, p. 40. The rockets that entered the building barely missed the vital equipment that was targeted, damaging a girder instead. 'Schüsse auf Superphénix', *Atom Express*, no. 28 (March/April 1982), p. 63.

[2] Francillon and Régent, 'Roquettes', *Le Monde*, 20 January 1982.

[3] Chaïm Nissim, *L'amour et le monstre* (2004).

Malville in 1976 and 1977. (He also served as a Green deputy in the Geneva city parliament from 1985 to 2001.) Today, he insists that the bazooka attack, like the thirty or so power tower bombings in which he participated, was a peaceful act consistent with his non-violent views.

AT: Was it important to you at the time [whether an action was violent or not]?

CN: VERY important, very! Crucial! If it was violent, I couldn't support it. There was a fundamental divergence within the movement between adherents of violence and of non-violence. I was among the non-violent ones. But for us, non-violence [meant] it was OK, the use of a bazooka or explosives. The thing was that there couldn't be any people there. That's where we drew the line. [. . .] We were practically the only group that thought like that. All the others were more vague [*flous*] on that question. With limits, always with limits, but [. . .] they found the Brigate Rosse or the Rote Armee Fraktion and all those groups heroic.[4]

'Armed struggle' or 'terrorist' groups like the West German Rote Armee Fraktion (RAF) and (to a lesser extent) France's Action Directe (AD) tend to dominate public memory of political violence in the 1970s because of the sensational nature of the violence they perpetrated. However, the overwhelming majority of acts of political violence during the period fell far short of kidnapping and murder. Skirmishes between police and demonstrators were relatively common at anti-nuclear protests, and acts of non-violent protest much more so. Chaïm saw himself as firmly committed to non-violence. At the same time, he too was fascinated by a certain romantic image of revolutionary heroism à la Che Guevara. He remembers seeing the Claude Chabrol film *Nada* in the cinema and identifying with its protagonist, the fictional 'terrorist' Buenaventura Diaz.

CN: I wanted to be like that. I wanted to be clandestine. To kill Pinochet and survive. [. . .] There was something attractive about this guy all dressed in black who had killed. I didn't like the idea of killing cops, I didn't like that. But we're all contradictory. There was a fascination all the same—even if one doesn't agree ideologically—there was a romantic side to it.[5]

The contradictions of the anti-nuclear movement were such that at least some activists could conceive of an attack using heavy weaponry obtained

---

[4] Chaïm Nissim, interview with the author, Geneva, 28 January 2010.
[5] Nissim, interview.

from what many considered to be 'terrorist' groups as 'non-violent' because it harmed property but not people.[6] By 1982, even respected, non-violent anti-nuclear groups were at least partially willing to accept contradictions like these. After the disastrous demonstration of 1977, various Comités Malville were succeeded by the Association de la Région de Malville Opposée à Super-Phénix, which promoted peaceful protest and exemplary alternative projects in an effort to dissociate itself from the violence that had marred the 1977 demonstration. Yet this same group issued only a tepid condemnation of the bazooka attack, arguing that 'recourse to such methods' (which did not correspond to 'those that [we] ordinarily use') was understandable given the 'disappointment and bitterness engendered by a government that has betrayed its promises'. They also used the publicity surrounding the attack to promote a march 'from Malville to the Élysée' being led by committed non-violent activists from Lyon.[7] The Coordination Nationale Anti-Nucléaire, a national umbrella group backing the same non-violent march, even explicitly refused to condemn the bazooka attack, or any of the similar acts of sabotage committed in places like Golfech and Chooz.[8]

The lack of distance between 'non-violent' discourse and apparently 'violent' practice such as bazooka, bomb, or arson attacks was the product of a development that few could have foreseen when anti-nuclear protest first took off in the early 1970s. The earliest anti-nuclear protests were overwhelmingly peaceful, as activists managed to achieve their goals by taking their opponents by surprise and occupying construction sites with minimal force. The West German and French states responded by quickly and dramatically escalating the situation, which prompted a polarizing debate over violent versus non-violent strategy within the movement. Two seemingly diametrically opposed positions dominated the discussion. Some activists argued that the use of violence (in any form) would harm their cause, distracting from the real issue, wrecking the movement's legitimacy in the eyes of the public, and turning protest into a militarized confrontation where the state would always have the upper hand. Others argued that a non-violent, moral appeal to the public was unlikely to have any effect when such powerful interests were at stake, that protesters

---

[6] The rocket launcher was obtained through West German 'armed struggle' networks via their allies in the Belgian Cellules Communistes Combattantes. Nissim, *L'amour et le monstre*, pp. 94–7.

[7] Before Mitterrand became president, the Parti Socialiste had backed a moratorium on the construction of new nuclear power stations. In government, however, it only froze construction at most sites for a few months. 'Les enquêteurs n'ont aucune piste', *Le Monde*, 21 January 1982, p. 23; 'Schüsse auf Superphénix', *Atom Express*, no. 28; Michel Bernard, interview with the author, Lyon, 22 January 2010.

[8] 'Aucune piste', *Le Monde*, 21 January 1982.

needed to demonstrate their resolve with militancy, and that they should be ready to defend both their views and themselves at protests.

This chapter explores the discourses and practices of violent and non-violent protest. It argues that, though activists discursively cast violence and non-violence as mutually exclusive strategies, in actual practice the distinction between them was subjective, context-dependent, and highly unstable. A first section on the so-called 'violence debate' explains how and why anti-nuclear protest came to be associated with a discourse of 'official non-violence', highlighting the role of internal power relations within the movement. A second, chronological section examines how practices of protest evolved over time in three periods: escalation in the years 1975–7, a 'search for alternatives' around 1977–9 and, thereafter, a partial truce in which certain contradictions were tolerated.

THE DEBATE

Debates over the appropriateness and efficacy of violent and non-violent protest tactics were, of course, neither unique to the anti-nuclear movement nor completely new to its members at the time: in 1977, the non-violent activist Hartmut Gründler wrote to Jens Scheer, a member of the Kommunistische Partei Deutschlands (KPD), that much of the discussion was 'still very familiar to us from the years after 1968'.[9] Such debates, a perennial fixture of social movements, are seldom (if ever) fully resolved, not least because individual activists may have sharply different understandings of what actually constitutes 'violence' or 'non-violence'.[10] Indeed, these two terms only weakly grasp the essence of the poles in the debate within the anti-nuclear movement of the 1970s. For most of those who understood themselves (and are here referred to) as 'non-violent activists'—especially those organized in non-violent action groups like Mouvement pour une Alternative Non-violente, Gewaltfreie Aktion Freiburg (GAF), or similar local groups elsewhere—non-violence never meant the merely tactical abstention from the use of physical force.[11] Driven by a moral impulse, these activists saw non-violent civil disobedience as a uniquely effective and morally consistent form of resistance against perceived injustices, a means that was itself part of its end.

---

[9] Hartmut Gründler, letter to Jens Scheer, 18 January 1977, AA, Brokdorf 76/77 JS.
[10] Dieter Rucht notes that definitions of violence as applied to protest are often stretched to the point of being 'unclear and ultimately unusable'. 'Gewalt', in *Internationales Handbuch der Gewaltforschung*, edited by Wilhelm Heitmeyer and Günter Albrecht (2002).
[11] This is expressed directly in German in the words *Gewaltfreiheit* (freedom from violence) versus *Gewaltlosigkeit* (the absence of violence). In French, the distinction is occasionally communicated by the use of the terms *non-violence* and *sans violence*.

The opposing position in this debate was not necessarily less morally inspired,[12] but led from a similar point of departure to fundamentally different conclusions: nuclear power was an affront and an injustice against ordinary people, a matter serious enough to require 'active' and 'offensive' (rather than merely 'passive') resistance. Such resistance could take at least two different forms. Communist groups (*K-Gruppen, gauchistes*) held that violence must come 'from the masses'. They therefore worked to promote large-scale demonstrations where protesters would resolutely and collectively stand up against authorities. Later in the decade, autonomist groups encouraged a slightly different practice of 'counter-violence' that could be undertaken by individuals or ad hoc groups independent of the larger movement, according to their own free choices. At demonstrations, this frequently took the form of attacks against construction sites or police and security personnel; in other contexts, it most often meant anonymous acts of sabotage.[13] However, radical protesters of both the communist and autonomist varieties did not simply seek out violent conflict as a matter of principle or of pleasure, as they are often accused of doing. Rather, they refused to commit themselves to a nonviolent strategy that they felt played into the hands of the state, already at the level of discourse.[14] They thus thought of themselves (and so are referred to hereafter) as 'militant'[15] rather than 'violent', rejecting the latter label as an intentional simplification by non-violent groups.[16]

Militant activists nevertheless simplified matters in turn to antagonize their non-violent counterparts, accusing them of being timid, legalistic, and therefore ineffective.[17] Non-violent activists, however, were adamant that 'not everything that is legal is also non-violent [*gewaltlos*]' and that

---

[12] tageszeitung, *Gorleben-Dokumentation* (1980), p. 40.

[13] Nelkin and Pollak associate these two forms of violence (against persons at demonstrations versus against property in separate acts of sabotage) with West Germany and France, respectively. Dorothy Nelkin and Michael Pollak, *Atom Besieged* (1981), p. 74. However, the prevalence of these strategies in each country changed over time, linked in part to the decline of *gauchistes* and the rise of autonomists, a change which began earlier in France than in West Germany.

[14] Dieter Halbach and Gerd Panzer, *Zwischen Gorleben & Stadtleben* (1980), p. 165.

[15] In Gorleben, for example, some activists went by the nickname 'die Millies', a shortened form of *Militanten*. See Günter Zint, ed., *RFW* (1980), p. 63.

[16] Michel Bernardy de Sigoyer, *La Contre-information dans les luttes urbaines : un système d'expression, le cas de Grenoble* (1980). Cited in Pièces et Main d'Oeuvre, 'Memento Malville : une histoire des années soixante-dix', essay, 31 pp., 14 June 2005, http://www.piecesetmaindoeuvre.com/IMG/pdf/MementoMalville.pdf (accessed 15 November 2009), p. 6.

[17] See, for example, 'Wie geht es weiter mit der Anti-AKW-Bewegung?', *Arbeiterkampf*, no. 102 Beilage (4 April 1977), pp. 1–3.

'not everything that is non-violent [*gewaltfrei*] is also legal.'[18] Many of them considered civil disobedience and the firm, disciplined, non-violent obstruction of nuclear projects to be 'militant' acts too. Furthermore, many (if not most) non-violent activists felt that small-scale property damage could be 'justified and necessary' under certain conditions (such as when activists used tools to cut through a fence).[19] The debate within the anti-nuclear movement as a whole thus revolved around what limits should be placed on property damage and what methods were appropriate to resist police at demonstrations. Though the matters at stake were of clear, concrete importance to many of those involved, the debate was also fuelled by its wider implications. As the non-violent activist Bernadette Ridard (b. 1947) puts it, 'everyone wanted to fight against the same thing, but they didn't have the same approach. [. . .] There was a sort of rivalry: "Who will organize the anti-nuclear movement?" And beyond that, ideological differences. The non-violent action groups [*Gewaltfreie Aktionsgruppen*] wanted non-violent actions and wanted to impose a tactic, a non-violent strategy. And the others weren't ready to submit themselves to anything whatsoever.'[20] The debate over violence was thus in part a struggle over power and influence within the anti-nuclear movement.

Aside from their very different positions on violence, the non-violent and militant factions were in many ways similar. The main point of convergence was the idea that protest practice should consist of direct action capable of concretely preventing nuclear programmes from advancing; for much of the 1970s, this meant occupying sites (or attempting to do so). A certain moral drive, a propensity for direct action, and a willingness (or even eagerness) to step outside the law were common to both blocs. Significantly, non-violent, communist, and autonomist protesters were all generally regarded as outsiders to the local communities where anti-nuclear protest was primarily based. Indeed, the entire debate about violence and non-violence was largely brought in 'from outside'[21] by groups like these. As the non-violent activist Wolfgang Hertle succinctly summarizes it, 'the local people were', at many larger meetings, 'more the audience over whose heads the other factions argued'.[22]

It is not at all clear that the rest of the movement ever fully supported either the non-violent or militant factions, however much they dictated the terms of the strategy debate. Irritation with the radical left was

---

[18] 'Anregungen zu einem Flugblatt zur Demo vom 13. November', flyer, 2 pp., undated 1976, AA, Brokdorf 76/77 JS.
[19] 'Anregungen'.
[20] Bernadette Ridard, interview with the author, Hamburg, 25 August 2010.
[21] Nina Gladitz, interview with the author, Berlin, 2 June 2010.
[22] Wolfgang Hertle, interview with the author, Hamburg, 22 July 2010.

certainly never hard to find, and often had as much to do with the political positions that *K-Gruppen* represented or with the manner in which autonomists presented themselves as it did with real or imagined violent propensities. When activists in Wyhl voted twenty-six to one to banish the 'violence-advocating KPD/ML' from the occupied site, 'violence' was but one of many reasons for doing so.[23] Violent activity did have important, concrete implications, but accusations of violent intent could also be tied to other resentments towards radicals. Perhaps more surprising is the resentment some felt towards non-violent activists. These activists held themselves to a very high moral standard that others did not always manage (or necessarily want) to achieve, sometimes making them appear arrogant or holier-than-thou. Lanza del Vasto, an inspirational figure of non-violence in France, came across to some as a 'patriarch' full 'of false modesty [...] who exudes arrogance'.[24] A broad coalition of anti-nuclear activists in Gorleben was irritated to no end when the non-violent groups they invited to join them went off and secretly prepared their own, separate actions 'in order to be able to carry them out in the purest manner possible'.[25]

Rather than drawing a black-and-white distinction between non-violence and violence, many activists positioned themselves in the grey area in between. Some were simply ambivalent. Ginette Skandrani (b. 1938), a committed anti-imperialist who joined anti-nuclear protests in Alsace, describes her own position as follows:

> GS: I've always had a rather ambiguous attitude. I agreed with advo-
>   cating non-violence, because non-violence permitted one to
>   respond in an intelligent manner. What I liked about the non-
>   violent movement was the intelligence within it. [...] But on the
>   other hand, I wasn't against people who employed violence.
>   I respected them all the same. [...] I didn't criticize them—on
>   the contrary, if I could protect them, I protected them.[26]

Many activists found something to dislike about both violence and non-violence—or at least about their respective proponents. One edition of the Wyhl squatters' newspaper *Was Wir Wollen* included a humorous 'test' asking readers to match cartoons with the organizations that advocated the strategies illustrated. The obvious answers ridiculed non-violent activists for their naïve martyrdom as well as communist groups for their

---

[23] '„Mer setze uns durch, weil mer recht hen"', *Spiegel*, no. 14 (31 March 1975), pp. 36–41 (p. 41).

[24] Yves Hardy and Emmanuel Gabey, *L... comme Larzac* (1974), pp. 76, 79.

[25] Halbach and Panzer, *Zwischen Gorleben & Stadtleben*, p. 61.

[26] Ginette Skandrani, interview with the author, Paris, 11 January 2010.

hypocrisy and condescension. The only group to be spared mockery was the local *Bürgerinitiative*.[27]

With both the militant and non-violent factions inspiring various degrees of antipathy, anti-nuclear activists routinely turned for guidance to local activists as the only grouping to command enough legitimacy to hold the movement together. Locals were the ultimate authorities within the movement, for several reasons. Because anyone might happen to live close to a prospective nuclear power station, local residents constituted something like a representative cross-section of society, transcending generations and political categories more so than the anti-nuclear movement as a whole.[28] When 'ordinary people' like these rebelled against state and industry, politicians and the public took notice in a way that they did not when protest appeared to originate among 'the usual suspects'.[29] One anonymous activist writing about Wyhl insisted that only the local *Bürgerinitiative* could determine protest strategy because its members could assess the urgency of matters better than 'university groups from nearby cities who rush to a planned construction site more out of principled understanding [*prinzipieller Einsicht*] than from direct, existential necessity'.[30] Locals were 'directly affected' and therefore supposedly not tainted by the suspect 'political' or 'ideological' concerns that animated others.[31] Putting local people at the forefront was in part natural, in part a calculated appeal to the broader public.

Accordingly, each faction within the violence debate argued that it had the local population squarely on its side. Non-violent activists claimed that 'whoever is in solidarity with the local population will show this through his or her non-violent action [*sein gewaltfrei-aktives Verhalten*]'.[32] It seemed apparent to them that violence could repel ordinary people and

---

[27] 'Test. Thema: Gewalt', *WWW*, no. 13 (23 October 1975), p. 21. Groups were matched to the following drawings: a lone demonstrator being dragged off by police says 'Surely everyone will join in!' (GAF); a demonstrator charges at police while shouting 'Where does violence come from?' and another, proudly showing an injury inflicted by police, says 'Finally proven: capitalism is brutal. Any questions?' (KBW/KPD); the last drawing contains no text and shows people massing stoically in front of police (BI).

[28] It helped that, in practice, not just anyone actually did live in such areas. The German small towns and French rural communities where planners placed nuclear power stations were thought to be conservative and politically docile, peopled by proportionally more families and older people than larger cities or university towns. (See Chapter 2.)

[29] The so-called *Wutbürger* continues to command this kind of attention in Germany today. See Dirk Kurbjuweit, 'Der Wutbürger', *Spiegel* (11 October 2010).

[30] '„. . . mehr Demokratie überhaupt". Ein Bericht von den Bürgerinitiativen um Wyhl', brochure, 68 pp., January 1977, IISG, Bro 2188/16, p. 54.

[31] See, for example, BBU, 'Liebe Freunde [. . .]', press release, 2 pp., 19 February 1977, APO, S 37.

[32] 'Anregungen'.

no one wanted to risk the departure of the movement's most valuably ordinary members. In 1976, Chaïm Nissim (who was then just beginning to participate in small-scale sabotage actions) told *Libération* that anti-nuclear activists in Malville were committed to keeping demonstrations non-violent 'because the peasants like this notion for a start.'[33] Militant activists asserted precisely the opposite with equal or greater vehemence. Autonomist satirists from Grenoble responded to the non-violent declarations of the Malville coordinating committee with sarcasm: '"Violence scares the peasant. It cuts us off from the population." Let's not joke around, boys. The peasant knows perfectly well that there's nothing like a shot from an old gun to change the agenda of a council of ministers.'[34] Communists argued that local populations might be 'against violence' for various practical reasons (they might be afraid or not physically up to the task), but that this by no means meant they subscribed to the 'ideology' of non-violence.[35] According to them, the anti-nuclear movement needed to defend itself, keep its strategic options open, and agitate near sites to prepare the local terrain, so that by the next protest, 'there should be 100,000 of us. No "fence" can withstand that!'[36] Activists advocating divergent strategies in the violence debate all claimed to do so in tandem with authentic, local people.

What did the locals actually think? The contradictory claims and counter-claims of each group all had a ring of truth to them. Most local activists probably preferred some form of non-violence, but some also saw utility in violence, so long as it did not slip out of control. The positions expressed by Georges David (b. 1943) and Marie-Jo Putinier (b. 1937), two activists from Malville who worked closely together for many years, are typical of disagreements on the matter. Georges argues that acts of sabotage like the destruction of electricity towers and even the rocket attack against Super-Phénix 'allowed [us] to keep talking about Malville in a semi-permanent manner',[37] keeping the issue on the agenda. Marie-Jo acknowledges that sabotage 'got information out, it made people talk [about Malville]', but she points out that it 'could only be a one-off thing. That's not what would stop the process. The process was political.'

---

[33] Chantal Desprez, 'Malville : une bataille qui durera cinq ans', *Libération*, 6 October 1976.

[34] 'Ne pas confondre, trou du cul et pastille de menthe', *Casse-Noix*, no. 4 (9 July 1976), p. 2.

[35] 'Wie geht es weiter mit der Anti-AKW-Bewegung?', *Arbeiterkampf*, no. 102 (Beilage), p. 1.

[36] 'Wie geht es weiter mit der Anti-AKW-Bewegung?', *Arbeiterkampf*, no. 102 (Beilage), p. 1. *Casse-Noix* made the same argument more pointedly, with a satirical survey of opinions on the question 'Êtes-vous pour la non-violence ?', showing agreement from 95 per cent of CRS riot police, 93 per cent of special brigades, and 92 per cent of *Gardes mobiles*. 'Sondage exclusif !', *Casse-Noix*, no. 4 (July 1976), p. 4.

[37] Georges David, interview with the author, Lhuis, 27 January 2010.

She also feared the practical consequences of sabotage, which could be unpredictable and affect those who were not involved.

> MJP: Georges David always used to say 'Yeah, we're not in favour of [sabotage], but we understand them.' Yes, we understand, but we mustn't encourage them. [...] Because afterwards, who's going to pay? [...] They'll come, they'll blow up their bomb or do their thing, they'll leave, and we, the locals, are there. So who will be held responsible? Us![38]

Those who had to live with the consequences of violence committed by others were not always in agreement over its effects.

Violence was, however, never solely the work of 'outside agitators'. Sometimes the frustration and anger of farmers and townspeople spilled over into acts of violence; many still recall today the bitterness they felt at the surveillance, harassment, and intimidation to which police patrolling nuclear sites subjected their communities.[39] Axel Mayer (b. 1955), a young man from the Kaiserstuhl region who became involved in the Wyhl protests, observes that 'There's really a difference between this nuanced violence debate of the left and the instinctive anger [*unreflektierte Wut*] of a farmer who says "I've got a gun at home."'[40] Nor was violence necessarily an out-of-control response to frustration. Some local activists saw it as strategically advantageous. Heinrich Voß (b. 1951), a farmer who lives directly next to the Brokdorf nuclear power plant, remembers thinking back in 1976 that violence against property 'was necessary in order to wake up the public':

> HV: We had slogged away for three years prior to that [...] And now, precisely because of this violence, because of these images from Brokdorf, the discussion got going. In the media they only talked about violence [...] But deep down it did trigger reflection for some people. My thinking back then was, well, violence has to occur before people will even start to think [about] nuclear energy. Though today I think it would be rather damaging here if there were violence.[41]

Far from presenting a single, unequivocal answer to the question of violence, local anti-nuclear activists held a range of conflicting views.

---

[38] Marie-Jo Putinier, interview with the author, Bourgoin-Jallieu, 26 January 2010.

[39] Interviews with Maurice and Chantal François, Marie-Jo Putinier, Ali and Marlene Reimers, Heinrich Voß, and Christine Scheer. See also Chapter 2.

[40] Axel Mayer, interview with the author, Freiburg, 12 April 2010.

[41] Heinrich Voß and Christine Scheer, joint interview with the author, Wewelsfleth, 21 August 2010.

It is likely that most local, concerned citizens—and plenty of other, unaffiliated anti-nuclear activists—were above all pragmatic, willing to support whatever strategy seemed more promising in a given situation. They wanted neither to bind their hands by committing themselves to strict non-violence, nor to dirty them by committing violent acts. The position broadly taken by local activists was therefore one that was officially non-violent in its discourse, but not consistently so in practice. As the movement's public face, the *comités d'action* and *Bürgerinitiativen* could ill afford to imperil their public standing by openly employing or condoning violence. Overt and covert forms of protest had to be kept distinct, but they nevertheless coexisted, as the leading Flamanville and La Hague activist Didier Anger (b. 1939) recalls:

DA: Within the associations, it was [. . .] systematic opposition to any violence against people. With things [*matériel*] it was more nuanced. What was said was that it can't be up to the associations to do it. But it was the principle of the Resistance [. . .]: small groups, compartmentalization—and don't get caught. [. . .] There were groups that formed—no one said 'you must form a group', but *voilà*.[42]

Non-violent activists were naturally disappointed by what appeared to them to be the half-hearted or quite simply opportunistic application of principles they held dear. When local activists supported illegal civil disobedience only so long as they themselves didn't get caught or when they refused to distance themselves from violent acts, this was doubly problematic. Such seemingly hypocritical behaviour undermined the moral authority on which effective non-violent action depended, while simultaneously making those who did stick to their principles look like sanctimonious martyrs.[43] For locals, though, the discourse of non-violence gave them a moral position from which to criticize the state (and break its laws) while preserving the threat that worse things could (be made to) happen.

The selective application of non-violence served another important purpose: it offered local activists a valuable means of controlling who could protest in their name.[44] Particularly in anti-communist West Germany, the *K-Gruppen* inspired great antipathy. Preventing these disciplined, hierarchically organized outsiders from seizing control was a high priority. Making participation contingent on non-violence was a way of either forcing communist and autonomist groups to adapt or allowing the

---

[42] Didier Anger, interview with the author, Les Pieux, 22 September 2010.
[43] Hertle, interview.
[44] See also Pauline Vuarin, 'Une lutte originale' (2005), p. 57.

local community to distance itself from radicals (and radical politics) with which it did not wish to be identified. Though non-violence could thereby function to exclude these supporters, it also left the door open for them to participate—so long as they did so on terms dictated by the local activists. Non-violence could thus be a pragmatic tool for shoring up local authority within the movement—at least when it worked.

ESCALATING (NON-)VIOLENCE

The anti-nuclear movement became a popular phenomenon in the mid-1970s largely as a result of a series of sensational mass demonstrations that took place in West Germany and France in the years 1975–7. Throughout this period, developments in each country had effects beyond their national borders, with communication among police and protesters contributing to a more or less synchronized escalation of conflict in both countries. Indeed, protesters and authorities were both engaged in learning processes that were translocal and often transnational, with each side responding in part to developments elsewhere. While many studies of the anti-nuclear movement portray this escalation as the takeover of a non-violent movement by militant opportunists, such analyses fail to take seriously the extent to which militant actors became involved or their motivations for doing so. They also ignore the ways in which non-violence and violence 'enabled' one another by turns:[45] militant action drew strength from the outrage over police brutality against non-violent demonstrators, but the 'civil war'-like clashes at certain demonstrations also increased the appeal of non-violent protest. Instead of presenting a unidirectional development, the use of non-violent or violent tactics often overlapped or alternated in cycles—at least until the situation escaped activists' control entirely in late 1977.

The earliest site occupations, which took place in Marckolsheim (France) and then Wyhl (West Germany) in 1974 and 1975, were conceived explicitly as non-violent actions. This owed much to the careful preparation by Alsatian and German pacifists who had prior training in non-violent direct action, some of whom had been involved in anti-nuclear protest since the first demonstration against the nuclear site in Fessenheim in 1971. Many of these activists were inspired by the non-violent example of anti-militarist protesters on the Larzac, with whom they established direct and indirect links.[46] In August 1974, Alsatian and

---

[45] William Marotti, 'Japan 1968', *American Historical Review* (February 2009), p. 128.

[46] See 'Le Larzac rencontre l'Alsace à Marckolsheim', flyer, 1974, ASB, 24416; Walter Moßmann, *Realistisch sein* (2009), pp. 176–82.

German activists openly announced their intention to engage in civil disobedience and jointly occupy building sites in both Marckolsheim and Wyhl whenever construction began.[47] The French authorities took no notice and were thus surprised when activists actually did set up tents on the unsecured site of the future Chemische Werke München lead processing plant in Marckolsheim in late September 1974. Though French governments aggressively defended the nuclear sites of the state-owned power company EDF, they did not bother to intervene on behalf of this West German company. Protesters used the space they had taken over to train others in methods of passive resistance by role-playing an eviction: participants were divided arbitrarily into 'demonstrators' and 'police', the latter armed with 'batons' made from rolled-up newspapers and the former charged with peacefully resisting efforts to remove them.[48] Though the real police never evicted protesters in Marckolsheim, the exercise provided useful preparation for those who went on to occupy the nuclear power site in Wyhl a few months later. In this way, the two struggles 'complemented each other perfectly', with Marckolsheim serving as a 'dress rehearsal' for the larger battle across the border.[49]

In Wyhl, non-violent activists and local citizens attempted to repeat the Marckolsheim formula for success, setting up camp on the prospective nuclear site on 18 February 1975. However, the element of surprise was no longer on their side the second time around, and the West German authorities proved less patient than their French counterparts. Only two days later, police employed tear gas, water cannon, and physical force to remove the squatters from the site. For a rural community like Wyhl, which had little experience of protest, the 'brutal' eviction came as a profound shock: the demonstrators had been strictly non-violent and visibly defenceless.[50] Perhaps more importantly, many of those roughly

[47] Badisch-Elsässische Bürgerinitiativen, 'Erklärung der 21 Bürgerinitiativen an die badisch-elsässische Bevölkerung / Déclaration des 21 organismes de sauvegarde de l'environnement aux populations Badoises et Alsaciennes', poster, August 1974, ASB, 00017652.

[48] This was modelled on non-violence training that Marie-Reine Haug, Raymond Schirmer, and Jean-Jacques Rettig had all undergone in Strasbourg under the guidance of another figure of religious non-violence, Jean Goss. Marie-Reine Haug and Raymond Schirmer, joint interview with the author, Rammersmatt, 17 April 2010; Jean-Jacques Rettig, interview with the author, Fréconrupt, 19 April 2010. A similar role-playing activity was conducted in Gorleben in 1980 prior to protesters' eviction by police. See Zint, *RFW*, pp. 112–15.

[49] RS in Haug and Schirmer, interview; Badisch-Elsässische Bürgerinitiativen, 'Wyhl. Ein Jahr danach', brochure, 1976, PA Tompkins, p. 2.

[50] Bernd Nössler and Margret de Witt, eds, *Kein Kernkraftwerk in Wyhl* (1976), p. 92. Walter Moßmann argues that this confrontation with the police was as much of a shock to people in small towns as the violent conflict in Malville was for activists who had come from Hamburg. Walter Moßmann, interview with the author, Freiburg, 1 April 2010.

dragged off were older women and mothers with children, some of the only people available to occupy the site on a Thursday morning. According to Ulla Bonczek (b. 1957), a Freiburg student who participated in the Wyhl protests, 'the brutality of the police against these women—that heated up the mood incredibly'.[51] Especially when women acted in consciously traditional roles, the violence perpetrated against them by police was perceived as a violation of norms and thus a sign of particular brutality.

When a new protest was held the following weekend, 28,000 people showed up, including outraged farmers and militant protesters from nearby Freiburg who had fewer inhibitions about pushing their way past police and onto the site. Though the perception that protest in Wyhl was strictly non-violent is central to the success story that anti-nuclear activists have constructed surrounding this struggle, some violence certainly did take place as the crowd occupied the site. Non-violent activists later expressed regret that the situation had got out of control, though they nevertheless argued that Wyhl, like Marckolsheim, was a case of 'nonviolence triumphant'.[52] At the same time, Maoist students cast it as an example of the 'just violence of the people's resistance'.[53] According to the KPD, the site was reoccupied, 'but not as a peaceful stroll like the first time. It was taken by storm, in a quite rough [*recht handgreiflich*] struggle that ended with the retreat of the police. Do the ideologues of absolute non-violence want to claim that it was only passive resistance?'[54] The memories of former activists (though these too may be questioned) suggest that the reality lay somewhere in between. The young Kaiserstühler Axel Mayer remembers there were non-violent activists near the front lines, but also, behind them, farmers throwing rocks.[55] Nina Gladitz (b. 1946), who made a well-known film about the Wyhl struggle, observes that 'If it hadn't turned out the way it did, I wouldn't rule out that they

---

[51] Ulla Bonczek, interview with the author, Freiburg, 26 April 2010. See also Nössler and de Witt, *Kein Kernkraftwerk in Wyhl*, pp. 100–4.

[52] Solange Fernex, 'Non-Violence Triumphant', *The Ecologist*, vol. 5, no. 10 (December 1975), pp. 372–85. Other non-violent activists were uncomfortable with the violence they felt had taken place at the site occupation: 'Je reconnais que nous n'aurions peut-être pas réoccupé le terrain si certains d'entre nous ne s'étaient pas montrés agressifs, mais je suis sûr que nous aurions pu éviter en grande partie les violences qui se sont produites.' 'Einige fühlten sich verantwortlich, hatten aber Angst, überrannt zu werden, es gab Gewalt bei der Besetzung, viele Menschen, zu wenig Ordner.' 'Wyhl : l'enjeu nucléaire', *Ionix*, no. 10 (March 1975), p. 28; 'Interview zur Entwicklung der gewaltfreien Bewegung im Elsass', summary transcript of interview, 1 p., 1975, AA, 'Ökologiebewegung im Elsass'.

[53] KPD, 'Nein zu den Atomkraftwerken!', brochure, 50 pp., December 1976, ASB, 12-A5-5, p. 40.

[54] KPD, 'Kein Kernkraftwerk in Wyhl! Arbeitereinheit, Volkseinheit – im Kampf für den Sozialismus!', 1975, DfuL, D01215, p. 32.

[55] Mayer, interview.

[the farmers] would have "gotten ideas." [...] It would be a mistake to believe that they were pilgrims on Gandhi's path.'[56] Roland Burkhart (b. 1956), a young protest singer from the Kaiserstuhl, candidly admitted that local farmers were 'more violent [*gewaltbereiter*], fundamentally':

RB: The people living there, they were like that. Obviously, that was unofficial [*unter der Hand*] and one knew it. [...] The new form of non-violence was a learning process for many in the *Bürgerinitiative*, absolutely. They had to learn that—and they enjoyed doing it. They obviously saw the success in it.[57]

The legendary site occupation that began on 23 February 1975 would not have come about without non-violent protesters, whose mistreatment at the hands of police the week before had attracted attention and outraged the public. However, it might not have succeeded without the (limited) violence of angry farmers and militant protesters. The success of Wyhl lay in this critical mass of very different demonstrators—some of them throwing rocks at police, others calling the police afterwards to apologize—who managed to force their way onto the site and initiate the legendary site occupation that lasted several months.[58] Violence and non-violence were entangled even in Wyhl, though the violence was not intense enough to damage the credibility of non-violent discourse. Wyhl thus became, almost immediately, the model for 'officially' non-violent protest elsewhere.

The contradictions of this entanglement would become much more apparent, and much more dangerous, as the West German state dramatically escalated the situation at the next major anti-nuclear demonstration. Determined to prevent Brokdorf from becoming the 'second Wyhl' that activists of every orientation (from communists to student groups to local BIs) announced it would be, police in the federal state of Schleswig-Holstein made a careful study of the earlier site occupation in Baden-Württemberg.[59] Leaving nothing to chance, authorities brought construction equipment to Brokdorf under cover of the night and with heavy police escort, only hours after official government approval for the project had quietly been announced. At 4.30 a.m. on 26 October 1976, workers set about turning the site into what activists frequently described as a 'fortress', complete with a moat-like ditch, pyramids of barbed wire and high, concrete-reinforced

---

[56] Gladitz, interview.
[57] Roland Burkhart, interview with the author, Freiburg, 22 April 2010.
[58] KPD, 'Kein KKW in Wyhl!', p. 32; Einsatztagebuch Wyhl, 23 February 1975, LASH, Abt. 621, Nr. 552.
[59] BUU, *Brokdorf* (1977), p. 183; Landespolizei Schleswig-Holstein, 'Dokumentation über die Polizeieinsätze in Brokdorf (Band 1)', 1977, LASH, Abt. 621, Nr. 534, pp. 13–14, 26–30.

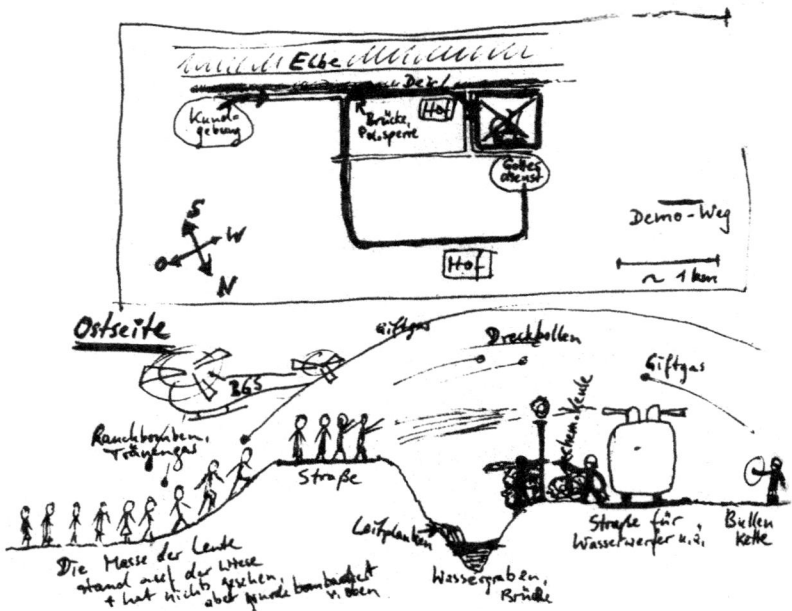

Fig. 5.1. The battle of Brokdorf II. This drawing depicts the pitched battle between demonstrators and police in Brokdorf on 13 November 1976. The bulk of demonstrators are at the bottom of the hill to the left, unable to see the altercations going on between angry demonstrators on the street (throwing, as police reports confirm, some rocks but mostly mud) and the police stationed on the construction site, across a ditch. Police fire tear gas through water cannon from behind the fence and drop tear gas canisters from helicopter onto the distant bystanders at the bottom of the hill. Reproduction courtesy ASB.[60]

fencing (see Fig. 5.1).[61] When nuclear energy opponents came to the site to protest on 30 October ('Brokdorf I') and again on 13 November ('Brokdorf II'), police beat them back with a degree of force never witnessed in Wyhl. At these two demonstrations combined, police used 6,828 canisters of tear gas and fired an additional 1,928 litres of tear gas mixture from water cannon. Units mounted on horseback were sent into the crowd, and private security personnel employed dogs and Chemical

[60] H., 'Brokdorf', p. 3.
[61] Polizeihauptkommissar, 'Verlaufsbericht (2. Fassung)', 3 November 1976, StHH, 331–1 II, Abl. 17, 1976 Band 8b.

Mace against demonstrators.[62] Looking back today, it is clear that the state regarded anti-nuclear protest in Brokdorf 'strategically as a confrontation, much more so than many of the people who went to demonstrate'.[63] Local farmer and anti-nuclear activist Heinrich Voß remembers that police '[dropped] tear gas on retreating demonstrators out of helicopters, which was completely idiotic. Of course [that] politicized a great many people. [. . .] It resembled civil war.'[64]

In such a chaotic situation, it was impossible to occupy the site using only gentle force, as had been done in Wyhl. Yet many anti-nuclear protesters were unwilling to abandon the idea. Non-violent discourse even exacerbated the practical problems of protest in Brokdorf. Activists from Freiburg tried to encourage their comrades in Brokdorf with the argument that 'This is the hour of just resistance [. . .] of non-violent action, the hour of civil disobedience.'[65] During the demonstration on 13 November, activists with non-violent intentions and those involved in violent action bled together (literally): Lutheran pastors, dressed in frocks, exhorted militant protesters not to throw rocks at the police, but accepted or perhaps even encouraged attacks on the perimeter fence.[66] A theology student who participated in the mêlée later told a church publication that 'We didn't throw mud and rocks in order to deliberately hurt police. It was a defensive measure for those of us in front who were working [to dismantle] the fence.'[67] By late evening on 13 November 1976, eighty-one police officers and as many as 700 demonstrators had been injured.[68] Violence on this scale at an environmental protest had previously been unknown and practically unthinkable. The mainstream press too compared it to 'civil war' and

---

[62] Landespolizei Schleswig-Holstein, 'Brokdorf-Dokumentation', p. 132; Landespolizei Schleswig-Holstein, 'Zusammenfassender Bericht', 20 January 1977, LASH, Abt. 621, Nr. 599, p. 7.

[63] Markus Mohr, interview with the author, Hamburg, 19 August 2010.

[64] HV in Voß and Scheer, joint interview. See also Landespolizei Schleswig-Holstein, 'Zusammenfassender Bericht', p. 19.

[65] GAF, 'Wyhl ist überall! (oder ist Brokdorf überall?)', flyer, 2 pp., October 1976, ASB, 12.1.9.1.I-vi.

[66] 'Überhaupt waren die ganze Zeit über Pfarrer vorne an der Straße, mit Talar, Gasmaske und Megaphone. Sie forderten immer wieder auf, keine Steine zu schmeißen und auch keinen Schlamm [. . .] Von dem, was die Pfarrer zu uns sagten, sind mir noch folgende Sätze in Erinnerung: „Keine Panik, wir schaffens auf jeden Fall, wir sind genug!" „Keine Gewalt gegen Personen, Gewalt gegen Sachen, ja. Keine Gewalt gegen Personen!" „Keine Steine, lieber besetzen wir den Platz nicht!"' H., 'Brokdorf – 13.11.76', report, 1976, ASB, 00024386, p. 6.

[67] Hans-Jürgen Benedict, 'Staatsgewalt oder Protest „gewalt" in Brokdorf. Hat die gewaltfreie Bewegung noch eine Chance?', no. 1/77 Beiheft 'Von Wyhl nach Brokdorf' (1977), p. 7.

[68] Landespolizei Schleswig-Holstein, 'Zusammenfassender Bericht', p. 21; BUU, *Brokdorf*, p. 122.

quoted disgusted protesters declaring 'That was my last non-violent demonstration.'[69] The escalation of violence initiated by authorities in Brokdorf prompted demonstrators to respond with actions that made their own officially non-violent discourse less and less credible.

It was at this point that some activists began to loudly promote a new discourse of militancy. After Brokdorf II, autonomists argued that 'we experience blatant injustice and naked violence every day at the hands of the nuclear industry and the state. The "violence question" is thus answered for us before it has even been posed.'[70] Echoing Che Guevara's 1967 battle cry in support of Vietnam, the organ of the Kommunistischer Bund (KB), *Arbeiterkampf*, called upon protesters to 'Create two, three, many Brokdorfs!'[71] Activists from one Hamburg group circulated a Christmas 'wish list' of equipment useful for invading the site at the next protest: a warm scarf, thick boots, an oilskin jacket, area maps, lemon juice (to use against tear gas), a motorcycle helmet, pickaxe, shovel, rope with grappling hook, aluminium kite (to interfere with police radio and helicopters), and so on.[72] Hamburg police feared that the next scheduled demonstration on 19 February 1977 would be so violent that their trade union wrote to the government to ask that 'no police forces be called in for protection of the construction site in Brokdorf', which they proposed 'could be cleared of valuable material and equipment' in advance.[73] Instead, the government clumsily and unsuccessfully attempted to ban the demonstration, with Chancellor Helmut Schmidt even appearing on television to warn 'serious' anti-nuclear activists not to join the 'deliberately destructive, illegal action' expected in Brokdorf.[74] Local activists within the Bürgerinitiative Umweltschutz Unterelbe (BUU), which had publicly praised Brokdorf II as 'a great success' that 'showed that our movement is stronger than ever and growing stronger daily', privately feared a further escalation and therefore pushed for the demonstration to take place in the nearby town of Itzehoe, away from the

[69] Horst Bieber, '„Bürgerkrieg" in der Wilster Marsch', *Zeit*, no. 48 (19 November 1976), p. 2; 'Das war meine letzte gewaltlose Demonstration', *Stern* (16 December 1976).
[70] AKPÖ, *Bilanz und Perspektiven* (1978), p. 1.
[71] 'Schafft zwei, drei, viele „Brokdorf"!', *Arbeiterkampf*, no. 96 (10 January 1977), p. 1. See also KB, 'Rundbrief des Leitenden Gremiums', 4 January 1977, reproduced in AKPÖ, 'Zur Klein-Bürgerlichen Politik des KB. Das Verhalten des KB in der Anti-AKW-Bewegung', May 1977, HIS, SBe 731: 1985/317.
[72] 'Wunschliste für Weihnachten 76 für jeden Brokdorf-Besucher!', flyer, 2 pp., 1976, APO, S 37.
[73] Vorsitzender des Landesverbands Hamburg der Polizeigewerkschaft im Deutschen Beamtenbund Joachim Münstedt, letter to Ministerpräsident des Landes Schleswig-Holstein Gerhard Stoltenberg, 11 February 1977, StHH, 331–1 II, Abl. 17, 1977 Bd. 8c.
[74] See *Wehrt Euch. Brokdorf 19.2.1977*, 1977, 40 mins.

construction site in Brokdorf. Activists thus found themselves facing a choice between competing 'Brokdorf' and 'Itzehoe' demonstrations, the one an unpredictable affair backed by the radical left, the other seemingly a nod to the movement's opponents. Not satisfied with either option, some non-violent activists drove instead to the site of a heretofore largely uncontested nuclear power station in Grohnde to occupy it symbolically for the day.[75] In the end, all three protests remained peaceful; the costs, though, were enormous. For the month of February alone, authorities spent 5,425,600 DM (not including ongoing expenses thereafter).[76]

One month later, militant activists took their turn in Grohnde, holding the most violent demonstration so far. What one sociological observer described as a 'senseless and bloody clash'[77] was, however, thoroughly invested with meaning by those who led it, and consistent with their militant discourse. Members of the Hamburg-based KB organized a mass action to tear down the fence around the site (making no attempt to keep it occupied thereafter). According to former member Günter Hopfenmüller (b. 1944), the KB rejected the autonomist method of having groups or individuals use tools to take apart the fence because 'sawing away at an iron post for hours' was 'anything but mobilizing' and 'didn't have the mass character we were thinking of'.[78] Instead, they brought a 100-metre-long rope that they connected to the fence with grappling hooks; with more than a hundred people pulling on it at once, they were able to tear down huge sections of fencing in a matter of minutes.[79] However, in order to reach the fence, activists first had to break through the police line. This was handled by specially trained groups of KB cadres who, according to police, 'ruthlessly, without scruples and often disregarding every natural inhibition [. . .] sought "man to man" combat' with police. KB members reportedly attacked in rows, under coordinated command, with those behind using long sticks to hit police from above and those in front attacking police with truncheons when they raised their shields to defend themselves.[80] As 'ruthless' as this violence against persons might seem to

---

[75] Hamburger Initiative kirchlicher Mitarbeiter und Gewaltfreie Aktion, 'Wir sind Protestleute gegen den Tod! Ein Erfahrungsbericht', booklet, May 1979, HIS, SBe 731, p. 29.

[76] Landespolizei Schleswig-Holstein, 'Brokdorf-Dokumentation', pp. 157–8. For the three Brokdorf protests in October, November, and February, the total cost was 9,162,600 DM.

[77] Dieter Rucht, *Von Wyhl nach Gorleben* (1980), p. 90.

[78] Günter Hopfenmüller, quoted in Michael Steffen, *Geschichten vom Trüffelschwein* (2002), p. 190.

[79] Inspekteur der Bundespolizei, 'Konzept zur Auswertung Einsatz „Grohnde"', 1977, LASH, Abt. 621, Nr. 569.

[80] Landespolizei Niedersachsen, 'Erfahrungsbericht über den polizeilichen Großeinsatz am 19.3.1977 in Grohnde', 12 August 1977, Nds, 100 Acc. 149/97 Nr. 111, p. 22.

the police, the KB felt amply justified in undertaking it. Former KB member Hans-Hermann Teichler (b. 1947) explains:

> HHT: The attack against the police line was absolutely an attack against people. However, that wasn't discussed in such general terms. The police were well-armed, well-protected, and never held themselves to any such [restrictions]. The state always arrogated to itself the right to use its truncheons against even unprotected people. Defending against—and in this case also an attack against—the police was thoroughly accepted. [. . .] Otherwise, there was to be no gratuitous violence against people.[81]

This carefully planned and executed violence was a strategy that duly reflected the KB's ideological perspective. It permitted the KB both to foster the kind of action 'from the masses' that its members held to be just while simultaneously positioning the organization as an avant garde that could lead the movement.

Following the protests in Brokdorf and Grohnde, mass demonstrations in France also underwent a sudden shift towards greater violence, on the part of both demonstrators and police. As late as July 1976, French anti-nuclear activists had hosted a short-lived but attention-getting peaceful occupation of the site of the future fast breeder reactor (FBR) in Creys-Malville. Video footage from 1976 shows protesters pushing a police van out of the mud as a gesture of goodwill; anti-nuclear activists even held a friendly football match with a few members of the Compagnies Républicaines de Sécurité (CRS, riot police).[82] However, when activists attempted to repeat the site occupation on a larger scale the following year, it was an entirely different affair, leading to a violent altercation between autonomists with Molotov cocktails and police who launched tear gas and stun grenades (*grenades offensives*) indiscriminately into the crowd. French authorities long insisted that such weapons were 'inoffensive', but they can be lethal at close range: following the death of another environmental demonstrator, Rémi Fraisse, at Sivens in 2014, the Interior Ministry has now banned their use at demonstrations.[83] In Malville, stun grenades and tear gas grenades resulted in hundreds of injuries, including

---

[81] Hans-Hermann Teichler, interview with the author, Hamburg, 20 August 2010.

[82] *Juillet 76 à Malville*, 1976, 40 mins; Nissim, *L'amour et le monstre*, pp. 26–7.

[83] Mediapart, 'Cazeneuve interdit définitivement les grenades offensives', 2014, http://www.mediapart.fr/journal/france/131114/cazeneuve-interdit-definitivement-les-grenades-offensives (accessed 25 February 2015); Nouvel Observateur, 'Rémi Fraisse, Vital Michalon : quand l'histoire se répète', 2014, http://tempsreel.nouvelobs.com/planete/20141113. OBS4959/infographie-remi-fraisse-vital-michalon-quand-l-histoire-se-repete.html (accessed 25 February 2015).

several serious ones: Manfred S., a nineteen-year-old from Bremen, had his right hand blown off as he picked up a grenade to throw it back towards police lines;[84] Michel Grandjean (a left-wing demonstrator from Lyon) had to have his right leg amputated below the knee after a stun grenade exploded near his foot; and Fernand Touzeau, a brigadier in the *gendarmes mobiles* who failed to throw a stun grenade quickly enough, lost his right hand.[85] Worst of all, the thirty-one-year-old demonstrator Vital Michalon was killed when a stun grenade exploded at very close range.

The violence in Malville in 1977 was directly related to developments across the border, as French police and protesters both took cues from their West German counterparts. The industrial consortium responsible for building Super-Phénix sent observers to the Brokdorf and Grohnde protests, who came back with strategic recommendations for protests in Malville.[86] Based on 'lessons communicated by the Federal Republic of Germany' (specifically 'what was observed at Wyhl, Brokdorf, and Grohnde'), French police established two concentric security cordons around the construction site in order to keep protesters as far away from it as possible.[87] West German authorities also screened a video about violent protesters in Brokdorf for their French counterparts, presumably sharing their horror at the 'attacks of heretofore unknown determination and brutality on the part of demonstrators' that they described in their written reports.[88] Brokdorf thus cast a shadow over Malville, leading French police to expect violence at the 1977 demonstration—especially from visiting West German protesters.

As for the protesters, many hoped to 'retake Malville' more durably in 1977 than they had in 1976 by bringing far more people to the site.[89]

---

[84] Manfred's last name is given as 'Schulte', 'Schultz', 'Schutz', or 'Schulze' in different sources. It is unclear whether the grenade in question was an exploding tear gas grenade (*grenade lacrymogène instantanée*, GLI) or a stun grenade (*grenade OF*), both of which were used at the demonstration. Gewerkschaft Erziehung und Wissenschaft, *Kriminalisierung* (1977), p. 46.

[85] *Aujourd'hui Malville* (1978), pp. 86–108; 'Les obsèques de Vital Michalon ont eu lieu dans le recueillement', *Le Monde*, 10 August 1977.

[86] NERSA, 'Compte rendu', report to the Prefect of Isère, 26 May 1977, AD Isère, 6857 W 35.

[87] 'Rapport d'analyse sur la Manifestation de Malleville [sic]', police report, undated 1977, AD Isère, 6857 W 36.

[88] Landespolizei Schleswig-Holstein, 'Brokdorf-Dokumentation', p. 57. It was not possible to obtain a copy of the video in question, though it appears to have been shown to visiting foreign delegations on several occasions as part of presentations given by Police Captain Karlheinz Müller. See 'Besuch ausländischer Polizeiführer', 1976–7, LASH, Abt. 621, Nr. 599.

[89] 'Malville : objectif 100.000', *GO*, no. 159 (26 May 1977), p. 1. The number was jokingly revised downwards after Brice Lalonde, media figure and leader of the Paris-based Amis de la Terre, announced that he would not attend. 'Malville : objectif 99.999', *GO/ CNV*, no. 167 (21 July 1977), p. 7.

Fig. 5.2. *Super-Pholix* no. 12. The drawing shows a 'peaceful non-violent group', 'peaceful self-defence group', and 'peaceful offensive group' all converging on Malville: 'All who want to march, will march.' Reproduced by permission of Georges David (director of publication, *Super-Pholix*).

However, a substantial portion of the energetic newcomers who joined the Comités Malville after the 1976 protest were less committed to non-violence. They argued that protests like those in Wyhl, Grohnde, and

Marckolsheim had shown that 'anti-nuclear resistance with "violent" and "non-violent" [protesters] united' was possible.[90] Some French militant protesters referred explicitly to Brokdorf as their model for militancy: in *Super-Pholix*, the shared newspaper of the ideologically diverse Comités Malville, they reprinted a photo of helmeted West Germans at the barricades, bearing the caption 'Brokdorf—not bad, huh?'[91] Different factions issued contradictory protest appeals, sending out mixed signals about the strategy the protesters would pursue. One edition of *Super-Pholix* proclaimed 'unanimity' regarding the 'necessity to penetrate the site in order to destroy everything that it is possible to destroy of the power station', while the next argued that 'what will stop Malville is not the damage we might be able to do but the political weight of the rally', which should therefore be non-violent 'so that everyone can come'.[92] The result was a protest that was to be 'peaceful but offensive', a discursive mélange that proved, under the circumstances, to be very dangerous in practice (see Fig. 5.2).

With different activists pursuing militant and non-violent strategies side by side, Malville wound up clearly illustrating the failings of both: no one had control and everyone got in everyone else's way, ultimately resulting in Vital Michalon's death. Vital, a high school physics teacher, had gone to the demonstration together with his younger brother Paul (b. 1955), an enthusiast of non-violence who had been inspired by the previous year's protest, in which Lanza del Vasto himself had participated. (Del Vasto quietly absented himself in 1977.) The July 1977 demonstration was one of the first protests either of the brothers had attended. Paul recalls the complex mix of impressions that the demonstration and its sudden, violent turn made on him at the time:

PM: I had never seen a crowd like that in my life. [. . .] We were among the first [to arrive] and in front of us there were thousands of police. Everything had been well prepared, they were waiting for us. There was no way to go back because the roads were full with all the marchers, who couldn't advance any further [either]. We were trapped. But [. . .] I didn't feel any concern about that, maybe even a bit curious [. . .] We were jammed in there and the battle started in front of us [. . .] We

---

[90] 'Discussion avec Françoise [d'Eaubonne] et ses amis à Paris', *Casse-Noix*, no. 6 (July 1977), pp. 6–7.

[91] 'Brokdorf : c'était pas mal hein !', *Super-Pholix*, no. 13 ([July] 1977), p. 4.

[92] 'Propositions soumises à la discussion des comités par la coordination du 2 avril 77', *Super-Pholix*, no. 12 ([May?] 1977), pp. 6–7; Kaim [Nissim], 'L'esprit du rassemblement', *Super-Pholix*, no. 13 ([June/July?] 1977), pp. 6–7 (p. 2).

were there, thousands upon thousands, watching what happened, [unable to] do anything. We were witnessing a spectacle. It lasted maybe an hour, an hour and a half. [...] And then, visibly, the police [...] began [...] to fire stun grenades and tear gas grenades. [...] I was with Vital when [...] we heard an explosion and screaming—really close to us, 10–20 metres away! And we saw people carrying [Michel] Grandjean, whose leg had been torn off. It was dreadful. And Vital said something curious to me. He said: 'It's appalling! The next time, we'll leave.' 'The next time.' It means that deep down, this spectacle was fascinating too. It disgusted us, it fascinated us.[93]

The spectacle and circumstances of violence drew all participants in, even those like Paul who had come with specifically non-violent intent. The kind of non-violence he and others had envisioned was impossible in Malville. The effective practice of non-violent protest requires careful preparation, self-control, and cooperation among demonstrators, not to mention a modicum of restraint on the part of police. None of these were present in Malville. Paul says that, as police began to attack, his brother and a number of non-violent activists sat down in an attempt to de-escalate the situation:

PM: And we were seated for *ten seconds*! It was impossible [...] It was, instantaneously, the defeat [*échec*] of Lanza del Vasto, [Martin] Luther King, all that. [...] It was a kind of war: you saw this guy with his leg torn off, injured people everywhere, people screaming. It was terrible! We asked ourselves 'Where in the world are we?' We talk about militancy, about ideals and all that, and they shoot at us. [... It] was a *total* defeat! A strategic failure [*échec*] if you will, we didn't even see the power station. A failure of everything we had dreamed of. You know? A non-violent demonstration that was supposed to be exemplary—not at all! Utter failure, brutality, aggression. Many people started shouting 'CRS—SS!' like in '68. [...] It was, for many, the feeling of absolutely total defeat. Everything was falling to pieces.[94]

If Malville was a defeat for non-violent demonstrators, it was no less of one for militant anti-nuclear activists. Even the most well-armed and aggressive demonstrators came no closer to catching so much as a glimpse of the

[93] Paul Michalon, interview with the author, Valence, 30 January 2010.
[94] Michalon, interview.

construction site that protesters had hoped to occupy; the innermost police cordon was positioned a full 2 kilometres beyond its perimeter.

A lasting occupation under these circumstances was impossible, but even if demonstrators had managed to make it onto the site and destroy equipment, the impact would have been minimal: a letter from the Prefect's office from February 1977 stated that 'nothing is planned for this year but infrastructural works of civil engineering. No sensitive material will be put in place'.[95] Jean-Luc Pasquinet (b. 1953), an autonomist participant in the demonstration, recognizes today that 'Super-Phénix was still under construction at the time, so there wasn't all that much to do [. . .] It was entirely a symbol.'[96] Yet the FBR was a symbol of the utmost importance for all sides. For the French state, it was a prestigious *bien national* to be defended at all costs,[97] a special technology that produced plutonium which could be used to power other reactors—or to build bombs. For demonstrators, Malville was the central and most repugnant element of the entire system of nuclear power, an especially expensive, high-risk, and unproven technology that produced 'the most toxic substance the world has ever known'.[98] But even if the stakes were high, no one was prepared for what actually happened.

PM: These [grenades] were falling all the time, all around us. You had to keep moving because they were falling. And we saw, very well, that the police were shooting [straight at us . . .][99] And that was scary. But we couldn't really move around that much. And then I suppose there was the desire to stand fast, to stay! So many of us had come, and under such difficult conditions. We weren't going to run off like rabbits! And then the order was given to the police to attack. [. . .] At that moment, there was panic. [. . .] We heard the explosions getting closer and we set off running. [. . .] I turned around and Vital wasn't there. [. . .] I told myself, 'He must have got through [. . .] he'll manage.' Now I know. I realized later that when I looked back, it was when my brother had just died. [As] he was climbing the embankment on all fours, a grenade fell in front of him and exploded. And the

---

[95] Cabinet du Préfet, letter to 'Monsieur le Directeur', 18 February 1977, AD Isère, 6857 W 35.

[96] Jean-Luc Pasquinet, interview with the author, Paris, 17 November 2009.

[97] Prefect René Jannin, speaking on 'Interdiction manifestation Creys-Malville', 28 July 1977, Antenne 2.

[98] 'Le saut dans . . . l'inconnu', *Politique Hebdo* (1 April 1976).

[99] This is a reference to police illegally shooting *tirs tendus* of tear gas and stun grenades, that is to say firing directly at demonstrators rather than shooting grenades parabolically into the air. *Aujourd'hui Malville*, p. 115.

blast, reflected by the ground, is deadly. He was killed like that, almost instantly.[100]

The violent repression of the demonstration in Malville on 31 July led to a wave of protests across France, West Germany, and Europe. In nearby Geneva, the first solidarity march began within hours of the Malville demonstration's tragic end. In the days that followed, protesters temporarily changed the inscription on the monument to war dead in the French consulate's garden from 'they died for France' to 'Malville 77—Vital Michalon died for us', and attempted to present a bouquet of flowers in Michalon's honour to the consul.[101] Along the Franco-German border in Alsace, protesters held a torchlight procession over the Rhine near one of France's hydroelectric power stations.[102] In Hamburg, up to 1,000 people came together the night of 31 July for a spontaneous demonstration in front of the French consulate, vandalizing it before police could arrive.[103] In these and other cities, protesters marched through the streets with banners bearing Vital Michalon's name. Despite all this organized, public solidarity, the events of Malville were a profound shock at the level of the individual. This was an environmental protest in Western Europe, not a demonstration against Franco or the military dictatorship in Greece. As Suzanne d'Hernies, a member of the Organisation Communiste des Travailleurs, put it, 'In Malville, no one was going to risk his or her neck [...] it just wasn't the goal.' Back in West Germany, KB member Hans-Hermann Teichler remembers that Malville was 'a level of escalation [...] that we didn't have. And it was absolutely shocking. No one wanted that.'[104]

For German activists, the shock was reinforced only two months later by the intimidation they experienced on the way to a protest in Kalkar. The West German government, not content to merely insinuate a link between protest and 'terrorism',[105] chose the date of a much-anticipated anti-nuclear protest in Kalkar to conduct an unprecedented, nationwide manhunt for members of the RAF, involving more than 8,000 police

---

[100] Michalon, interview.

[101] Consul général Lucien Balthazar, letter to l'Ambassadeur de France en Suisse, 10 August 1977, AD Isère, 6857 W 35.

[102] EDF responded by sending Jean-Jacques Rettig a bill for 4,800 francs, supposedly to cover the costs of cleaning its parking lot thereafter. Memo, 17 November 1977, AD Haut-Rhin, 1391 W 17.

[103] Memos, 1 August and 8 August 1977, StHH, 331-I II, Az. 20.37-3, Abl. 17, 1977, Bd. 14.

[104] SDH in Bernard Dréano and Suzanne d'Hernies, joint interview with the author, Paris, 20 January 2010. Teichler, interview.

[105] Karrin Hanshew, *Terror and Democracy* (2012), pp. 173–4.

officers.[106] On 24 September 1977, checkpoints with armoured vehicles and machine gun-toting police were set up throughout the country. Though the RAF was the official target, police were at least as interested in thwarting the protest. They confiscated truckloads of equipment from anti-nuclear protesters, including thousands of helmets and gas masks, hundreds of tools that might be used against perimeter fences at the site, sticks and pocketknives that could potentially be used as weapons, camping equipment, flyers, loudspeakers, and reportedly even protesters' lunches.[107] According to Teichler, if anti-nuclear activists had wanted to attempt to occupy the site under such circumstances, 'one would almost have had to change over to military methods'.[108]

The goal for militant demonstrators was to protest with resolve and determination, 'not to fight out a war with the police'.[109] Non-violent demonstrators were equally shocked, if not more so. For them, Malville and Kalkar provided the final proof that the 'fence fixation'[110] had to end. Autonomists too increasingly argued that mass demonstrations were not the way forward, that activists would have to find new, less predictable ways to fight nuclear power. The escalation of violence at demonstrations had made the mismatch between discourse and practice all too apparent. Within all quarters of the anti-nuclear movement, the events of 1977 led to a pause for reflection and a 'search for alternatives'[111] to mass demonstrations and the contradictions they entailed.

BEYOND DEMONSTRATIONS

Non-violent and militant activists moved further apart in the late 1970s, as the practice of mass demonstrations no longer lived up to the officially 'non-violent' discourse that most of the anti-nuclear movement (especially local activists) propagated. Rather than demonstrating side by side as before, each

---

[106] Ermittlungsausschuss der Bürgerinitiativen gegen Kernenergie, *Wir, das Volk* (1977), p. 30. The demonstration was planned before the RAF kidnapping of Hanns Martin Schleyer occurred on 5 September 1977.

[107] Polizei Hamburg, 'Verlaufs- und Erfahrungsbericht', 25 September 1977, StHH, 331-1 II, Az. 20.37-3, Abl. 17, 1977, Bd. 15, p. 4. Among the items that police reportedly confiscated were tomatoes, eggs, and '5 Frikadellen'. When asked about these apparently arbitrary seizures, the Interior Minister of Nordrhein-Westfalen, Burkhard Hirsch, responded that it was better 'that one tomato too many be confiscated' than risk anyone being killed or injured at the demonstration. Ermittlungsausschuss der Bürgerinitiativen gegen Kernenergie, *Wir, das Volk*, pp. 53, 30.

[108] Teichler, interview.   [109] Teichler, interview.

[110] Hamburger Initiative kirchlicher Mitarbeiter und Gewaltfreie Aktion, 'Protestleute gegen den Tod', p. 16.

[111] Rucht, *Von Wyhl nach Gorleben*, p. 92.

bloc adopted practices more in line with its own preferred discourse of non-violence or militancy. The common denominator of their divergent protests was the avoidance of mass action, with a consequent reduction in scale. Whether as a small crowd, a closed group, or individually, anti-nuclear activists in the late 1970s attempted to keep the nuclear issue on the public agenda through attention-getting forms of protest.

In the aftermath of Malville and Kalkar, many activists explored the possibilities of non-violent protest. One option they pursued was the use of partial boycotts that withheld 10–15 per cent of energy bills.[112] By 1978, boycotts were planned or underway in cities across France, such as Bordeaux, Chambéry, Colmar, Lille, Nantes, and Toulouse; and in West Germany from Bonn to Bremen, Frankfurt, Freiburg, Hamburg, Kassel, Kiel, Köln, München, Nürnberg, Oldenburg, Stuttgart, and Wiesbaden—not to mention West Berlin, where no commercial nuclear power plant was planned, but where activists similarly argued that energy production should be scaled back and decentralized.[113] Many boycott actions were inspired by experiences abroad, such as American, Italian, and Dutch tax boycotts against the Vietnam War or government nuclear programmes.[114] Especially in West Germany, where anti-nuclear protest was frequently framed in terms of 'protecting life', boycotts were conceived in explicitly non-violent terms: a means consistent with the ends to be achieved and an act in which anyone could participate.[115] In Hamburg, non-violent activists working together with the Lutheran church argued that such actions were necessary 'because we have seen that mass demonstrations are only one way, with an extremely short half-life'.[116] In Freiburg, a boycott was justified in part by the fact that 'the most important means of resistance since Wyhl: the prevention of construction through site

---

[112] Some French activists even attempted a *grève du zèle* whereby they paid their electricity bills in full, but divided up into many small payments in order to complicate EDF's accounting. 'Grève du zèle : mode d'emploi', flyer, 2 pp., 1979, PA Lalanne; 'Astérix antinvcléaire', February 1979, BnF, 4°WZ-13630.

[113] Comité Malville de Grenoble, 'Autoréduisons 15 %', brochure, 12 pp., undated [1977], Gryffe, Malville etc; Initiativgruppe Stomzahlungsboykott im LBU-Berlin, 'Stromzahlungsboykott nun auch in Berlin', *Berliner Strobo-Kurier*, no. 1 (September 1978); Initiativgruppe Stomzahlungsboykott im LBU-Berlin, 'Strobo!', *Berliner Strobo-Kurier*, no. 1 (undated [1978]).

[114] Stromboykottgruppe der gewaltfreien BI Stuttgart, 'Kein Atomkraftwerk mit unserem Geld!', flyer, 4 pp., 1977, ABEBI, 13HL/13; Hamburger Initiative kirchlicher Mitarbeiter und Gewaltfreie Aktion, 'Protestleute gegen den Tod', pp. 59, 73–5; Comité Malville de Grenoble, 'Autoréduisons 15 %', p. 9.

[115] Initiativgruppe Stomzahlungsboykott im LBU-Berlin, 'nun auch in Berlin', *Berliner Strobo-Kurier*, no. 1.

[116] Claus Ifflaender, '10 Argumente für den Stromzahlungsboykott', flyer, 2 pp., 29 October 1979, AA, Strobo Prozesse.

occupation' had been 'taken' from activists.[117] Actions like these helped maintain protest over the long term, especially during the lull of large-scale anti-nuclear activity in 1978–9. However, they often fell short of their goals. Hamburg activists initially planned to maximize impact and minimize risk to participants by waiting to begin the boycott until 1,000 households had signed on. After more than six months of campaigning, they decided to go ahead with only 300 participants instead.[118] Faced with the threat of lawsuits or electricity shut-offs, far fewer people joined boycotts than had been willing to attend demonstrations.[119]

Other creative forms of non-violent protest complemented these and assured that the nuclear issue did not disappear from public discussion even in the absence of large protest. In Berlin, activists placed 1,600 bottles in front of a nuclear industry supplier's offices to protest against cheap energy tariffs for the packaging industry.[120] In Hamburg, sixty friends and members of the local Gewaltfreie Aktion lay down in front of the entrance to the electric utility's offices, forcing employees to step symbolically over their bodies to get to work.[121] In Alsace, activists proved even more creative. One Alsatian woman involved in anti-nuclear struggles on both sides of the Rhine remembers how activists there tried to use imaginative, 'unusual actions' in an attempt to 'get beyond demonstrations' even before the tragedy in Malville.[122] In the weeks before and after the Fessenheim power plant start-up on 8 March 1977, they focused on forcing the French government to publish its classified emergency evacuation plans. On 7 March, activists stole West German evacuation plans from an administrative office in Lörrach, which they then published in German and in French translation.[123] A couple of weeks later (the night of

---

[117] GAF, 'Wie geht es weiter? Neue Möglichkeiten des Widerstands gegen Atomenergie', flyer, 2 pp., 6 March 1978, StAF, W100/1 Nr. 98.

[118] Hamburger Initiative kirchlicher Mitarbeiter und Gewaltfreie Aktion, 'Protestleute gegen den Tod', pp. 61–2.

[119] Hamburger Initiative kirchlicher Mitarbeiter und Gewaltfreie Aktion, 'Wir boykottieren weiter! Denn Gerichte können nicht über unser Gewissen entscheiden', flyer, 2 pp., May 1978, APO, S 37.

[120] 'Flaschen . . . und „Leichen"', *GWR*, no. 40 (March/April 1979), pp. 30–1 (p. 30). This may have been inspired by a 1971 protest by Friends of the Earth in Britain. See Joachim Radkau, *Ära der Ökologie* (2011), p. 131.

[121] '[Die Aktion] sollte vor allem symbolisch ausdrücken, daß die HEW „über Menschen geht"'. 'Teppich mit Löchern', *GWR*, no. 38 (October 1978); Hertle, interview.

[122] The examples cited hereafter were given in response to a question about her personal experiences of the 1977 Malville demonstration: 'J'ai pas trop de souvenir de ça. [. . .] J'ai plutôt envie de parler [. . .] de l'imagination qui s'est développée à partir de 75 jusqu'en 77 dans le mouvement anti-nucléaire.' E., interview with the author, Zässingue, 17 April 2010.

[123] Écologie et Survie, 'Plan ORSEC allemand traduit — commenté — édité', brochure, 40 pp., 1977, PA Skandrani, p. 2. German militants later took this sort of action a step further, posting relevant sections of the emergency plans for Esenshamm nuclear power

26–7 March 1977), a small group of activists went from town to town throughout the region setting off emergency sirens, leaving behind notes asking what people would have done in the event of a real accident. Shortly thereafter (on 16–17 April 1977), activists pasted the name 'Fessenheim' over road signs at the entrance and exit of every town in the region in order to communicate the idea that they would all share the same fate in the event of an accident.[124] This action would later be copied in Germany on a much larger scale, with the phrase 'Gorleben is every-where' being pasted over road signs from Lüchow-Dannenberg to Hann-over, West Berlin, Hamburg, Stuttgart, and München.[125] The Gorleben road sign protest was the first element of a wave of momentum-building actions that took place during the month of March 1979, timed to coincide with the start of the (Larzac-inspired) tractor journey by local activists to the state capital of Hannover. The idea, promoted by envir-onmentalists and non-violent activists together, was to demonstrate against the centrally important nuclear waste disposal site in Gorleben first and foremost in a decentralized manner, making protest more diffi-cult for police to quash. Such ideas were also enthusiastically promoted in France, where the 'centralizing' nature of nuclear power fed decentralized and especially regional(ist) opposition. By conducting creative, attention-getting actions in rapid succession, non-violent activists kept the nuclear issue on the agenda while advancing a discourse of non-violence.

However, the emotions unleashed by Kalkar and Malville did not lead everyone to conclude that non-violence was the way forward. Even environmentalists who were predisposed to non-violence found the situ-ation challenging. Perhaps Mireille Caselli (b. 1948), who attended the Malville protest together with friends from a non-violent group (of which she was not a member), expresses this most clearly:

> MC: [Malville] is something I don't like to talk about, it was very traumatizing for me. [. . .] I think it wasn't difficult at that time to become totally radical. To become violent. I'm not that type of person, I've never really been for violence, but it rendered legitimate every form of illegality [. . .] A thing like Malville, it was revolting. [. . .] It made one want to be violent. It made one want to no longer belong to this society.

---

plant in public locations within each of the plan's three different evacuation zones. AKPÖ, *Bilanz und Perspektiven*, p. 110.

[124] E., interview.

[125] Telex, 15 March 1979, Nds, 100 Acc. 2003/116 Nr. 66.

If Malville made activists like Mireille have their doubts, for militant demonstrators it was the consummate proof that non-violence led nowhere. They blamed the non-violent organizers of the Malville protest, arguing that they had 'either exaggerated the horror of Super-Phénix or their actions were not commensurate with that horror'.[126] Autonomists argued that sabotage was the most appropriate and effective response. In the months that followed Vital Michalon's death, anonymous militants in France bombed EDF property repeatedly, claiming responsibility under names like *les rescapés de Malville* and *Groupe autonome du 31 juillet*.[127] Sabotage in West Germany, though much less common, was sometimes inspired by acts committed in France.[128] Indeed, one 1978 catalogue of direct actions against nuclear power assembled by West German autonomists is littered with French examples and explicitly suggests that Germans should learn from their foreign friends.[129] The frequency of sabotage in West Germany appears to have increased in the early 1980s, with one 1982 flyer from Schleswig-Holstein listing nearly thirty acts of sabotage in connection with the Brokdorf nuclear power plant during the preceding eighteen months (ranging from broken windows and graffiti at one supplier's offices to arson and bomb attacks against cement mixers and building equipment). Hoping to incite others to commit similar acts, the flyer's authors provided a list of construction companies working on the Brokdorf site.[130]

Acts of sabotage like these were powerful displays of militancy and often served multiple purposes at once. On a practical level, they hindered or slowed the construction of nuclear power plants. Symbolically, they communicated to the movement's enemies that autonomist action was unpredictable, capable of striking anywhere and at any time—a violent version of 'decentralized' opposition that avoided the head-on, losing confrontations with police that had come to characterize mass

---

[126] Pièces et Main d'Oeuvre, 'Memento Malville', p. 1.

[127] The latter argued that 'Malville n'est pas la fin du combat anti-nucléaire, mais d'une certaine forme de lutte (non-violence) qui n'a amené que des défaites'. Claude Courtes and Jean-Claude Driant, *Golfech* (1999), pp. 80–2.

[128] There appear to have been perhaps twice as many bomb and arson attacks in France for the period 1975–1981 than in Germany for the period up until 1986, based on a comparison of acts of sabotage recorded in the (non-exhaustive) chronologies in 'Actions directes contre le nucléaire, 1973–1996', 2008, http://infokiosques.net/spip.php?article553 (accessed 6 Feb 2010) and Atom Express, *Und auch nicht anderswo!* (1997).

[129] AKPÖ, *Bilanz und Perspektiven*, pp. 17, 88–117. Of the approximately fifty actions described, more than a third took place in France.

[130] weiße Rose, 'Anschläge', *Bauplatzwacheninfo*, no. 3 (1982), p. 3.

demonstrations.[131] Referring to sabotage in the region around Grenoble, 'Yannick' from the militant satirical paper *Casse-Noix* wrote:

> 50 million [francs] in damages at St.-Maurice-l'Exil, 20 million in Monta-lieu. And that doesn't include everything! Bravo and thanks, comrades! You give us hope! You show us an example! [. . .] Sabotage is very good! It's effective! LONG LIVE DIRECT ACTION![132]

Within the movement, sabotage was also meant to encourage a radical understanding of the struggle against nuclear power, with attacks directed 'by no means only against the nuclear industry' but also 'against the state and all forms of repression'.[133] Whether sabotage actually convinced local activists to reconceive their struggle in such terms is doubtful. After protesters in northern Germany detonated a pylon carrying electricity from Esenshamm nuclear power plant, autonomists went to the area to ask local people what they thought. 'Everyone spoke of their "secret pleasure" [*klammheimliche Freude*], but some looked around to make sure no one was observing them'; they did not want 'to make themselves [appear] suspect, to be somehow associated with the attacks, to outwardly display approval'.[134] For local activists and organizations fearful of reper-cussions, the expressions of solidarity with imprisoned RAF members that occasionally appeared in some statements of responsibility were particu-larly difficult to digest. However, real connections between anti-nuclear activists and 'terrorists' were exceedingly rare and tentative at best.[135] One supporter of 'low-intensity armed opposition' to nuclear power wrote retrospectively that 'Excepting mistakes, none of these actions entailed the slightest drop of blood, proof of the self-restraint and humanity of anti-nuclear [activists].'[136] Anti-nuclear arson and bomb attacks pushed vandal-ism and the discourse of militancy to the extremes, but they did not ordinarily spill over into violence against persons.

---

[131] AKPÖ, *Bilanz und Perspektiven*, pp. 16–17.

[132] Yannick, '. . . Vive l'action directe !', *Casse-Noix*, no. 8 (September 1977), p. 14.

[133] 'Atomkraftwerk Esenshamm: Strom-Masten gesprengt', *Anti-AKW-Telegramm*, no. 24 (September 1981), pp. 25–8 (p. 25).

[134] 'Atomkraftwerk Esenshamm: Strom-Masten gesprengt', *Anti-AKW-Telegramm*, no. 24, p. 25.

[135] One interviewee claimed that West German 'terrorist' groups had provided *matériel* for an act of sabotage in Fessenheim in 1975, which would explain why responsibility was claimed by the 'Commando Puig Antich-Ulrike Meinhof' (jointly honouring a victim of Franco and the imprisoned RAF member). Chaïm Nissim's group also received its RPG-7 via 'armed struggle' networks, but Nissim insists that it was received as a gift, with no exchange of material, financial, or other support. Nissim, *L'amour et le monstre*, pp. 97–8.

[136] The text continues: 'On ne saurait évidemment en dire autant des tueurs de Vital Michalon, des naufrageurs du *Rainbow Warrior*, des matraqueurs de tant de manifestants désarmés.' Pièces et Main d'Oeuvre, 'Memento Malville', p. 29. The anonymous author was a contributor to *Casse-Noix* in the late 1970s.

Non-violence could also take extreme forms, as in the case of self-starvation. By refusing to eat, activists turned the violence of power inward on themselves to show its destructiveness. Certainly, such actions were not the sole preserve of non-violent activists, as the hunger strikes of imprisoned Irish Republican Army and RAF members during the 1970s demonstrate.[137] However, admirers of Gandhi portrayed self-starvation as the 'strongest means of non-violent resistance',[138] a particularly demanding act that communicated their resolve and the seriousness of their cause. During the most famous such action against nuclear power, seven activists from Alsace gathered in the Maison de la Nature in Roggenhouse in February 1977 and collectively stopped eating to protest the impending start of the first, recently completed reactor at Fessenheim. They explained that their decision 'must be seen as a sign of readiness, of personal commitment and not of aggression. [...] We all love life very much [...]. The struggle we are leading is a struggle for life. [...] The choice of a hard and unlimited fast shows how important the problem is to us.'[139] Though the protesters would undoubtedly have preferred to stop the reactor's start-up entirely, their official demands for an independent monitoring commission (with participation from both French and German activists), publication of the evacuation plans, alarm drills, and a public consultation were more moderate. After twenty-four days, they ended their fast, even though only the first of these demands had been met. Rémy Verdet (b. 1956), a university student at the time and one of the seven participants, felt ambivalent about stopping, not only because of what it represented for the movement but also because he found the form of protest so appealing.

RV: We stopped at the end of twenty-four days. Should we have continued, should we not have continued? Maybe we should have continued except that the doctors, they didn't want us to continue. They said, 'You've got spots reserved for you at the hospital.' [...] But it was a great experience! I don't regret any of it and if I could have, I would have started again. Really.

It is nevertheless clear what a toll such a long fast took on its participants.

RV: At the beginning, we wrote letters to all the mayors [...] in Alsace. We had plenty of energy. And little by little, we became a bit more tired. The thing I'll always remember is: we thought

---

[137] See Leith Passmore, 'Art of Hunger', *German History* 27, no. 1 (2009).

[138] Raymond Schirmer, quoted in Thomas Lehner, 'Hungerstreik aus Protest gegen „Zünden" in Fessenheim', *Badische Zeitung*, 11 February 1977, p. 6.

[139] Flyer quoted in Christoph Büchele et al., *Der Widerstand* (1982), p. 91.

about nothing but food [*la bouffe*]! It was crazy! We dreamed about it, we talked about it, we exchanged recipes—it was incredible! [. . .] And little by little, we began to get a bit more tired and by the end, people who moved, who bustled about, who talked—it was almost violent! For [us]! It was tiring.[140]

The serious risk involved in this kind of self-starvation did not always inspire enthusiasm on the part of even sympathetic anti-nuclear activists. Writing about an earlier hunger strike in 1975, German activists who fasted for three days in solidarity with French comrades questioned 'whether [it was] the right time for a life-and-death hunger strike. To enter into an unlimited hunger strike is certainly one of the last means that one should employ [in the service of a] just cause.'[141] The 1975 hunger strikers had demanded more unbiased information about nuclear power, and decided their demands had been met when French television agreed to broadcast a previously censored, critical documentary film.[142] After the hunger strike was over, one sympathetic activist wrote that 'it is regrettable that one has to go on hunger strike for a month just to be able to get a little information'.[143] Extreme forms of non-violence—like extreme forms of violence—raised the question of ends and means in a different way: while self-starvation might be powerful as moral discourse, many viewed it as excessive given the ends it could practically achieve.

Different audiences responded to such acts in very different ways; whether one portrayed self-starvation as a 'hunger strike' or as 'fasting' could determine how much attention activists might attract, and from whom. For instance, the Trotskyist paper *Rouge* referred either to the *grève de la faim* in Roggenhouse or, mockingly, to the « *jeûne* » (the latter term always appearing in quotation marks). However, within Alsace itself, religious language helped garner widespread support, as manifested in the hundreds of letters to the 1977 fasters, the more than twenty 'solidarity fasts' elsewhere, and the joint declaration of support by over 100 Catholic and Protestant priests (or *ministres du culte*, as the Trotskyists referred to them).[144] Even the practised, well-managed, and usually

---

[140] Rémi Verdet, interview with the author, Neuviller-la-Roche, 19 April 2010.

[141] 'Warum wir 3 Tage nichts aßen', *WWW*, no. 5 ([May] 1975), pp. 5–6. On the matter of 'whether all other means had previously been exhausted', these German activists decided they 'didn't know enough to say', because they could not judge the situation in France.

[142] Claude Otzenberger, *Les atomes nous veulent-ils du bien ?*, 1975, 60 mins.

[143] 'Hungerstreik der 10 Franzosen nach einem Monat endlich beendet', *WWW*, no. 6 ([May/June?] 1975), p. 9.

[144] See 'Centrale nucléaire de Fessenheim', AD Haut-Rhin, 1391 W 17; Büchele et al., *Der Widerstand*, p. 91; 'Nucléaire : un manifeste de prêtres alsaciens', *La Croix*, 19 February

short-term fasts of non-violent leader Lanza del Vasto met with highly different fates depending on where and when they took place: his fast for the Larzac is widely credited with strengthening the unity and resolve of local farmers against the military camp, but other fasts in Marckolsheim, Malville, and elsewhere passed largely unnoticed.[145] The strength and weakness of the hunger strike as a form of protest lay in its very seriousness: once non-violent protest had reached that level, there was little activists could do to increase the pressure on their opponents.

Few were willing to take the discourse of non-violent self-sacrifice to its ultimate, fatal conclusion. The aforementioned hunger strikes ended with their moderate demands only partly fulfilled because participants could ill afford to push their protest any further: whatever the rhetoric, it was not an issue most people were ready to die for. Vital Michalon may have been hailed by *Libération* as the 'first death of the ecological struggle', but he had clearly not gone to Malville seeking martyrdom.[146] However, only a few months later, a teacher from Tübingen named Hartmut Gründler did choose to sacrifice his life in protest against nuclear power. On 16 November 1977, during a Social Democratic convention on energy policy in Chancellor Schmidt's hometown of Hamburg, Gründler walked to the St. Petri church in the city centre, doused himself in gasoline, and set himself ablaze. In a letter addressed to the Hamburg police, he had written:

After exhausting all other means, even that of the hunger strike, I now reach to the last and most extreme form of protest. For the sake of the human dignity that has been disgraced for years, I want to die.[147]

Gründler had taken this extreme step and become a 'human torch of protest' because he hoped it would shake the consciences of politicians and the public.[148] Previous instances of self-immolation, like those of Pastor

1977; 'Alsace : 4e dimanche d'occupation et de fête sur le site de Gerstheim', *Rouge*, 21 February 1977. Lutheran pastors in Germany also separately expressed their solidarity. 'Nachprüfungen in Fessenheim', *Badische Zeitung*, 5–6 March 1977, p. 9.

[145] See, for example, 'Interview zur Entwicklung'; Report, July 1976, AD Isère, 6253 W 37.

[146] 'Vital Michalon, le premier mort de la lutte écologique', *Libération*, 1 August 1977. This statement, including especially the comparison to Gilles Tautin (a seventeen-year-old who drowned in the Seine after fleeing police at a demonstration on 10 June 1968) and Pierre Overney (a Maoist shot in front of a Renault factory by security guard Jean-Antoine Tramoni on 25 February 1972), was seized upon for mockery by the right-wing press. See 'Malville : le sang après la boue', *L'Aurore*, 1 August 1977.

[147] 'Infobericht 126/77', 17 November 1977, StHH, 331-I II, Az. 20.37-3, Abl. 17, 1977, Bd. 20.

[148] Herbert Bruns, ed., *Hartmut Gründler* † (Wiesbaden, Biologie-Verlag, 1977), p. 5.

Oskar Brüsewitz in East Germany (1976), Jan Palach in Prague (1968), Norman Morrison in front of the Pentagon in Washington, D.C. (1965), or Thich Quang Duc in Saigon (1963) had received abundant press coverage and initiated public debates about the misdeeds perpetrated in the name of communism or anti-communism. Dissatisfied that Gründler's death seemed not to have the same effect, activists wondered aloud if nuclear power simply failed to fit the Cold War agenda that drove opinion makers.[149]

However, sympathy was not to be confused with approval. Non-violent activists were particularly appalled at Gründler's act and emphasized that he, unlike Gandhi, was a 'loner' [*Einzelgänger*] whose individual actions seldom had any connection to the broader movement.[150] Nevertheless, non-violent and militant anti-nuclear activists alike who had known him insisted that Gründler was not insane: he was someone who 'trusted in the power of arguments', who 'took seriously the liberal promises' of politicians and parties, and who sought to hold them to their word through exemplary, individual protest.[151] Two years earlier, Gründler had initiated an indefinite fast in an attempt to appeal to the conscience of Minister of Research and Technology Hans Matthöfer, insisting that Matthöfer's 'Citizen's Dialog' (*Bürgerdialog*) should take nuclear energy opponents more seriously. Many non-violent activists had 'considerable objections' at the time as to whether hunger strike was 'an appropriate means under the circumstances and for the objectives'.[152] In 1976, Gründler went on a second fast, this time appealing directly to Chancellor Schmidt on the basis of Schmidt's own (election-year) book about Christian responsibility in politics. After breaking his fast in response to a call from the Chancellery, Gründler was disappointed when no concrete action followed.[153] The 'most unusual form of resistance' that Gründler's final protest took was 'for him' the only means left that might be capable of increasing the pressure. Some activists even implied that Gründler's form of protest might be the last *legal* recourse available after 'site occupations, sit-ins, passive resistance in general [have] long since [become] criminalized'.[154] Though

[149] BI Lübeck, 'Selbstverbrennung', flyer, 1977, DfuL, D 1813.

[150] 'Hartmut Gründler †', *GWR*, no. 33 (1978), pp. 1, 11.

[151] 'Hartmut Gründler †', *GWR*, no. 33; BI Lübeck, 'Selbstverbrennung'; Sozialistisches Zentrum Tübingen, 'Hartmut Gründlers Verbrennung. Ein deutscher Tod!', flyer, 20 November 1977, DfuL, D 7400 (SZ 03 26), p. 3.

[152] 'Hartmut Gründler †', *GWR*, no. 33.

[153] Helmut Schmidt, *Als Christ in der politischen Entscheidung* (1976). At his funeral, Gründler's supporters fulfilled one of the deceased's final requests and nailed Schmidt's book to the coffin. Bruns, *Hartmut Gründler †*, p. 86.

[154] 'Schließt euch fest zusammen, leistet Widerstand!', flyer, 1977, ABEBI, 13HL/13; BI Lübeck, 'Selbstverbrennung'; Sozialistisches Zentrum Tübingen, 'Ein deutscher Tod'.

no one chose to imitate Gründler's act, the desperation and frustration behind it were familiar to other anti-nuclear activists at the time.

If few people thought that opposing nuclear power was a cause worth dying for, those prepared to kill for it were almost as rare. No faction within the anti-nuclear movement openly advocated the kinds of kidnappings, hijackings, and murder executed by groups such as the RAF or AD. Nevertheless, there were isolated incidents where militant action became fatal or nearly so. The first such case occurred in France in early July 1977, as violent conflict over nuclear power was escalating in parallel in France and West Germany. A group calling itself the Comité d'Action Contre les Crapules Atomiques (CACCA) planted a bomb outside the flat of Marcel Boiteux, CEO of the French power company EDF. Boiteux and his family were unharmed, but only by chance.[155] Organized anti-nuclear groups distanced themselves from the act publicly, but not even all non-violent activists took pity on Boiteux. The ecologist newspaper *La Gueule ouverte* (then recently merged with *Combat non-violent*) published a satirical 'Open Letter to a Badly Housed Civil Servant' in which the author professed:

> I can't quite manage to show solidarity with the press that condemns this 'murderous attack'. Normally I should, I who am incapable of shortening the life of a fly. But there's nothing that can be done. [Nothing] comes out. I'll leave it to the unions, parties, and Paris branch of Les Amis de la Terre to testify their virtuous horizontal solidarity, class solidarity.[156]

This 'open letter' was reminiscent of the controversial 'obituary' published in West Germany only two months earlier, in which an anonymous radical leftist expressed 'secret pleasure' (*klammheimliche Freude*) at the death of Chief Federal Prosecutor Siegfried Buback, even while unequivocally condemning his assassination by the RAF.[157] However, 'armed struggle' groups like the RAF (much more prominent in West Germany than in France) showed little or only belated interest in the issue of nuclear power, claiming instead to fight in the name of struggles against imperialism and repression.[158]

---

[155] 'Atome : la croisade des jeunes', *Le Point* (8 August 1977).

[156] Arthur [pseud.], 'Lettre ouverte à un fonctionnaire mal logé', *GO/CNV*, no. 166 (14 July 1977), p. 16.

[157] Mescalero [pseud. Klaus Hülbrock], 'Buback. Ein Nachruf', *Göttinger Nachrichten*, 25 April 1977. According to one observer, 'Die „klammheimliche Freude" war weit verbreitet, trauern tat niemand, aber lauten Jubel gab es ebenfalls nicht.' 'Das Jahr 1977', *ak*, no. 447 (22 February 2001), p. 4.

[158] The first nuclear-related RAF attack was the murder of Karl Heinz Beckurts on 9 July 1986. RAF declarations from the 1970s mention nuclear power only twice, and then only in relation to anti-imperialist struggle. RAF, *Texte und Materialien zur Geschichte der*

The Revolutionäre Zellen (RZ) constituted an exception, though they too admitted that 'The movement against nuclear power that emerged in 1974/75 was foreign to us' and its non-working-class social base 'very suspect'.[159] In 1981, RZ planned an action to intimidate and incapacitate Hessen's Business Minister Heinz Herbert Karry by shooting him in the leg. The goal was thereby to 'hinder him for a longer period from pursuing his repulsive and destructive projects', foremost among them the Biblis nuclear power plant and Frankfurt airport's Startbahn West expansion.[160] In the event, the attack went much further than intended: one of the shots fired at Karry as he slept hit an artery, causing him to bleed to death. Actions like this dramatically demonstrated the potential for violence against persons to spin out of control. Nevertheless, the RZ statement claiming responsibility for the attack ended with a call for sabotage 'against machines, institutions, persons. Against everything that breaks us, destroys us, and oppresses us.'[161] What seemed to work well as rhetoric was not nearly so attractive in practice. In a statement ten years later announcing their dissolution, the RZ assessed that sabotage against nuclear projects and Startbahn West had made successful interventions in these 'single-issue movements' (*Teilbereichsbewegungen*)—until, 'through one single, fatal error, the murder of Karry', the RZ's concept of revolutionary action plummeted in popularity.[162]

At the extremes, the militant discourse of RZ and the non-violent discourse of Hartmut Gründler could not be matched to practice without alienating supporters. More mild forms of protest such as boycotts and sabotage also ran up against limits, bringing attention to the nuclear issue but doing little to expand or mobilize the movement's base.

RAF (1997), pp. 157, 256. In France, AD does not appear to have carried out attacks against nuclear power. However, the anti-nuclear struggle was a centrally important theme for some autonomists, including future AD founder Jean-Marc Rouillan.

[159] RZ, 'Subversiver Kampf in der Anti-AKW-Bewegung', *Autonomie*, no. 4/5 (1980), pp. 30–5. RZ sabotaged facilities belonging to nuclear industry suppliers MAN and KSB in August 1977, arguing notably that 'Der einkalkulierte und vollendete Mord in Malville macht für den Widerstand neue Qualitäten notwendig.' RZ, 'Anschlag gegen Klein, Schanzlin & Becker AG', *BUG-Info*, no. 172 (5 September 1977).

[160] RZ, 'Aktion gegen den hessischen Wirtschaftminister Karry', May 1981, http://www.freilassung.de/div/texte/rz/zorn/Zorn38.htm (accessed 26 September 2012).

[161] RZ, 'Aktion gegen Karry'.

[162] '(Durch einen einzigen verhängnisvollen Fehler, den Mord an Karry, wurde dieses Konzept von Popularität schlagartig desavouiert.)' Note that the text here refers specifically to Startbahn West rather than anti-nuclear protest, though both issues are also described as '(fast) beliebig und austauschbar'. RZ, 'Das Ende unserer Politik', January 1992, http://www.freilassung.de/div/texte/rz/zorn/Zorn05.htm (accessed 26 Sept 2012).

LIVING WITH CONTRADICTION

However much such alternatives may have brought the discourse and practice of either non-violence or militancy into line, they did not bring anti-nuclear activists themselves together. After the Harrisburg nuclear accident in 1979, a new wave of mass protests around local sites would do so, reintroducing some of the contradictions that anti-nuclear activists had worked to eliminate. Unlike during the 1970s, though, these contradictions caused the violence debate to recede rather than intensify, as many activists decided that success (determined largely by the support of the local community) was more important than moral consistency. Though 'violent' French protests such as those in Plogoff and 'non-violent' West German ones in Gorleben appeared to diverge, each represented a different path leading towards the same conclusion: effective action should not be prevented by endless debate. Non-violent, militant, and other activists thus found ways to protest alongside one another again, even if this did not mean they marched shoulder to shoulder.

In France, activists' defeat at the 1977 demonstration in Malville had crushed the nascent national movement and forced a retreat back to local and regional protests like those that took place during the public consultation (*enquête d'utilité publique*, EUP) in Plogoff in 1980. Coming after more than five years of anti-nuclear protest throughout France and West Germany, activists in Plogoff learned from others, developing practices that were guided less by a moral discourse and more by trial-and-error experience.[163] Both nuclear energy opponents and police had learned from protests against the EUP in Le Pellerin and neighbouring Cheix-en-Retz in 1977: when the mayors of both towns refused to post notices about the planned nuclear facility as formally required, central authorities sent a sub-prefect in to do it in their stead; when the mayors closed city hall for the entire six weeks of the EUP, the prefect had police escort impromptu 'Town Hall Annex' vans to the area to display information for public comment; when protesters stole and subsequently destroyed the register of citizens' comments, authorities made a habit of producing certified copies nightly. In Plogoff, this cat-and-mouse game would be carried to a new level. Upon receiving planning documents for display, the mayor of Plogoff hosted a bonfire on the town's main square and tossed them in. The night before the EUP was to begin, activists built such elaborate barricades to block the

---

[163] Plogoff 'était en bout de course, donc c'était l'expérience des autres qui pouvait alimenter notre expérience à nous'. Gérard Borvon, interview with the author, via telephone, 10 March 2010.

arrival of the 'Annex' vans that it took hundreds of police almost four hours to clear them the next morning. During the six weeks the EUP lasted, the laying of increasingly odious obstacles became an almost daily ritual for activists as they sought to demoralize the police. So too did participation in the so-called '5 o'clock mass', when protesters 'escorted' police, under a volley of projectiles, back to the seminary where they were temporarily accommodated. These regular confrontations escalated rapidly: most people 'came with empty hands' during the short first week of the EUP, then rocks began to fly on Monday 4 February, followed by paint-filled yoghurt pots and beer cans on Tuesday, which were then launched from slingshots starting Wednesday; the first Molotov cocktails made their appearance on Friday, 8 February. It was small consolation to police that, 'in this fever that rose in a crescendo, [protesters] did not get the guns out'.[164]

Today, Plogoff is remembered for the intensity with which protesters (overwhelmingly local citizens and regional youth) opposed the police during the EUP. This became a model for the 'local violence' that would continue in places like Chooz and Golfech. However, that violence was always relative. The local community of tiny, remote Plogoff was subjected to an overwhelming display of force by the state, which residents compared (unfavourably) to the German occupation during the Second World War.[165] The massive contingent of heavily armed security forces (consisting of as many as two squadrons of militarily trained *gendarmes mobiles* and five CRS units, approximately 900–1,000 men in total)[166] came into the town every weekday for six weeks and responded to protesters' various improvised projectiles by launching round after round of tear gas and stun grenades (the same kind that killed Vital Michalon in Malville). Against this backdrop, many felt that the local community was more restrained than violent, an idea that found expression in the title of a popular film about the struggle: *Des pierres contre des fusils*.[167] Months after the EUP was over, military intelligence reported that Plogoff was still 'haunted' by the memory of the security intervention. When a few military vehicles with no connection to the nuclear dispute happened to pass through town one day in October 1980, local citizens sounded an alarm to report the 'troop movements' and sent groups of men armed with hunting rifles to take up positions at the edge of town. Authorities worried

---

[164] RG, 'Réflexions sur l'Enquête d'Utilité Publique', March 1980, AD Finistère, 1235 W 24; Gérard Borvon, 'Plogoff occupé', in *Histoire lacunaire de l'opposition à l'énergie nucléaire en France*, edited by Association contre le nucléaire et son monde (2007), pp. 61, 64–7; Memo, 13 July 1977, AD Finistère, 1347 W 164-2, pp. 7–9.

[165] Hélène Crié, 'Ende der gewaltfreien Utopie?', *tageszeitung*, 17 March 1980, p. 12.

[166] Report, 135 pp., undated, AD Finistère, 1235 W 25/2, pp. 113–14.

[167] Nicole Le Garrec, *Plogoff : des pierres contre des fusils*, 1980, 90 mins.

that Plogoff was descending into 'anarchic autonomy' from the central state and that the local anti-nuclear committee that had been behind the protests could not keep control over its own members.[168] Though 'rocks against guns' hardly constituted a non-violent strategy, authorities' disproportionate use of force put public opinion squarely on the side of the underdog local community.

Protest in Plogoff was certainly intense, but was it 'the end of a non-violent utopia', as the German *tageszeitung* and much of the French media seemed to think?[169] While autonomist activists in Paris and West Germany eagerly celebrated the use of 'guerilla tactics' in Plogoff, other activists from Alsace described the *Plogoffistes* as 'energetically non-violent'.[170] Both were projecting their own discourse onto a conflict whose reality was complex and ambiguous. In fact, the protests in Plogoff pulled every available lever, usually under the direction of the local community and its *comité de défense*. Much was learned or copied from the Larzac struggle, considered at that time to be the epicentre of non-violent protest. To raise money and complicate expropriation proceedings, Plogoff activists created a *groupement foncier agricole* on the Larzac model, selling thousands of tiny parcels of land all around the site to their outside supporters. They also illegally built a barn on the site of the future power plant (see Fig. 5.3), transplanting both the idea and the sheep that lived there from the Larzac. As in Marckolsheim and Wyhl, older women exploited the public's preconceived notions about their age and gender in order to condition perceptions of the protest movement, but here their intent was not to make a non-violent, moral appeal by portraying themselves as innocent, passively resisting victims. Instead, they hurled a constant stream of verbal abuse at police while demonstratively knitting, sending the public the message that the heavy-handed police presence had exhausted even the patience of kindly grandmothers.[171] The same message was communicated even more dramatically in a photo showing an elderly woman picking up a rock and handing it to a young demonstrator,

---

[168] Monthly report for October 1980, 3 pp., 2 November 1980, AD Finistère, 1347 W 85, p. 2; Memo, 9 February 1981, AD Finistère, 1235 W 25; RG, 'Réflexions', p. 17.

[169] Félix le Garrec argues that it was the national television media above all 'who wanted to distort' the story and thus played up the violence. FLG in Félix et Nicole Le Garrec, joint interview with the author, Plonéour Lanvern, 26 September 2010. Crié, 'Ende der gewaltfreien Utopie?', *tageszeitung*, 17 March 1980.

[170] 'Eine Einführung in die Guerillataktik des bretonischen Dorfes Plogoff im Widerstand gegen den Atomwahn', brochure, 43 pp., 1981, PA Tompkins; Rettig, interview.

[171] Police wrote of 'les « tricoteuses » de Plogoff, dont l'hostilité ne dépasse guère le stade du harcèlement verbal permanent, et souvent ordurier et provocateur'. RG, 'Réflexions', p. 8.

Fig. 5.3. Illegal barn in Plogoff, 2010. The full text on the barn door reads *L'avenir? C'est notre affaire.* ('The future? It's our affair.') Photo: Andrew Tompkins.

presumably to throw it at police.[172] Yet far from being in favour of violence, many local people were 'shocked' when the first rocks were thrown.[173] One local woman stated, 'I certainly didn't expect that at all. But I understood why they did it. It was their only defence.'[174] In other situations, though, protester violence was more an implied threat than a reality. When young protesters were put on trial for attacking police in Plogoff, townspeople stood outside the courtroom, symbolically holding slingshots in their hands. Was this a threatening and therefore 'violent' act or was it a display of restraint and therefore 'non-violent'? The protesters in Plogoff seem not to have concerned themselves greatly with such questions. Jean Moalic (b. 1953), an environmentalist protester who worked with the local action committee, felt it was closer to the latter, but he stresses that protest in Plogoff did not conform to any ideology.

> JM: There was no ready-made response. An adapted response was found—that is to say, a form of violence, verbal or physical, but one that was controlled. There were no autonomists, [but] at the same time 'extreme' non-violent demonstrations so to speak didn't take place either. [...] It's because the local population, in its overwhelming majority, was opposed and led the struggle

---

[172] 'Einführung in die Guerillataktik', p. 66; Renée Conan and Annie Laurent, *Femmes de Plogoff*, 2010 republished edn (1981), p. 29.

[173] Conan and Laurent, *Femmes de Plogoff*, pp. 28–31.

[174] Le Garrec, *Pierres contre fusils*.

[...] *the way they wanted to*, which sometimes left the confines of being straightforward to people who came from outside—'Listen, it's our struggle, we're the ones who lead it'—and [because] everyone hit their own register that it was able to succeed. [...] That was the 'brand name' of Plogoff: a local population that defends itself with greater or lesser [violence], sometimes with contradictions too.[175]

Gérard Borvon (b. 1944), another activist from Bretagne but not from Plogoff, describes it succinctly in other terms: the struggle in Plogoff was 'not violent, but sensational'.[176] However one chose to describe it, protest in Plogoff demonstrated that practical success was more important than discursive consistency.

Only a few months after the confrontation over the EUP in Plogoff, West Germans made equally sensational headlines, but this time through a display of sensational *non*-violence in Gorleben. On 3 May 1980, 5,000 activists walked onto an unsecured area designated for test drilling for the planned nuclear waste disposal site and called into being the Republik Freies Wendland (RFW). Over the course of the next four weeks, activists organized in small, independent affinity groups would illegally build more than fifty structures, ranging from architecturally expressive huts to shared kitchen, bathroom, and event facilities as well as an improvised wooden church, observation towers, and a gigantic swing set. Life in the 'village' was organized along non-violent, democratic principles. Each affinity group was entitled to send a representative to the Council of Speakers (*Sprecherrat*), where collective decisions were made on the basis of consensus. A so-called 'consensus paper' drafted during the three months of advance preparations declared that the occupation would be 'an expression of the local community's resistance' and therefore had to remain non-violent; no one was to organize sabotage actions from the site and, in the event of eviction by police, activists were to exercise only passive resistance.[177] In this particularly conservative region along the East German border, the local community was highly suspicious of outsiders and had repeatedly tried to limit radical protest through non-violence. At a first demonstration in 1977, they had told people to come 'without helmets, with flowers' and declared, 'Gorleben: a second Brokdorf? Never!'[178] In

---

[175] Jean Moalic, interview with the author, Mahalon, 29 September 2010.
[176] Borvon, interview. [177] Zint, *RFW*, p. 55.
[178] Bürgerinitiative Umweltschutz Lüchow-Dannenberg (BI L-D), 'Gorleben ein 2. Brokdorf? Nein! Niemals!', flyer, 1 p., 12 March [1977], HIS, SBe 730 Box 01. The BI L-D at one time considered writing a clause into its statutes to permanently exclude radicals from membership. The group's long-time leader, Marianne Fritzen, repeatedly distanced

effect, the calm, passive resistance of protesters during the eviction was to be perhaps the greatest achievement of RFW, leading to more effective cooperation between locals and outside supporters at subsequent protests and effectively dramatizing the state's overreaction to anti-nuclear protest.

On 4 June 1980, more than 8,000 police surrounded the village from all sides, coming on horseback, in armoured vehicles, and by helicopter. Even more than in 'violent' Plogoff, this overwhelming display of force stood in marked contrast to the demonstrators' own armaments: none wore helmets and some even stripped off their clothes to show they were unarmed.[179] Police hit demonstrators with truncheons, pulled them by the hair and dragged them through the dirt; though they did not make use of the ample water cannon, tear gas, and pepper spray at their disposal, this predictably rough handling of visibly defenceless activists seemed out of all proportion. As police bulldozed RFW buildings, protesters remained seated in rings in front of the village's central towers. Over a loudspeaker system, council members spoke words of encouragement, directed activists to sit in strategically useful places, appealed to police not to use their truncheons, and played music to which protesters sang along.[180] When police finally stormed the last tower, those holed up inside it jokingly offered them a glass of wine as a reward. The good humour of these peaceful demonstrators placed the violence and destructiveness of the authorities in stark relief. The banner on one of the last structures left standing drove the point home: 'You can destroy towers and a village, but not [the] energy that created them' (see Fig. 5.4).

That this non-violent protest would go off so well was, however, never a foregone conclusion. The organizers themselves were among those most surprised. Success in Gorleben was initially the product less of cooperation than of an accepted *separation* between militant and non-violent protest: after the same 'old and unproductive'[181] debates over violence resurged at multiple planning meetings, activists on both sides of the debate decided that 'the diversity of the movement should not lead, via forced unity, to anaemic compromises for which no one takes responsibility'.[182] Some (but not all) militant demonstrators chose to pull out and, from then on, environmentalists with non-violent propensities took charge of planning.[183] Nevertheless, debates about the appropriate level of militancy (and the

the BI from radical actions with which she disagreed and alarmed even non-radical supporters by, for example, serving tea and strawberry cake to the police in their barracks. See Halbach and Panzer, *Zwischen Gorleben & Stadtleben*, p. 110.

[179] Zint, *RFW*, p. 190.   [180] Zint, *RFW*, pp. 203–10.
[181] Zint, *RFW*, p. 10.   [182] Zint, *RFW*, p. 11.
[183] 'Gorleben 1004. Erfolg? Niederlage?', *Anti-AKW-Telegramm*, no. 22 (August 1980), pp. 4–9 (p. 5).

Fig. 5.4. Demonstrators at the Republik Freies Wendland. Visible in the background are numerous buildings, including the tower bearing the banner *Turm und Dorf könnt ihr zerstören, aber nicht unsere Kraft, die es schuf.* Reproduced by permission of Günter Zint.

balance of power among activists at the site) continued throughout the preparations, during the occupation, and even long after the protest was over. Just days before it was to begin, the occupation almost had to be called off after activists with militant inclinations (apparently unaware of the occupation plans) set up their own camp on the site before others arrived.[184] As the village was being built, there were constant fights: a group was authorized by the Speakers' Council to build barricades, then ordered to stop so the matter could be debated again; the observation towers that came to be icons of the occupation were initially rejected out of hand by non-violent activists who saw them as a sign of aggression; protesters were allowed to bring gas masks and helmets but told not to wear them, please.[185] The eviction itself was the source of the greatest controversy: militant activists were not alone in asking whether it really made sense to stand by and passively watch as police bulldozed in a matter of hours the utopian community that it had taken activists weeks of work, months of

---

[184] Zint, *RFW*, p. 11. Some of them left when asked, others stayed put and thus became part of the larger occupation. Halbach and Panzer, *Zwischen Gorleben & Stadtleben*, p. 157.
[185] Zint, *RFW*, pp. 56, 62; tageszeitung, *Gorleben-Dokumentation*, pp. 11, 38.

preparation, and years of learning to develop.[186] Police added insult to injury by thanking the protesters over loudspeaker for making the eviction such a 'success'.[187]

Yet in the end phase of RFW, activists of different perspectives came together to make the protest work.[188] Some militant activists (the 'Millies'), while insisting on the principle that forceful resistance was necessary, declared they would cooperate with non-violent activists in the name of unity:

> Our conception of resistance [...] encompasses all possible forms and knows no separation of anti-nuclear activists into non-violent and militant action! We weigh from one situation to another what the most sensible action form of resistance is. Here in Gorleben, we have agreed with all the other groups on non-violent action in the event of an eviction![189]

In their interactions with the 'Millies', non-violent activists realized that they themselves 'carried around a lot of prejudices' towards the radical protesters, of which they had 'unconsciously awaited confirmation'. Non-violent and militant activists certainly did not resolve the 'violence debate' in Gorleben, but they did manage to set it aside for a time, such that some felt they had 'succeeded, in the concrete situation, in overcoming the existing split, the chronic illness of the left. The bridges that were thrown up across ideological divides must be developed.'[190] Within Gorleben itself, the experience of RFW established trust between outsiders of all ideological perspectives and members of the local community.[191] Indeed, Gorleben is now widely known as a place where anti-nuclear activists with divergent strategies have been able to contribute in their own ways for more than thirty years.[192] In 1984, activists described Wendland as a place

---

[186] 'Räumung des Dorfes: Das gleiche Geschehen — unterschiedliche Erfahrungen!', *Anti-AKW-Telegramm*, no. 22 (August 1980), pp. 11–12.

[187] tageszeitung, *Gorleben-Dokumentation*, pp. 44–5. According to one report, a sixty-year-old woman who chose to stand up and walk on her own rather than be carried off by police was thanked by an officer for her cooperation and told to 'persuade the young people to stand up'. In response, she reportedly attempted to pull an officer away from the demonstrator he was hitting with his truncheon—only to be promptly hit in the back herself for doing so and then dragged by the hair. 'Eindrücke von der Räumung', *Atom Express*, no. 21 (July/August 1980), pp. 15–16 (p. 15); Cornelia Frey, 'Lieder wurden zu Schreien', *Zeit*, 13 June 1980, p. 59.

[188] Zint, *RFW*, p. 29.

[189] Zint, *RFW*, p. 63.   [190] Zint, *RFW*, p. 62.

[191] 'Eindrücke', *Atom Express*, no. 21; *Gorleben-Dokumentation*, pp. 36–7.

[192] For a somewhat oversimplified view of this, see the comments on Germany in Sylvie and Denis, 'Aperçu sur l'histoire du mouvement antinucléaire en France', *Courant alternatif*, no. Hors-Série 15 (2010). Recent examples of parallel militant and non-violent campaigns include a series of non-violent blockades and an illegal campaign to remove ballast from rail sections in order to render them unusable. See 'gorleben365',

where local people still had a certain fear of 'anarchists', but where cooperation meant 'that the "anarchists" were asked what they imagined [as protest] and had to address the fears of the locals'.[193] For the broader anti-nuclear struggle elsewhere in Germany, RFW emptied the 'violence debate' of some of its irreconcilable moral conflict.[194] In the end, the experience proved to many that the violence debate itself was an unhelpful distraction. The guiding mantra for future protest was that, 'Whether non-violent or not, it must be successful.'[195]

CONCLUSION

The question of violence is one that plagues many (if not all) major social movements: is it more effective to protest peacefully in the hopes of winning sympathy and support or to use physical force to bring about practical change? Despite apparent incompatibilities between the two approaches, the anti-nuclear movement of the 1970s made liberal use of both. Their uneasy coexistence was not the result of any conscious decision by anti-nuclear activists, but rather of stalemate between the proponents of non-violent and militant action, both of whom failed to win over a clear majority. The local activists called upon to arbitrate in the strategy debate opted for an officially non-violent discourse, behind which lurked a practical reality that was much more ambiguous.

Over the course of the 1970s, forms of anti-nuclear protest changed repeatedly. Sincerely non-violent activists took the first step, occupying the construction site of a chemical plant in Marckolsheim. This form of direct action appeared even more promising in Wyhl, though a first, strictly non-violent site occupation quickly gave way to a situation in which gentle force had to be employed to retake the site. West German authorities learned from their mistakes, going out of their way to prevent another site occupation in Brokdorf. The measures that they undertook provoked outrage that boiled over into much more serious violence in 1977, both in nearby Grohnde and in distant Malville. By the end of that summer, the extreme repression that demonstrators faced in Malville and

---

http://www.gorleben365plusx.de (accessed 9 December 2015) and 'Castor? Schottern!', http://de-de.facebook.com/castorschottern (accessed 9 December 2015).

[193] 'Wendlandblockade!', *GF*, no. 5 (1984).

[194] tageszeitung, *Gorleben-Dokumentation*, p. 40.

[195] '[. . .] ob nun gewaltfrei oder nicht gewaltfrei, erfolgreich muß es sein'. B.W., 'Duell mit 2 Siegern? Thesen zur Platzbesetzung und was danach kommt', *Atom Express*, no. 21 (July/August 1980), pp. 20–1 (p. 20).

in Kalkar had made 'official non-violence' at mass protests implausible and unworkable.

Faced with these realities, different anti-nuclear activists sought to formulate a new strategy. Non-violent activists tried to match word and deed through boycotts, 'decentralized' actions, and hunger strikes. These strategies kept attention on the nuclear issue, but they failed to attract the large numbers that had previously supported demonstrations. The same can be said of sabotage, the form of protest that militant activists preferred. Even when sabotage met with expressions of 'private pleasure', local activists in particular were reluctant to publicly adopt the militant discourse that went along with it. At the margins, both non-violence and violence could spill over into extremes, as in the cases of Hartmut Gründler's self-immolation and the murder of Heinz Herbert Karry.

In a third phase, the anti-nuclear movement returned to mass protest, but this time under different circumstances. In France, the battle of Plogoff elevated ambiguity to a virtue, as the local population used practically every tool within its limited means to fight against the overbearing and invasive presence of the police and army in their community. The protest was not peaceful, but nor was it consciously violent; the local community was more occupied with resisting authorities than with defining the nature of that resistance. In West Germany, the protest at Tiefbohrstelle 1004 seemed to be almost the opposite: a deliberately non-violent protest so carefully cultivated that it survived serious internal squabbling. Yet the conclusions activists drew from Gorleben were remarkably similar to those in Plogoff: the success of protest counted more than its discursive, moral consistency.

Anti-nuclear protest during the 1970s and early 1980s alternated between violence and non-violence, sometimes taking forms of direct action that mixed both. No single strategy promised success in all situations, and every protest action was in part a reaction to past events (even ones that had occurred abroad). The history of protest in the period thus did not lead unambiguously towards either violence or non-violence, as narratives of 1970s 'terrorism' or 'new social movements' tend to imply. Rather, contradictory strategies remained (and remain) in constant tension. In the early 1980s, the violence debate had been pushed into the background, but nothing had been resolved: non-violent and militant protests would continue to take place alongside one another in places like Brokdorf, Chooz, and Wackersdorf over the next decades. These inconsistencies were part of what made the anti-nuclear movement so unpredictable to its opponents, driving up the nuclear industry's security costs and periodically shifting the balance of power and of public opinion in the movement's favour. According to Chaïm Nissim, who was closely involved in both official, non-violent movement activities and clandestine violence against property, 'Neither one was just in itself. The complementarity in all these actions was [what was] victorious. We didn't know outright which ones [were responsible]—and how it was all going to join up. We would never have thought, not one of us, that we could win.'[196] Whether and in what sense anti-nuclear activists did 'win' their struggle is the subject of the next chapter.

[196] Nissim, interview.

6

Legacies

Trajectories of Activism and Activists since the 1980s

What impact did the anti-nuclear protests of the 1970s and early 1980s actually have? Social scientists have repeatedly attempted to answer such questions by looking at the direct impact of protest on energy policy.[1] According to sociologist Felix Kolb's calculations, German anti-nuclear activists partially succeeded where their French counterparts completely failed: by the time of the Chernobyl accident in 1986, West Germany's nuclear programme was 34 per cent smaller than had been planned in 1973, while France's remained more or less unchanged.[2] As of 2015, France relies on nuclear energy more than any other country in the world: its fifty-eight reactors produce 76.9 per cent of the electricity generated there, far more than its nearest competitors and vastly more than the

---

[1] See Herbert Kitschelt, 'Political Opportunity Structures', *British Journal of Political Science* 16, no. 1 (1986); Wolfgang Rüdig, *Anti-Nuclear Movements* (1990); Felix Kolb, *Protest and Opportunities* (2007). This focus on policy impact is not exclusive, but it is widespread. A summary of different assessments of anti-nuclear protest outcomes can be found in Hein-Anton van der Heijden, 'Great Fear', in *A History of Environmentalism*, edited by Marco Armiero and Lise Sedrez (2014), pp. 192–8. For a review of some of the exceptions to this focus on intended, political outcomes in the social movements literature—as well as repeated laments about their dearth—see Marco G. Giugni, 'Personal and Biographical Consequences', in *The Blackwell Companion to Social Movements*, edited by David A. Snow, et al. (2004), pp. 489–507 (p. 490); Jennifer Earl, 'Cultural Consequences', in *Blackwell Companion* (2004), pp. 508–30 (p. 509); Nancy Whittier, 'Consequences for Each Other', in *Blackwell Companion* (2004), pp. 531–51 (p. 548).

[2] Kolb, *Protest and Opportunities*, pp. 196–8. The relative lack of impact in France is explained in terms of the 'unfavorable political environment' there. Wolfgang Rüdig estimates the impact in both countries to have been even lower. See *Anti-Nuclear Movements*, p. 350. On the question of protest impact generally (regardless of the issue), Charles Tilly has argued that 'Taken strictly as a means-ends action on behalf of stated demands, social movement activity is inefficient, even self-defeating.' It is therefore necessary to consider 'the possibility that the major effects of social movements will have little or nothing to do with the public claims their leaders make.' 'From Interactions to Outcomes', in *How Social Movements Matter*, edited by Marco G. Giugni et al. (1999), pp. 262, 270.

15.8 per cent of electricity generated in Germany by that country's remaining nine reactors.[3]

These numbers are valuable for comparison, but they do not tell the whole story. In France, one of François Mitterrand's first acts as president in 1981 was the abandonment of Plogoff nuclear power station (along with the planned expansion of the Larzac military base);[4] no replacement site in Bretagne was ever proposed, and a nearby project at Le Pellerin (Loire-Atlantique), though approved, was later dropped. Activists also achieved a partial victory in Fessenheim, which was the first new pressurized water reactor to be built in France, but also the last nuclear facility of any kind in Alsace; other sites considered within the region were dropped in the planning phase, at least in part due to the vociferous opposition of local protesters. Though the construction moratorium imposed by Mitterrand's government was very brief (July–November 1981), it also led to an immediate deceleration of construction of new reactors (from nine to six for the years 1982–3).[5]

In West Germany, nuclear energy opponents were far more successful. Construction of the power plant in Wyhl remained blocked for many years before ultimately being abandoned in the 1980s. Only one new project was initiated after the first wave of planning in the 1970s (Isar, built 1982–8), and nine planned reactors at six sites were never built.[6] Nevertheless, German nuclear energy opponents did not always win: in particular, the centrally important struggle over a nuclear waste disposal site at Gorleben continues to this day. A fitting testament to the mixed success of the anti-nuclear movement in West Germany can be found in Kalkar. The fast breeder reactor that stands there today was built at incredible expense and over the objections of tens of thousands of Germans (as well as their Dutch neighbours), but it was never put into operation. It has since been converted into a theme park, complete with its

---

[3] In terms of the proportion of electricity generated from nuclear sources, France is followed mostly by much smaller countries, such as Slovakia (second, 56.8 per cent), Hungary (third, 53.6 per cent), and Belgium (fifth, 47.5 per cent). The only other country with a population of more than 15 million in the top twelve nuclear producers (by percentage) is Ukraine (fourth, 49.4 per cent); Germany is placed twentieth. Prior to the Fukushima disaster in 2011, nineteen reactors were producing 28.4 per cent of Germany's domestically generated electricity. Thereafter, Chancellor Angela Merkel announced Germany's definitive abandonment of nuclear energy by 2022—only a year after she had extended operations for the country's nuclear facilities until as late as 2036 (reversing an existing plan from the year 2000 to withdraw from nuclear energy by 2021). IAEA, *Reactors in the World 2015*; IAEA, *Reactors in the World 2011*.

[4] The plan was announced on 27 May 1981 following the first meeting of the new government's *Conseil des ministres*.

[5] 'Des promesses d'arrêt au dégel des sites', *Libération*, 26 November 1981.

[6] Dieter Rucht, 'Anti-AKW-Bewegung', in *Die sozialen Bewegungen in Deutschland seit 1945*, edited by Roland Roth and Dieter Rucht (2008), pp. 264–5.

Fig. 6.1. Wunderland Kalkar theme park. Photo: Andrew Tompkins.

own mascot ('Kernie'), hotel accommodation (in the former control centre), and carousel (in the cooling tower; see Figs 6.1, 6.2). In Kalkar, activists were unable to prevent construction of the FBR, but the power station has since been turned into a parody of itself.

There is at least one other sense in which numbers do not tell the whole story: even where activists suffered their worst defeats, protesters deem their engagement to have been worthwhile. Heinrich Voß (b. 1951) lives practically next door to Brokdorf nuclear power plant, which he has opposed since 1973. In spite of repeated protests of up to 100,000 people there over the course of a decade, Brokdorf went online in October 1986, only a few months after the Chernobyl disaster. The reactor dome behind Heinrich's house—hidden from view by a row of tall trees he planted—stands as a concrete reminder of the failure of protesters' efforts. Across the Rhine, Georges David (b. 1943) lived for many years with a similar defeat. Mass demonstrations (1975–7), sabotage (1977–82), two marches to Paris (1984, 1994), and even international lawsuits pursued by the Swiss canton of Geneva failed to stop the FBR in Malville. It too went online in 1986 (before Chernobyl), remaining in operation (between breakdowns and outages) for a decade thereafter. Yet neither Heinrich nor Georges looks back with regret on the many years each invested in protest. In fact, both conclude, in almost the same words, that protest was, 'on balance, positive'.[7]

---

[7] 'Das Fazit ist positiv.' 'Le bilan est plutôt positif.' HV in Heinrich Voß and Christine Scheer, joint interview with the author, Wewelsfleth, 21 August 2010; Georges David, interview with the author, Lhuis, 27 January 2010.

This is not simply a rationalization of 'failure'. Across France and West Germany, opponents of projects that were cancelled as well as those that were completed are convinced that protest had its greatest impact in the long term rather than in particular siting decisions. Though immediate outcomes differed considerably between France and West Germany, both Heinrich and Georges see the anti-nuclear movement as having changed society in similar ways. As Georges puts it, nowadays 'we talk about alternative energy, we talk about consumer society, we talk about healthy eating. And they're themes that we had already brought up in the 1970s, but back then we were preaching in the desert.' Heinrich too speaks of how wind farms, once dismissed as a crackpot idea, have become common (far more so in West Germany than in France, one might add). Both men also explain that anti-nuclear protest changed their own lives. Like nearly everyone else interviewed for this research, Heinrich claims that he 'met people who I would otherwise never have got to know' and had encounters 'that wouldn't have happened at all that way'. Georges agrees: 'even at the local level', protest networks brought together 'people who wouldn't have met if it hadn't been for the anti-nuclear movement, people who wouldn't have evolved the way they did' without it (himself expressly included).[8]

Assessments like these reveal two ways in which the impact of protest cannot be reduced simply to 'success' or 'failure'. First, what protest accomplished in the immediate sense was not always as important as what it achieved over the long term. As this chapter will argue, anti-nuclear protest served as an incubator for diverse protest traditions, catalysing important political changes and making an impact not only on the number of power stations built, but also on politics inside and outside of parliaments. Second, what protest achieved politically was not always the same as what it meant personally. Indeed, political and personal impacts of activism could be poles apart, with protest changing participants' lives for better *and* for worse, regardless of whether 'their' particular site was built. The remainder of this chapter explores the trajectories of protest and protesters after the 1970s by separately examining these 'political' and 'personal' legacies of activism (bearing in mind that the boundaries between the two were particularly fluid). As it will attempt to show, the impact of protest was neither wholly positive nor wholly negative, but it altered understandings of 'politics' and the trajectories of individuals.[9]

---

[8] David, interview; Voß and Scheer, joint interview.
[9] Because many 'political' changes remain more visible in Germany than in France, this chapter uses several extended examples from the latter to counter the notion that 'nothing happened' there.

CHANGING THE WORLD

Of the many enduring legacies of the anti-nuclear movement, parliamentary Green parties are most often singled out for attention. Though they may now seem like a logical outgrowth of anti-nuclear protest (a view the parties themselves have encouraged), it is worth remembering just how controversial party formation was. At its origins, the anti-nuclear movement was extra-parliamentary, whether out of desperation (as in the case of those local activists who took to protest after authorities proved unresponsive) or out of conviction (as for protesters who saw nuclear energy as a symbol of the state, capitalism, or society's ills). The repression protesters young and old experienced in 1975–7 strengthened the antipathy of all participants towards politicians who were willing not only to trample on democratic principles, but to employ massive intimidation and lethal force in doing so. The shift from anti-nuclear activism to parliamentary participation was therefore neither automatic nor easy. Heinrich Voß, who currently sits for Die Grünen in his local council, recalls joining the party early on in order to 'support the parliamentary path [. . .] according to the principle that "it won't change anything, *but . . .*"' Today, he says, 'I'm a member of Die Grünen, but I have some critical distance. I'm not a soldier of the party.'[10] Among anti-nuclear activists themselves, a certain ambivalence persists to this day about whether Green parties are the most desirable or effective means of opposing nuclear energy.

It is nevertheless clear why anti-nuclear protest is so closely associated with such parties. Though Die Grünen and Les Verts were both formed from a heterogeneous base that took (and continues to take) positions on a variety of different issues, frustration with nuclear policy was most directly formative.[11] In both France and West Germany, a pro-nuclear consensus among political elites extended from governments to their parliamentary opponents, from parties of the political right well into the established left. Those anti-nuclear activists who became Green party proponents were driven by a desire to respond to parties like these, especially social democrats, who (activists felt) 'always said, "they'll wind up voting for us in the end"'.[12] As the slogan of one proto-Green campaign put it, 'This time, we'll vote for ourselves!' Especially in the aftermath of the extreme repression in Malville and Kalkar in 1977, some, like Kommunistischer

---

[10] HV in Voß and Scheer, joint interview.
[11] Guillaume Sainteny, *Les Verts*, 2nd edn (1992), p. 11; Silke Mende, *Nicht rechts, nicht links* (2011), pp. 37–71.
[12] Didier Anger, interview with the author, Les Pieux, 22 September 2010.

Bund (KB) member Günter Hopfenmüller, began to see a Green party as something 'that had a certain future. Because with large demonstrations, we had become stuck. That had come to a certain end.'[13] Not everyone agreed with him, though, and the controversy over electoral participation cut across all existing divisions within the anti-nuclear movement. Within the KB, the electoral question caused a major split that led Günter and others (the so-called Gruppe Z) to depart en masse. Among non-violent activists too, certain individuals (such as Solange Fernex) energetically helped found the Greens, while others (including Wolfgang Hertle) kept their distance. Though Die Grünen and Les Verts claim to represent the broader legacy of the anti-nuclear movement, they do so only for a certain fraction of those activists who participated in the early anti-nuclear movement.

Nor was unity easy to achieve among those who did go along with party formation. Electoral participation posed a number of questions that the different constituencies of the anti-nuclear movement (not to mention their allies in feminist, gay, peace, and other movements that helped found Green parties) did not all answer in the same way. Did protesters want to accede to power and, if so, how would they choose to wield it? Were coalitions an option? With whom? Questions like these were highly divisive. In Alsace, where the group Écologie et Survie played a pioneering role in electoral participation, some began to speak of a 'Balkanization' of the ecological movement around 1977–9.[14] Because of the controversy surrounding whether and how to participate in elections, most proponents of electoral participation initially advocated only a limited engagement with official politics, one that would augment, but not replace, other forms of protest. Speaking of the Bunte Liste that he and other members of the KB helped found in Hamburg, Günter Hopfenmüller argued that it was 'absolutely a parliamentary attempt, but one that was explicitly defined in such a way that we wanted to give these movements a mouthpiece, an additional platform. In no way was it that we had now converted to parliamentarianism and wanted to join in the game.'[15] Even moderate environmentalists such as Solange Fernex, who went on to serve as a Member of the European Parliament for Les Verts, initially justified electoral participation primarily in terms of getting the message out. In her view, participation in the 1976 cantonal elections had allowed Écologie et Survie to reach a much broader audience via the more than 30 newspaper opinion pieces, 1,000 election posters, and 124,847

---

[13] Günter Hopfenmüller, interview with the author, Hamburg, 23 August 2010.
[14] Memo, 12 January 1978, AD Bas-Rhin, 1743 W 186.
[15] Hopfenmüller, interview.

'very radical' pamphlets that the election permitted them to produce and distribute throughout Alsace. Since Écologie et Survie candidates garnered more than 10 per cent of the vote in their constituencies, they were entitled to reimbursement of election costs, meaning, as Solange stressed to her friends, that they got 'all this *for free*'.[16] At the outset, Green parties were less interested in power than in a platform that would allow them to magnify the impact of anti-nuclear and related protest.

Contrary to a common assumption, Green parties were not a West German invention when they took off in that country in the 1980s; French activists had taken an interest in the possibilities of electoral participation at least five years earlier and their experiences were a conscious point of reference for many West Germans.[17] René Dumont's one-off 1974 presidential campaign (supported by Les Amis de la Terre and managed by Brice Lalonde, who later ran for president himself) was the first nationally and internationally visible indication that ecology might become a political force. However, Écologie et Survie had already participated in the 1973 legislative elections a year prior to Dumont's campaign, and Alsace was the birthplace of 'political ecology' in both France and West Germany. Indeed, after the group's success in the 1976 cantonal elections, Solange Fernex raved to her German non-violent comrade Wolfgang Hertle that 'We in Alsace have once again shown the rest of France what one can do when we fight the state in its own way.'[18] Some in West Germany interpreted these successes in a similar manner: the KB, for instance, regarded the Alsatian example as a 'point of departure for discussions and reflection' about electoral participation.[19]

As with anti-nuclear protest strategies more generally, the idea of electoral participation that emerged in Alsace (partly in response to the difficulties ecologists there faced within the highly centralized French system) found a more conducive environment in West Germany than at home. When, for example, in 1979, Green parties in both countries participated in elections to the European Parliament, they received 4.4 per cent of the vote in France, but only 3.2 per cent in West Germany. Nevertheless, quirks of the electoral system meant that German Greens were reimbursed for their election costs, whereas French activists (having fallen below a 5 per cent threshold within the enlarged national constituency) wound up saddled with debt: in mid-1979, Écologie et Survie owed

[16] Solange Fernex, letter to Wolfgang Hertle, undated [1976], AA, 'Ökologiebewegung im Elsass'. Original emphasis.

[17] See Mende, *Nicht rechts, nicht links*, pp. 69, 338.

[18] Fernex, to Hertle, undated [1976].

[19] 'Wie geht es weiter mit der Anti-AKW-Bewegung?', *Arbeiterkampf*, no. 102 (Beilage) (4 April 1977), pp. 1–3.

more than 100,000 francs, which had to be paid back using 'foreign (notably German) loans, gifts and donations'. Proportional representation also meant that West German Greens could gain substantially from partial victories, whereas French groups had to win outright in a two-phase process. Critically, federalism meant that West German Greens had more and better opportunities to affect policy than their French counterparts: getting into a Landtag was both easier and more meaningful than making it onto the Conseil Régional. As with many other consequences of anti-nuclear activism, the idea of using elections to advance the cause of ecology was first tested in France, but came to greater fruition across the border in Germany.[20]

The differing degrees of electoral success that Die Grünen and Les Verts experienced have magnified other consequences of anti-nuclear protest. Whether Die Grünen put ecological issues on the media agenda or not, journalists can pitch stories about environmentalist protest to their editors more easily in Germany than in France; whether Die Grünen themselves advance environmentalism in parliament, other parties occasionally poach these issues; and whether Die Grünen actually change policy or not, they can redirect party funds to pet projects within civil society. Green parties constitute only the most visible part of a broad infrastructure of environmentalism, but their successes (far greater in Germany than in France) draw attention to the wider movement and its concerns.

If the anti-nuclear movement contributed to the emergence of new, reformist politics in the form of Green parties, it also played a part in the decline of the revolutionary, Marxist–Leninist parties that participated in it. Some of this was directly related to the question of electoral participation, which crystallized multiple internal conflicts within radical Marxist groups, leading to large numbers of individual departures and serious organizational splits. Hans-Hermann Teichler (b. 1947) was responsible for the KB's Anti-Nuclear Commission in the 1970s and chose to remain with the organization until its dissolution in 1991 rather than join Die Grünen. Looking back, he regards the radical left's initial support for Die Grünen as something that 'damaged the KB and other left-wing [groups]. That is undeniable, [...] that it damaged the left-wing spectrum.'[21] Yet if

[20] Bundeswahlleiter, 'Wahl zum 1. Europäischen Parlament am am 10. Juni 1979', 2012, http://www.bundeswahlleiter.de/de/europawahlen/fruehere_europawahlen/ew1979. html (accessed 1 June 2012); 'Elections européennes 1979', http://www.france-politique. fr/elections-europeennes-1979.htm (accessed 1 June 2012); Memos, 15 June 1979 and 9 May 1979, AD Bas-Rhin, 1743 W 186. See also Jean-Luc Bennahmias, 'De la marge au pouvoir', *Autres Temps*, no. 49 (1996).

[21] He continues: 'Und dem Land hat es natürlich nicht geschadet, dass es die Grünen gegeben hat.' Hans-Hermann Teichler, interview with the author, Hamburg, 20 August 2010.

the Greens might appear in some sense to have inaugurated the decline of *gauchisme* and of the *K-Gruppen*, they are in truth but a symbol of more ambiguous changes that were already underway on the radical left— changes which were both cause and effect of Marxist-Leninists' engagement with the anti-nuclear movement (as well as feminism, gay rights, and other NSMs).

Maoists, Trotskyists, and others had joined anti-nuclear protests for a variety of reasons, many of them principled (*mouvementisme*, anti-capitalism, and social aspects of the nuclear issue), others more instrumental (recruitment of new members, 'entrism', and the aspiration to lead). As one environmental historian has (somewhat cynically) put it, anti-nuclear activism was 'a rather good investment' from an organizational standpoint.[22] After enthusiastically taking up the anti-nuclear cause following the first attention-getting protests in Malville and Brokdorf in 1976, the *K-Gruppen* (first and foremost the highly engaged KB) grew to their peak size in West Germany the following year, as did their French counterparts in groups like the Organisation Communiste des Travailleurs (OCT).[23] Anti-nuclear protest broadened not just the membership base but also the thematic scope of these groups, making nuclear and environmental issues into perennial topics in party organs like *Arbeiterkampf* or the *Quotidien du Peuple* and opening a dialogue between Marxism and environmentalism.[24] Indeed, the extensive coverage of 'new' issues like nuclear power boosted sales of *Arbeiterkampf* to their peak in 1977, giving the paper a readership well beyond its radical and working-class target audience.[25] Yet anti-nuclear protest also sharpened certain contradictions within radical Marxist groups, which suffered a precipitous decline after 1977: according to (very rough) police estimates, KB lost nearly half its membership and

---

[22]   Frank Uekötter, *Am Ende der Gewissheiten* (2011), p. 108.

[23]   There are no reliable records of the exact number of members of these groups (nor of their larger networks of sympathizers). Michael Steffen (in the unpublished version of his doctoral dissertation) provides indicative figures based on police estimates (which he suggests are too low) that show the KB growing steadily throughout the early 1970s to 1,500 members by 1976, then rapidly increasing to a peak of 2,500 in 1977 before dropping down to 1,450 in 1978 and then to 900 by 1979 as the 'Gruppe Z' split off. 'Geschichten vom Trüffelschwein' (2002), p. 323. French police estimated the combined forces of Gauche ouvrière et populaire and Révolution ! at 900 members in 1976, growing to 1,500 members as they merged to form the Organisation Communiste des Travailleurs in 1977, before declining to 1,000 members in 1979 and plummeting to 200 by 1981. See 'Partis, syndicats et mouvements divers', annual index of organizations and estimated sizes, PPP, G^A br 11.

[24]   See, for example, 'Ökologie und Marxismus', *Arbeiterkampf*, no. 136 (21 August 1978), pp. 10–11.

[25]   Michael Steffen, *Geschichten vom Trüffelschwein* (2002), pp. 175–6. Though the KB no longer exists, *Arbeiterkampf* lives on (under the same acronym) as *analyse & kritik*.

OCT declined by around one-third in the following year; by 1981, they had respectively dwindled to a quarter and one-eighth of their peak strength. The loss of members after 1977 had many causes, but one of them was that the anti-nuclear movement in which *gauchistes* and *K-Gruppen* participated came to be seen by some as a more attractive outlet for the energies of existing members and potential recruits than these organizations themselves.[26]

This was the case for the documentary film-maker Daniel Coche (b. 1950), who quit Maoism as the anti-nuclear movement was gaining ground. The son of two teachers who sympathized with the Parti Communiste Français (PCF), Daniel was a student in Strasbourg until May '68 intervened. He subsequently abandoned the ambitions expected of him, leaving university to work in the factories as an *établi* for the Maoist group Front rouge.[27] The factory work in particular was a transformative experience that he says he would repeat if given the opportunity, but the political organizing of which it was a part was extraordinarily demanding. For several years, Daniel had to suspend his passion for film, as there was never time to go to the cinema. Though he does not repudiate his past as some '68ers have done, Daniel became disillusioned with Maoism towards the mid-1970s, feeling that it no longer resonated with the world around him.

> DC: I began to perceive that this political group—[like] all the political groups—was completely out of touch. [In Alsace, there was] a renewal of regional culture and we saw it and so we said to ourselves, 'You must establish the dictatorship of the proletariat, yes, yes' [and] we discussed whether that dictatorship should be centralized or decentralized, [while] people were saying 'We don't want a chemical plant' and doing something about that. I experienced the same thing in my factory: the righteous struggle of the Angolan people against social imperialism didn't interest anyone.

Daniel's disillusionment was further accentuated when Marxism-Leninism brushed up against the nascent anti-nuclear movement. Front

---

[26] Figures are calculated from the sources cited above. On the *K-Gruppen* losing members to anti-nuclear and other 'new social movements', see Polizeieinsatzinspektion Lüchow, 'Organisationen und Planungen im Landkreis Lüchow-Dannenberg seit NEZ-Standortbenennung im Februar 1977', report, 20 December 1979, Nds, 100 Acc. 2003/116 Nr. 67. See also Gerd Koenen, *Das rote Jahrzehnt* (2001), pp. 294, 308–9, 490–2. Even for groups like KB and OCT, which had moved away from strict Maoism, the death of Mao Zedong in 1976 and subsequent arrest of the 'Gang of Four' accentuated ideological dissonance. See '„Wie geht's weiter?" Debatte auch bei der OCT', *Arbeiterkampf*, no. 141 (31 October 1978), p. 60. On other difficulties faced by the *K-Gruppen*, see Steffen, *Geschichten vom Trüffelschwein*, pp. 269–73.

[27] On the practice of *établissement* more generally, see Robert Linhart, *L'établi* (1978); Virginie Linhart, *Volontaires pour l'usine* (1994); Marnix Dressen, *De l'amphi à l'établi* (2000).

rouge participated at the margins of anti-nuclear protest, showering attention on the movement in its national newspaper and distributing flyers at
protests in Fessenheim.[28] Yet to Daniel it seemed that the anti-nuclear
movement quickly surpassed everything the Maoists had achieved, and
without any help from them.

> DC: They retook the site [. . . they] won in Wyhl. [. . .] Having a
>   favourable balance of power on the ground and winning a battle
>   [. . .] that's completely different from distributing a pamphlet
>   and saying 'down with the government', etc. [. . .] It was a
>   popular movement. And that was very important because for
>   years, we had always said 'The masses aren't ready, they must be
>   educated', etc. And then we perceived that these people, well
>   they simply said they don't want a nuclear power plant. [. . .]
>   There was no need for our educational work.

As time went on, Daniel came to feel that 'The ecologist movement
represented everything that had not succeeded among the Maoists.'[29]
When he broke his connection with Front rouge, he joined a documentary
film collective whose first project was a film about the occupation of a
potential nuclear site in Gerstheim (Alsace); a year later, the group made a
documentary about the environmentalist pirate radio programme Radio
Verte Fessenheim.[30] Daniel later moved on to other cinematic activities
that were likewise infused with political content: he has been active in the
organization of human rights film festivals and continues to make documentaries on topics such as the *engagé* Alsatian poet André Weckmann,
the life and death (by cancer) of anti-nuclear activist Solange Fernex,
French and German surgeons working in Laos, and the plight of asylum
seekers in Strasbourg.[31] Today, he is a member of Les Verts and an
admirer of former Franco-German Green MEP Daniel Cohn-Bendit.

---

[28] Front rouge Alsace, 'Notre vie, notre santé sont plus précieux que le profit', A5
pamphlet, 8 pp., 1975, ABEBI, 84RC/4. Front rouge splintered off from the Parti
Communiste Marxiste-Léniniste de France, taking the name of the group's central organ
with them. A subsequent transformation led to the creation of the Parti Communiste
Révolutionnaire (Marxiste-Léniniste). Its organ, *Le Quotidien du Peuple*, provided substantial coverage of the anti-nuclear movement from a French radical left perspective, with
articles like 'Tout a commencé à Marckolsheim' (14 April 1977) and 'Ici Radio Verte
Fessenheim' (12 September 1977). On the history of these organizations, see Christophe
Bourseiller, *Maoïstes*, 2nd edn (2008).
[29] Daniel Coche, interview with the author, Strasbourg, 20 April 2010.
[30] Daniel Coche, *Écoutez RVF vous écoute*, 2006 1978, 30 mins; Daniel Coche, *Ni ici ni
ailleurs*, 1977, 25 mins.
[31] See Dora Films, 'Daniel Coche', 2011, http://www.dorafilms.com/article-556-dan
iel-coche (accessed 9 December 2015).

However, he remains deliberately aloof from the party's internal squabbling, a decision he traces back to his frustrating experience with Maoism in the 1970s: back then, he says, 'you discussed every morning [...] whether to put the comma before "proletariat" or after "proletariat" [...] Put it wherever you want!'[32] Daniel's views are not necessarily representative of (former) *gauchistes* generally: some would support a similar 'radical reformism', others see this as a poor substitute for the far-reaching ideals of socialism, and still others now reject left-wing politics more emphatically.[33] However, Daniel's experience partly illustrates why a certain kind of revolutionary politics declined, how anti-nuclear protest catalysed that process, and why new parties and movements were able to profit from it.

If anti-nuclear activism constituted a point of origin for the Greens and marked the decline of revolutionary politics in its Maoist form, it also contributed greatly to the emergence of autonomism as an extra-parliamentary foil to the former and a radical successor to the latter.[34] The concept of 'autonomy' from which such movements take their name has a long prehistory (going back to Italian demands for *autonomia operaia* in the 1950s), but the term itself is difficult to define and hotly debated among its proponents. There is thus no coherent 'ideology' that united autonomists, but the practice of protest in the anti-nuclear, feminist, and urban squatting movements of the 1970s and 1980s was directly formative of this protest tradition, which rejects established organizations (inter-group autonomy), social hierarchies (inter-personal autonomy), and cultural norms (intrapersonal autonomy).[35] Autonomist protest grew rapidly within the anti-nuclear movement, becoming the dominant force within its radical wing as *K-Gruppen* and *gauchistes* declined after 1977.[36] Today, autonomists

---

[32] Coche, interview.

[33] On the related question of how former '68ers now reflect on their past (such as by repenting, defending, or rethinking radical politics), see James Mark et al., 'Reflections', in *Europe's 1968*, edited by Robert Gildea et al. (2013).

[34] Like the anti-nuclear movement generally, autonomist movements became, particularly for the radical left, a more attractive alternative to *gauchisme*. See Christian Joppke, *Mobilizing against Nuclear Energy* (1993), pp. 160–1; 'L'extrême gauche et les autonomes', 10 February 1979, PPP, B^A 2332.

[35] Darcy K. Leach, 'The Way is the Goal' (2006), p. 122.

[36] HKS13, ed., *hoch die kampf dem* (1999), pp. 173–5. On the competition between *K-Gruppen* and *Autonomen* within the anti-nuclear movement in Hamburg, see AKPÖ, 'Zur Klein-Bürgerlichen Politik des KB. Das Verhalten des KB in der Anti-AKW-Bewegung', May 1977, HIS, SBe 731: 1985/317; Geronimo [pseud.], *Feuer und Flamme*, 6th edn (2002), pp. 103–15; Steffen, *Geschichten vom Trüffelschwein*, pp. 184–6. In France, the *gauchistes* had already begun to decline earlier. Police observed a close relationship between anti-nuclear protest and the early autonomist movement in that country. See Georges Marion, '« On m'appelait l'étudiant »', *Nouvel Observateur* (23 January 1982), pp. 14–18; 'Violence politique : thèmes d'actions des « autonomes »', police report, 2 February 1978, PPP, B^A 2332.

(often associated in the media with 'anarchists') remain marked by the emphasis on 'personal concern', preference for direct democracy, and desire to effect concrete change through direct action that were such an integral part of early anti-nuclear protest. The longevity of autonomist protest over time has been ensured by the roots it put down within urban 'scenes' and projects loosely associated with them, such as squats, youth centres, or newspapers. These frequently address multiple political issues and therefore have a longer lifespan than any single protest campaign.[37]

During the 1980s, autonomism increased in size and importance, both within and beyond the anti-nuclear issue. In France, autonomists joined militant anti-nuclear demonstrations in Chooz and repeatedly sabotaged suppliers to the Golfech nuclear power station.[38] In West Germany, autonomist groups built up a substantial infrastructure of squats in major cities across the country, which fed into larger (sometimes trans-national) networks.[39] They mobilized these networks repeatedly to oppose West Germany's planned nuclear fuel reprocessing centre as it was moved from Gorleben (1977–9) to possible sites in Dragahn (1981–5) and Wackersdorf (1981–9) before being ultimately abandoned. One issue could, and often did, lead to another. Markus Mohr (b. 1962), who started out as an opponent of the Brokdorf nuclear power plant near his home, became involved in numerous autonomist campaigns over the years.

> MM: I continued organizing in the militant wing of the anti-nuclear
>   movement until around 1986. We did Gorleben [...] and
>   Wackersdorf [...] And then we, as an anti-nuclear group, got
>   involved in this anti-IMF campaign and hoped we could mobilize
>   part of the anti-nuclear movement to come to Berlin for it. [...]
>   When I came to Berlin in September 1985 I participated in an
>   anti-apartheid demonstration and I knew the people with the
>   megaphones from the anti-nuclear movement. It was like déjà vu.

As this suggests, networks initially tied to anti-nuclear protest were frequently reactivated and repurposed. Though the issue changed, the opponents often did not.

---

[37] George N. Katsiaficas, *Subversion of Politics*, updated edn (2006), pp. 11–12, 80–8; Geronimo [pseud.], *Feuer und Flamme*, p. 128; Sebastian Haunss, *Identität in Bewegung* (2004), p. 107; Darcy K. Leach and Sebastian Haunss, 'Scenes and Social Movements', in *Culture, Social Movements, and Protest*, edited by Hank Johnston (2009), pp. 273–4.

[38] See *Un récit de lutte de Chooz* (1998); Claude Courtes and Jean-Claude Driant, *Golfech* (1999).

[39] See Freia Anders, 'Wohnraum, Freiraum, Widerstand', in *Das Alternative Milieu*, edited by Sven Reichardt and Detlef Siegfried (2010); Jake P. Smith, 'Häuserkämpfe' (forthcoming).

MM: Then there was [...] German unification [...] these pogroms, I went to Hoyerswerda, to Rostock.[40] I later discovered that the entire police command in Rostock was the same as from Brokdorf. In that sense, the confrontation continued for me.[41]

Autonomists have continued to be an active force in more recent protests, including within the so-called Global Justice Movement that has contested neoliberal globalization since the 1990s. Like the anti-nuclear networks of the 1970s, autonomists today are informally networked but not hierarchically organized. They have been most visible in cases where protest could be localized in space, either in relation to particular local struggles or to specific protest events. In Germany, France, and beyond, international summits of the G8 (Heiligendamm, 2007), NATO (Strasbourg, 2009), IMF, and EU have been magnets for autonomists, often in the form of the so-called 'black bloc'. However, this term and the representations associated with it in the media are one-dimensional and dismissive, casting participants as little more than violent youth. Autonomist protest practice is not so much violent as it is unpredictable.[42] As in the 1970s anti-nuclear movement, autonomists today often cooperate with other groups at large demonstrations, but they refuse to let others dictate, control, or direct their own actions.

Jean-Luc Pasquinet (b. 1953) is an anti-nuclear activist who took part in autonomist protests during the 1970s. His trajectory shows how another radical left emerged, with its own understanding of militancy and political engagement. Around 1968, he says, 'We [*on*] believed that there could be a revolution. I no longer believe in it now, I think we must change society without taking power. [...] I believed in a revolutionary movement and that we were going to change the world, even though the opposite happened. But me, I was one of those naïve people.'[43] Like many other autonomists, Jean-Luc's perspective was tinged with Marxist anti-capitalism, but he did not feel at home with authoritarian Leninism.

---

[40] Following the absorption of East Germany into the Federal Republic of Germany in 1990, a wave of racist riots directed at asylum seekers, 'guest workers', and other immigrants occurred, notably in Hoyerswerda (Sachsen) from 17 to 23 September 1991 and in Rostock-Lichtenhagen (Mecklenburg-Vorpommern) from 22 to 26 August 1990. Police in Rostock did little to prevent the attacks or protect its victims, even withdrawing completely at one point, but they did organize a show of force when left-wing and anti-racist activists came to Rostock to demonstrate. These attacks in the former East Germany were also followed by arson attacks in the West in Mölln (Schleswig-Holstein) on 23 November 1992 and Solingen (Nordrhein-Westfalen) on 29 May 1993, in which a total of eight Turkish immigrants (including infants and children) were murdered.

[41] Markus Mohr, interview with the author, Hamburg, 19 August 2010.

[42] Martin Winter, *Politikum Polizei* (1998), p. 328 (of pdf version).

[43] Jean-Luc Pasquinet, interview with the author, Paris, 17 November 2009.

Somewhat younger than the generational cohort that became involved in Maoist groups in the aftermath of 1968, he became a radical anti-nuclear activist, but without joining any particular group.[44] His studies were likewise different from those of older peers. Rather than being interested in China, as many '68ers had been, Jean-Luc chose to study Japan and write his thesis about peasant revolts in the Edo period. At the time, some autonomists considered the ongoing struggle of Japanese peasants against Narita airport to be a possible model for protests in Malville and elsewhere.[45]

When Jean-Luc became involved in anti-nuclear protest in the 1970s, he 'did not separate the anti-nuclear struggle from the global struggle [...] against the system'. It is in part for this reason that he considered violent resistance legitimate, though that violence was of a particular kind. Authorities often portray autonomists as opportunists seeking confrontation with the police or engaging in violence for its own sake rather than pursuing legitimate political goals.[46] Jean-Luc explains that autonomist conceptions of violence were about both resisting a violent system and taking control of one's own destiny.

JLP: On the other side, they [i.e. authorities] were very, very violent. It was really the right, as we see it again today [with Sarkozy]—very authoritarian, violent. [In Malville,] they had prepared for war. [...] We thought that violence was the only thing that paid off faced with such a violent government, so it was necessary to use violence. But rather collectively. We were against terrorism, let that be clear. Even if we looked at what was going on in Germany, we were against terrorism.[47] Rather, we were in favour of spontaneous,

---

[44] On autonomist disinterest in Maoism, see also Yann Moulier-Boutang, interview with Sébastien Schifres, 2004, http://sebastien.schifres.free.fr/moulier.htm (accessed 15 May 2012). Informal organization is typical of autonomist protest, which tends to be based on ad hoc cooperation rather than work within lasting organizational structures. See, for example, 'Bruno', interview with Sébastien Schifres, 2004, http://sebastien.schifres.free.fr/bruno.htm (accessed 15 May 2012).

[45] 'Narita mon amour', *Casse-Noix*, no. 5 (June 1977), p. 7.

[46] 'Autonomie — Autodéfense. La violence, un moyen d'expression politique devenu trop fréquent et systématique : les difficultés de sa répression', 24 January 1978, PPP, BA 2332.

[47] Autonomists in France and West Germany were attentive to the activities of the Rote Armee Fraktion and joined protests against the alleged mistreatment of RAF members in prison and against the extradition of RAF lawyer Klaus Croissant from France back to West Germany. However, it is important not to equate a certain sympathy and *klammheimliche Freude* with support, as autonomists usually kept a critical distance from 'terrorist' groups. An important exception is the case of Jean-Marc Rouillan, who was involved in anti-nuclear and anti-imperialist protests with autonomist groups prior to founding the 'armed struggle' group Action directe.

collective violence. The idea was . . . *conseillisme*.[48] That is to say, taking possession of our own daily lives rather than, say, factories— a generalized self-management [*autogestion*] of our lives.[49]

Jean-Luc's biography (like Markus's) demonstrates that autonomist opposition to nuclear power was not similarly about ephemeral thrill-seeking, but part of an enduring political commitment. After moving between Japan and France for his studies in the early 1980s, Jean-Luc continued opposing nuclear power, first with the Franco-Japanese review *Cultures plurielles* (for which he prepared an issue on nuclear energy), later with the group 'Irradiés de tous les pays, unissons-nous' as well as the Association Contre le Nucléaire et son Monde, and more recently with a group seeking to shut down the Nogent-sur-Seine nuclear power plant near Paris. A self-described *objecteur de croissance*, he has also been closely associated with the 'degrowth' movement since 2006, which argues for an alternative to ever-increasing capitalist consumption.[50] Jean-Luc even ran for a seat in the European Parliament as part of an attempt to get the message out.[51] However, he and many others within this movement are critical of mainstream Green politicians like Daniel Cohn-Bendit (for accommodating to capitalism and liberal democracy) and of so-called 'green capitalist' projects (for giving the false impression that current levels of consumption can continue, if only one consumes differently).[52] Even if Jean-Luc no longer wears a motorcycle helmet to protests, his biography demonstrates a radical, deeply political opposition to nuclear power that has remained consistent over time.

The anti-nuclear movement also represented an important phase in the development of protest traditions beyond the radical left. Non-violent practices associated with anti-nuclear protest subsequently spilled over (or out[53]) into the 'new' peace movement of the 1980s. Here again, the

---

[48] The term *conseillisme*, frequently used by French autonomists to describe their ideological perspective, derives from 'council democracy' of the kind employed during the Russian Revolution or the German Revolution of November 1918. See, for example, Jean-Marc Rouillan, interview with Robert Gildea, 17 April 2008, http://around1968. modhist.ox.ac.uk/ (accessed 27 Oct 2008); Moulier-Boutang, interview with Schifres.

[49] Pasquinet, interview.

[50] 'Growth objector' is a word play on the French term for conscientious objection to military service. See 'La Décroissance', web page and monthly paper, http://www. ladecroissance.net/ (accessed 19 June 2012). This movement also has the sympathy of some German activists. See the interview with Jean-Luc in Rudolf Balmer, 'Französische Konsum-Verweigerer: Vive la Crise!', *tageszeitung*, 3 December 2009.

[51] Neither he nor the public regarded this as a serious attempt to obtain a parliamentary seat: as head of the list for Europe Décroissance in the Île-de-France voting district, he received 0.04 per cent of the vote.

[52] See, for example, 'Dany, casse-toi', *La Décroissance*, no. 67 (March 2010), p. 1.

[53] On this concept, see Jennifer Hadden and Sidney Tarrow, 'Spillover or Spillout?', *Mobilization* 12, no. 4 (2007).

Table 6.1. Estimated sizes of major West German peace demonstrations[54]

Location	Date	Size
Hamburg (Kirchentag)	20 June 1981	100,000
Bonn	10 October 1981	300,000
Bonn	10 June 1982	400,000
throughout West Germany	1–3 April 1983	780,000
throughout West Germany	22 October 1983	1,000,000 or more
Hasselbach/Hunsrück	11 October 1986	150,000

effects were far more visible in West Germany than in France. Peace activism has a long (and international) tradition in Germany, but the movement that emerged in response to the NATO double-track decision[55] constituted a fundamental renewal: whereas peace protests in the 1970s had been relatively small (especially compared to anti-nuclear energy ones), those that took place in the years 1981–3 sometimes attracted hundreds of thousands of participants (see Table 6.1).[56] Independent of their size, these demonstrations were dramatic in their mise en scène: the blockade in Mutlangen by 150 prominent individuals (including Günter Grass, Heinrich Böll, Oskar Lafontaine, and Petra Kelly) from 1 to 3 September 1983 and the 'human chain' formed by 250,000–400,000 people along the 100 kilometres from Stuttgart to Neu-Ulm on 22 October 1983 to encircle US military bases both represented symbolic politics of the highest order. Like the non-violent occupations of nuclear construction sites in the mid-1970s, these involved activists placing their own bodies in the way of heavy weapons transports or symbols of militarism, thus dramatizing their own vulnerability while simultaneously rendering the abstract threat of nuclear war concrete in their own physical environments.[57] Actions like these brought non-violent practices to the masses, further 'normalizing' civil disobedience as an effective strategy for demonstrations large and small up to the present day.[58] The illegal

---

[54] Drawn from Rüdiger Schmitt, *Friedensbewegung* (1990), p. 14.

[55] On 12 December 1979, NATO decided that it would station intermediate-range nuclear weapons in Europe if the Soviet Union did not agree, in negotiations with the United States, to withdraw its own SS-20 missiles. The US deployment of Cruise and Pershing missiles, which began in 1983, prompted widespread protests in Western Europe and especially in West Germany.

[56] On the global history of peace activism, see Lawrence Wittner, *Toward Nuclear Abolition* (2003). On West Germany specifically, see Holger Nehring, *Politics of Security* (2013); Andrew Oppenheimer, 'Conflicts of Solidarity' (2010).

[57] Tim Warneke, 'Aktionsformen und Politikverständnis der Friedensbewegung', in *Das Alternative Milieu* (2010), pp. 455–7; Susanne Schregel, *Atomkrieg vor der Wohnungstür* (2011), pp. 229–35.

[58] Wolfgang Hertle, interview with the author, Hamburg, 22 July 2010; Jan Stehn, interview with the author, Blütlingen, 24 August 2010.

occupations of public space associated with Occupy Wall Street, Blockupy Frankfurt, and related protests that attracted widespread participation in 2011–13 further testify to this spread of non-violent protest practices.

The peace movement's new appeal in the 1980s was based in part on its adoption of the rhetoric and strategies of the 1970s anti-nuclear energy movement, particularly the emphasis on 'personal concern' and local action (described by one contemporary as *lebensräumliche Betroffenheit*).[59] Certain distinctive action forms associated with 1980s peace protests in West Germany and elsewhere have also flowed back into subsequent demonstrations against nuclear energy, with human chains being used as early as 1984 in Gorleben (20,000 participants) and more recently in 2010 from Krümmel to Brunsbüttel (120,000 over 120 kilometres)—not to mention a similar chain in 2012 in France's Rhône Valley (60,000 people over 230 kilometres).[60] Discursively, protesting against nuclear weapons naturally complemented the fight against nuclear energy, and the West German peace movement piggybacked on some of the structures of the anti-nuclear movement, though it was ultimately organized very differently. The BBU, an umbrella organization of anti-nuclear and other citizens' initiatives (known for its role in organizing the 1979 post-Harrisburg demonstration in Bonn) became a leader within the peace movement, present (alongside Die Grünen) in the Koordinierungsausschuß der Friedensbewegung. The latter functioned as a centralized and 'professional' body, orchestrating mass protest at the national level in a way that had not been possible within the anti-nuclear energy movement, and propelling apparent leaders such as Petra Kelly to fame.[61] The West German peace movement of the 1980s thus built on earlier anti-nuclear networks, but shifted leadership away from the grassroots and towards media-savvy professionals.

Like the earlier opposition to nuclear energy, the peace movement of the 1980s was a transnational phenomenon in which French activists also

---

[59] Harald Müller, 'Ökologiebewegung und Friedensbewegung', in *Die neue Friedensbewegung. Analysen aus der Friedensforschung*, edited by Reiner Steinweg (1982). See also Schregel, *Atomkrieg vor der Wohnungstür*, pp. 42–77.

[60] 'Menschenkette im Wendland', *tageszeitung*, 3 February 1984; Ketten(re)Aktion, 'Größte Proteste in der Geschichte der Anti-AKW-Bewegung', 2010, http://2010.anti-atom-kette.de/pressemeldungen/pressemitteilungen/artikel/302826667e/groesste-proteste-in-der-geschichte-1.html (accessed 21 May 2012); Chaîne humaine, 'une mobilisation historique pour la sortie du nucléaire !', 2012, http://chainehumaine.org/mobilisation-historique (accessed 21 May 2012). The French protest built in part on the momentum of earlier German demonstrations in 2010–11 and benefited from organizational support by German activists. 'Frankreichs bisher größte Demonstration gegen Atomkraft', *Hamburger Abendblatt*, 12 March 2012.

[61] See Thomas Leif, 'Friedensbewegung zu Beginn der 80er', *Gewerkschaftliche Monatshefte*, no. 6 (1989); Geronimo [pseud.], *Feuer und Flamme*, pp. 125–39; Saskia Richter, *Die Aktivistin* (2010), p. 145.

participated. Indeed, the Alsatian anti-nuclear activist and Green MEP Solange Fernex even helped initiate international protests like the Fast for Life, a hunger strike that took place for forty days in Paris, Bonn, Rome, San Francisco, and Toronto starting on 6 August 1983 (the anniversary of the Hiroshima bombing).[62] French activists mobilized in solidarity with peace protesters across Europe and also against their own country's nuclear testing in the Pacific, but they remained far less visible than their neighbours. On the Europe-wide day of protest against the stationing of American missiles on 22 October 1983, a million or more West Germans participated in various actions throughout the country; across the Rhine, only about 30,000 French protesters came together for the occasion.[63] Just as West German anti-nuclear activists had once looked towards France for inspiration, so too did French peace activists in the 1980s look to their counterparts in West Germany. Patrice Bouveret (b. 1955), a long-time anti-military activist from Lyon who also protested against Super-Phénix, remembers that 'we watched what happened outside [France...] and we tried to see why these movements developed in Germany, in Belgium, in the United Kingdom but not in France'. One reason seemed to be that foreign activists had better access to academic research in the field of Peace Studies, which became established in West Germany and elsewhere in the 1970s.[64]

> PB: In those countries, they had developed an informational expertise. People didn't work solely from an ideological, political approach [...] but from an approach that was much more pragmatic: from dossiers, from facts. And they tried to mobilize [based] on the facts rather than mobilizing solely on ideology.

---

[62] Within France itself, Fernex and her friends founded the Maison de vigilance (located in Taverny until the closure of the French nuclear air base there in 2011), which has held demonstrations and short-term fasts annually since 1984 (likewise on 6 August).

[63] The reasons for the weakness of French peace activism are many, including France's inactive role within NATO, popular support for the *force de frappe*, and especially the narrow space left between the Communist Party on the left and the Gaullists on the right. See Sudhir Hazareesingh, *Political Traditions* (1994); Hanspeter Kriesi et al., *NSMs in Western Europe* (1995), pp. xi–xii; Claus Leggewie, 'Keine Friedensbewegung in Frankreich?', in *Vom Krieg der Erwachsenen gegen die Kinder*; Wilfried von Bredow and Rudolf Horst Brocke, *Krise und Protest* (1987), pp. 135–43. Whereas the internal rift within the West German SPD over the Euromissiles controversy was powerful enough to induce long-term changes in German social democracy, Parti Socialiste members (like their PCF comrades) were reluctant to openly criticize their party once it gained power in May 1981 for the first time under the Fifth Republic. See Jan Hansen, *Abschied vom Kalten Krieg?* (2016). See also Jan Willem Duyvendak, *Power of Politics* (1995), pp. 3–6, 149–55.

[64] See the preface and foreword in Dieter Lutz, *Guerre mondiale*, trans. Philippe Lacrois (1983), pp. 7–37.

In 1984, Patrice and two friends thus created the Centre de Documentation et de Recherche sur la Paix et les Conflits (now the Observatoire des Armements), which produces information and analysis about nuclear weapons, nuclear testing, and the arms trade.[65] Even if the peace movement was incomparably weaker in France than in the rest of Western Europe, its members saw themselves as part of a broader movement and sought to learn from their foreign allies.

The professionalization of activism that reached new heights with the peace movement also fed back into the anti-nuclear movement, as the story of Patrice's friend Michel Bernard (b. 1958) demonstrates. Like others who have found (or created) work for themselves with NGOs since the 1970s, Michel began as a grassroots, rank-and-file activist and went on to become a 'movement professional'. Unlike for the slightly older cohort of activists who had been in their early twenties around 1968, Michel's path to activism did not involve an anti-authoritarian revolt against parents or professors. In fact, he was introduced to the anti-nuclear movement by his father, a university professor of physics in Lyon who helped organize one of the first protests against the FBR in Malville: an 'anti-nuclear picnic' on the (not yet fenced-in) site in 1975. Michel also became involved with conscientious objector groups, drifting between the Mouvement pour une Alternative Non-violente (which he felt was too Christian) and the 'much more radical' Groupe d'Action et de Résistance à la Militarisation (which he found too violent). While studying to become an engineer, Michel remembers his professors being supportive, even encouraging his activism; indeed, many of them were themselves '68ers, only a bit older than Michel. Nevertheless, he ran into difficulties with his engineering school's administration as a result of his political engagement. Michel was eventually able to complete his studies, but says he did not receive his diploma because he refused to do an internship with any of the university's partners: 'I saw the list of companies that they proposed and it was basically: multinational, multinational, multinational.'[66]

Instead of launching himself into the engineering career for which he had been educated, Michel and a friend organized a march 'from Malville to the Elysée', timed to start over the 1982 Easter break on the third anniversary of the Harrisburg nuclear accident. Though supported by well-known groups (including CSFR and the peasants of the Larzac), the march attracted few participants and little attention in Paris. Nevertheless, it marked Michel's shift from grassroots participant to organizer. Upon returning to Lyon, one of his first actions was to found the journal *Silence*,

---

[65] Patrice Bouveret, interview with the author, Lyon, 23 January 2010.
[66] Michel Bernard, interview with the author, Lyon, 22 January 2010.

intended to 'fill the gap in means of communication and [exchange] of information between groups' that had cooperated on the march. Initially a bi-weekly bulletin for Lyon and the surrounding area, it has since grown into a full-colour monthly magazine devoted to ecology and non-violence, sold at organic co-ops and alternative bookshops across France.[67] As a long-time member of the journal's editorial team, Michel remains closely involved in anti-nuclear and environmental protests, though they have changed substantially in form since the mass demonstrations of the late 1970s. Referring to protests against the nuclear power plant in Malville during the 1980s, Michel recalls that 'Every time there was a demonstration, there were 5,000 people. [. . .] In fact, it was always the same 5,000 people.' In order to reach a broader audience, Michel and his colleagues began to focus more on 'small, media-savvy [*médiatiques*] actions that got them talking about us in the papers', such as occupying a street in downtown Lyon for a weekend. 'We did a lot of small actions like that [which . . .] gave [journalists] a pretext to talk about the issue.' In 1994, Michel and others planned a new march to Paris, but this time it was 'completely different': instead of marching 30 kilometres per day along a direct route, which left marchers too exhausted for protests and interviews, they marched half as long and focused on prefectural capitals, carefully timing their departures and arrivals to coincide with maximum pedestrian traffic and holding picnics before nuclear-related facilities to draw attention from the media. Between 1982 and 1994, Michel says, 'We made a lot of progress in terms of efficacy.'[68]

Anti-nuclear activists have also worked to change society through means other than protest, most notably by developing constructive alternatives to nuclear energy. Many such projects were designed not only to generate electricity without splitting nuclei, but also to exemplify broader ideals: they were thus deliberately small, independent of centralized structures, and relatively cheap to operate. One example was the device Maurice François built to trap methane gas produced by his farm animals, which could then be used to produce electricity. According to his son Yves, plans for the project had been drawn up years before, but it was the construction of Super-Phénix next door that actually gave the family the 'kick in the ass' to turn the idea into a reality.[69] After the 1977 demonstration in Malville, regional activists opposed to Super-Phénix built an

[67] 'Appel pour la marche Malville-Élysée', 4 pp., 1982, Gryffe, dossier 'Super-Pholix'; 'Acceuil de la Marche Malville-Paris', flyer, 17 April 1982, BnF, 4°WZ-13632; 'Compte-rendu de la réunion du Collectif d'opposition à Superphénix', 7 pp., 24 April 1982, Gryffe, dossier 'Super-Pholix'; *Silence*, no. 0 (14 May 1982). See also http://www.revuesilence.net/.
[68] Bernard, interview.
[69] Yves François, interview with the author, Creys-Mépieu, 24 January 2010.

environmentally friendly house (given the tongue-in-cheek name *maison autonome*), which they then used for informational and protest-related events.[70] Protesters from Plogoff installed a wind power generator atop the barn they had illegally built, organized a group to elaborate new projects (Plogoff-Alternatives), and formulated a comprehensive energy plan for Bretagne (Alter Breton). French activists developed numerous alternative projects like these, though most were eventually abandoned for lack of funding or state support to carry them through in the long term.[71]

West German anti-nuclear activists, enjoying a more conducive atmosphere (and sometimes financial or political backing from Die Grünen), went further in pushing for the adoption of wind and solar energy. One of the places in which alternative energy most firmly implanted itself was in Sasbach, a German town directly across the border from Marckolsheim. Already mobilized against the chemical plant on the French side, many of the town's residents took up the anti-nuclear cause with alacrity when plans for the power station in Wyhl were announced. In February 1975, the local electrician Werner Mildebrath set up a loudspeaker system on the French side of the Rhine, which announced news and information to squatters in Wyhl and played protest songs to encourage demonstrators when West German police evicted the first occupation.[72] As protests continued in the following months and years, Mildebrath experimented with solar energy and built his own prototype photovoltaic panels, some of which are still to be found today on the roofs of houses in the region around Wyhl;[73] he subsequently reoriented his business towards solar power (under the name Mildebrath Sonnenenergie). In 1976, shortly after the site occupation in Wyhl ended, Mildebrath and his neighbours in Sasbach joined up with anti-nuclear activists from throughout the region to host the first of a series of expositions for solar energy, the Sasbacher Sonnentage. Like the Volkshochschule Wyhler Wald—which had already hosted informational meetings about solar energy in October 1975[74]— the Sonnentage mixed information, protest, and culture together into a proper *Volksfest*, with Alsatian poets and musicians providing

---

[70] 'Malville: une maison pas comme les autres', *Super-Pholix*, no. 24 (3 April 1979); 'Compte-rendu'. Like the *maison autonome* in Plogoff, the name represented a deliberate irony, invoking principally energy autarchy but also the militancy of the *autonomes*.

[71] See Gérard Borvon, *Plogoff* (2004), ch. 16.

[72] Bernd Nössler and Margret de Witt, eds, *Kein Kernkraftwerk in Wyhl* (1976), pp. 90–1.

[73] Carola Bury, interview with Anna von der Goltz, Bremen, 22 June 2010, http://around1968.modhist.ox.ac.uk/ (accessed 10 March 2011); Walter Moßmann, *Realistisch sein* (2009), pp. 187–90.

[74] See VHSWW, '7. Programm', schedule flyer, 2 pp., 2–24 October 1975, ASB, 12.1.11.I.

accompaniment.[75] The first expo attracted as many as 12,000 visitors, and the event grew in size with repetition. It eventually became too large for Sasbach and had to be moved to Freiburg; according to Axel Mayer, the Sasbacher Sonnentage were a direct forerunner of Intersolar Europe, which now takes place annually in Munich and bills itself as the world's largest solar exhibition (in 2015, it attracted 38,000 visitors from 165 countries).[76] Renewable energy projects such as these constitute some of the most visible evidence of the anti-nuclear movement's impact on society.

Anti-nuclear activists have also tried to change society in less obvious ways, according to the maxim that in order to change the world, they had to change themselves. Paul Michalon (b. 1955), whose brother Vital was killed at the 1977 Malville demonstration, is one of those who have tried to construct alternatives in their everyday lives. A teacher of history and geography in Valence today, Paul strengthened his commitment to Christian pacifism after the tragic demonstration. Together with his wife Françoise, he is involved in the promotion of fair trade with Africa and especially Burkina Faso, where Paul performed voluntary service in the late 1970s (Vital had previously done a similar *coopération* in Algeria).[77] The couple even took a group of high school students to Nairobi in 2007 to observe and participate in that year's World Social Forum.[78] However, the most tangible evidence of the Michalons' commitment to changing society is their home. Paul describes the large building as 'not a commune, but a shared house' where his and other families live together. In the spacious basement and dining room, they host jazz concerts and invite local associations to hold meetings or social events. For Paul Michalon, this home is 'a utopia that works', an alternative to the norm, but one that is nevertheless compatible with life in modern society.[79] Jan Stehn (b. 1957) is another anti-nuclear activist who has tried to put utopian ideals into practice in his everyday life. In the 1970s, Jan travelled frequently from his home near Hamburg to Brokdorf and Gorleben for protests. Since 1995, he has lived in the Wendland region, in a multigenerational home where everyone contributes to a shared household budget and cooks for one another. Jan sees

[75] Christoph Büchele et al., *Der Widerstand* (1982), p. 63.
[76] Axel Mayer, interview with the author, Freiburg, 12 April 2010; Intersolar Europe, 'Messebilanz', 2015, http://www.intersolar.de/fileadmin/Intersolar-Europe/2_Exhibitor_Material_2016/ISE2016_Messebilanz_2015.pdf (accessed 15 December 2015).
[77] Paul Michalon, interview with the author, Valence, 30 January 2010.
[78] 'Compte-rendu FSM Nairobi', 2007, http://www.ac-grenoble.fr/admin/spip/spip.php?article485 (accessed 7 May 2012).
[79] Michalon, interview.

himself in a different light now than he did as an anti-nuclear protester during the 1970s.

> JS: Back then we essentially tried to change society from outside. We took direct action with the goal of throwing a spanner into the works. And with the idea of calling into being another society through the modest alternatives that we had developed. Today I would see myself as someone who is *within* society and not so much trying from outside to change it, but rather [working] with those involved in society.[80]

Anti-nuclear protest did not stop nuclear energy in its tracks, much less produce a revolution or a utopian society as many activists would have liked. However, activism has had an effect on subsequent forms of extra-parliamentary protest, and the changes activists have made in their daily lives have helped pull society in the direction of the utopia they once envisaged.

CHANGING THEMSELVES

Anti-nuclear protest not only changed politics and society; its greatest impact was arguably on the life trajectories of activists themselves. Particularly in the domains of family, continued activism, career, and community, the consequences for individual activists were deeply ambivalent, as protest impinged on certain social activities while providing a space for the development of others. Personal consequences of activism were thus seldom wholly negative or completely positive, but almost always formative.

During the 1970s, opposition to nuclear power was something that was capable of 'splitting up families', as one activist wrote at the time.[81] The reasons were multiple. The most immediate was the clash that resulted when political polarization was carried into the family environment. In directly affected communities such as Wyhl, the potential for familial conflict was great: Jürgen Nössler remembers how 'entire families tore themselves apart' over the question of whether a nuclear power plant would bring high-paying jobs to town or destroy existing winegrowers, improve local infrastructure or poison the local environment.[82] However, it

---

[80] Stehn, interview.
[81] Nössler and de Witt, *Kein Kernkraftwerk in Wyhl*, p. 38.
[82] Martin Kaul, 'Die Wunden von Wyhl', *tageszeitung*, 18 September 2010. See also Bernd-A. Rusinek, 'Wyhl', in *Deutsche Erinnerungsorte*, edited by Etienne François and Hagen Schulze (2001), p. 663.

was not only political controversy that was argued out within families, but the appropriate degree of political commitment: whether anti-nuclear activists won or lost their battles, activism took time away from family relationships. G., the son of a prominent activist in Wyhl, remembers growing up in a family that struggled to balance work and politics (both present in abundance) and a household that stood at the centre of attention for outside activists and the media. Fourteen years old at the time of the site occupation, he remembers that 'We didn't really have it, family, in my parents' house. No time! [. . .] Family life didn't happen.' G.'s father became well known for good-humoured acts of civil disobedience, but these often had serious consequences that were borne by the family as a whole: his father was arrested and threatened with outrageous fines, his sister lost her job because of the family's political engagements, and G. remembers the 'very unpleasant' experience of police searching their home. Growing up under these circumstances has had long-term consequences for him: though he shares his father's interest in political issues, today he argues that 'I don't want to involve myself politically, because of the experience in my parents' house. Because I don't want the stress.'[83]

In Wyhl, the political victory for the anti-nuclear cause might have been some consolation for the personal trials families like his endured. However, where activists were less fortunate, political and personal problems could compound one another. Asked to reflect on how they look back on their own anti-nuclear activism during the 1970s, one couple living near an operational power plant openly showed signs of tension. As the husband struggled to find words to describe his own feelings, his wife interjected by saying to him, 'For you it changed your whole life, your personality! Let's be completely honest about it: it set us back a great deal. All the cheer has gone out.' Intense activism could place serious strain on families, especially where the demands of protest interfered with existing relationships.

At the same time, activism was also capable of bringing some couples together. For example, Heinrich Voß (b. 1951) and his partner Christine Scheer (b. 1953) live in a house directly next to Brokdorf nuclear power station, where they also raised their children. The couple met around 1976 through work in a local chapter of the Bürgerinitiative Umweltschutz Unterelbe (BUU). Though their family homes are less than 15 kilometres apart, Heinrich, a farmer descended from generations of farmers, says his wife comes from a 'completely different world': her father was a lawyer and local councillor, Christine herself is an architect. Given their different

---

[83] G., interview with the author, Weisweil, 24 April 2010.

social backgrounds, Heinrich and Christine might never even have met, much less got to know one another under such favourable circumstances, had it not been for the BUU.[84] Several other activist couples also met within the social space that activism provided, whether in the intimate quarters of site occupations (e.g. Marie-Reine Haug and Raymond Schirmer, who met in Marckolsheim), at meetings and protests (like Conny Baade and Christian Petty, Freiburg residents who protested in Wyhl), or via circuitous paths that crossed at nuclear sites (such as Yves and Kuniko François, who live in Malville). Whether their protests stopped a particular reactor from being built does not seem to have had any bearing on whether these activist couples found happiness. Rather, how and when protest interacted with their relationships seems to have been more important: it was almost certainly easier to meet a new partner through activism than to adjust an existing relationship to accommodate protest. Relationships could be helped or harmed by activism, but they did not necessarily rise and fall with the fortunes of the anti-nuclear movement.

A recurring theme in interviews with former activists is their struggle to balance politics with the rest of their lives. Several of those interviewed for this project have maintained a lifelong commitment to anti-nuclear and related struggles. Wolfgang Hertle's persistent political engagement can be traced through the durable institutions he helped found. In the early 1970s, he created *Graswurzelrevolution* as a newspaper for non-violent anarchism. After becoming heavily involved in the anti-nuclear movement during the 1970s, he founded the Kurve Wustrow near Gorleben as a centre to help train nuclear energy opponents in methods of civil disobedience. After returning to Hamburg in 1989, he helped found Archiv Aktiv, an archive devoted to the history of non-violent protest. All three of these institutions still exist today, but, like Wolfgang himself, they remain close to the grassroots and largely aloof from the professional NGO sector and its lobbying activities. Wolfgang thus never earned much money from his own activism, though he always got by. After many years spent organizing for political causes, he found it difficult to obtain a 'normal' job and has received only a very modest pension since reaching retirement age.[85] Wolfgang still participates regularly in anti-nuclear and other protest, but his high level of commitment has entailed making certain sacrifices in terms of economic stability.

Not everyone remained as committed as Wolfgang. For some, difficulties reconciling the personal and the political led them to give up on the

---

[84] Voß and Scheer, joint interview.
[85] Hertle, interview.

latter entirely. Their stories tend to pass under the radar of most studies of protest, since they disappear from the narrative that social movements tell about themselves. During the 1970s, Lison de Caunes (b. 1948) was romantically involved with Brice Lalonde, the future national politician, when both were active in Les Amis de la Terre (ADLT) in Paris. Over time, though, political activism strained their relationship. When Brice Lalonde inherited a large flat in central Paris, he and Lison turned half of it over to ADLT for associational activities, but the (literal) lack of separation between personal and political space became a burden to which each reacted differently. According to a book in which Lison relates her experiences, 'Our house had become a meeting space [*un local*]', where 'all the rooms ended up being invaded', where five people sat at the table during 'lovingly prepared one-on-one dinners'. In part as a means of distancing herself from this 'invasion', Lison began directing more and more of her energies towards her work as an artisanal producer of straw furniture. She withdrew from activism while Brice plunged further in, and their different levels of commitment to ecology worsened other problems within their relationship, which ended in 1976.[86] It is perhaps not surprising, then, that Lison was happy to move on from the life she associated with activism. At a recent reunion of former ADLT activists, Lison says she saw friends who 'had stayed the same twenty years later, with the same taste for discussion, for activism. [. . .] And I said to myself, No, I don't want that anymore: eternal discussions, four-page letters . . . ' Lison learned certain skills from activism that she says she later put to use (how to write articles, speak on the radio, etc.), but on the whole she concludes that 'it is very, very interesting to be an activist for a time. But not for your whole life!'[87] For Lison, activism belongs to a phase of her life that she has since left behind.

For most of those interviewed for this project, activism was neither a permanent activity nor one that ever disappeared completely from their lives. They were often intensely involved with anti-nuclear activism for a time, but also experienced periods of relative inactivity and shifts of orientation, even while remaining interested in political developments. This was particularly true for those who found themselves in the spotlight as a result of activism. For example, Odile Wieder (b. 1947) was centrally

---

[86] Lison de Caunes, *Les Jours d'après* (1980), pp. 80–5, 99, 163. Though billed as a novel, this book directly describes Lison's relationship with Brice Lalonde, presenting details consistent with information available elsewhere; only the names are omitted (Lalonde is alternately addressed as *tu* or referred to as an anonymous 'he'). Lison herself was listed as secretary of ADLT in the group's newspaper *La Baleine* as late as the end of 1976, but her name no longer appears in later editions consulted (from mid-1977).

[87] Lison de Caunes, interview with the author, Paris, 17 March 2010.

involved in planning the 1977 protest against Super-Phénix that ended in a terrible defeat for the non-violent protesters with whom she felt an affinity. Seriously depressed in the demonstration's aftermath, Odile decided to reorganize her life and set up a bookstore in Annecy, La Bise noire. This was not activism in the same sense, but nor was it apolitical: the bookstore eschewed bestsellers in favour of stocking political literature (e.g. Éditions Maspero), the works of women authors, philosophy, and poetry; it quickly became a centre of cultural and political activity in Annecy. However, during the 1980s, Odile withdrew from this and similar projects in order to concentrate professionally on her new passion: singing and giving voice lessons. Then, in 1989, after what felt like a ten-year absence from activism, she joined environmentalist friends on a Green voting list for the municipal elections. Odile was elected to Annecy's city council and served for six years, but she did not seek a second term. As with anti-nuclear activism twenty years earlier, she felt the need to limit her political involvement for her own emotional well-being.[88] Like Odile, many anti-nuclear activists remain politically interested, but have moved on to other themes or recalibrated their level of commitment since the 1970s.

Anti-nuclear protest also had ambivalent consequences for the professional development of many activists. Sociological studies (mostly of the New Left) have shown that many committed activists tend to have lower incomes than their peers and experience more ruptures in their careers as a result of balancing politics and work.[89] However, some individuals 'professionalize' their activism in different ways, capitalizing (consciously or not) on the experiences of political struggle.[90] The careers of several activists involved in the Wyhl struggle illustrate just how divergent the effect of protest on professional trajectories could be. Some, like Bernd Nössler (b. 1953), speak openly of the sacrifices they made for the cause. As a native son of Wyhl, Bernd was closely involved in protest there from the start. Among other things, he helped edit a book to promote the cause, writing many of the chapters about the development of the local movement himself.[91] He remembers that, 'As a young man, I actually wanted to work in development aid or to study theology. And then these struggles started. That turned everything on its head. And so I wasn't able to realize my own life's dream.' Instead, he took over the family baking business from his father. Despite this sacrifice, he nevertheless felt that opposing

---

[88] Odile Wieder, interview with the author, Annecy, 29 April 2010.
[89] Giugni, 'Personal and Biographical Consequences', pp. 494–6.
[90] Mark et al., 'Reflections' pp. 296–302.
[91] Nössler and de Witt, *Kein Kernkraftwerk in Wyhl*.

the nuclear power plant was 'necessary. [One] didn't think about whether one got something material or whatever—one knew that it was simply altruistic engagement, and one felt obliged to be there on a daily basis.'[92] For other activists, it was possible to eliminate the tension between work and protest by combining the two. Like Michel Bernard in Lyon, Axel Mayer (b. 1955) eventually found a job for himself in the NGO sector: he was thus able to turn his 'hobby' into a career. However, the path leading there involved detours from more secure employment prospects. Originally trained as a surveyor (a civil service job that carried substantial benefits), he later took night classes to become a social worker (he wrote his dissertation on political learning within the Wyhl protest movement). After abandoning that in turn, he came to the Freiburg office of the environmental organization Bund für Umwelt und Naturschutz Deutschland, where he is now regional director. As of 2015, he has been involved in environmental protest for more than forty years.[93]

However, activism was not always a hindrance to employment, nor did paths that began with it lead only towards NGO work. Many people developed reputations through activism that they were then able to take with them elsewhere. For example, Nina Gladitz (b. 1946) was fresh out of film school when she returned to her parents' home near Freiburg in September 1974 to make a film about the protest brewing in Wyhl. For many years the only full-length documentary about the struggle, *Lieber heute aktiv als morgen radioaktiv* premiered at, and was subsequently shown repeatedly as part of, the Volkshochschule Wyhler Wald (for which Nina and her mother had previously hosted several events).[94] The film was prized by anti-nuclear activists, who invited Nina to show and discuss her film at sites across West Germany, and demand was high enough to merit the publication of an accompanying book.[95] This was spectacular success for a first-time film-maker, and for a woman in a profession heavily dominated by men. Nina's follow-up film focused on uranium mining on aboriginal land in Australia, and subsequent

---

[92] Bernd Nössler, interview with the author, Freiburg, 14 April 2010.

[93] Mayer, interview; Axel Mayer, 'Politisches Lernen und politische Sozialisation – dargestellt am Beispiel der Badisch-Elsässischen Bürgerinitiativen' (Diplomarbeit, Evangelische Fachhochschule für Sozialwesen, 1982); Axel Mayer, 'Ich erinnere mich', 2010, http://www.mitwelt.org/print.php?=569 (accessed 12 April 2010); 'Über uns – Regionalgeschäftsstelle Südlicher Oberrhein', http://www.bund-bawue.de/?id=2050 (accessed 26 October 2012).

[94] These included an account of Anne Gladitz's 1974 trip to China, readings of Bertolt Brecht, and the projection of a film about Mexican copper mine workers. See VHSWW, '19. Programm', schedule flyer, 2 pp., 31 October–25 November 1976, ASB, 12.1.11.I.

[95] Nina Gladitz, ed., *Lieber heute aktiv* (1976).

documentaries dealt with the history of the Second World War.[96] As Nina puts it, her documentary about Wyhl founded her career and established her reputation as a politically engaged film-maker.[97]

Activist experience could also wander far from its political home, with individuals putting skills earned in the context of anti-nuclear protest to use in unexpected ways. In 1974, Peter Modler (b. 1955) came to Freiburg to study law, but he quit school abruptly the following year in order to participate more actively in the site occupation in Wyhl. After several years of work with local activists and the Gewaltfreie Aktion Freiburg, Peter returned to university as a student of Catholic theology. Hoping to teach religious classes, he found his career prospects blocked as a result of his political engagement.[98] Switching to carpentry instead, he found an apprenticeship through the help of local activists. Protest connections proved useful once again when he decided to undertake doctoral studies, as activist friends helped him obtain a scholarship from the Friedrich-Ebert-Stiftung (closely associated with the Social Democrats). In the late 1980s and 1990s, he moved through a series of jobs in publishing that eventually led to his career as an independent business consultant. Today, he says, 'I restructure businesses. And it's clear for me when I take on a restructuring contract that I do not want jobs to be lost.' Perhaps surprisingly, he says he is 'rather certain that I wouldn't be able to do my job as a business consultant without the period with the citizens' initiatives'. Within the framework of activism, he says, he learned how to work closely with people from wildly different backgrounds and to forge political coalitions with them.[99] At many different stages in his circuitous career, Peter has drawn on skills and contacts that he initially developed through anti-nuclear activism.

As with regard to families and careers, anti-nuclear activism also affected activists' relationships to their communities in contradictory ways. Particularly in small towns near nuclear projects, protest could redraw social boundaries, pitting neighbours against one another but also facilitating contact with like-minded individuals further afield. Within these local communities, the positions for and against a local nuclear power plant tended to harden over time, especially as money came into play. A new nuclear plant held out the promise of large tax revenues, a source of

[96] *Das Uran gehört der Regenbogenschlange*, 1979, 44 mins; *Zeit des Schweigens und der Dunkelheit*, 1982, 94 mins; *Perlasca*, 1993, 94 mins.
[97] Nina Gladitz, interview with the author, Berlin, 2 June 2010.
[98] Peter used the term *Berufsverbot* to describe this, though this is usually applied only to communists. According to Peter, the local bishop who was responsible for appointing Catholic religious instructors demanded that Peter sign a statement declaring he would not publicly take a position 'on ecological questions', which Peter refused to do.
[99] Peter Modler, interview with the author, Amoltern, 21 April 2010.

employment (often desperately needed), and new infrastructure. Activists who fought tooth and nail to prevent the transformation of their home region into a purportedly ultra-modern paradise were not always popular with their neighbours. Marie-Jo Putinier (b. 1937) remembers how local support for the protests in Malville waxed and waned.

> AT: What were relations like with the people who didn't participate in the protests?
>
> MJP: In the beginning [. . .] we were well regarded. [. . .] No one wanted this fast breeder. They were happy that someone was engaged, but they didn't dare. They stayed home, but in spirit they supported us. [. . .] On the other hand, they expected—they were promised—that there would be jobs [. . .] So we were the ugly ducklings who prevented the jobs from coming.

After the disastrous protest of 31 July 1977 at which Vital Michalon was killed, Marie-Jo felt her relationship to her neighbours change for the worse.

> MJP: When the demonstration failed, the terrible one, afterwards we—or at least I, the way I experienced it—I felt terribly guilty and I didn't dare look my neighbours in the eye. It was difficult to approach them about it. There were really [two] camps [. . .] With time, that's faded. But it took a long time.[100]

Even in places where anti-nuclear activists won out in the end, the wounds that protest left could run deep: in Wyhl and Plogoff, many local citizens are hesitant to be interviewed today about what they remember as a difficult and divisive period.[101] Outside supporters, journalists, and researchers who think of these struggles primarily in terms of activists' 'success' are not always aware of how bitter it was to live through them on an everyday basis. Conflict among the local community in Wyhl sometimes became visible in the form of slashed tyres and smashed windows; when it remained more civil, proponents and opponents of a nuclear power plant might boycott one another's businesses or refuse to serve their political adversaries.[102] On occupied sites, squatters were occasionally attacked by pro-nuclear mobs; during one infamous incident, a German anti-nuclear activist was hospitalized with burn wounds after political opponents armed with iron bars and Molotov cocktails attacked

---

[100]   Marie-Jo Putinier, interview with the author, Bourgoin-Jallieu, 26 January 2010.

[101]   Rusinek, 'Wyhl', pp. 663–5; Vincent Porhel, *Ouvriers bretons* (2008), pp. 224–8.

[102]   Nössler and de Witt, *Kein Kernkraftwerk in Wyhl*, pp. 37–8, 120. Similar divisions were reported elsewhere. See 'Braud-Saint Louis : pas d'atome dans le bordeaux', *Témoignage chrétien* (10 July 1975).

a camp occupying the power tower in Heiteren (Alsace).[103] However, anti-nuclear activists could give as well as they received: in 1981, a meeting called by the PCF to support one of its pro-nuclear members in Plogoff was disrupted by 350–400 anti-nuclear activists. They blocked PCF members from leaving, cut their phone line, vandalized cars, and barri-caded the surrounding roads for hours until a truce was negotiated.[104] The wounds left by incidents like these could indeed take a long time to heal.

It would, however, be a mistake to assume that activism had only (or even primarily) a destructive effect on activists' sense of community. Protest could certainly polarize, but shared political commitments some-times allowed activists to transcend existing social hierarchies. Didier Anger (b. 1939), a leading organizer of the protests in La Hague, remem-bers that 'we had people against us, but at the same time we had people with us', including people from very different backgrounds. Didier him-self was a teacher, but says the grassroots of the Comité de Réflexion, d'Information et de Lutte Anti-Nucléaire (CRILAN) which he led for many years was composed primarily of farmers and fishermen. They were joined by some workers (including PCF members), but also by the lord (*châtelain*) of the sixteenth-century manor in nearby Sotteville. Didier tells the story of how a fisherman's wife was visibly moved upon being kissed on the hand by the lord as he invited her inside for a CRILAN meeting at the manor. For Didier, stories like these about encounters between activists from different extremes of social class testify to the 'important [. . .], interesting mixing of populations' that occurred as a result of activism, and which 'changed things beyond just the anti-nuclear strug-gle.'[105] In Gorleben, too, activists tell similar stories about their local aristocrat. One account of the 1980 occupation of Tiefbohrstelle 1004 describes Count Andreas von Bernstorff sitting down with an 'anarchist with a punk haircut and a grubby leather jacket' to tell the newspapers about the positive atmosphere of protest.[106] One need not believe every word to recognize that activism provided one of the few spaces in which such unlikely interactions could take place under favourable conditions.

---

[103] Préfet du Haut-Rhin, 'La centrale nucléaire de Fessenheim', 4 August 1977, AD Haut-Rhin, 1391 W 17; 'Französische Chauvinisten gegen deutsche KKW-Gegner', flyer, 3 pp., 1977, ASB, 12.1.7/00024377. Similar incidents of less gravity also occurred elsewhere. See Wasserschutzpolizei Wyhl, telex, 22 March 1975, StAF, G 114/1 Nr. 1.

[104] Préfet du Finistère, memo to Ministère de l'Intérieur, 9 February 1981, AD Finistère, 1235 W 25.

[105] Anger, interview.

[106] Ingrid Müller-Münch et al., *Besetzung* (1981), p. 167. For more recent information on this aristocratic family's anti-nuclear engagement, see Astrid Geisler, 'Adel verzichtet', *tageszeitung*, 29 October 2010.

In addition to fostering 'improbable encounters' like these, protest provided shared experiences that changed the quality of social interactions among activists, sometimes leading to remarkably durable friendships. In Malville, for example, the activists who planned, led, and subsequently shouldered the blame for the 1977 demonstration grew closer together as a result of the hardships they endured. Many of them continued to see each other socially many years later.[107] Maryse Budin (1944–2013) recalled how she became connected to other activists through the unpleasant experiences that they shared of being interrogated by police and having their homes searched.

> MB: It connected us. One year, [. . .] we took a trip together along the Danube. It was Georges [David], his wife, Marie-Jo [Putinier], and me in the car, singing. *[MB laughs.]* Yes, yes, it connected us. It was incredible. And afterwards [. . . many things] followed on the heels of Malville . . . one group met for a long time with Marie-Jo and the François family and a Jesuit.[108] All that comes from Malville. It joined us strongly for years and years.

Protest fostered contact not only with fellow activists nearby, but with distant and different people who came to participate in meetings and protest actions. Among the local activists interviewed for this project, many described the period of anti-nuclear activism in the 1970s as one of *ouverture* or *Öffnung*. Maryse recalled how the protests in Malville 'brought all kinds of people to us. It opened our family, our milieu [. . . to] people from all sorts of countries [. . .], often with a higher social standing than ourselves.'[109] Across the Rhine in Wyhl, Bernd Nössler also says that activism was 'the most important experience of my life as far as people are concerned', because it permitted him to 'get to know hundreds of [politically] involved people [*Engagierten*] from all over the world' and taught him about how people tick.[110] Indeed, when former anti-nuclear activists are asked today to take stock of the period of intense protest in the 1970s, the single most common response they give is that it was a period in which they 'met so many people'. Political activism created an alternative social environment where shared commitments enabled people to reach beyond traditional social and geographic boundaries and tap into a broader, political community.

---

[107] During interviews, several former Malville activists brought up (unprompted) a recent meeting they had attended together about the Israeli–Palestinian conflict.

[108] See 'Rencontre Malville d'un groupe de Chrétiens', minutes of meeting, 10 May 1977, PA Putinier.

[109] Maryse Budin, interview with the author, Vézeronce, 27 January 2010.

[110] Nössler, interview.

The expansion of community was not limited to the local activists who in interviews most often express their excitement at the 'opening' that anti-nuclear protest produced in their lives. For outside activists too, anti-nuclear protest connected them to a broader community through a political dimension—though 'politics' became more about shared opposition than about a precise ideological perspective. This was the case, for example, for the Hamburg-based anti-nuclear protester Günter Hopfenmüller (b. 1941). Günter's radical, left-wing political orientation was moulded at an early age: in the 1950s, he says, he was a member of a youth group with clandestine links to the illegal Freie Deutsche Jugend;[111] in secondary school, he took part in Easter marches for disarmament and claims to have helped smuggle American deserters over the border into Denmark in the early 1960s; just after 1968, he became chairperson of the left-dominated student assembly at the University of Hamburg before subsequently joining the Sozialistisches Arbeiter- und Lehrlingszentrum and then its successor, the KB.[112] By the time he became heavily involved with the opposition to nuclear energy (serving, among other things, as the public face of the KB at all major anti-nuclear demonstrations),[113] Günter's identity as a radical leftist was firmly established. So too was the anti-fascist tradition of which his own left-wing politics were a part: in 1977, Günter's organization published a brochure describing at length the fascist backgrounds of founding members of a right-wing anti-nuclear group, the Weltbund zum Schutze des Lebens (WSL), and criticizing the group for failing to distance itself from its former, brown leadership: 'We have no understanding for a chummy [*kumpelhaft*] relationship to such people.'[114]

Yet when Günter helped found Die Grünen in the late 1970s (before serving in the party leadership from 1983 to 1986), he worked closely with members of another right-wing group that partially overlapped with WSL, the Aktionsgemeinschaft Unabhängiger Deutscher (AUD).[115] AUD leader August Haußleiter briefly served as one of Die Grünen's first speakers until he was forced to resign in 1980, when propagandistic articles he had published

---

[111] The FDJ was a mass organization of the Moscow- and GDR-aligned post-war Communist Party and thus banned along with the party in West Germany.

[112] Hopfenmüller, interview; Steffen, *Geschichten vom Trüffelschwein*, pp. 360–1.

[113] Günter led KB actions in Brokdorf, Grohnde, and Kalkar. See, for example, 'Veranstaltungen BUU („Solidarität mit den Opfern von Malville!")', protest registration files, 6 August 1977, StHH, 331-1 II, Az. 20.37-3, Abl. 17, 1977, Bd. 14.

[114] KB, '„Dritter Weg" im Umweltschutz?', brochure, 30 pp., 22 July 1977, AK, p. 3. For background on WSL, see Mende, *Nicht rechts, nicht links*, pp. 102–5. On the entry of SALZ into the KB, see Steffen, *Geschichten vom Trüffelschwein*, pp. 28–32.

[115] Mende, *Nicht rechts, nicht links*, pp. 94–134; Richard Stöss, *Vom Nationalismus zum Umweltschutz* (1980).

during the Second World War came to light.[116] Günter nevertheless remembers Haußleiter fondly and claims to have worked together 'very much in solidarity' with AUD members. This was possible largely because of the way people changed and opened up as a result of shared involvement in protest.

> GH: I knew, for example, an older woman from Hamburg whom I very much liked. She and her father [. . .] would probably have subscribed to 80 per cent of National Socialist ideas.[117] But I witnessed how these people said goodbye to all that, to so many things at this time. It was a situation—comparable to '68—when once again everything was possible. Where people were again ready to question everything that they had held to be true in their lives up to that point. And to throw a lot of it overboard.[118]

Nor were AUD members the only ones to open up. So too did many radical leftists, who opened themselves to the very different activists who they encountered within the movement.[119] As Günter recalls, AUD members 'knew what burdens they had to free themselves of and we also knew we had to let go of some baggage. We knew that we weren't founding a Marxist–Leninist party—which none of us wanted anymore anyway.'[120] For activists on all sides, participating in the broad-based antinuclear movement forced them to re-examine their own political goals, required them to cooperate with unlikely partners, and enabled them to form friendships with people who, under other circumstances, would have been their mortal enemies.

Like many of the other activists discussed above, Günter's biography deviates from sociological norms in ways that imply sacrifices made for activism. He left university without the teaching degree he had studied for, expecting that he would never be able to find work in that field because of West Germany's *Berufsverbot* policy towards communists. Instead, he earned a living through odd jobs before becoming a landscape architect, which allowed him to continue pursuing political activism on

---

[116] 'Warm und ehrlich', *Spiegel*, no. 27 (1980), pp. 85–7.

[117] 'Das waren Leute, die durchaus . . . dem Nationalsozialismus kritisch gegenüber gestanden haben, aber eben nicht sehr weit entfernt waren. Die hatten unterschiedliche Motive, warum sie zum Nationalsozialismus kritisch waren [. . . , z.B.] weil sie die Euthanasie für falsch und für verbrecherisch gehalten haben. Aber ansonsten hätten sie wahrscheinlich 80% der nationalsozialistischen Ideen durchaus unterschrieben.'

[118] Hopfenmüller, interview.

[119] This does not imply a repudiation of left-wing politics. Though 'right turns' of the kind undertaken by André Glucksmann or (at the extremes) Horst Mahler receive disproportionate attention in the media, they are rare. Érik Neveu, 'Trajectoires', in *Mai–Juin 68*, edited by Dominique Damamme et al. (2008), p. 317.

[120] Hopfenmüller, interview.

the side and travel extensively. He has continued to work freelance past retirement age, since 'with political work, one doesn't earn a pension from which one can live'. He has been with his partner since 1983, though they did not marry until 2003 (when they bowed to practical necessities created by the German health and pension systems) and have no children. However, Günter does not look back upon his lifetime of political engagement with sadness: 'I'm not sorry for anything, I don't regret any of it. I always did what I held to be right and necessary.' Nor does he regret the defeats and failures endured by protesters as they have fallen short of achieving their goals.

> GH: I have never been a person who thought that his goals or desires or visions would somehow be fulfilled in his lifetime. [...] Like I said, through this school of hard knocks—I mean in the 1950s in Germany, during the Cold War period, if you held your ground, stood up to [it all]—you never believed you would win. Instead, you said, first you have to be able to look in the mirror, to look at yourself. [...] In my youth I was very strongly marked by people, [...] communists, who had survived concentration camps, who may have been in wheelchairs, but who said they don't regret it, that what they did was necessary. And that every single step, in the end, somehow changed society.[121]

As in many other protest movements, anti-nuclear opponents measured their own success not exclusively in terms of policy change, but morally, in terms of acting in accord with their principles.[122] This, they felt, was capable of changing society at a more profound level.

In the end, whether activists actually managed to halt the expansion of nuclear power at a given site was less important than the fact and extent of their resistance. Step by step, they created unforeseen alternatives, pulled politics and society closer to their ideals, and allowed themselves to be changed in the process. Whether they became professional activists or took skills with them to other activities, individuals at the grassroots were the motors of real change, bringing ideas, issues, and experiences from anti-nuclear protest into their daily lives and, through that, to a broader community. By making many small changes in these domains, they

---

[121] Hopfenmüller, interview; Steffen, *Geschichten vom Trüffelschwein*, pp. 360–1.
[122] Eric Schlosser makes this argument about 'success' in relation to Catholic pacifists protesting against American nuclear weapons installations. 'Break-in at Y-12', *New Yorker* (9 March 2015).

amplified the impact of protest well beyond the achievements of any particular demonstration or campaign.

CONCLUSION

In assessing the impact of anti-nuclear protest, it would be a mistake to focus strictly on whether protesters achieved their stated goal of immediately halting nuclear technology. In the words of Chaïm Nissim, who was closely involved in years of (largely 'unsuccessful') protest against the FBR in Malville, 'We didn't win—but we did win, actually.'[123] This ambivalence testifies to the mix of outcomes to which anti-nuclear protest contributed: some victories, some losses, and a great many more ambiguous changes.

As a broad-based movement in which people of very different social and political backgrounds briefly came together before often parting ways again, it is fitting that the consequences of anti-nuclear protest should follow multiple trajectories. For some, the next logical step at the beginning of the 1980s was to make protest more effective, either by directly engaging in political decision-making as part of Green parties or by exerting pressure on politicians through NGO activity. Another set of activists has focused instead on keeping alive different extra-parliamentary protest traditions that developed within the anti-nuclear movement, for example by cultivating autonomy as a successor to earlier Marxist forms of radicalism or by bringing non-violent civil disobedience to ever greater masses. A further set of activists has focused on proposing, developing, and promoting alternatives, not only within the domain of energy production but also in their everyday lives, ultimately creating a niche for themselves and their ideals within mainstream society. Anti-nuclear activists may not have stopped Brokdorf or Malville, but in trying to do so, they established new organizations, created alternative infrastructures, and cultivated protest traditions that continue to have a political impact today, beyond the sole issue of nuclear energy.

For those who participated in it, anti-nuclear activism also had important consequences on a personal level. The biographies of many committed activists are marked by their years of political engagement. Time devoted to protest could take away from relationships to partners and children, sometimes leading to break-ups, divorces, or strained family relationships,

---

[123] Chaïm Nissim, interview with the author, Geneva, 28 January 2010.

such as Lison and others experienced. However, political activism also brought people into closer contact with others who shared their concerns and passions, leading to durable and satisfying partnerships for people like Heinrich and Christine. Careers too could be affected for better and for worse. Some, like Bernd, look back with regret on unrealized hopes, abandoned studies, and obstacles to advancement that resulted from political engagement. Yet others, such as Nina, met with success in their careers precisely as a result of activities connected to protest. Indeed, a given individual could experience both professional setbacks and advantages as a result of activism, as Peter did. Finally, activism had mixed effects on communities. Activists in the small towns closest to nuclear projects might find their circle of friends shrink within the local community just as it expanded to encompass members of a new, geographically disparate community of activists; the lasting friendships between Maryse, Marie-Jo, Georges, and others involved in the Malville protests constitute but one example. Even highly politicized, urban activists like Günter could see their definition of community change, as they formed personal friendships in spite of political differences. The 'opening up' that all of these activists experienced as a result of working together may be the most important legacy to result from the anti-nuclear protest of the 1970s, even as it is the most difficult to measure.

These personal and political consequences of activism were, of course, deeply intertwined. Anti-nuclear protest may not have led to either the

Fig. 6.2. The carousel at Wunderland Kalkar. Photo: Andrew Tompkins.

immediate changes to nuclear policy or the total transformation of society that activists envisioned, but participating in this movement led individuals to make changes in their own lives that they took with them past the 1970s. What happened on a small scale in the lives of those described here was repeated by the hundreds of thousands throughout France, West Germany, and elsewhere. Their improbable encounters within this movement shaped their interactions beyond it, allowing them to carry ecological arguments, ideas, and alternatives to a broader public.

Conclusion

On 11 March 2011, an earthquake and massive tsunami hit Japan, killing more than 15,000 people, injuring thousands more, and destroying or damaging more than one million buildings.[1] In the midst of this terrible natural disaster, the emergency cooling systems at a coastal nuclear power plant in Fukushima failed, leading to dangerous core meltdowns in three separate reactors that it took crews months to bring under control. More than four years later, many of the problems created by this nuclear accident were still not resolved. Although the radioactive release was apparently not as great as during the 1986 Chernobyl accident, this was a dire emergency, worse even than many anti-nuclear activists expected. In Germany, the weeks that followed were marked by repeated demonstrations against nuclear energy, culminating in protests by almost 150,000 people across the country on the weekend prior to 26 April (which marked the twenty-fifth anniversary of the Chernobyl accident). In France, by contrast, protest was far more limited. Only 1,000 people showed up to demonstrate in Paris in the wake of the disaster—one twentieth the number that took to the streets in Berlin. As during the 1970s, protests were stronger in the provinces: up to 10,000 nuclear energy opponents came to Fessenheim (Alsace) and 5,000 to Cattenom (Lorraine). However, French and German media unanimously reported that the majority of those protesters were Germans who had come from Baden-Württemberg, Saarland, and Rheinland-Pfalz. By 2011, the anti-nuclear movement in Germany appeared vibrant, its French counterpart moribund or non-existent by comparison.[2]

---

[1] National Police Agency of Japan, 'Damage Situation and Police Countermeasures Associated with 2011 Tohoku Earthquake', 2015, http://www.npa.go.jp/archive/keibi/biki/higaijokyo_e.pdf (accessed 15 December 2015).

[2] AFP, 'Plus de 100 000 manifestants contre le nucléaire en Allemagne et en France', 25 April 2011; 'Près de 10 000 personnes antinucléaires réunies à Fessenheim, un millier à Paris', Le Monde, 22 March 2011; Andreas Gandzior, 'Marsch gegen die Atomkraft', Berliner Morgenpost, 29 May 2011, p. 12; AFP, 'Pique-nique au bord du Rhin pour demander l'arrêt de la centrale de Fessenheim', 10 April 2011; dapd, 'Gemeinsam gegen Cattenom', 25 April 2011. See also 'Manifestation antinucléaire franco-allemande', 2011,

Many commentators extrapolated from the present backwards through time, drawing on clichés, stereotypes, and some of the more malleable aspects of history to explain developments in both countries: it was assumed that 'France doesn't (yet) have an anti-nuclear movement', whereas 'an irrational fear of nuclear energy runs deep in Germany'; Germans are supposedly haunted by the knowledge that Hiroshima could have been Hannover, while the French, mindful of their wartime defeat, purportedly regard nuclear technology as a 'symbol of freedom'; a rationalist, pro-technology legacy of the French Revolution contrasts with 'the Romantic worship that is traditionally shown in Germany towards nature and not science'. Vague cultural traits and 'lessons of history' painted in very broad strokes were made to account for apparent differences in protest today.[3] Whatever grains of truth these sweeping generalizations may contain, they all create a false sense of inevitability. France's *nucléarisation* and Germany's *Atomausstieg* were not foreordained decades or centuries ago. They were the outcomes of intense political conflict—fought across national borders—over the course of many years. While the odds for nuclear energy opponents may never have been as good in centralist France as they were in federalist West Germany, it was certainly not a lost cause from the outset in France, and there was little to indicate that protest in West Germany would catch on the way it did. During the 1970s, opponents of nuclear power found their footing in West Germany, but stumbled in France. Things could have turned out differently (and they may yet change again).

The distortions cited above, though exaggerated in news media, result from the common tendency—even in the field of 'transnational' history— to conceptualize and interpret social movements primarily in relation to national frameworks. Transnational phenomena cannot be grasped merely by lining up national case studies, studying the itineraries of mobile leaders and the agendas of international organizations, or highlighting transfers from one context to another. All of these approaches tend to reify what Marc Bloch once called the 'obsolete topographical

---

http://www.ina.fr/video/4446666001009/manifestation-antinucleaire-franco-allemande-video.html (accessed 2 February 2015). The strength of protest in Germany was due in no small part to Angela Merkel's decision only a few months earlier to decelerate the country's phase-out of nuclear energy.

[3] Laura Hofmann, 'Madame Anti-Atom', *Berliner Zeitung*, 29 June 2011, p. 1; Alan Cowell, 'Germans' Deep Suspicions of Nuclear Power Reach a Political Tipping Point', *New York Times*, 2 June 2011, p. 11; Daniel Johnson, 'Why Germany Said No to Nuclear', *Daily Telegraph*, 31 May 2011, p. 15; Matthias Horx, 'Die deutsche Kernfrage', *Focus*, no. 17 (24 April 2011), p. 70; Guy Sorman, 'Jenseits von Fukushima: Der Boom grüner Ideologie wird nicht ewig halten', *Welt*, 23 June 2011.

compartments in which we pretend to enclose social realities'.[4] As this book has argued, the opposition at the grassroots level to nuclear energy in West Germany was never entirely distinct from that in France. National differences were often not as salient as other differences, such as between urban and rural areas or between violent and non-violent protesters. French and German activists belonged to the same networks, learned from one another, and sometimes demonstrated together—notably at the protests in Wyhl and Malville, both of which were decisive for the development of protest in each country (albeit in diametrically opposed ways). Indeed, the escalation of violence between these two demonstrations was itself a transnational development, neither fully French nor fully German, but synchronized across borders, with effects felt in multiple countries. In the 1970s, transnational anti-nuclear protest was based on decentralized, largely informal networks such as those that also characterize more recent protests like Occupy, and it thrived even in the absence of the internet-based communication that has since come to be seen as vital to working across borders.[5] Nevertheless, national contexts were never fully irrelevant, not least because activists could and did put them to use. The importance of border-crossing to protest was not limited to the 'national diversity' or 'international solidarity' that activists themselves often celebrate. Moving across borders could provide creative resources for protesters, a foil that could be used for reinterpreting one's local situation, or an escape from the constraints of a familiar context. In places such as Marckolsheim and Wyhl along the Franco-German border, activists even shifted protest between contexts in order to pit states against one another. Naturally, working across borders also introduced certain distortions into the equation, many of which remain relevant to protest today. Selective interpretations, projections, translation problems, and cultural differences meant that French and German activists were not always on the same page, even if (they thought) they were reading from the same script. This had serious negative consequences at the 1977 Malville protest, where Germans' unfamiliarity with the French context added to the confusion that reigned there and made it easier for authorities to isolate German protesters. The opposition to nuclear power, like most other social movements, cannot be fully understood without taking into account transnational factors and the complexities they introduce.

[4] Marc Bloch, 'Pour une histoire comparée', in *Mélanges historiques*, p. 36, cited in William H. Sewell, 'Marc Bloch and Comparative History', *History and Theory* 6, no. 2 (1968), pp. 211–12.
[5] On the 'fetishization' of social media in relation to protest, see Paolo Gerbaudo, *Tweets and the Streets* (2012), pp. 5–6.

In many ways, transnational protest can seem exotic or exceptional. However, as the individual stories of transnational protesters illustrate, cross-border contact could be an ordinary part of who they were and what they did. Not everyone was born in a border region like Jean-Jacques Rettig or grew up in a family that moved around like Bernadette Ridard, but for such individuals, taking advantage of language skills and contextual differences could come almost naturally. For others, especially young people growing up in post-war West Germany like Conny Baade and Wolfgang Hertle, looking or going abroad could result from dissatisfaction with the political environment at home. In part through activism, they found elsewhere approaches to life and politics that suited them better. Moving frequently across borders was not always easy, as the complicated identities of activists such as Christian Petty and Bernadette Ridard demonstrate. However, activism was one activity that provided them with an alternative identity, which gave greater continuity to lives otherwise marked by repeated ruptures. Finally, activism itself fostered transnational contact that could be of great personal consequence: for some, like Yves François, this could be as simple as falling in love with a distant stranger whose path crossed one's own as a result of protest. In all of these ways, transnational protest could be both a normal activity and one with powerful potential.

National borders were not the only ones across which this movement worked: the political divisions within it were often considerable. The motivations of local activists in affected communities and of outside anti-nuclear activists were sometimes very different. Those who lived near projected nuclear power stations were most concerned with the social, economic, and environmental consequences for their community of a leap from farming and fishing to a high-tech, post-industrial world. However, the anger they expressed towards state and industry intervention in their lives could be (mis-)read by outside activists as a validation of their own opposition to the state, the military, capitalism, repression, and/or consumerism. Anti-nuclear networks intersected with those of movements focused on other issues, such as feminism or peace activism, and such intersections were often mutually reinforcing. Borrowing freely from one another's arguments, diverse groups of outsiders and locals framed their common cause in terms of a fundamental critique of state and society rather than in terms of a parochial 'single issue'. They claimed to face a *choix de société* in France and a struggle against a multi-faceted, dystopian *Atomstaat* in West Germany. By the 1980s, the 'anti-nuclear movement' had become a recognizable social force in both countries, even if anti-nuclear activists themselves came in many different shapes and sizes.

The key division between 'local' and 'outside' activists was often conflated with a difference between rural and urban or, more accurately, between small towns and larger cities. Protest in rural space did not always work the way outside activists expected it to, sometimes leading to serious miscalculations such as occurred in Malville. Much like with transnational communication, contact between urban and rural activists was plagued by misunderstandings, as outsiders projected their own aspirations onto local farmers and townspeople. Their imaginings of rural life were conditioned by the ideologies and attitudes of left-wing youth after 1968: radical activists latched onto tropes of peasant revolt that associated the rural with revolution, while hippie environmentalists looked to the countryside as an authentic, marginal space outside of consumer society. However, local farmers and townspeople were usually too constrained by work, family, and community responsibilities to fulfil all of the hopes invested in them; local activists thus depended on outside support as much as other anti-nuclear activists depended on them. This interdependency created tensions, especially within the close space of site occupations, but it also forced people from different backgrounds to cooperate in spite of the 'interruptions' that resulted from misunderstandings and cultural clashes.

As with communication across national borders, cooperation between rural and urban activists could produce unexpected and important changes on both sides. In the eyes of many protesters, dialogue across this divide was 'democracy' of a kind that did not take place in society at large. Whether or not their own interactions were always as participatory as activists claimed, activists contrasted them with what they perceived as the sham democracy of the West German government's *Bürgerdialog* and French *enquêtes d'utilité publique*. Encounters between city and country could also have an impact on personal trajectories, as anti-nuclear protest brought individuals into closer contact with urban and rural spaces that offered very different things. Dieter Halbach, who grew up in West Berlin, eventually found a 'second home' for himself in a small town near Gorleben, and Markus Mohr left the countryside for the urban scenes of Bremen, Hamburg, and West Berlin. Finally, protest changed the rural areas to which it came, as local activists in need opened their communities, their homes, and themselves to a highly politicized segment of the outside world. Especially for country women like Marie-Jo Putinier, this could be powerfully emancipatory: taking on new responsibilities, confronting political authorities, and working in solidarity with feminists from nearby cities all helped her refashion herself into a more assertive, self-directed woman.

If the differences between town and country or between West German and French protest cultures were, on balance, constructive, the same was not always true of those between non-violent and militant activists. Like participants in other post-war protest movements from '68 to the Global Justice Movement and beyond, anti-nuclear activists in the 1970s were strongly divided over the question of strategy. A majority always favoured some form of non-violence, as illustrated by the memorable, mythical protests that took place in Wyhl and Gorleben (to say nothing of the related protests in Marckolsheim and on the Larzac). Groups dedicated specifically to non-violent action promoted forms of protest that included boycotts and hunger strikes, decentralized demonstrations, and especially site occupations, their preferred form of direct action. They consistently opposed militant activists, who committed acts of sabotage (another form of decentralized, direct action) and who clashed with police in their attempts to occupy construction sites by force. By 1977, protests over nuclear power had escalated dramatically, as authorities went to extremes to prevent site occupations from occurring. When militant and non-violent factions pursued opposing strategies in the same space at an international demonstration that year in Malville, tragedy ensued. Non-violent and militant activists subsequently blamed one another for the disaster, deepening the split within the movement.

Yet outside the extreme context of Malville (where problems of violence were exacerbated by the confusion of urban activists in a rural environment and West German demonstrators' unfamiliarity with French protest norms), violence and non-violence managed to coexist with less contradiction than advocates of either were willing to admit. Indeed, dedicated non-violent activists and their militant counterparts were both a minority within the movement and resembled one another in their moral drive and emphasis on direct action. Moderately 'violent' practices such as property damage or rock-throwing were widely toler-ated, and forms of non-violence up to and including hunger strikes commanded great respect. However, extreme protest practices of any kind repelled other activists, such as when self-sacrifice ended in suicide or, worse, when militancy spilled over into murder. Activists from outside the militant and non-violent blocs were frequently ambivalent or resentful towards both, and many local activists were indifferent to a debate that largely took place among outsiders. As the movement's public representatives, local activists insisted on an official discourse of non-violence, but their own practices of protest were ambiguous and inconsistent. Throughout the 1970s and early 1980s, violence and non-violence enabled one another by turns, making protest unpredictable and costly for authorities to police. In spite of their discursive incom-patibility, non-violent and militant practices could thus be to some extent complementary.

Just as the anti-nuclear movement's membership was broad and contradictory, so too was the impact it had on politics and society. Within the realm of 'official' politics, anti-nuclear activists contributed directly (if controversially and sometimes reluctantly) to the development of Green parties such as Die Grünen and Les Verts, which carried ecological themes into regional and national parliaments. These have turned out to be more durable than the revolutionary Maoist parties of the 1970s, which declined in part because anti-nuclear and other 'new social movements' presented a more attractive alternative to potential recruits. Beyond the domain of 'politics' in its strictest sense, opponents of nuclear energy also cultivated vigorous traditions of extra-parliamentary protest. Autonomist practices incubated within the anti-nuclear movement and have since become a visible fixture of demonstrations on a number of issues. At the same time, the anti-nuclear movement helped develop, test, and spread non-violent protest strategies that are now much more common than they were in the 1970s. Alongside protest, many activists also worked to construct viable alternatives to 'nuclear society', particularly in the field of renewable energy. Their alternatives and the ecological critiques animating them have since found much wider resonance within society. Though anti-nuclear activists may not have stopped nuclear power as quickly or as completely as they would have liked, they initiated long-term changes that continue to have an effect today.

Arguably the greatest impact of protest has been felt in the lives of those who made it happen. As in other domains, the results were neither wholly positive nor wholly negative, but the changes activism induced were far-reaching. The intense commitment that protest demanded took time away from family and relationships, sometimes straining them to the point of collapse; on the other hand, protest also brought some couples together in the first place, including many who would otherwise never have met. Activism created an alternate social environment in which the usual boundaries of class and nation did not always apply. Within that environment, it was not unusual for a farmer to meet an architect near Brokdorf or for Franco-German couples to form during site occupations in Wyhl and Marckolsheim. Protest could be a launching pad or a hindrance to one's professional development, or a combination of both. For some nuclear energy opponents, activism got in the way of pursuing their desired careers, but for others, it gave them skills and credentials that could later be 'professionalized' in various ways. Finally, protest networks created a different kind of community, where the values that reigned were not the same as those in one's small town or in one's political organization. Shared struggle fostered unexpected friendships across political and other divides, as interaction forced people on all sides to question their assumptions about themselves and one another.

Interactions like these were a driving force behind the social changes that we now recognize as resulting from the 1970s. It was one thing to reason about the merits of nuclear power, ecological thinking, or alternative visions of society based on what one read in a book or newspaper. Forging alliances with people one might otherwise never have met, debating strategy with them, and dragging shared concerns into the mainstream of society were an entirely different affair, one which involved active engagement and which could alter one's personal trajectory. By integrating change into their everyday lives, individual participants in the anti-nuclear movement changed politics, culture, and society—and not just in their own country. Like other, more recent movements, anti-nuclear protest in the 1970s was not confined to particular organizations or contained within distinct national movements. Rather, it was a global network of local struggles driven primarily by activism at the grassroots. Even if one accepts the premise that protesters in France 'lost' their fight to stop the construction of nuclear power plants—a battle that their German counterparts are sometimes seen to have 'won'—the impact of their efforts clearly did not stop at the border.

Selected Bibliography

PRIMARY SOURCES

Principal Archive Collections

Abbreviation	Archive	Main items consulted
AA	Archiv Aktiv (Hamburg, Germany)	Various boxes on: Frankreich, Larzac, Brokdorf, Gorleben, Stromzahlungsboykott
ABEBI	Archiv der Badisch-Elsässischen Bürgerinitiativen (Weisweil, Germany)	Various binders and book collections
AD Aveyron	Archives départementales de l'Aveyron (Rodez, France)	747 W 6–8 and 10–14
AD Bas-Rhin	Archives départementales du Bas-Rhin (Strasbourg, France)	1743 W 54, 57, and 186
AD Finistère	Archives départementales du Finistère (Quimper, France)	1235 W 24 and 25 1347 W 83, 85, 164-1, and 164-2
AD Haut-Rhin	Archives départementales du Haut-Rhin (Colmar, France)	1391 W 17, 18, 26, and 27
AD Isère	Archives départementales de l'Isère (Grenoble, France)	6253 W 37; 6299 W 15; 6857 W 35 and 36
AD Manche	Archives départementales de la Manche (Saint-Lô, France)	1515 W 72 and 73; 1516 W 49, 51, and 52
AGG	Archiv Grünes Gedächtnis (Berlin, Germany)	Various personal collections and journals
AK	ak-Archiv (Hamburg, Germany)	Journal and brochure collections
AN	Archives nationales (Fontainebleau, France)	19850718, art. 25; 19940274, art. 24
APO	Archiv „APO und soziale Bewegungen" (Berlin, Germany)	S 29, 36–9, 42–4, 46, and 48 (Anti-AKW) S 231, 234, 235, and 237 (Frankreich) S 636 and 637 (KB)
ASB	Archiv der sozialen Bewegungen in Baden (Freiburg, Germany)	12.1.4–11, 'Wyhl: Die Anfänge' CD-ROM, brochure and journal collections

BArch	Bundesarchiv (Berlin and Freiburg, Germany)	Various GDR documentation
BDIC	Bibliothèque de documentation internationale contemporaine (Paris, France)	Recueils; book and journal collections
BM	Bibliothèque municipale (Millau, France)	Various Larzac-related material
BnF, INA	Bibliothèque nationale de France and Institut national de l'audiovisuel (Paris, France)	Recueils de tracts; book and journal collections: film and television archives
CEDRATS	Centre de ressources sur les alternatives sociales (Lyon, France)	Miscellaneous boxes
CHS-XXe	Centre d'Histoire Sociale du XXᵉ siècle (Paris, France)	Fonds 'Mai 68'
DfuL	Dokumentationsstelle für unkonventionelle Literatur (Stuttgart, Germany)	Brochure collections
FNSP	Fondation nationale des sciences politiques (Paris, France)	Press clippings 1967–83
Gryffe	Archives de la librairie « La Gryffe » (Lyon, France)	Miscellaneous dossiers, posters, and journals
HIS	Hamburger Institut für Sozialforschung (Hamburg, Germany)	SBe 730, 731; miscellaneous cartons, unsorted brochures, and journals
IISG	Internationaal Instituut voor Sociale Geschiedenis (Amsterdam, Netherlands)	Various collections, including Arbeiterkampf, IDS, Knastarchiv, WRI, WISE; brochure and newspaper collections
LASH	Landesarchiv Schleswig-Holstein (Schleswig, Germany)	Abt. 621, Nr. 474, 534, 552, 569, and 599
MPZ	Medienpädagogik Zentrum (Hamburg, Germany)	Film collection
Nds	Niedersächsisches Landesarchiv (Hannover and Pattensen, Germany)	Nds. 100 Acc. 149/97 Nr. 111 and 119; Nds. 100 Acc. 2003/116 Nr. 66, 67, and 71

PA	Private archives of...	Didier Anger
		Frank Baum
		Maryse Budin
		Georges David
		Lison de Caunes
		Bernard Dréano
		Wolfgang Hertle
		Robert Joachim
		Dominique Lalanne
		Félix le Garrec
		Joseph Pineau
		Marie-Jo Putinier
		Albert Reimers
		Ginette Skandrani
PapierTiger	PapierTiger (Berlin, Germany)	Various collections and posters
PPP	Préfecture de Police de Paris (France)	B^A 2330, B^A 2332; Série F and F^D; G^A br 7 and G^A br 11
RF	Archiv der Sozialen Bewegungen in der Roten Flora (Hamburg, Germany)	15, 15.130, 15.200, 15.230; miscellaneous brochures and journals
StAF	Staatsarchiv Freiburg (Freiburg, Germany)	Various collections including F 22/58 Nr. 1, 25, 34, 36, and 44; F 39/2 Nr. 52, 55, 208, and 293; W 100/1 Nr. 97, 98
StHH	Staatsarchiv Hamburg (Hamburg, Germany)	136-3, Nr. 414, 653, 858, and 890; 331-1 II, Abl. 17, Az. 20.37-3

Activist Press

Anti-AKW-Info, 1977–8
Anti-AKW-Telegramm, 1977–81
Arbeiterkampf, 1973–82
Atom Express, 1977–83
Le Casse-Noix, 1975–8
Combat non-violent, 1971–3
L'Etincelle, 1976–7
Gardarem lo Larzac, 1975–80
Gazette nucléaire, 1976–7
Graswurzelrevolution, 1973–82

La Gueule ouverte, 1975–8 (incl. *La Gueule ouverte/Combat non-violent*, 1977–8)
Die Internationale, 1973–7
Ionix, 1971–5
Le Lien du Ried, 1973–7
Nouvelles de l'Arche, 1958–78
L'Outil des travailleurs d'Alsace, 1974–5
Révolution/L'Outil des travailleurs, 1976
Lip-Info/Larzac-Info, 1980–2
Radikal, 1978–9
Super-Pholix, 1976–82
Was Wir Wollen, 1974–7

Interviews
Anger, Didier and Paulette: 22 September 2010 in Les Pieux, France.
Baade, Conny: 19 September 2010 in St-Jean-de-Buèges, France (joint interview with Christian Petty).
Baum, Frank: 21 April 2010 in Staufen, Germany.
Bernard, Michel: 22 January 2010 in Lyon, France.
Bonczek, Ulla: 26 April 2010 in Freiburg, Germany.
Bonnet, Jacques: 29 January 2010 in Montmiral, France.
Borvon, Gérard: 10 March 2010 via telephone from Paris, France.
Bouveret, Patrice: 23 January 2010 in Lyon, France.
Bouvier, Claude: 25 January 2010 in Passins, France.
Budin, Maryse: 27 January 2010 in Vézeronce, France.
Burkhart, Roland ('Buki'): 22 April 2010 in Freiburg, Germany.
Caselli, Mireille: 12 April 2010 in Freiburg, Germany.
Coche, Daniel: 20 April 2010 in Strasbourg, France.
Cochet, Yves: 9 December 2009 in Paris, France.
David, Georges: 27 January 2010 in Lhuis, France.
de Boissieu, Pierre-Yves: 15 September 2010 in Nant, France.
de Caunes, Lison: 17 March 2010 in Paris, France.
D'Hernies, Suzanne: 20 January 2010 in Paris, France (joint interview with Bernard Dréano).
Dréano, Bernard: 20 January 2010 in Paris, France (joint interview with Suzanne D'Hernies).
E.: 17 April 2010 in Zaessingue, France.
Feuillet, Marcel: 25 January 2010 in Passins, France.
Fiedler, Ulf: 8 April 2010 in Freiburg, Germany.
François, Chantal and Maurice: 25 January 2010 in Creys-Mépieu, France (joint interview).
François, Yves: 24 January 2010 in Creys-Mépieu, France.
G.: 24 April 2010 in Weisweil, Germany.
Gladitz, Nina: 2 June 2010 in Berlin, Germany.
Göpper, Siegfried: 18 April 2010 in Weisweil, Germany.

Göpper, Siegfried: 24 April 2010 in Weisweil, Germany (group interview with Luise Däschner, Heinz Ehrler, Marie Stöcklin, Anne Witzelmaier, and Frieda Zimmerman).

Halbach, Dieter: 23 August 2010 via telephone, Germany.

Haug, Marie-Reine: 17 April 2010 in Rammersmatt, France (joint interview with Raymond Schirmer).

Hertle, Wolfgang: 22 July 2010 in Hamburg, Germany.

Hopfenmüller, Günter: 23 August 2010 in Hamburg, Germany.

Joachim, Robert: 23 April 2010 in Haguenau, France.

Lalanne, Dominique: 25 February 2010 in Orsay, France.

Laponche, Bernard: 11 March 2010 in Paris, France.

Le Coeur, Alain: 13 January 2010 in Paris, France.

Le Garrec, Félix and Nicole: 26 September 2010 in Plonéour Lanvern, France (joint interview).

Lemaire, Gilles: 16 March 2010 in Paris, France.

Lepoittevin, Paul: 23 September 2010 in Tollevast, France.

Luquet, Jean-Marc: 24 January 2010 in Lyon, France.

Mahlke, Gottfried: 24 August 2010 in Luckau, Germany.

Mayer, Axel: 12 April 2010 in Freiburg, Germany.

Michalon, Paul: 30 January 2010 in Valence, France.

Moalic, Jean: 29 September 2010 in Mahalon, France.

Modler, Peter: 21 April 2010 in Amoltern, Germany.

Mohr, Markus: 19 August 2010 in Hamburg, Germany.

Moßmann, Walter: 1 April 2010 in Freiburg, Germany.

Nissim, Chaïm: 28 January 2010 in Geneva, Switzerland.

Nössler, Bernd: 14 April 2010 in Freiburg, Germany.

Ott, Hervé: 18 September 2010 in St-Martin-du-Larzac, France.

Pasquinet, Jean-Luc: 7 December 2009 in Paris, France.

Petitjean, Patrick: 23 February 2010 in Paris, France.

Petty, Christian: 19 September 2010 in St-Jean-de-Buèges, France (joint interview with Conny Baade).

Putinier, Marie-Jo: 26 January 2010 in Bourgoin-Jallieu, France.

Reimers, Marlene and Albert: 21 August 2010 in Wewelsfleth, Germany (joint interview).

Rettig, Jean-Jacques: 19 April 2010 in Fréconrupt, France.

Ridard, Bernadette: 25 August 2010 in Hamburg, Germany.

Scheer, Christine: 21 August 2010 in Wewelsfleth, Germany (joint interview with Heinrich Voß).

Schirmer, Raymond: 17 April 2010 in Rammersmatt, France (joint interview with Marie-Reine Haug).

Sené, Monique and Raymond: 13 December 2009 in Orsay, France (joint interview).

Skandrani, Ginette: 11 January 2010 in Paris, France.

Stehn, Jan: 24 August 2010 in Blütlingen, Germany.

Teichler, Hans-Hermann: 20 August 2010 in Hamburg, Germany.

Verdet, Rémi: 19 April 2010 in Neuviller-la-Roche, France.
Voß, Heinrich: 21 August 2010 in Wewelsfleth, Germany (joint interview with Christine Scheer).
Vuarin, Pierre: 26 November 2009 in Paris, France.
Wandschneider, Sönke: 26 August 2010 in Hamburg, Germany.
Wieder (Lanza), Odile: 29 January 2010 in Annecy, France.

Published Interview Material
'Bruno', interview with Sébastien Schifres (2004) [http://sebastien.schifres.free.fr/bruno.htm (accessed 15 May 2012)].
Jean-Marie Burguière, interview with Robert Gildea (21 May 2008) [http://around1968.modhist.ox.ac.uk/ (accessed 5 June 2009)].
Pierre Burguière and Christiane Burguière, joint interview with Robert Gildea (22 May 2008) [http://around1968.modhist.ox.ac.uk/ (accessed 5 June 2009)].
Carola Bury, interview with Anna von der Goltz, Bremen (22 June 2010) [http://around1968.modhist.ox.ac.uk/ (accessed 10 March 2011)].
Yann Moulier-Boutang, interview with Sébastien Schifres (2004) [http://sebastien.schifres.free.fr/moulier.htm (accessed 15 May 2012)].
Jean-Marc Rouillan, interview with Robert Gildea (17 April 2008) [http://around1968.modhist.ox.ac.uk/ (accessed 27 Oct 2008)].

Audiovisual Material
Albrecht, wir kommen, 1979, 45 mins.
Die Herren machen das selber, dass ihnen der arme Mann Feyndt wird, 1979, 126 mins.
Juillet 76 à Malville, 1976, 40 mins.
Kalkar. Ein Schritt auf dem Weg zum Polizeistaat, 1977, 45 mins.
Larzac 73, 1973, 48 mins (audio).
Wehrt Euch. Brokdorf 19.2.1977, 1977, 40 mins.
Weil ich das Leben liebe, 1977, 34 mins.
s' Weschpenäscht. Die Chronik von Wyhl (1972–1982), 1982, 111 mins.
Coche, Daniel, *Écoutez RVF vous écoute*, 1978, 30 mins.
Coche, Daniel, *Ni ici, ni ailleurs*, 1977, 25 mins.
Gladitz, Nina, *Lieber heute aktiv als morgen radioaktiv*, 1976, 63 mins.
Jacquemain, François, *Condamnés à réussir*, 1976, 60 mins.
Le Garrec, Nicole, *Plogoff: des pierres contre des fusils*, 1980, 90 mins.
Otzenberger, Claude, *Les atomes nous veulent-ils du bien ?*, 1975, 60 mins.

Published Primary Sources
Aujourd'hui Malville, demain la France (Claix: La Pensée Sauvage, 1978).
Nur wer sich bewegt, spürt seine Fesseln. Erfahrungen aus der Bewegung gegen die Startbahn West (Offenbach: Verlag 2000 GmbH, 1982).
Un récit de lutte de Chooz (Bogny-sur-Meuse: La Question Sociale, 1998).
AKPÖ, *Bilanz und Perspektiven zum Widerstand gegen Atomanlagen* (Hamburg: 1978).

Arbeitsgruppe Schadstoffbelastung am Arbeitsplatz und in der Industrieregion Unterweser, *Zum richtigen Verständnis der Kernindustrie. 66 Erwiderungen* (Berlin: Oberbaumverlag, 1975).

Arens, Roman, Beate Seitz, and Joachim Wille, *Wackersdorf. Der Atomstaat und die Bürger* (Essen: Klartext, 1987).

Atom Express, . . . *Und auch nicht anderswo! Die Geschichte der Anti-AKW-Bewegung* (Göttingen: Die Werkstatt, 1997).

Borvon, Gérard, *Plogoff : un combat pour demain* (Saint-Thonan: Cloître, 2004) http://seaus.free.fr/spip.php?article131 (accessed 9 March 2010).

Büchele, Christoph, Irmgard Schneider, and Bernd Nössler, *Der Widerstand geht weiter. Der Bürgerprotest gegen das Kernkraftwerk von 1976 bis zum Mannheimer Prozess* (Freiburg: Dreisam-Verlag, 1982).

Burmeister, Heidi and Volker Tonnätt, *Zu kämpfen allein schon ist richtig. Larzac* (Frankfurt: Jugend & Politik, 1981).

BUU, *Brokdorf. Der Bauplatz muß wieder zur Wiese werden!* (Hamburg: Association, 1977).

Centre d'action paysanne, *Le Mouvement de la jeunesse et les paysans de l'Ouest : l'expérience militante de 120 étudiants et jeunes ouvriers révolutionnaires dans les campagnes durant l'été 1970* (Paris: Hallier, 1970).

Collin, Claude, *Écoutez la vraie différence ! Radio verte Fessenheim, radio S.O.S. emploi-Longwy et les autres* (Claix: La Pensée sauvage, 1979).

Conan, Renée and Annie Laurent, *Femmes de Plogoff,* 2010 republished edn (Baye: La Digitale, 1981).

Courtes, Claude and Jean-Claude Driant, *Golfech le nucléaire : implantation et résistances* (Toulouse: CRAS, 1999).

CRILAN, *140 dessins contre le nucléaire* (St-Lô: CRILAN, 1980).

Daum, Nicolas, *Mai 68 raconté par des anonymes* (Paris: Amsterdam, 2008).

de Caunes, Lison, *Les Jours d'après* (Paris: J.-C. Lattès, 1980).

del Vasto, Lanza, *Technique de la non-violence* (Paris: 1978).

Ehmke, Wolfgang, *Zwischenschritte. Die Anti-Atomkraft-Bewegung zwischen Gorleben und Wackersdorf* (Köln: Volksblatt, 1987).

Ermittlungsausschuss der Bürgerinitiativen gegen Kernenergie, *„Wir, das Volk . . ." Eine Dokumentation* (Köln: Graphischer Betrieb Henke, 1977).

Fernex, Solange, 'Non-Violence Triumphant'. *The Ecologist*, December 1975.

Gewerkschaft Erziehung und Wissenschaft, *Kriminalisierung von AKW-Gegnern am Beispiel: Malville* (Berlin: Oktoberdruck, 1977).

Gladitz, Nina, ed., *Lieber heute aktiv als morgen radioaktiv. Wyhl: Bauern erzählen. Warum Kernkraftwerke schädlich sind. Wie man eine Bürgerinitiative macht. Und wie man sich dabei verändert* (Berlin: Wagenbach, 1976).

Groupement des scientifiques pour l'information sur l'énergie nucléaire, *Électronucléaire, danger* (Paris: Seuil, 1977).

Halbach, Dieter and Gerd Panzer, *Zwischen Gorleben & Stadtleben. Erfahrungen aus 3 Jahren Widerstand im Wendland und in dezentralen Aktionen* (Berlin: AHDE, 1980).

Hardy, Yves and Emmanuel Gabey, *Dossier L . . . comme Larzac* (Paris: Alain Moreau, 1974).

Hertle, Wolfgang, *Larzac, 1971–1981. Der gewaltfreie Widerstand gegen die Erweiterung eines Truppenübungsplatzes in Süd-Frankreich* (Kassel: Weber Zucht & Co., 1982).

International Atomic Energy Agency, *Nuclear Power Reactors in the World* (IAEA, 2011) http://www-pub.iaea.org/MTCD/Publications/PDF/RDS2_web.pdf (accessed 14 July 2014).

International Atomic Energy Agency, *Nuclear Power Reactors in the World* (IAEA, 2015) http://www-pub.iaea.org/books/IAEABooks/10903/Nuclear-Power-Reactors-in-the-World-2015-Edition (accessed 15 December 2015).

Jean [pseud.], *Elsass: Kolonie in Europa* (Berlin: Wagenbach, 1976).

Jund, Thierry, *Le nucléaire contre l'Alsace* (Paris: Syros, 1977).

Jungk, Robert, *Der Atomstaat. Vom Fortschritt in die Unmenschlichkeit* (Hamburg: Rowohlt, 1977).

Lalonde, Brice, *Sur la vague verte* (Paris: Laffont, 1981).

Lalonde, Brice, *L'écologie en bleu* (Paris: l'Archipel, 2001).

Lambert, Bernard, *Les paysans dans la lutte des classes* (Paris: Seuil, 1970).

Lambert, Bernard, *Bauern im Klassenkampf* (Berlin: Wagenbach, 1971).

Linhart, Robert, *L'établi* (Paris: Éditions de Minuit, 1978).

Lutz, Dieter, *La guerre mondiale malgré nous ? La controverse des euromissiles*, trans. Lacrois, P. (Paris: La Découverte-Maspero, 1983).

Mao Zedong, *Report of an Investigation into the Peasant Movement in Hunan* (Peking: Foreign Languages Press, 1953).

Mao Zedong, *Quotations from Chairman Mao Tse-tung* (Peking: Foreign Languages Press, 1966).

Marx, Karl, *The Eighteenth Brumaire of Louis Bonaparte*, trans. Padover, S. K. (Pacifica, CA: Marx/Engels Internet Archive, 1999), http://www.marxists.org/archive/marx/works/1852/18th-brumaire/.

Moßmann, Walter, 'Der lange Marsch von Wyhl nach Anderswo'. *Kursbuch*, no. 50 (1977): 1–22.

Moßmann, Walter, *Realistisch sein: Das unmögliche Verlangen. Wahrheitsgetreu gefälschte Erinnerungen* (Berlin: Freitag, 2009).

Mohr, Markus, *Alles wie geplant. Die katastrophale Industrialisierung von Brunsbüttel/Unterelbe* (Brünsbuttel: Arbeitskreis Umweltschutz, 1985).

Müller-Münch, Ingrid, Wolfgang Prosinger, Sabine Rosenbladt, and Linda Stibler, *Besetzung – weil das Wünschen nicht geholfen hat* (Reinbek: Rowohlt, 1981).

Nissim, Chaïm, *L'amour et le monstre : roquettes contre Creys-Malville* (Lausanne: Favre, 2004).

Nordmann, Charlotte and Bernard Laponche, 'Entre silence et mensonge : le nucléaire, de la raison d'État au recyclage « écologique »'. *La Revue internationale des livres et des idées*, November–December 2009, pp. 6–13.

Nössler, Bernd and Margret de Witt, eds, *Kein Kernkraftwerk in Wyhl und auch sonst nirgends. Betroffene Bürger berichten* (Freiburg: Inform-Verlag, 1976).

RAF, *Texte und Materialien zur Geschichte der RAF* (Berlin: ID-Verlag, 1997).

Saitcevsky, Boris, 'Creys-Malville : les accords de coopération européenne entre producteurs d'électricité'. *Revue générale nucléaire*, no. 6 (November–December 1979): 597–8.

Schroeren, Michael, *Zum Beispiel Kaiseraugst. Der gewaltfreie Widerstand gegen das Atomkraftwerk: Vom legalen Protest zum zivilen Ungehorsam* (Zürich: Schweizerischer Friedensrat, 1977).

Schulthess, Élisabeth, *Solange Fernex, l'insoumise : écologie, féminisme, non-violence* (Barret-sur-Méouge: Y. Michel, 2004).

Sternstein, Wolfgang, 'Der Alltag des Widerstands. Probleme einer langandauernden Platzbesetzung'. In *Ökologiebewegung und ziviler Widerstand*, edited by Ebert, T., W. Sternstein, and R. Vogt (Stuttgart: Umweltwissenschaftliches Institut, 1978), pp. 34–50.

Sternstein, Wolfgang, *Mein Weg zwischen Gewalt und Gewaltfreiheit. Autobiographie* (Norderstedt: Books on Demand, 2005).

Strohm, Holger, *Friedlich in die Katastrophe. Eine Dokumentation über Kernkraftwerke* (Hamburg: Association, 1973).

tageszeitung, *Gorleben-Dokumentation* (Berlin: taz, 1980).

Union des communistes de France marxiste-léniniste, *Le livre des paysans pauvres : 5 années de travail maoïste dans une campagne française* (Paris: Maspero, 1976).

Zint, Günter, ed., *Republik Freies Wendland. Eine Dokumentation* (Frankfurt: Zweitausendeins, 1980).

Zint, Günter, Wolf Biermann, Otto Köhler, Klaus Traube, and Günter Wallraff, eds, *Gegen den Atomstaat* (Frankfurt: Zweitausendeins, 1979).

Zint, Günter, Claus Lutterbeck, and Wolf-Dietmar Stock, *Atomkraft. Fotodokumente vom 'Bürgerdialog' um Atomenergie*, 2nd edn (Fischerhude: Atelier im Bauernhaus, 1979).

Secondary Sources

Anders, Freia, 'Wohnraum, Freiraum, Widerstand. Die Formierung der Autonomen in den Konflikten um Hausbesetzungen Anfang der achtziger Jahre'. In *Das Alternative Milieu*, edited by Reichardt, S. and D. Siegfried (Göttingen: Wallstein, 2010), pp. 473–98.

Aron, Raymond, *La Révolution introuvable : réflexions sur les évènements de mai* (Paris: Fayard, 1968).

Aust, Stefan, *Der Baader-Meinhof-Komplex*, 3rd edn (Hamburg: Hoffmann und Campe, 2008).

Bardelli, Alexandre, 'Contribution à l'appréciation de l'impact d'une centrale électronucléaire dans une région transfrontalière en crise, à travers le cas de Cattenom' (thèse, Metz, 1997).

Bennahmias, Jean-Luc, 'De la marge au pouvoir'. *Autres Temps*, no. 49 (1996): 22–6.

Berstein, Serge and Jean-François Sirinelli, eds, *Les années Giscard : Valéry Giscard d'Estaing et l'Europe, 1974–1981* (Paris: Armand Colin, 2006).

Bess, Michael, *The Light-Green Society: Ecology and Technological Modernity in France, 1960–2000* (Chicago, IL: University of Chicago Press, 2003).

Bhabha, Homi, *The Location of Culture* (London: Routledge, 1994).

Biard, Roland, *Dictionnaire de l'extrême-gauche : de 1945 à nos jours* (Paris: Belfond, 1978).

Bloch, Marc, 'Pour une histoire comparée des sociétés européennes'. In *Mélanges historiques* (Paris: SEVPEN, 1928), pp. 16–40.

Boggs, Carl, 'Rethinking the Sixties Legacy: From New Left to New Social Movements'. In *Social Movements: Critiques, Concepts, Case-Studies*, edited by Lyman, S. M. (London: Macmillan, 1995), pp. 331–55.

Bourseiller, Christophe, *Les Maoïstes : la folle histoire des gardes rouges français*, 2nd edn (Paris: Points, 2008).

Bracke, Maud, *Which Socialism, Whose Détente? West European Communism and the Czechoslovak Crisis, 1968* (Budapest: Central European University Press, 2007).

Bramwell, Anna, 'Blut und Boden'. In *Deutsche Erinnerungsorte*, edited by François, E. and H. Schulze (München: C. H. Beck, 2001), pp. 380–91.

Brand, Karl-Werner, Detlef Büsser, and Dieter Rucht, *Aufbruch in eine andere Gesellschaft. Neue soziale Bewegungen in der Bundesrepublik* (Frankfurt: Campus, 1983).

Brown, Timothy Scott, '"1968" East and West: Divided Germany as a Case Study in Transnational History'. *American Historical Review* vol. 114, no. 1 (February 2009): 69–96.

Brown, Timothy Scott, *West Germany and the Global Sixties: The Antiauthoritarian Revolt, 1962–1978* (Cambridge: Cambridge University Press, 2013).

Brüggemeier, Franz-Josef, 'Umweltgeschichte – Erfahrungen, Ergebnisse, Erwartungen'. *Archiv für Sozialgeschichte* vol. 43 (2003): 1–18.

Brüggemeier, Franz-Josef, Mark Cioc, and Thomas Zeller, eds, *How Green Were the Nazis? Nature, Environment, and Nation in the Third Reich* (Athens, OH: Ohio University Press, 2005).

Buton, Philippe, 'L'extrême-gauche française et l'écologie'. *Vingtième siècle*, no. 113 (2012): 191–203.

Calhoun, Craig, 'Occupy Wall Street in Perspective'. *British Journal of Sociology* vol. 64, no. 1 (2013): 26–38.

Cans, Roger, *Petite histoire du mouvement écolo en France* (Paris: Delachaux et Niestlé, 2006).

Caute, David, *1968: The Year of the Barricades* (New York: HarperCollins, 1988).

Châtellier, Hildegard, 'Moloch Großstadt'. In *Deutsche Erinnerungsorte*, edited by François, E. and H. Schulze (München: C. H. Beck, 2002), pp. 567–83.

Clavin, Patricia, 'Defining Transnationalism'. *Contemporary European History* vol. 14, no. 4 (2005): 421–39.

Clavin, Patricia, 'Time, Manner, Place: Writing Modern European History in Global, Transnational and International Contexts'. *European History Quarterly*, no. 40 (2010): 624–40.

Conway, Martin, 'The Rise and Fall of Western Europe's Democratic Age, 1945–1973'. *Contemporary European History* vol. 13, no. 1 (2004): 67–88.

Conway, Martin and Volker Depkat, 'Towards a European History of the Discourse of Democracy: Discussing Democracy in Western Europe, 1945–60'. In *Europeanization in the Twentieth Century*, edited by Conway, M. and K. K. Patel (New York: Palgrave Macmillan, 2010), pp. 132–56.

Conze, Werner, 'Bauer'. In *Geschichtliche Grundbegriffe*, edited by Brunner, O., W. Conze, and R. Koselleck (Stuttgart: Klett, 1972), pp. 407–39.

Corbin, Alain, 'Paris-Province'. In *Les Lieux de mémoire*, edited by Nora, P. (Paris: Gallimard, 1992), pp. 776–823.

Corbin, Alain, *Les Cloches de la terre* (Paris: Flammarion, 1994).

Davis, Belinda, 'What's Left? Popular Political Participation in Postwar Europe'. *American Historical Review* vol. 113, no. 2 (April 2008): 363–90.

Davis, Belinda, 'A Whole World Opening Up: Transcultural Contact, Difference, and the Politicization of "New Left" Activists'. In *Changing the World, Changing Oneself*, edited by Davis, B., W. Mausbach, M. Klimke, and C. MacDougall (New York: Berghahn Books, 2010), pp. 255–73.

della Porta, Donatella, Hanspeter Kriesi, and Dieter Rucht, *Social Movements in a Globalizing World* (New York: St. Martin's Press, 1999).

della Porta, Donatella and Dieter Rucht, 'Left-Libertarian Movements in Context: A Comparison of Italy and West Germany, 1965–1990'. In *The Politics of Social Protest: Comparative Perspectives on States and Social Movements*, edited by Jenkins, J. C. and B. Klandermans (Minneapolis, MN: University of Minnesota Press, 1995), pp. 229–72.

Diani, Mario and Hein-Anton van der Heijden, 'Anti-Nuclear Movements across States: Explaining Patterns of Development'. In *States and Anti-Nuclear Movements*, edited by Flam, H. (Edinburgh: Edinburgh University Press, 1994), pp. 355–82.

Doering-Manteuffel, Anselm and Lutz Raphael, *Nach dem Boom. Perspektiven auf die Zeitgeschichte seit 1970* (Göttingen: Vandenhoeck & Ruprecht, 2008).

Dominick, Raymond H., *The Environmental Movement in Germany: Prophets and Pioneers, 1871–1971* (Bloomington, IN: Indiana University Press, 1992).

Dressen, Marnix, *De l'amphi à l'établi : les étudiants maoïstes à l'usine, 1967–1989* (Paris: Belin, 2000).

Duyvendak, Jan Willem, *The Power of Politics: New Social Movements in France* (Boulder, CO: Westview, 1995).

Earl, Jennifer, 'The Cultural Consequences of Social Movements'. In *The Blackwell Companion to Social Movements*, edited by Snow, D. A., S. A. Soule, and H. Kriesi (Oxford: Blackwell, 2004), pp. 508–30.

Ehrenreich, Barbara and John Ehrenreich, *Long March, Short Spring: The Student Uprising at Home and Abroad* (New York: Monthly Review Press, 1969).

Eley, Geoff, *Forging Democracy: The History of the Left in Europe, 1850–2000* (Oxford: Oxford University Press, 2002).

Engels, Jens Ivo, 'Gender Roles and German Anti-Nuclear Protest: The Women of Wyhl'. In *Le démon moderne : la pollution dans les sociétés urbaines et industrielles d'Europe*, edited by Bernhardt, C. and G. Massard-Guilbaud (Clermont-Ferrand: Presses Universitaires Blaise-Pascal, 2002), pp. 407–24.

Engels, Jens Ivo, *Naturpolitik in der Bundesrepublik. Ideenwelt und politische Verhaltensstile in Naturschutz und Umweltbewegung, 1950–1980* (Paderborn: Schöningh, 2006).

Ferguson, Niall, 'Crisis, What Crisis?'. In *The Shock of the Global: The 1970s in Perspective*, edited by Ferguson, N., C. Maier, E. Manela, and D. J. Sargent (Cambridge, MA: Belknap, 2010), pp. 1–21.

Fraser, Ronald, Daniel Bertaux, Bret Eynon, Ronald Grele, Béatrix le Wita, Danièle Linhart, Luisa Passerini, Jochen Staadt, and Annemarie Tröger, *1968: A Student Generation in Revolt* (London: Chatto & Windus, 1988).

Frei, Norbert, *1968. Jugendrevolte und globaler Protest* (München: dtv, 2008).

Freytag, Nils, '„Eine Bombe im Taschenbuchformat"? Die „Grenzen des Wachstums" und die öffentliche Resonanz'. *Zeithistorische Forschungen*, no. 3 (2006): 465–9.

Gasnier, Thierry, 'Le Local : Une et indivisible'. In *Les Lieux de mémoire*, edited by Nora, P. (Paris: Gallimard, 1992), pp. 462–525.

Gebauer, Annekatrin, 'Apokalyptik und Eschatologie. Zum Politikverständnis der Grünen in ihrer Gründungsphase'. *Archiv für Sozialgeschichte* vol. 43 (2003): 405–20.

Gerbaudo, Paolo, *Tweets and the Streets: Social Media and Contemporary Activism* (London: Pluto, 2012).

Geronimo [pseud.], *Feuer und Flamme. Zur Geschichte der Autonomen*, 6th edn (Berlin: ID-Verlag, 2002).

Geyer, Michael and Charles Bright, 'World History in a Global Age'. *American Historical Review* vol. 100, no. 4 (October 1995): 1,034–60.

Gilcher-Holtey, Ingrid, *Die 68er Bewegung. Deutschland, Westeuropa, USA* (München: C. H. Beck, 2001).

Gilcher-Holtey, Ingrid, 'Der Transfer zwischen den Studentenbewegungen von 1968 und die Entstehung einer transnationalen Gegenöffentlichkeit'. In *Transnationale Öffentlichkeiten im 20. Jahrhundert*, edited by Kaelble, H., M. Kirsch, and A. Schmidt-Gernig (Frankfurt: Campus, 2002), pp. 303–25.

Gildea, Robert, *The Past in French History* (New Haven, CT: Yale University Press, 1994).

Gildea, Robert and James Mark, 'Introduction: Voices of Europe's '68'. *Cultural and Social History* vol. 8, no. 44 (2011): 441–8.

Gildea, Robert, James Mark, and Niek Pas, 'European Radicals and the "Third World": Imagined Solidarities and Radical Networks, 1958–1973'. *Cultural and Social History* vol. 8, no. 4 (2011): 449–72.

Gildea, Robert, James Mark, and Anette Warring, eds, *Europe's 1968: Voices of Revolt* (Oxford: Oxford University Press, 2013).

Gildea, Robert and Andrew Tompkins, 'The Transnational in the Local: The Larzac Plateau as a Site of Transnational Activism since 1970'. *Journal of Contemporary History* vol. 50, no. 3 (2015): 581–605.

Giugni, Marco G., 'Personal and Biographical Consequences'. In *The Blackwell Companion to Social Movements*, edited by Snow, D. A., S. A. Soule, and H. Kriesi (Oxford: Blackwell, 2004), pp. 489–507.

Hadden, Jennifer and Sidney Tarrow, 'Spillover or Spillout? The Global Justice Movement in the United States after 9/11'. *Mobilization* vol. 12, no. 4 (2007): 359–76.

Hansen, Jan, *Abschied vom Kalten Krieg? Die Sozialdemokraten und der Nachrüstungsstreit (1977–1987)* (München: De Gruyter Oldenbourg, 2016).

Hanshew, Karrin, *Terror and Democracy in West Germany* (New York: Cambridge University Press, 2012).

Hasenöhrl, Ute, *Zivilgesellschaft und Protest. Eine Geschichte der Naturschutz- und Umweltbewegung in Bayern 1945–1980* (Göttingen: Vandenhoeck & Ruprecht, 2011).

Hatzfeld, Hélène, *Faire de la politique autrement : les expériences inachevées des années 1970* (Rennes: Presses Universitaires de Rennes, 2005).

Haunss, Sebastian, *Identität in Bewegung. Prozesse kollektiver Identität bei den Autonomen und in der Schwulenbewegung* (Wiesbaden: VS Verlag für Sozialwissenschaften, 2004).

Haunss, Sebastian and Markus Mohr, 'Die Autonomen und die anti-deutsche Frage oder: „Deutschland muss . . . "'. In *„Sie warn die Antideutschesten der deutschen Linken". Zu Geschichte, Kritik und Zukunft antideutscher Politik*, edited by Hanloser, G. (Münster: Unrast, 2004).

Hazareesingh, Sudhir, *Political Traditions in Modern France* (Oxford: Oxford University Press, 1994).

Hecht, Gabrielle, *The Radiance of France: Nuclear Power and National Identity after World War II* (Cambridge, MA: MIT Press, 1998).

Herberich-Marx, Geneviève and Freddy Raphaël, 'Les incorporés de force alsaciens : déni, convocation et provocation de la mémoire'. *Vingtième siècle*, no. 6 (1985): 83–102.

Herbert, Ulrich, 'Liberalisierung als Lernprozeß. Die Bundesrepublik in der deutschen Geschichte – eine Skizze'. In *Wandlungsprozesse in Westdeutschland. Belastung, Integration, Liberalisierung 1945–1980*, edited by Herbert, U. (Göttingen: Wallstein, 2002), pp. 7–49.

HKS13, ed., *hoch die kampf dem. 20 Jahre Plakate autonomer Bewegungen* (Hamburg: Libertäre Assoziation, 1999).

Hockenos, Paul, *Joschka Fischer and the Making of the Berlin Republic: An Alternative History of Postwar Germany* (Oxford: Oxford University Press, 2008).

Horn, Gerd-Rainer, *The Spirit of '68: Rebellion in Western Europe and North America, 1956–1976* (Oxford: Oxford University Press, 2007).

Inglehart, Ronald, *The Silent Revolution: Changing Values and Political Styles among Western Publics* (Princeton, NJ: Princeton University Press, 1977).

Jacquiot, Pierre, 'Comparaison des processus de formation et de diffusion du mouvement écologiste en RFA et en France'. *Cahiers internationaux de sociologie* vol. 123, no. 2 (2007): 217–44.

Jarausch, Konrad, ed., *Das Ende der Zuversicht? Die siebziger Jahre als Geschichte* (Göttingen: Vandenhoeck & Ruprecht, 2008).

Jobs, Richard I., 'Youth Movements: Travel, Protest, and Europe in 1968'. *American Historical Review* vol. 114, no. 2 (2009): 376–404.

Joppke, Christian, *Mobilizing against Nuclear Energy: A Comparison of Germany and the United States* (Berkeley, CA: University of California Press, 1993).

Kaelble, Hartmut, 'Die Debatte über Vergleich und Transfer und was jetzt?'. *H-Soz-u-Kult* (8 February 2005) http://hsozkult.geschichte.hu-berlin.de/forum/type=diskussionen&id=574&view=print (accessed 3 June 2010).

Kalmbach, Karena, 'Meanings of a Disaster: The Contested "Truth" about Chernobyl. British and French Chernobyl Debates and the Transnationality of Arguments and Actors' (PhD dissertation, European University Institute, 2014).

Katsiaficas, George N., *The Subversion of Politics: European Autonomous Social Movements and the Decolonization of Everyday Life*, updated edn (Oakland, CA: AK Press, 2006).

Keck, Margaret E. and Kathryn Sikkink, *Activists beyond Borders: Advocacy Networks in International Politics* (Ithaca, NY: Cornell University Press, 1998).

Kedward, Rod, *La Vie en Bleu: France and the French since 1900* (London: Penguin, 2006).

Kenney, Padraic, *A Carnival of Revolution: Central Europe 1989* (Princeton, NJ: Princeton University Press, 2002).

Kießling, Rolf, 'Der Bauernkrieg'. In *Deutsche Erinnerungsorte*, edited by François, E. and H. Schulze (München: C. H. Beck, 2001), pp. 137–53.

Kirchhof, Astrid and Jan-Henrik Meyer, 'Global Protest against Nuclear Power: Transfer and Transnational Exchange in the 1970s and 1980s'. *Historical Social Research* vol. 39, no. 1 (2014): 165–90.

Kitschelt, Herbert, 'Political Opportunity Structures and Political Protest: Anti-Nuclear Movements in Four Democracies'. *British Journal of Political Science* vol. 16, no. 1 (1986): 57–85.

Klandermans, Bert, Jacquelien van Stekelenburg, Marie-Louise Damen, Dunya van Troost, and Anouk van Leeuwen, 'Mobilization without Organization: The Case of Unaffiliated Demonstrators'. *European Sociological Review* vol. 30, no. 6 (2014): 702–16.

Klimke, Martin, *The Other Alliance: Student Protest in West Germany and the United States in the Global Sixties* (Princeton, NJ: Princeton University Press, 2010).

Kocka, Jürgen, 'Comparison and Beyond'. *History and Theory* vol. 42, no. 1 (February 2003): 39–44.

Koenen, Gerd, *Das rote Jahrzehnt. Unsere kleine deutsche Kulturrevolution, 1967–1977* (Köln: Kiepenheuer & Witsch, 2001).

Kolb, Felix, *Protest and Opportunities: The Political Outcomes of Social Movements* (Frankfurt: Campus, 2007).

Koopmans, Ruud, *Democracy from Below: New Social Movements and the Political System in West Germany* (Boulder, CO: Westview, 1995).

Kriesi, Hanspeter, Ruud Koopmans, Jan Willem Duyvendak, and Marco G. Giugni, *New Social Movements in Western Europe: A Comparative Analysis* (Minneapolis, MN: University of Minnesota Press, 1995).

Kupper, Patrick, *Atomenergie und gespaltene Gesellschaft. Die Geschichte des gescheiterten Projektes Kernkraftwerk Kaiseraugst* (Zürich: Chronos, 2003).

Lafaye, Françoise, 'Une centrale pas très . . . nucléaire : Revendications territoriales et processus identitaires lors de l'implantation de la centrale nucléaire du Blayais à Braud-et-Saint-Louis' (thèse, Paris X, 1994) [https://tel.archives-ouvertes.fr/tel-00286639/fr/(accessed 4 February 2015)].

Lavie, Smadar and Ted Swedenburg, 'Between and Among the Boundaries of Culture: Bridging Text and Lived Experience in the Third Timespace'. *Cultural Studies* vol. 10, no. 1 (1996): 154–79.

Le Roux, Thomas, *Le Laboratoire des pollutions industrielles : Paris, 1770–1830* (Paris: Albin Michel, 2011).

Leach, Darcy K., 'The Way is the Goal: Ideology and the Practice of Collectivist Democracy in German New Social Movements' (PhD dissertation, University of Michigan, 2006).

Leach, Darcy K. and Sebastian Haunss, 'Scenes and Social Movements'. In *Culture, Social Movements, and Protest*, edited by Johnston, H. (Aldershot: Ashgate, 2009), pp. 255–76.

Léger, Danièle and Bertrand Hervieu, *Le retour à la nature* (Paris: Seuil, 1979).

Leggewie, Claus, 'Keine Friedensbewegung in Frankreich? Zehn Gründe für ihre relative Unterentwicklung'. In *Vom Krieg der Erwachsenen gegen die Kinder*, edited by Steinweg, R. (Frankfurt: Suhrkamp, 1984).

Leif, Thomas, 'Die Friedensbewegung zu Beginn der achtziger Jahre – Themen und Strategien im Spannungsfeld von basisdemokratischem Anspruch und Spektren-Interessen'. *Gewerkschaftliche Monatshefte*, no. 6 (1989): 369–83 http://library.fes.de/gmh/main/pdf-files/gmh/1989/1989-06-a-369.pdf.

Lemercier, Claire, 'Analyse de réseaux et histoire'. *Revue d'histoire moderne et contemporaine* vol. 52, no. 2 (April–June 2005): 88–112.

Linhart, Virginie, *Volontaires pour l'usine : vies d'établis, 1967–1977* (Paris: Seuil, 1994).

Locher, Fabien and Grégory Quenet, 'L'histoire environnementale : origines, enjeux et perspectives d'un nouveau chantier'. *Revue d'histoire moderne et contemporaine* vol. 56, no. 4 (2009): 7–38.

McAdam, Doug and Dieter Rucht, 'The Cross-National Diffusion of Movement Ideas'. *Annals of the American Academy of Political and Social Science* vol. 528 (July 1993): 56–74.

McCormick, John, *The Global Environmental Movement*, 2nd edn (Chichester: Wiley, 1995).

McNeill, J. R., *Something New under the Sun: An Environmental History of the Twentieth-Century World* (New York: Norton, 2000).

McNeill, J. R. 'Observations on the Nature and Culture of Environmental History'. *History and Theory* vol. 42, no. 4 (December 2003): 5–43.

McNeill, J. R. 'The Environment, Environmentalism, and International Society in the Long 1970s'. In *The Shock of the Global: The 1970s in Perspective*, edited by Ferguson, N., C. S. Maier, E. Manela, and D. J. Sargent (Cambridge, MA: Belknap, 2010), pp. 263–78.

Mark, James, Anna von der Goltz, and Anette Warring, 'Reflections'. In *Europe's 1968*, edited by Gildea, R., J. Mark, and A. Warring (Oxford: Oxford University Press, 2013), pp. 283–325.

Marotti, William, 'Japan 1968: The Performance of Violence and the Theater of Protest'. *American Historical Review* (February 2009): 97–135.

Martin, Jean-Philippe, *Histoire de la nouvelle gauche paysanne : des contestations des années 1960 à la Confédération paysanne* (Paris: La Découverte, 2005).

Marwick, Arthur, *The Sixties: Cultural Revolution in Britain, France, Italy, and the United States, c.1958–c.1974* (Oxford: Oxford University Press, 1998).

Massard-Guilbaud, Geneviève, 'La France, une « société vert claire » ? Retour sur *The Light Green Society*'. *Vingtième siècle* vol. 113, no. 1 (2012): 205–10.

Mende, Silke, *'Nicht rechts, nicht links, sondern vorn': Eine Geschichte der Gründungsgrünen* (München: Oldenbourg, 2011).

Mendras, Henri, *La Fin des paysans : innovations et changement dans l'agriculture française* (Paris: S.é.D.é.I.S., 1967).

Meyer, Jan-Henrik, 'Challenging the Atomic Community: The European Environmental Bureau and the Europeanization of Anti-Nuclear Protest'. In *Societal Actors in European Integration*, edited by Kaiser, W. and J.-H. Meyer (Basingstoke: Palgrave Macmillan, 2013), pp. 197–220.

Milder, Stephen, *Greening Democracy: The Antinuclear Movement and Political Environmentalism in Western Europe, 1968–1983* (Cambridge: Cambridge University Press, 2016).

Mohr, Markus, *Die Gewerkschaften im Atomkonflikt* (Münster: Westfälisches Dampfboot, 2001).

Mohr, Markus and Hartmut Rübner, *Gegnerbestimmung: Sozialwissenschaft im Dienst der 'innereren Sicherheit'* (Münster: Unrast, 2010).

Müller, Harald, 'Ökologiebewegung und Friedensbewegung: Zur Gefährdung des Lebensraums'. In *Die neue Friedensbewegung: Analysen aus der Friedensforschung*, edited by Steinweg, R. (Frankfurt: Suhrkamp, 1982), pp. 177–88.

Nehring, Holger, 'National Internationalists: British and West German Protests against Nuclear Weapons, the Politics of Transnational Communications and the Social History of the Cold War, 1957–1964'. *Contemporary European History* vol. 14, no. 4 (2005): 559–82.

Nehring, Holger, *Politics of Security: British and West German Protest Movements and the Early Cold War, 1945–1970* (Oxford: Oxford University Press, 2013).

Nelkin, Dorothy, 'L'énergie nucléaire dans le discours féministe'. *Sociologie et sociétés* vol. 13, no. 1 (1981): 147–60.

Nelkin, Dorothy and Michael Pollak, *The Atom Besieged: Extraparliamentary Dissent in France and Germany* (Cambridge, MA: MIT Press, 1981).

Neveu, Érik, 'Trajectoires de « soixante-huitards ordinaires »'. In *Mai–Juin 68*, edited by Damamme, D., B. Gobille, F. Matonti, and B. Pudal (Ivry-sur-Seine: l'Atelier, 2008), pp. 306–18.

Nicholls, Walter, 'Place, Networks, Space: Theorising the Geographies of Social Movements'. *Transactions of the Institute of British Geographers* vol. 34, no. 1 (2009): 78–93.

Oberkrome, Willi, *„Deutsche Heimat". Nationale Konzeption und regionale Praxis von Naturschutz, Landschaftsgestaltung und Kulturpolitik in Westfalen-Lippe und Thüringen (1900–1960)* (Paderborn: Schöningh, 2004).

Olsen, Jonathan, *Nature and Nationalism: Right-Wing Ecology and the Politics of Identity in Contemporary Germany* (Basingstoke: Macmillan, 1999).

Oppenheimer, Andrew, 'Conflicts of Solidarity: Nuclear Weapons, Liberation Movements, and the Politics of Peace in the Federal Republic of Germany, 1945–1975' (PhD dissertation, University of Chicago, 2010).

Passmore, Leith, 'The Art of Hunger: Self-Starvation in the Red Army Faction'. *German History* vol. 27, no. 1 (2009): 32–59.

Patel, Kiran Klaus, *Nach der Nationalfixiertheit. Perspektiven einer transnationalen Geschichte* (Berlin: Humboldt-Universität, 2004).

Pichardo, Nelson, 'New Social Movements: A Critical Review'. *Annual Review of Sociology* vol. 23 (1997): 411–30.

Plotke, David, 'What's So New about New Social Movements?' In *Social Movements: Critiques, Concepts, Case-Studies*, edited by Lyman, S. M. (London: Macmillan, 1995), pp. 113–36.

Poneman, Daniel, *Nuclear Power in the Developing World* (London: George Allen & Unwin, 1982).

Porhel, Vincent, *Ouvriers bretons : conflits d'usines, conflits identitaires en Bretagne dans les années 1968* (Rennes: Presses Universitaires de Rennes, 2008).

Portelli, Alessandro, 'The Peculiarities of Oral History'. *History Workshop Journal*, no. 12 (August 1981): 96–107.

Radkau, Joachim, *Aufstieg und Krise der deutschen Atomwirtschaft, 1945–1975* (Reinbek: Rowohlt, 1983).

Radkau, Joachim, *Natur und Macht. Eine Weltgeschichte der Umwelt* (München: C. H. Beck, 2000).

Radkau, Joachim, *Die Ära der Ökologie. Eine Weltgeschichte* (München: C. H. Beck, 2011).

Radkau, Joachim, 'Mythos German Angst'. *Blätter für deutsche und internationale Politik*, no. 5 (May 2011): 73–82.

Radkau, Joachim and Frank Uekötter, eds, *Naturschutz und Nationalsozialismus* (Frankfurt: Campus, 2003).

Reichardt, Sven, *Authentizität und Gemeinschaft. Linksalternatives Leben in den siebziger und frühen achtziger Jahren* (Berlin: Suhrkamp, 2014).

Richter, Saskia, *Die Aktivistin. Das Leben der Petra Kelly* (München: DVA, 2010).

Rivat, Emmanuel, 'The Continuity of Transnational Protest: The Anti-Nuclear Movement as a Precursor to the Global Justice Movement'. In *Understanding European Movements*, edited by Fominaya, C. F. and L. Cox (London: Routledge, 2013), pp. 61–75.

Rivat, Emmanuel, 'La transnationalisation de la cause antinucléaire en Europe : une approche comparée de la France et des Pays-Bas, 1970–2010' (thèse, Bordeaux 4, 2013).

Rootes, Christopher, 'Environmental Movements'. In *The Blackwell Companion to Social Movements*, edited by Snow, D. A., S. A. Soule, and H. Kriesi (Oxford: Blackwell, 2004), pp. 617–40.

Ross, Kristin, *May 68 and its Afterlives* (Chicago, IL: University of Chicago Press, 2002).

Rucht, Dieter, *Von Wyhl nach Gorleben. Bürger gegen Atomprogramm und nukleare Entsorgung* (München: C. H. Beck, 1980).

Rucht, Dieter, 'The Anti-Nuclear Power Movement and the State in France'. In *States and Anti-Nuclear Movements*, edited by Flam, H. (Edinburgh: Edinburgh University Press, 1994), pp. 129–62.

Rucht, Dieter, 'Gewalt und neue soziale Bewegungen'. In *Internationales Handbuch der Gewaltforschung*, edited by Heitmeyer, W. and G. Albrecht (Wiesbaden: Westdeutscher Verlag, 2002), pp. 461–78.

Rucht, Dieter, 'On the Sociology of Protest Marches'. In *The Street as Stage*, edited by Reiss, M. (Oxford: Oxford University Press, 2007), pp. 49–57.

Rucht, Dieter, 'Anti-Atomkraftbewegung'. In *Die sozialen Bewegungen in Deutschland seit 1945*, edited by Roth, R. and D. Rucht (Frankfurt: Campus, 2008), pp. 245–66.

Rüdig, Wolfgang, *Anti-Nuclear Movements: A World Survey of Opposition to Nuclear Energy* (Harlow: Longman, 1990).

Rusinek, Bernd-A., 'Wyhl'. In *Deutsche Erinnerungsorte*, edited by François, E. and H. Schulze (München: C. H. Beck, 2001), pp. 652–66.

Sainteny, Guillaume, *Les Verts*, 2nd edn (Paris: Presses Universitaires de France, 1992).

Sainteny, Guillaume, *L'introuvable écologisme français ?* (Paris: Presses Universitaires de France, 2000).

Schlosser, Eric, 'Break-in at Y-12'. *New Yorker*, 9 March 2015.

Schmitt, Rüdiger, *Die Friedensbewegung in der Bundesrepublik Deutschland: Ursachen und Bedingungen der Mobilisierung einer neuen sozialen Bewegung* (Opladen: Westdeutscher Verlag, 1990).

Schregel, Susanne, *Der Atomkrieg vor der Wohnungstür. Eine Politikgeschichte der neuen Friedensbewegung in der Bundesrepublik, 1970–1985* (Frankfurt: Campus, 2011).

Sewell, William H., 'Marc Bloch and the Logic of Comparative History'. *History and Theory* vol. 6, no. 2 (1968): 208–18.

Sharp, Gene, 'The Meanings of Non-Violence: A Typology (Revised)'. *Journal of Conflict Resolution* vol. 3, no. 1 (March 1959): 41–66.

Siegfried, Detlef, '„Einstürzende Neubauten": Wohngemeinschaften, Jugendzentren und private Präferenzen kommunistischer „Kader" als Formen jugendlicher Subkultur'. *Archiv für Sozialgeschichte*, no. 44 (2004): 39–66.

Simon, Gilles, *Plogoff : l'apprentissage de la mobilisation sociale* (Rennes: Presses Universitaires de Rennes, 2010).

Smith, Jake P., '*Häuserkämpfe*: Squatting, Urban Renewal, and the Crisis of Dwelling in West Germany, 1970–1995' (PhD dissertation, University of Chicago, forthcoming).

Sommier, Isabel, 'Les gauchismes'. In *Mai–Juin 68*, edited by Damamme, D., B. Gobille, F. Matonti, and B. Pudal (Ivry-sur-Seine: l'Atelier, 2008), pp. 295–305.

Steffen, Michael, 'Geschichten vom Trüffelschwein' (Doktorarbeit, Philipps-Universität Marburg, 2002) [http://archiv.ub.uni-marburg.de/diss/z2002/0060/ (accessed 4 March 2015)].

Steffen, Michael, *Geschichten vom Trüffelschwein. Politik und Organisation des Kommunistischen Bundes, 1971–1991* (Berlin: Assoziation A, 2002).

Stöss, Richard, *Vom Nationalismus zum Umweltschutz. Die Deutsche Gemeinschaft, Aktionsgemeinschaft Unabhängiger Deutscher im Parteiensystem der Bundesrepublik* (Opladen: Westdeutscher Verlag, 1980).

Suri, Jeremi, *Power and Protest: Global Revolution and the Rise of Detente* (Cambridge, MA: Harvard, 2003).

Tartakowsky, Danielle, *Manifester à Paris, 1880–2010* (Seyssel: Champ Vallon, 2010).

Tauer, Sandra, *Störfall für die gute Nachbarschaft? Deutsche und Franzosen auf der Suche nach einer gemeinsamen Energiepolitik (1973–1980)* (Göttingen: V&R unipress, 2012).

Terkel, Studs, *Division Street: America* (London: Penguin, 1968).

Thomas, Nick, *Protest Movements in 1960s West Germany: A Social History of Dissent and Democracy* (Oxford: Berg, 2003).

Thompson, Paul, *The Voice of the Past: Oral History*, 3rd edn (Oxford: Oxford University Press, 2000).

Thomson, Alistair, 'Unreliable Memories? The Use and Abuse of Oral History'. In *Historical Controversies and Historians*, edited by Lamont, W. M. (London: UCL Press, 1998), pp. 23–34.

Tilly, Charles, 'From Interactions to Outcomes in Social Movements'. In *How Social Movements Matter*, edited by Giugni, M. G., D. McAdam, and C. Tilly (Minneapolis, MN: University of Minnesota Press, 1999), pp. 253–70.

Tompkins, Andrew, 'Transnationality as a Liability? The Anti-Nuclear Movement at Malville'. *Revue Belge de Philologie et d'Histoire/Belgisch Tijdschrift voor Filologie en Geschiedenis* vol. 89, no. 3/4 (2011): 1,365–80.

Topçu, Sezin, 'Nucléaire : de l'engagement « savant » aux contre-expertises associatives'. *Natures Sciences Sociétés* vol. 14 (2006): 249–56.

Topçu, Sezin, *La France nucléaire : l'art de gouverner une technologie contestée* (Paris: Seuil, 2013).

Tosi, Simone and Tommaso Vitale, 'Explaining How Political Culture Changes: Catholic Activism and the Secular Left in Italian Peace Movements'. *Social Movement Studies* vol. 8, no. 2 (1 April 2009): 131–47.

Touraine, Alain, Zsuzsa Hegedus, François Dubet, and Michel Wieviorka, *La prophétie anti-nucléaire* (Paris: Seuil, 1980).

Touraine, Alain, Zsuzsa Hegedus, François Dubet, and Michel Wieviorka, *Anti-Nuclear Protest: The Opposition to Nuclear Energy in France*, trans. Fawcett, P. (Cambridge: Cambridge University Press, 1983).

Uekötter, Frank, 'Wie neu sind die Neuen Sozialen Bewegungen? Revisionistische Bemerkungen vor dem Hintergrund der Umwelthistorischen Forschung'. *Mitteilungsblatt des Instituts für soziale Bewegungen* vol. 31 (2004): 115–38.

Uekötter, Frank, *Am Ende der Gewissheiten. Die ökologische Frage im 21. Jahrhundert* (Frankfurt: Campus, 2011).

van der Heijden, Hein-Anton, 'The Great Fear: European Environmentalism in the Atomic Age'. In *A History of Environmentalism: Local Struggles, Global Histories*, edited by Armiero, M. and L. Sedrez (London: Bloomsbury, 2014), pp. 185–211.

van Hüllen, Rudolf, *Ideologie und Machtkampf bei den Grünen* (Bonn: Bouvier, 1990).

Varon, Jeremy, *Bringing the War Home: The Weather Underground, the Red Army Faction, and Revolutionary Violence in the Sixties and Seventies* (Berkeley, CA: University of California Press, 2004).

Vigna, Xavier, 'Lip et Larzac : conflits locaux et mobilisations nationales'. In *68 : une histoire collective*, edited by Artières, P. and M. Zancarini-Fournel (Paris: La Découverte, 2008), pp. 487–94.

Vigna, Xavier and Michelle Zancarini-Fournel, 'Les rencontres improbables dans « les années 68 »'. *Vingtième siècle* vol. 101, no. 1 (2009): 163–77.

von Bredow, Wilfried and Rudolf Horst Brocke, *Krise und Protest. Ursprünge und Elemente der Friedensbewegung in Westeuropa* (Opladen: Westdeutscher Verlag, 1987).

von Hirschhausen, Ulrike and Kiran Klaus Patel, 'Europeanization in History: An Introduction'. In *Europeanization in the Twentieth Century*, edited by Conway, M. and K. K. Patel (New York: Palgrave Macmillan, 2010), pp. 1–18.

Vuarin, Pauline, 'Larzac 1971–1981 : la dynamique des acteurs d'une lutte originale et créatrice' (maîtrise, Paris 1 Panthéon Sorbonne, 2005).

Warneke, Tim, 'Aktionsformen und Politikverständnis der Friedensbewegung. Radikaler Humanismus und die Pathosformel des Menschlichen'. In *Das Alternative Milieu*, edited by Reichardt, S. and D. Siegfried (Göttingen: Wallstein, 2010), pp. 445–72.

Weber, Reinhold and Hans-Georg Wehling, *Geschichte Baden-Württembergs* (München: C. H. Beck, 2007).

Weir, Lorna, 'Limitations of New Social Movement Analysis'. *Studies in Political Economy*, no. 40 (Spring 1993): 73–99.

Werner, Michael and Bénédicte Zimmermann, 'Penser l'histoire croisée : entre empirie et réflexivité'. *Annales* vol. 58, no. 1 (2003): 7–36.

Whittier, Nancy, 'The Consequences of Social Movements for Each Other'. In *The Blackwell Companion to Social Movements*, edited by Snow, D. A., S. A. Soule, and H. Kriesi (Oxford: Blackwell, 2004), pp. 531–51.

Winter, Martin, *Politikum Polizei. Macht und Funktion der Polizei in der Bundes-republik Deutschland* (Münster: Lit-Verlag, 1998) http://www.hof.uni-halle. de/mar-win/Winter_Martin_Politikum_Polizei_1998.pdf (accessed 23 May 2012).

Wirsching, Andreas, Göran Therborn, Geoff Eley, Hartmut Kaelble, and Philippe Chassaigne, 'The 1970s and 1980s as a Turning Point in European History?'. *Journal of Modern European History* vol. 9, no. 1 (March 2011): 8–26.

Wittner, Lawrence, *Toward Nuclear Abolition: A History of the World Nuclear Disarmament Movement, 1971 to the Present* (Stanford, CA: Stanford University Press, 2003).

Zahra, Tara, 'Imagined Noncommunities: National Indifference as a Category of Analysis'. *Slavic Review* vol. 69, no. 1 (2010): 93–119.

Zancarini-Fournel, Michelle, 'Aléria (1975) et Montredon (1976) : deux mani-festations régionalistes'. In *68 : une histoire collective*, edited by Artières, P. and M. Zancarini-Fournel (Paris: La Découverte, 2008), pp. 719–24.

Zancarini-Fournel, Michelle, *Le moment 68 : une histoire contestée* (Paris: Seuil, 2008).

Zhao, Dingxin, *The Power of Tiananmen: State–Society Relations and the 1989 Beijing Student Movement* (Chicago, IL: University of Chicago Press, 2001).

Index